THE POLITICS OF SECURITY SECTOR REFORM

Dedicated to the memory of Witold Patoka (1957-2010)

The Politics of
Security Sector Reform
Challenges and Opportunities for the
European Union's Global Role

MAGNUS EKENGREN AND GREG SIMONS
Swedish National Defence College

ASHGATE

Published by
Ashgate Publishing Limited
Wey Court East
Union Road
Farnham
Surrey, GU9 7PT
England

Ashgate Publishing Company
Suite 420
101 Cherry Street
Burlington
VT 05401-4405
USA

www.ashgate.com

British Library Cataloguing in Publication Data
The politics of security sector reform : challenges and
   opportunities for the European Union's global role.
   1. European Union. 2. National security--European Union
   countries. 3. Peace-building--International cooperation.
   4. Security, International.
   I. Ekengren, Magnus. II. Simons, Greg.
   327.1'72-dc22

Library of Congress Cataloging-in-Publication Data
Ekengren, Magnus.
   The politics of security sector reform : challenges and opportunities for the European
Union's global role / by Magnus Ekengren and Greg Simons.
      p. cm.
   Includes index.
   ISBN 978-1-4094-1028-7 (hardback) -- ISBN 978-1-4094-1029-4
(ebook) 1. Security, International--European Union countries. 2. National security--
European Union countries. 3. European Union countries--Defenses. I. Simons, Greg. II.
Title.
   JZ6009.E85E54 2010
   355'.03304--dc22

2010028780

ISBN 9781409410287 (hbk)
ISBN 9781409410294 (ebk)

Printed and bound in Great Britain by the
MPG Books Group, UK

Contents

PART III CASE STUDIES OF SSR POLITICS IN PRACTICE

Notes on Contributors

Caroline Bahnson holds a Master of Science degree from the London School of Economics. She has worked for the past ten years on security and development with the European Union (Commission and Council), the United Nations, the World Bank and the British Department for International Development.

Alyson J.K. Bailes is currently a visiting professor at the University of Iceland. She graduated from Oxford in 1969 with a Bachelor of Arts degree (First Class Honours) in Modern History and a Master of Arts degree in 1971. She started her diplomatic career in the British Foreign and Commonwealth Office (FCO) in 1969. She served in several posts in the FCO – in Budapest, delegation to NATO, Bonn, Beijing and Oslo as well as in London, plus the Ministry of Defence. In between posts she served as a researcher at the Royal Institute for International Affairs in London, the vice-President for the European Security Programme at the Institute for East-West Studies (now East-West Institute) in New York and Political Director of the Western European Union in Brussels. Returning to the Diplomatic Service, she became Britain's Ambassador to Finland from November 2000 until June 2002. She left that position and resigned from the FCO in order to begin her post as Director of the Stockholm Peace Research Institute (SIPRI) from July 2002 until 2007.

Malena Britz holds a doctorate from the University of Stockholm. She is a lecturer and researcher at the Swedish National Defence College. Her research interests include EU security policy in a broad perspective as an example of European integration and Europeanization.

Fredrik Bynander is an associate professor at the Department of Government at Uppsala University, and retains links with the Swedish National Defence College. He has articles published in a number of refereed journals, including: *Political Psychology*, *Public Administration* and *Government and Opposition*.

Gemma Collantes-Celador is a lecturer in International Security at the Department of International Politics, City University London. She holds a PhD in International Politics from the University of Wales, Aberystwyth (now Aberystwyth University). Her research is related to human security, Security Sector Reform in the Western Balkans, and policing practices within peacekeeping missions.

Magnus Ekengren is Associate Professor, Director of the 'Programme for European Security Research' (EUROSEC) at the Swedish National Defence College, and co-Director of the international research programme 'Building Societal Security in Europe'. He is a former Swedish diplomat and was previously deputy Director at the Policy Planning Unit of the Swedish Ministry for Foreign Affairs. Ekengren has worked at the European Commission and was posted at the Swedish representation to the Council of Europe, Strasbourg. He was educated at Uppsala University, Johns Hopkins University (Bologna), and College of Europe (Bruges), receiving his PhD at Stockholm University. Ekengren has published in the area of European foreign and security policy, crisis management and the Europeanization of the nation-state. His recent publications include an article on transboundary threats and new forms of EU co-operation (*European Security*) and the book *The Time of European Governance* (Manchester University Press). His latest book is *The EU as Crisis Manager – Patterns and Prospects* (forthcoming).

Andrea Johansson is a former student and research assistant at the Swedish National Defence College. She has a Bachelor of Arts degree in Political Science, Crisis Management and International Cooperation. Her specialization was in Russian and Ukrainian security policy. Currently she is working for the Swedish Ministry of Defence.

Ana E. Juncos is Lecturer in European Politics in the School of Sociology, Politics and International Studies at the University of Bristol. Previously, she was a Postdoctoral Research Fellow at the University of Bath, working on a project on the 'EU's Global Role'. She holds a PhD in Politics, International Relations and European Studies from Loughborough University. Her research interests include EU foreign and security policy and security sector reform in the Western Balkans. With Eva Gross, she is the co-editor of *EU Conflict Prevention and Crisis Management* (Routledge, forthcoming).

Magnus Jörgel holds a Master of Arts degree in War Studies from King's College in London and is in the process of finishing his doctoral thesis (also at King's College). Jörgel is a Lt-Colonel in the Swedish Armed Forces and works as a researcher at the Swedish National Defence College. His research focus is on Sub-Saharan Africa, conflicts and ethnicity.

Ana Kantor is currently a security and justice sector reform consultant. She has been working with the International Security Sector Advisory Team (ISSAT), part of the Geneva Centre for the Democratic Control of the Armed Forces (DCAF). Previously, she worked as a Security Sector Reform Analyst at EUROSEC at the Swedish National Defence College, Department of Security and Strategic Studies. Her principal areas of work include policing in post-conflict settings and assessment and evaluation of SSR strategies. Ana has a Honours Bachelor of Arts in Peace and Conflict Studies from the University of Toronto, and a Master of Arts degree in International Studies from Uppsala University.

Witold M. Patoka (†) held a PhD in Political Science from the University of Umeå in Sweden. Dr Patoka was a senior researcher at the Swedish National Defence College, and then a researcher at the University of Umeå. He specialized in strategic decision-making, civil-military coordination, crisis management, Security Sector Reform and European studies.

Mariam Persson holds a Master of Arts in Peace and Conflict Research from Uppsala University. Her areas of interest include African conflicts, informal security provision/vigilantism, gender, and post-war rebel structures. She has fieldwork experience from Liberia, Sierra Leone, and the Central African Republic. Currently, she is working within the Africa Programme at the Swedish National Defence College.

Mark Sedra is a research assistant in the Department of Political Science at the University of Waterloo, Canada. He is also a research fellow at the Centre for International Governance Innovation (CIGI), which is also located in Waterloo. Sedra holds a Bachelor of Arts degree (Honours) in Political Science and History from the University of Toronto and a Master of Science degree in International History from the London School of Economics (LSE). He is currently a PhD candidate in the Political Studies Department at the School of Oriental and African Studies (SOAS) at the University of London. His research focuses upon the issue of post-conflict state-building, with an emphasis on the security sector.

Greg Simons holds a doctoral degree from the French/Russian Department at the University of Canterbury in New Zealand. Dr Simons is a senior researcher at the National Centre for Crisis Management Research and Training at the Swedish National Defence College, a researcher at the Centre for Russian and Eurasian Studies at Uppsala University and a lecturer at the Department of Communication Science at Turiba University in Riga (Latvia).

David Spence is currently the First Counsellor for Security and Disarmament at the European Commission Delegation to the United Nations and other international organizations in Geneva, Switzerland. His previous responsibilities in the EC include work on terrorism, enlargement, European security and defence policy, and general security issues. He has also been Head of Training for the EC External Service and was secretary of the EC's Task Force on German Unification. Before joining the EC he was Head of European Training at the UK Civil Service College and Academic Advisor to the FCO's Conference Centre at Wilton Park. Spence has lectured at the Sorbonne, the Ecole Normale Supérieure and the Institut d'Etudes Politiques in Paris. He is a graduate of the Universities of Sussex, Oxford and Nice.

Carl-Einar Stålvant is Director of Studies in Political Science at the Swedish National Defence College. Stålvant has been a participant on a number of public enquiries as an expert. He has published extensively within the subject of Swedish foreign policy, European integration, Nordic politics, environmental politics and Baltic Sea area affairs.

Preface

Security is a precondition for development and democracy. Democracy and respect for human rights make nations, regions and the international community secure and prosperous. This is the simple logic that has made Security Sector Reform (SSR) a cornerstone of international security and development cooperation. The challenge is to make policies for security, development and democratization work together for sustainable results in developing nations, countries in transition from post-authoritarian rule to democracy, and post-conflict states.

As Minister for International Development Cooperation, I am encouraged to see that a common understanding of the policy concept is evolving and that there seems to be a growing consensus on the need to shape policies for SSR in a coherent and mutually reinforcing way. It is equally crucial, however, to make a real difference in the countries that need it most. We have seen progress and good examples, but a great deal remains to be done. Successful SSR will depend on how well we manage to assess national conditions and understand different political preconditions and, based on this, adjust SSR efforts to address these realities in cooperation with domestic reformers.

With its focus on understanding and linking policies and practice – 'the politics of SSR' – this book makes an important contribution to the process of enhancing international capacity to address SSR challenges. Bringing together key thinkers and doers, it provides a valuable in-depth analysis of SSR experiences and prospects. It highlights the need for balance between respecting national ownership of reforms and providing support to democratic forces, and argues that international efforts should be guided to a greater extent by the long-term goals of democracy and regional cooperation rather than short-term security objectives in areas such as counter-terrorism.

The European Union (EU) is particularly well equipped to realize the objectives of SSR. Today, the EU supports reform processes in partner countries and regions all over the world, and across a wide range of policy areas including development, conflict prevention and crisis management, democracy and human rights, and EU enlargement. Greater priority is being given to SSR efforts. New policies, capacities and tools have been added. By drawing on their own regional experiences of SSR, the EU Member States, as a group, are well positioned to inspire, design and assist other countries in seeking reform rationales and incentives in regional solutions and the sharing of best practices.

Security sector reform needs to generate both national reform incentives and regional dynamics favouring security, democracy and development. The EU is in a unique position to develop this strategic SSR goal further. This book presents a set of ideas on how this important work can be taken forward.

Gunilla Carlsson
Minister for International Development Cooperation, Sweden

Acknowledgements

This book has grown out of an on-going research project, 'Security Sector Reform and the European Union', at the Swedish National Defence College (SNDC). We have benefited greatly from the helpful contributions of many who have discussed the project and engaged with us throughout the years. You know who you are – thank you!

We owe special thanks to Deputy Director Dr Philipp Fluri of the Geneva Centre for the Democratic Control of Armed Forces (DCAF), and David Spence, First Counsellor for Security and Disarmament at the European Commission Delegation to the United Nations in Geneva for their strong support ever since the start of the project. Our thanks also go to all the members of the Programme for European Security Research (EUROSEC) at the SNDC, in which the SSR project is an important part. We would like to extend our appreciation to the Swedish Ministry of Defence for its generous funding that has made the book possible and to the Swedish Ministry for Foreign Affairs for financial support in the crucial finalizing stage. We are of course also very grateful to all contributors to the current work for sharing their expertise and knowledge with us as well as the readers of this book.

We are equally indebted to Carl-Einar Stålvant and Anna Helkama-Rågård of the SNDC for their invaluable help in producing the report on the international conference on 'The EU and Security Sector Reform' in 2007 that provided an important basis for the book. Our thanks are also extended to Thomas Klementsson at the SNDC for his devotion to the SSR issues and assistance with the book and to Johan Carlsson at the Swedish Ministry for Foreign Affairs for his whole-hearted support of our project.

In June 2010, Witold Patoka, one of the authors of this book unexpectedly passed away and thus unfortunately did not get to see the final result of our joint work in print. Witold was a very vibrant and colourful person, a good colleague and friend. He shall be sorely missed. The editors dedicate this book to his memory.

Magnus Ekengren and Greg Simons
Stockholm, November 2010

Introduction

Magnus Ekengren and Greg Simons

Towards a Comprehensive SSR Analysis

Security Sector Reform (SSR) is increasingly becoming a key component in international security and development cooperation. Indeed, the concept has almost come to be seen as a panacea for many of the biggest threats to the world such as failed states, terrorism and poverty. In the political language SSR refers to the establishment and improvement of democratic governance of the security sector and to the close link between security and development. Much of today's SSR is driven by the conviction that security, development and democracy are intrinsically linked – we can not have development without security and there is no security without democracy and development. The objective is policy coherence to achieve effective and lasting change in developing countries, states in transition from post-authoritarian rule to democracy and post-conflict state building.

At the same time there are few subjects that have evoked more academic inquiries and discussions over the last couple of years than Security Sector Reform. The literature is steadily growing and broadening to include new disciplines of social and political sciences and international relations. SSR seems to be one of those subjects where many have an understanding of what it is and what it involves, but the diversity of opinion is large. Therefore, it can be said that SSR means different things to different actors, both as donors and as recipients, as well as observers.

There is a growing literature that covers the issue of SSR from different angles, from the broader theoretical issues, to more focused evaluations (Brzoska and Law, 2007; Law (ed.) 2007; Spence and Fluri (eds) 2008; Schnabel and Ehrhart (eds) 2005). However they all take a relatively broad approach, and lack specific case studies to support the policy and political observations. Other literature tends to focus on an aspect of SSR, such as a geographical area (Cottey (ed.) 1999; Jervell (ed.) 1992), issues and dilemmas that are faced by donors, one particular aspect of SSR (state building, capacity building, assistance and aid). These provide a valuable understanding of an aspect of the SSR process, and can give an in-depth appreciation of the complexities of the specific narrow topic. One of the interesting, and for the purposes of this book, relevant track of research analyses the role of complex actors (not single states but multinational groupings) in SSR. David M. Law states that the role of regional actors and inter-governmental organizations shall play an increasingly important role in shaping the future SSR agenda (2007: 21-26).[1] This comes at a crucial point in time for the European Union (EU) and its aspirations in becoming a world leader in providing effective assistance in SSR. As suggested in the title of the book, this involves not only opportunities, but challenges to be overcome as well.

The issue of economic development and democratization as key components of SSR has been embraced in the literature. The United Kingdom's Department for International Development produced 'Understanding and Supporting Security Sector Reform' in 2002 is one such example. This document also emphasizes the key role of understanding and measuring key indicators in order for the success or otherwise of the mission to be gauged. The human aspect to security is taken up by Mary Kaldor in *Human Security* (2007). This work emphasizing that SSR is far from just an exercise of a technical mission upon institutions, but has real life impacts for the citizens of the countries being assisted (and potentially their neighbours too).

But even though there is a growing consensus in the literature that there is a lack of understanding of local conditions in the implementation of international SSR support there has to date been very little literature provided on in-depth studies of the interplays between multilateral donors' policies and local political realities. SSR is a far from predictable process, and the best of plans can lie in ruin after coming into contact with the reality of conditions on the ground. One of the major problems that affect the outcome of SSR is a number of pre-existing assumptions that are held by not only the donor country or countries, but also by the recipients of the SSR help.

At times, it seems as though there is the perception of the need to create some kind of SSR 'template' that can be applied to all cases by donor states. To put this idea into a comparative aspect, one can look at the Bush Administration (2001-2009) Doctrine of *Transplanting Democracy*, the idea that a donor country's system can be transposed upon the recipient without any modification. Failures in the implementation process, especially a lasting change to the system, may be the result when the aspect of not adapting to the specifics of local conditions.

There can also be a failure or at least challenges to successful SSR through the level of expectations. What does the donor country expect the recipient to do? Does the recipient clearly understand those expectations? In some cases there may be a failure by the recipient country to understand what is exactly required of them. There may also be the case that the recipient country may not be able to

---

1   Ebnoether, A.H., Felberbauer, E.M. and Staničić, M. (eds) *Security Sector Reform in South East Europe: From a Necessary Remedy to a Global Concept*. Vienna and Geneva: National Defence Academy and Bureau for Security Policy at the Austrian Ministry of Defence in co-operation with Geneva Centre for the Democratic Control of Armed Forces, Switzerland, and PfP Consortium of Defence Academies and Security Studies Institutes, Garmisch-Partenkirchen, Germany, January 2007.

carry out what is required of them, for instance this may be the result of severe financial constraints or simply by lacking the required expertise to do so.

The aim of this book is to further a deepened understanding of the origins of the international SSR policy and the opportunities for EU SSR policies together with in-depth studies of how these policies play out in practice in the current politics of Western Balkans, Ukraine, Afghanistan, Liberia, Guinea-Bissau and Sub-Saharan Africa.

In this way the volume offers a broad perspective; stretching from post-authoritarian transition through to development issues in post-conflict states; including cases of SSR engagement in the 1990s in order to put the current lessons into perspective. But it also fills at least two gaps in the SSR study field. It gives a comprehensive and integrated approach through the use of the *Three Ps*; analysing SSR *Policy*, *Policies* and *Practice* as a way to provide a greater appreciation of the influences on the *process* of SSR, from conception to implementation. And it analyses perhaps one of the most important multilateral organizations in the field at a point in time when the EU is seeking to build its capacity in order to become a credible and viable global actor in the sphere of SSR. The book will end with a set of recommendations that are drawn from this analysis.

Consequently there are three core themes to this edited volume – *Policy*, *Policies* and *Practice* – *the politics of SSR* – which are also the basis for its disposition into three sub sections.

A Regional Approach to SSR

We agree with David Law's prediction that states and regions increasingly will carry out their SSR efforts within multinational organizations such as the UN, the EU and NATO. One of the normative reasons for a multilateral approach is today's need for strengthened strategic coordination of international SSR. The challenge is to build up a donor capacity able to provide broad, sustainable and legitimate support with clear long term goals for SSR. Moreover, international SSR needs to generate not only national reform incentives in receiving states but regional dynamics favouring security, democracy and development.[2] In practical life as well as the literature, the promotion of regional confidence building mechanisms is often seen as the most important tasks for SSR actors.[3]

---

2   Schnabel, A. and Ehrhart, H.-G. (eds) *Security Sector Reform and Post-Conflict Peacebuilding*. New York: United Nations University Press, 2005; Brzoska, M. and Law, D., *Security Sector Reconstruction and Reform in Peace Support Operations*. London: Routledge, 2007.

3   Schnabel and Ehrhart, 'Post-Conflict Societies and the Military: Challenges and Problems of Security Sector Reform' in Schnabel and Ehrhart (eds) *Security Sector Reform and Post-Conflict Peacebuilding*. New York: United Nations University Press, 2005, p. 8.

Resistance and obstacles to the security sector reforms in individual states are often originating in regional tensions and threats emanating outside national borders. Many times receiving states have simply other security and defence priorities that do not match with the SSR aid offered by external actors. A truly regional analysis and approach to SSR would help to improve donors' possibilities to shape its SSR more effectively and in ways that could also contribute to a change of individual states' security and defence priorities by efforts including other partners in the region. The final reason for a regional approach to SSR is the fact that coordination of SSR so far has been weak in existing regional and sub-regional organizations such as the Association of South-East Asian Nations (ASEAN), the African Union (AU) and the Southern African Development Community (SADC) and the New Partnership for Africa's Development (NEPAD).[4] A more coherent EU SSR could provide a new basis for an enhanced cooperation with these organizations.

The European Union and SSR

The EU in many respects has a number of advantages in the sphere of SSR. There is a wealth of experience in the individual membership of the states that make up the union, a number of whom have undergone the SSR process on their way to membership in the EU and NATO. The challenge is now to realize this potential internationally with regard to a more efficient interplay between donors' capacities and recipients' needs.

According to the International Security Information Service there are some 14 active EU missions within the Common Security and Defence Policy (CSDP)[5] as of October 2009. To-date there have been a total of 27 completed and on-going missions. Six of the on-going missions are in the Western Balkans, Caucasus and Eastern Europe; three in the Middle East; four in Africa and one in Central Asia. Of those 14 missions, 12 are civilian and two are military run. Eleven of the 12 civilian missions are to do with aspects of SSR.[6]

The aim of cooperation in the EU has ever since its creation been to further security, development and democracy. Although the term SSR has not been common in descriptions of the work of the organization, it includes nations who have experienced SSR and supported the very same reforms by passing on their expertise to neighbours in a wide range of areas. In this way, they constitute

---

4   Hendrickson, D. and Karkoszka, A., 'Security Sector Reform and Donor Policies' in Schnabel and Ehrhart (eds) *Security Sector Reform and Post-Conflict Peacebuilding.* New York: United Nations University Press, 2005, p. 30.

5   Technically speaking, the Common Security and Defence Policy only exists since the entering into force of the Lisbon Treaty, 1 December 2009. This chapter takes into account the history of the European Security and Defence Policy (which began in 1999) as well when referring to CSDP.

6   ESDP Mission Analysis Partnership, www.esdpmap.org, accessed 5 November 2009.

regional SSR examples from which other parts of the world can draw lessons. Indeed, one of the strongest strands in current efforts to understand the pre-conditions for successful SSR policies has been to recognize the fact that security and/or democratic governance in one country often is short-lived in the absence of similar developments in neighbouring countries.[7] In the case of both security and economic development this regional logic of mutually reinforcing reform is of course very strong. History has shown that the democratization of the defence sector and/or disarmament in one state imply reduced threats to its neighbours which in turn paves the way for reform also in these countries.[8]

Today's challenge is to make the most of this regional experience in the theory and practice of SSR, not least with regard to implementation. We need a deepened understanding of the contexts for successful SSR and frameworks of analysis for systematic comparisons of regional and sub-regional experiences. In practical life it is important not to make SSR just a matter for bi-lateral assistance but an important ingredient in multilateral security cooperation and in cooperation between international organizations such as the EU and the AU, including their SSR policies *vis-à-vis* other regions in the world.

Defining SSR

SSR is a complex process and it touches a number of different spheres and aspects in modern society, and especially those societies that are in need of reform in order to give them a capacity and sense of securing the state and population. For the purposes of this volume, SSR is to be understood not as a solely military or defence issue. It involves many different aspects including: police, customs, border control, politics, military forces and in some cases paramilitary forces. One of the observations that come out from this book is the need to approach the issue of SSR comprehensively and not piecemeal.

Figure I.1 demonstrates that there are likely to be problems encountered if SSR is approached from a piecemeal strategy. Each of these three aspects of the spectrum of SSR does not live in an isolated existence, which is detached from the others. As the various components that constitute the area of interest – state building, capacity building, and aid and assistance – assert a two way influence on each other. As a way to analyse the dynamics of this interplay, the first section of

---

7 Edited by Cawthra, G., du Pisani, A. and Omari, A., *Security and Democracy in Southern Africa*. Wits University Press, IDRC (The International Development Research Centre), 2007; *Appendix 1: Research Briefing: Democratic Governance and Common Security in Southern Africa*, http://www.idrc.ca/lacro/ev-132711-201-1-DO_TOPIC.html, accessed 5 June 2010.

8 Bailes, A.J.K., Haine J.-Y. and Lachowski, Z., 'Reflections on the OSCE-EU Relationship' in *SIPRI Yearbook 2007*. Baden-Baden: Nomos, 2008, pp. 65-77.

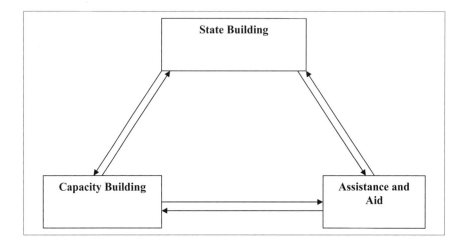

Figure I.1 Influences between the different spheres of SSR

this book discusses the components in the light of earlier experiences of forging an SSR policy, such as the ones of Poland and the Baltic states in the 1990s.

Some of the literature has concluded that international SSR support has had difficulties to meet the specific need of the donor countries (Dokos, 2007; Law, 2007; Schnabel and Ehrhart, 2005). A major problem has been that assisting actors have not clearly separated the three components. The presentation of the specific background and politics of various recipient countries around the globe will provide a unique basis for an improved analysis of how the three components relate to each other, both at the donor and the receiving end (Part III of this book).

The three aspects laid out in Figure I.1, state building, capacity building, and aid and assistance relate to specific SSR missions at the tactical level. On the strategic level, Stålvant defines three agents of SSR change (Chapter 2), which are *regionalization, stabilization and normalization*. Those agents that are proposed by Stålvant are closely related to the situation that occurred after the collapse of the Eastern Bloc. However, the agents have applicability to this volume and can be applied to the case studies analysed in this book (such as Afghanistan, Liberia and Guinea-Bissau). They provide an understanding for the wider, longer term issues that need to be considered.

As noted by Spence and Fluri (2008), the EU has been in the process of defining concepts and developing SSR policies for over one decade, but still does not have a unified approach to the issue. Instead, SSR does not rely on the EU per se, but rather the level of commitment and engagement by individual member states. This book analyses the pre-conditions for more comprehensive EU SSR policies with regard to the three components laid out above, that so far have been divided into the responsibility of different EU institutions in an unfortunate way (Part II).

Structure of the Book

The structure of this book is intended to follow the logic of the stated *Three Ps – Policy, Policies* and *Practice*. Thus a logical red thread can be traced from the *Policy* and inception of an approach to SSR, over how the policies of one of the most important donors are shaped, to how politics affects the implementation of the policy and the result or *Practice* as witnessed in a number of case studies of SSR. This is reflected in the organization of the sections and chapters, which cumulatively build upon these three primary themes in order to logically build the case for the EU's involvement in the process, and how to do this in a manner that tangibly brings about the desired outcomes.

Part I, 'Towards a Policy – Concept and Experiences', concerns the *Policy* element involved in the SSR process. As implied by the title of this part, it is an attempt to look at the issue of policy development and experiences and how those lessons can be incorporated into forming a comprehensive and integrated policy approach to the SSR issue. Three chapters constitute this part, looking at the issue of policy from a number of different angles. Chapter 1 presents a background by explaining the origins of the Security Sector Reform concept in three traditions; authoritarian transition, post-conflict rebuilding and development. By laying out the differences Carl-Einar Stålvant shows the evolution and inherent tensions of today's concept and how this understanding can be of help in clarifying roles and conditions for coordination in today's practical SSR work. In Chapter 2 the Nordic-Baltic SSR experiences and prospects for cooperation are placed in a broader framework of analysis. Stålvant analyses three driving forces behind change in the Baltic Sea area during the 1990s; *regionalization, stabilization, normalization*. The question of to what extent these experiences are applicable to other regions of the world has a bearing on the following analyses of different cases and the concluding remarks. In Chapter 3, Witold Patoka provides a framework for shaping and evaluating SSR in general through an analysis of the obstacles and facilitating factors in the transformation of the Polish security sector in the 1990s. This chapter also discusses the question of in what way the Polish experience has affected the country's current SSR policy.

Part II, 'EU Policies', begins to delve into the second of the stated *Three Ps* and how the shaping of policies can affect the overall policy of SSR. This part looks at the political opportunities and challenges that lie ahead for the EU on the road to forming a systematic approach to SSR. Is there an 'EU approach' to SSR? A total of four chapters make up this part of the book. In Chapter 4 Alyson Bailes echoes some of the same definitional issues as in Chapter 1, going on to conclude that the EU is one of the best potential actors to carry out SSR but that it cannot simply externalize the security success story of either its older or newer members to the rest of the world. Many of the countries in Africa, Asia and Latin America that Europeans want to help have quite different internal and external starting points from those of the EU's own nations, or even its nearer neighbours.

Malena Britz provides a comprehensive overview of the most recent SSR instruments established for the Union in Chapter 5. She focuses on how the key policy documents of the Union define SSR, when and where the EU is supposed to act and what resources are needed. She finds two different views on SSR expressed in the EU policies. The aim of SSR in the CSDP is security and the means are mainly the use of crisis management capacities for capacity building in receiving states, while the purpose of SSR in the documents produced by the European Commission is development and good governance through aid and assistance and 'state building'. She opens up the question of how this discrepancy affects the member states' allocation of resources to the EU's security policy. A more coherent EU SSR policy that might be achieved through the new high representative for the Union's foreign policy established through the Lisbon treaty, will most likely break up traditional lines of demarcations in national administration such as the one between security/defence and development. It will also make it more difficult for member states to 'choose' what direction for EU SSR they want to support: SSR through CSDP or the Commission? One thing, however, is clear according to Britz; the object of protection is the same for all EU SSR. Today EU reform efforts are not only aimed for state security but for safeguarding citizens of the Union and the world.

In the following chapter (Chapter 6), David Spence argues in favour of giving the Union a stronger SSR role. He sees the Union as guarantor for effective and sound SSR due to its creation of a European interest or model above national self-interests that is probably more acceptable in receiving states. The challenge for the Union is now to clearly define the aims of its SSR in security and development terms in order to reconcile all its instruments in the best possible way.

In Chapter 7, Magnus Ekengren analyses the implications of the Union's broadening security agenda for the content and process of EU SSR in other parts of the world. The Union's increasingly stronger focus on human, EU citizens' and 'societal' security will have great repercussions not only on its support of capability building but the way security is conceptualized in efforts for state building and enhanced regional cooperation. The Union is today trying to overcome divisions between policy fields and professions such as the police and the military, both for its security work abroad (CSDP) and at home (the Solidarity Clause of the Lisbon Treaty). The work of narrowing the gap between internal and external security leads to a broadening of the notion of international SSR and puts new demands on national provisions of SSR resources.

Part III, 'Case Studies of SSR – Politics in Practice', which forms the basis of the third P – *Practice*. There are a total of eight different chapters in this part of the book covering case studies from Afghanistan, Liberia, Guinea-Bissau, Sub-Saharan Africa, Ukraine and the Western Balkans. These cases highlight the need to understand and take into account the effect of realities before, rather than after attempting SSR, which can hinder or even cause failure of the SSR programme. The sample sheds light on both the different 'Ps' of SSR as laid out in this chapter and the main traditions of SSR outlined in chapter one: post-conflict rebuilding (Western Balkans), authoritarian transition (Ukraine) and development (Afghanistan, Africa). The selection of sector or issue 'cases' in each region is made on the following grounds: they are all significant examples of well-recognized SSR implementation *problematiques* such as international coordination with regard to the three spheres (aid and state and capacity building), the need for holistic and regional approaches, the security-democracy-development nexus, short vs. long term objectives for reforms. The studies will also provide material for a discussion of differences in dynamics between SSR in countries with a clear EU and/or NATO membership perspective compared to other states such as Afghanistan. The aim of all country studies is to include a clear political–practical perspective on SSR and recommendations for the future.

Gemma Collantes-Celador and Ana Juncos give a broad introduction of the political, security and economic challenges facing the international SSR community in the Western Balkans (Chapter 8). Many of the problems of individual states still have a strong regional dimension such as cross border criminality and tense inter-ethnic relations. Unfortunately, international SSR have been characterized by short term objectives in fields such as counter-terrorism and corruption at the expense of the longer term goals of good governance and democracy. Collantes-Celador and Juncos conclude that without a longer term strategy for common regional goals the link between SSR reform and wider reform processes will continue to be weak. A key challenge for international and European SSR is to foster regional confidence building in the form of sustainable security cooperation arrangements between the Western Balkans countries. A pre-requisite for coherence is, according to the authors, that the international community already at the planning stage jointly sets regional goals for all its SSR activities.

In Chapter 9 Fredrik Bynander underlines that SSR is not a 'neutral' concept independent from the donor's characteristics. He explains how a country's choice of international SSR partners is often heavily politicized and having great implications for its security identity. In the case of Ukraine, NATO has been the major provider of reform support which has resulted in a focus on the defence sector and the sharing of norms and standards for international military crisis management. Some Ukrainian political parties however wants to slow down the pace in the NATO Membership Action Plan at the same time as the EU is starting to help reforming the broader security sector. Bynander shows that the SSR question is not only a technical issue but of great signification for Ukraine's transatlantic cooperation, European vocation and relationship to Russia.

Greg Simons examines central historical, political and institutional issues that today affect international SSR in the area of Ukrainian border management (Chapter 10). He focuses on the impact of Russia, the NATO question, and the tense situation with the Autonomous Republic of Crimea. The disputed border issues with Russia together with the domestic debate on NATO membership and the problems spilling over from unstable Transdniestria and Georgia make SSR almost per definition a highly regional question. Although NATO and EU SSR efforts have gained some success at lower levels of administration, Simons reminds us of the need to identify domestic stakeholders, actual and potential, that could be driving forces for more strategic SSR. Of key importance is that the shaping of SSR is based on an in-depth understanding of Ukraine's relationship with its neighbours.

In Chapter 11, Andrea Johansson investigates the current problems of implementing international SSR for the strengthening of Ukrainian control of small arms and light weapons (SALW). She explains the modest international impact in this crucial area as a result of an underestimation of the complexity of the deep-seated political, institutional and legal obstacles to reform. Many times the international organization is to a higher degree driven by its own internal logic and programmes than by Ukrainian needs, which render a holistic approach involving also neighbouring states very difficult. Johansson accepts that the area is particularly difficult to reform due to the on-going power struggle in the country and calls for an 'outspoken', broader and coordinated international SSR policy that produces domestic incentives for reform.

Mark Sedra explores the potential role of the European Union in the Afghan security sector (Chapter 12). According to Sedra the EU should fill today's absence of donor leadership and provide the necessary support of the rule of law sector; the police and the court system. Stronger Union engagement would provide for a shift from expediency to the much needed long term reform goals. Sedra shows that the Union is well placed to coordinate the input of the EU member states in the field of SSR. This is due to the fact that the EU in Afghanistan is seen as the 'alternative' soft power to NATO and the US which gives it legitimacy.

Magnus Jörgel takes a closer look on some key SSR challenges specific to Sub-Saharan Africa (Chapter 13). Jörgel explains how the fragility of the state and the complexity of the conflicts in this region call for cautiousness in the application of a 'Western oriented' approach to SSR, both in theory and practice. It is of crucial importance for any SSR support to understand the root causes of conflicts in today's Sierra Leone, Liberia and Democratic Republic of Congo (DRC). Even though many reform needs are highly situation specific the most fundamental ones are according to Jörgel of a general character. International actors must realize that state structures are so weak that any reform endeavour needs to involve and build on the very people that are supposed to carry out the particular security functions, or indeed, establish the security institution. Formal institutions are dependent on social and informal networks which make it crucial for SSR to link security and development together. Jörgel shows that without economic progress there will be little incentive to participate in new or transformed security sectors. Without security for the man in the street there will be little economic life.

Caroline Bahnson tackles the issue of the EU's involvement in Guinea-Bissau from a practitioner's point of view in Chapter 14. The country was devastated by a civil war, and subsequently by a number of *coup d'état*s. These issues continue to plague Guinea-Bissau and stymie the efforts of the international community in their SSR programmes. In addition to the problems that arise from the formal sphere, there are numerous problems that arise from the informal settings too.

There has been a lot of international involvement and effort, but little result to date. Bahnson makes a strong case that donors need to pay as much (if not more) attention to these influences that exist beyond the formal structures if donors aid is going to be effective and attain its objectives.

Finally, in Chapter 15 Ana Kantor and Mariam Persson analyse the role of non-state actors in the provision of security in Liberia. Kantor and Persson look at the issue of SSR in post conflict Liberia and argue that it is necessary to look beyond the formal structures at times when implementing SSR. This is required due to lack of state capacity (or political will) and that it may be the informal structures and not the formal ones that are functioning.

In the conclusion Magnus Ekengren and Greg Simons compare the results of the empirical chapters with regard to the interaction and influence between policy, policies and implementation within the three spheres – state building, capacity building, assistance and aid. The chapter brings the potential and pitfalls of the SSR process to the fore. What lessons can be drawn for the future?

In the epilogue, Ekengren summarizes the policy-recommendations in the book for a more comprehensive SSR approach. This part suggests elements that should be included in the pursuit of a 'Regional Approach to SSR'. Ekengren argues that the elaboration of such an approach by the EU would serve two purposes. Firstly, it would help to make the Union's policies more coherent and point out ways and methods for other international donors. Secondly, it could function as a catalyst that could inspire receiving countries to follow regional paths towards effective SSR implementation.

References

Bailes, A.J.K., Haine, J.-Y. and Lachowski, Z., 'Reflections on the OSCE-EU Relationship' in *SIPRI Yearbook 2007*. Baden-Baden: Nomos, 2008, pp. 65-77.

Brzoska, M. and Law, D., *Security Sector Reconstruction and Reform in Peace Support Operations*. London: Routledge, 2007.

Cawthra, G., du Pisani, A. and Omari, A. (eds) *Security and Democracy in Southern Africa*. Wits University Press, IDRC (The International Development Research Centre), 2007. *Appendix 1: Research Briefing: Democratic Governance and Common Security in Southern Africa*, http://www.idrc.ca/lacro/ev-132711-201-1-DO_TOPIC.html, accessed 5 June 2010.

Cottey, A. (ed.) *Sub-Regional Cooperation in the New Europe: Building Security, Prosperity from the Barents to the Black Sea*. London/New York: Macmillan, 1999.

Department for International Development, 'Understanding and Supporting Security Sector Reform'. London, 2002.

Dokos, T., 'Security Sector Transformation in South-Eastern Europe and the Middle East', *NATO Science for Peace and Security Series*. Human and Societal Dynamics. Amsterdam: IOS Press, 2007.

Hendrickson, D. and Karkoszka, A., 'Security Sector Reform and Donor Policies' in Schnabel and Ehrhart (eds) *Security Sector Reform and Post-Conflict Peacebuilding*. New York: United Nations University Press, 2005.

Jervell, S. (ed.) *The Baltic Sea Area. A Region in the Making*. Karlskrona: Europa Programme in Cooperation with the Baltic Institute, 1992.

Kaldor, M., *Human Security*. Cambridge: Polity Press, 2007.

Law, D. (ed.) *Intergovernmental Organisations and Security Sector Reform*. LIT, The Geneva Centre for the Democratic Control of Armed Forces, 2007.

Schnabel, A. and Ehrhart, H.-G. (eds) *Security Sector Reform and Post-Conflict Peacebuilding*. New York: United Nations University Press, 2005.

Spence, D. and Fluri, P. (eds) *The European Union and Security Sector Reform*. London: John Harper Publishing, 2008.

PART I
Towards a Policy:
Concept and Experiences

Chapter 1

Three Traditions and the Concept of Security Sector Reform

Carl-Einar Stålvant

Notes on SSR as an Essentially Contested Concept

SSR is both a comprehensive but vague concept and a policy-making tool. As a vision it embodies a holistic message; a message about good and democratic governance of the basic functions of statehood. Efficient security should be provided both for the state and for human beings. Although the formula remains intact as it is framed within international programs, it is hardly surprising that its content keep shifting with the political environment and underlying assumptions. An examination of the theoretical understandings of SSR reveals how three different discourses about strategic needs and political motives coalesce in the conception. It contains different, perhaps contradictory views on the functions of security and its relationship to other ultimate political goals. The reference to reform intentionality is not uncontested; certain scholars rather prefer to talk about security sector governance. However the former notion brings back a lingering reminder that the security apparatus have been a cause of insecurity and costly overspending in many countries.[1] Thus the case is made for not prolonging such a state of affairs by the retention of a non-protective public good outside public scrutiny.

Somewhat simplistically we can say that these three discourses have their origins in a developmental, transitional and post conflict state building context. The underlying assertions and rationales could be spelled like this:

- SSR facilitates development: an insecure environment is an obstacle to progress, propels the misuse of resources and assistance, and creates few incentives for social and economic empowerment;
- SSR is conducive to democratization, reduces political authoritarianism and widens transparency and public accountancy of defence and security matters. Democracy, in turn, is essential for peace.[2]

---

1   Buzan, B., *People, States, and Fear: An Agenda for International Security Studies in the Post-Cold War Era*, 2nd edition. Boulder, CO: Lynne Rienner, 1993.

2   The reasoning is based on the democratic peace doctrine, posited by the scholar Rudolph Rummel (2002) as an empirical generalization of an analysis of states' war-proneness.

• SSR is a key ingredient in healing societal scars when reintegrating previous hostile groups into society and in rebuilding institutions that are legitimate and trusted by the citizens.

As noted, the chapters of this report demonstrate how SSR is working in all the three different strategic environments. Ukraine exemplifies the complexities of transition; certain African states the developmental and Bosnia those of a state in post-conflict circumstances while Afghanistan fulfils all the criteria.

Challenges of a Comprehensive SSR Concept

As an instrument for policy guidance SSR is much en vogue. Hänggi and Tanner claim that a broad agreement prevails on general principles and good practices.[3] While the former consensus is met by a list of institutional requirements, the latter criterion suggests that a woolly notion is validated through an intuitive acceptance of its manifestation.

The authors, emphasizing how security sector is subject to democratic governance, mention five components in an ideal type of rule:

• A constitutional and legal framework clarifying both separation of powers and the competencies of individual institutions;
• Civilian control and professional responsibility;
• Parliamentary control and oversight;
• Judicial control and accountability;
• Public control via media and various independent stakeholders.

However, the elasticity of SSR applications is evident when scrutinizing a number of case studies of attempted SSR programs. Abstract principles broken down into pointed projects, specific missions and advisory services subsume quite a number of diverse activities. The concrete and simplistic language interpreting particular actions and quick measures (a two-week training course, a one-week consultancy assessment team) as a SSR measure need not lead to misunderstandings although it is obvious that the underlying vision is easily lost. Even the reverse approach contains a trap. An effort to embrace all the elements of SSR when framing and implementing a policy program for a particular country risks achieving nothing. The particular parts prey on the sum.

These difficulties stem from a well meant but perhaps also overwhelmingly generous development of the concept. A number of attempts to arrive at definitions in and by international organizations have gradually ensured political support. However, any negotiated and approved concept risks enumerating a number of

---

3   Hänggi, H. and Tanner, F., *Promoting Security Sector Governance in the EU Neighbourhood*. Paris: Institute for Security Studies, 2005.

desiderata that ends up as a possible shopping list. Hence one can make the case that both the horizontal and vertical dimensions of SSR seem open-ended: the horizontal by expanding the numbers of actors and public functions addressed, and the vertical by opening up the entire question of state – society relations. A cursory overview of the generally accepted OECD – DAC definition reveals the many possibilities covered by SSR.

> SSR is another term used to describe the transformation of the security system– which includes all the actors, their roles, responsibilities and actions – working together to manage and operate the system in a manner that is more consistent with democratic norms and sound principles of good governance and this contributes to a well-functioning security framework.[4]

Hence the formula must be brought to life in the diagnosis for each country and situation. The ability to discriminate between various possible measures and to put actions in sequential order has a crucial impact on the likelihood of success. Hence SSR is no easily found and ready made panacea for transforming dire situations into safe environments.

So, in order to get a grip of the significance of SSR and its wide range of uses we have to ponder the particular meanings and applicability of each of the significant corners in a triangular term: security, sector and reform. For each term and corner we can imagine a number of polar possibilities:

- A classical military vs. a broadened understanding of security;
- A narrow concentration on public punitive and coercive powers vs. governance qualities and state capacity and responsive performance across-the – board;
- An incremental and piecemeal but selective strategy vs. drastic alterations and sweeping dismissals of old traditions and guards.

All three notions making up SSR (Security, Sector and Reform) carry more than one dimension and a range of operational alternatives. Functionally the element of security could also be expressed as a summary judgement on the country situation (whether it is domestic or foreign security that is the root of the matter or to what an extent the interplay of external and internal factors yield benign or malign challenges); institutionally as a dispersed or centralized lead agency structure and thirdly, as a choice and time order problem between many competing public concerns. National action plans are often volatile in times of rapid change and dwindling generosity on part of donors and partners.

When trying to comprehend the policy-making part of an alleged SSR attempt one could also make a number of additional distinctions. Crucial alternatives is the

---

4 *SSR and Governance; Policy and Good Practice*. Paris: OECD/DAC, 2004.

nature of the target, the degree and range of conditionality from donors or advisors and the scale of direct foreign involvement in the reforms:

- A narrow vs. wide support to public institution-building; i.e. favouring central ministries at the expense of executing authorities and local public offices. Administrative delineations are often obstacles, yet every country has a number of structures that need to be coordinated within this sector;
- A state centric vs. society centric approach;
- Autonomous driven change that is externally supported vs. change under foreign duress;
- Reform processes in failed states conditioned by various degrees of direct foreign presence.

However, the variability is great between different cases. Using the typology above and referring once again to the studies of the volume, in Afghanistan the scale of involvement encompasses war fighting, PSO and traditional development assistance. Bosnia is still under an international PSO that encompasses civil, police and military assistance. In Ukraine a large number of consultants and commissioned experts are docked into domestic institutions. Moldova illustrates yet another variety where SSR is addressed within various assistance and cooperation programs, but where security is propped up by the presence of a team of unarmed border observers. For the sake of the argument, the criticized Belorussian regime is not totally put into quarantine by EU neighbours and Brussels but substantial efforts are directed to cultivate relations with civil society and induce reform thinking as a prelude to change. As pointed out in the record of Baltic Sea cooperation, domestic circumstances and determination were decisive factors for national development and reforms of the security sectors, foreign advice and assistance only encouraged, complemented and enhanced the process.

Paradoxes of SSR

An activity and one-shot measure might be valuable by enhancing either security, sector efficiency or by inducing a reform package – without necessarily be regarded as means apt to realize SSR. As argued above one should be careful about 'overloading' SSR. When many objectives should be realized at the same time it is conceivable that unintended effects outmatch intentions: that democratic governance does not stabilize an unruly environment; that an operationally efficient and leaner security sector is little helpful for democratic control or that reforms of ordering institutions have little bearing on economic development. At least three paradoxes or difficult trade-offs could be mentioned, trade offs that requires both short and long term strategies:

- The 'local ownership' imperative is a condition for success but at least this author can see limits for its applicability in the short term: the extraordinary increase in drug trafficking from Afghanistan despite public campaigns and foreign advice to domestic efforts to curb the flows is but one example;
- Stability could be put against immature democratization. As the number of properly conducted elections yielding outcomes that enhances rather than diminishes potential conflicts are on the rise, fingers are crossed behind the doors of many donors and partners in SSR. The experiences of free elections in Algeria and Palestine have made it clear that good governance requires many reforms and additional institutions besides the plebiscite;[5]
- Massive foreign presence and investment in SSR activities within a dependent economy without self sustained economic growth run a risk of becoming the central ingredient of the local economy apart from crime, thereby perpetuating distress and diminishing the will to solve those cleavages that motivated the intervention in the first place, Kosovo being an example.

Conclusion

Closing this overview of concepts, alternatives and dilemmas one should ponder three things. Political environments, discursive contexts and institutional mind-sets matter when establishing the framework for SSR. A number of 'hidden assumptions', ultimate values and international and national objectives colour the three traditions and contexts alluded to above. Each tradition harbour their specific roots and supportive institutional background. A liberal-democratic agenda and cognitions about the desirability and nature of development reform is the driver behind the instrumental view on programming 'self to self-help' in partner/target countries. OECD/DAC is a central actor in this tradition. NATO has been the champion of re-educating and transforming military forces and of building defence institutions in countries of transition while paying regard to democratic and civilian control. As for internal safety and border control, EU has taken on a great responsibility. With regard to post-conflict reconstruction members of the UN family has been at the forefront together with more exclusive regional organizations such as NATO, EU and ECOWAS.

However, results in SSR work are susceptible to shifts in both ends of the interconnection. SSR is built on a donor receiver relationship or one of '*inter-actors*' interacting openly: EU 'transformatory power' and the inducements of Europeanization still function in Ukraine and Western Balkans – but since 2005 it is

---

5 An analogy could be made with the conventional wisdom of frozen conflicts. 'Peace has been held since the cease-fires'. The problem was conceptually solved in the early years of peace research when the popular distinction between positive and negative peace was coined by Johan Galtung (*Fredsforskning*. Stockholm: Prisma-Föreningen Verdandi, 1967).

generally known that the lures of membership are closed for foreseeable future. The apprehension is of course that willingness to reform and adapt also slows down. The European Neighbourhood Policy is adamant in pointing out that these partnerships do not equal a pre-accession road. Hence the inducements are less encouraging. In Afghanistan other values are at play, *viz.* the credibility of services rendered to the government and the long term commitment to the cause, a presence that easily is questioned by domestic opposition and opinion when met by violence.

For every substantial SSR component (police, armed forces, paramilitary troops, border guards, intelligence) there is a supply/demand relationship subject to a political calculus of costs/benefits on both sides. If the costs of change are high, and the inducements low, there is always a point of resistance beyond which change encouraged by an external agent will slow down, become nullified by other actions or simply dismissed and ignored. The window for influence is closed.

What is not SSR? There are realities which correspond to SSR but that are not identified as SSR as the underlying assumption are the wrong ones or the political context intuitively of a different nature.

The resurgence of a powerful defence sector within the so called power structures of the Russian Federation is not generally known as SSR despite a drastic overhaul of structures and a tightening of political control. The Federation has recently increased its defence budget, but in contrast to those new alliance members that also have invested more in traditional defence spending, a major power like Russia is not part of the SSR community. A number of bilateral arms control measures concluded with the US as well as a partnership in the combat against terrorism are not counted as merits.

A shift to a country where the political process unfolds outside of open foreign pressures also reveals the limits to SSR. An outdrawn and almost and stalemated competition between the Swedish MoD and Ministry of Justice concerning constitutional privileges and role in combating terrorism and surveillance of citizens' electronic transboundary messages are not generally understood as SSR. The label is confined to other areas of applicability and policy designs.

Neither could an imposed political solution and shock treatment SSR be treated as a proper receiver donor relationship: the dismantling of the then power institutions sustaining Saddam Hussein's regime comes to mind. It is only after a long passage of time, many unsuccessful trials and after successive Security Council resolutions legitimizing new realities that more actors in the international community have accepted the challenges. But the SSR discourse is hesitant, even absent on this particular threshold.

The conclusion is obvious: SSR is a political concept, susceptible both to its own achievements and external forces.

References

Buzan, B., *People, States, and Fear: An Agenda for International Security Studies in the Post-Cold War Era*, 2nd edition. Boulder, CO: Lynne Rienner, 1993.

Galtung, J., *Fredsforskning*. Stockholm: Prisma-Föreningen Verdandi, 1967.

Hänggi, H. and Tanner, F., *Promoting Security Sector Governance in the EU Neighbourhood*. Paris: Institute for Security Studies, 2005.

Rummel, R., *Power Kills: Democracy as a Method of Nonviolence*. New Jersey: Transaction Publishers, 2002.

SSR and Governance; Policy and Good Practice. Paris: OECD/DAC, 2004.

Chapter 2

Security and Safety in the Baltic Sea Region 1989-2004: Transformations and Three Agents of Change

Carl-Einar Stålvant

Introduction

Baltic Sea politics and developments have for two decades been driven by several national and collectively shared motives. Analytically they could be put into three overriding perspectives: *regionalization, stabilization and normalization.* Within a time-span of 15 years, the formation sprung from relative oblivion into a European success story. Achievements were noticeable in terms of transcending the divisive East-West barrier in the European North. Epochal changes in the late 1980s spurred regional activism and social dynamism to redefine, even to recast long-standing political identities and commonalties. An immense number of direct and close contacts were established between neighbouring peoples, communities and public institutions who have shared barriers but no bridges.[1]

Improvements in the strategic environment mattered much. A tacit but strong strategic dimension was present in redefinition of interests when the states in the region assessed unfolding events. In accordance with the sausage theory, the peace dividend of the Cold War was delayed in the Baltic flank area as much armour and large number of troops from Central Europe were at first deployed in its vicinity. Likewise, much of the strategic nuclear infrastructure remained intact on the Kola Peninsula. With the pullout of Russian troops from the Baltic States in 1994 and reduction in standing military force levels, the situation changed. The cardinal problem was hereinafter how to combine security with stability and political reform.

With regard to security governance the agenda bifurcated. Foreign policy reorientation coalesced with domestic reforms in stabilizing turbulent conditions. Strategies were devised, not the least by Nordic countries, which amplified the efforts of neighbouring countries to change and transform themselves. Such measures contributed to the reduction of tensions and dissolution of traditional enemy images. Shifts in perceived threats and risks conditioned the built-up of

---

1 Stålvant, C.-E., *Actors around the Baltic Sea: An Inventory*. Stockholm: Ministry for Foreign Affairs, 1996.

a more omnipotent, responsive and apt security sector. Soft power assistance propped up feeble state institutions across the entire field of public order and security tasks and thereby strengthened the processes of nation- and state-building. A number of scholars have hence claimed cooperation between Baltic Sea states as an illustrative laboratory for overcoming insecurity traps and for realizing a more secure environment. Bearing this in mind, the chapter explores the dynamics of the three titular perspectives introduced above.

Three Modes of Change: A Few Assertions and their Implications

Although cooperation is driven by a multitude of interests and covers substantive issues in all walks of life, the three perspectives give a sound basis for a theoretical interpretation of changes in Baltic Sea regional conditions. A certain sequential order is also expressed by the terms. This means that the chronology of events is to a certain extent subordinated to the logic of the perspectives. No exact temporal fixing points exist although certain actions and policy reversals stand out.[2]

The underlying preconception for *regionalization* is spurred by new concepts of political organization. A shared framework of action emerged, attracting various actors, visualized by a spatial core of untapped potentials. Dispersed contacts and uncoordinated interactions were soon given direction and purpose by *stabilization* policies providing security and assistance to policy-making. *Normalization* is trickier. It does not seem necessary to examine the political meanings of normalization beyond a few simple observations. The term is associated with legal and diplomatic practices connoting mutual recognition of states and the pursuit of 'correct' inter-state relations. It denotes courses of actions arriving at crossroads, turning from one pattern of conducting business in a tense way into a less confrontational mode. It is consonant with a propensity of regional members to assess, exploit and acquiesce to unfolding new political realities and alignments. The term is a relative one, not necessarily describing amicable relations, and might even be consistent with tension, divergent and even opposing political principles.

The implications could be spelled out in the following way. Each term emphasizes a particular category of actor sustaining Baltic Sea cooperation: civil society, states and international institutions. Secondly, they identify changing strategic nexuses on the regional agenda. Thirdly they are apt to discern shifts in bottom-up and top-down approaches to political and social cooperation. While all categories of actors influence the unfolding of developments, many indicators suggest that their relative import vary over time and within the three dimensions.

---

2   Some arguments, references and a sequential identification of trends are by and large in line with the consistently theory-based interpretation of Baltic Sea Region Security and Co-operation from post-Wall to post-Enlargement Europe presented by Fabrizio Tassinari in his dissertation 'Mare Europaeum'. Copenhagen: Department of Political Science, 2004.

To illustrate the claims, a few references are made to Swedish Baltic Sea programs in this paragraph. An established assertion maintains that civil society and local transnational structures were initially forceful agents in creating regionalization. This pattern was evident when environmental action groups took initiatives to ameliorate ambient conditions in Poland. In 1989 a crash program for *emergency aid* was launched. Public efforts coalesced with substantial private sacrifices in alleviating harsh living conditions and poverty. Although much popular concern and solidarity actions were concentrating on the three Baltic States, activities were also directed to vicinity areas in Russia and Poland as well. The reunification of Germany comprised a noteworthy Baltic Sea dimension as well.[3] Within a few years these different strands crystallized into political measures propping up *sovereignty support* for weak and reborn states.

Stabilization was long a rhetorical phrase rather than a straight strategy. Safety and security has been a matter primarily handled by national governments. The designation adopted by a Swedish assistance programme in 1995 – *security enhancing support* – epitomizes how focused inter-governmental relations in pursuit of *security and stability* tended to overshadow the role of social bonds and organizational networks created during the initial phase. Reading the story from a Polish or Baltic perspective periodization might be somewhat different. A campaign for the maximum objective of achieving stability via inclusion in the EU and NATO, even before these organizations declared open doors to an eastern enlargement, was already accepted among national priorities. Nor has the role and significance of security cum stability in the region remained a constant preoccupation. National governments have preferred to forego 'regional tables' and to link the harder issues to a wider international context as an assurance option.[4]

Both regional bodies and a number of international institutions contributed to region-building Assistance programmes foresaw the adoption of the rule of law principles and promoted general justice reform. OSCE as well as the Council of Baltic Sea States monitored how international standards in minority protection were respected. Support was rendered to democratic developments and to the adaptation of national economies to the rules and standards of market economies. *Development cooperation* later entered regional parlance as a comprehensive description for capacity building during pre-accession EU preparations (and for NATO, Membership Action Plans) in an increasingly multilateralized relationship.

The decisions taken in 2002 to expand NATO and to enlarge EU set a steady course with clear objectives and time targets. *Normalization* both proceeds and sustains this new post-enlargement agenda. It moreover entails the prospects of

---

3 Auffermann, B. and Visuri, P., *Nordeuropa und die Deutsche Herausforderung.* Baden-Baden: Nomos Verlag, 1995.

4 A number of such meetings on confidence building measures were held under the auspices of OSCE and the inspiration of French Prime Minister Balladur's stability pact.

many sub-regional matters coalescing at decision-making tables in dominant international and transatlantic structures.

Hence a few central questions emerge: What made the region tick? What achievements could one discern within each of the perspectives? How will regional affairs be affected by the post-enlargement agenda and decision-making in new constellations? What ideas and shared policies are likely to impact on national and regional policies? Of course, such questions are easier to pose than to answer. But an effort will be made to support these theoretical ideas by diverse evidence and to pinpoint how structural factors and political tendencies conceivably and reasonably interact under changing conditions.

Regionalization

Early Drivers

Regionalization is and remains an accomplishment. Churchill once located the iron curtain between Trieste and Lübeck, leaving Northern Europe as a less central area in the contest. Somewhat later the Berlin wall came to epitomize the division of all of Europe. Modern Baltic Sea regionalism could hence be rationalized as a policy and strategy for overcoming this barrier. Many forces and happenstance coalesced in creating this opportunity. During the late 80s, scholars of the arts and humanities emphasized with some justification that their intuitive grasp of overstretched Soviet ambitions and socialism's shaky cultural foundations were more accurate guides to understand accelerating events in East Europe than the categories and cognitions used by social scientists trained in the realist school of power relations. The relevance of explanations based on economic exhaustion and strategic checkmate to the demise of the socialist system should not be dismissed. It is a fact, however, that the banners of the velvet revolution – 'the contagious strength of new ideas in times of accelerating upheavals', to quote the renaissance historian Jacob Burckhardt – were in the Baltic Sea region carried by musicians, artists, poets and an electricity repair worker. Old political hands, bureaucrats or scientists played more marginal roles.

So, within a short period of time, the Baltic Sea area turned from a militarized borderland area into a sub-regional 'laboratory of all-European unification'[5] or even a 'microcosm of wider Europe society'.[6] The outer contours of the formation were and remain undetermined; an attribute that enhanced the attraction of the region as

---

    5   Hubel, H., 'The Baltic Dimension of European Unification' in Lahteenmäki (ed.) *Dimensions of Conflict and Cooperation in the Baltic Sea Rim*. Tampere: TAPRI Research Report No. 58, 1994, p. 59.
    6   Stålvant, C.-E., 'The Council of Baltic Sea States' in Cottey (ed.) *Sub-Regional Cooperation in the New Europe: Building Security, Prosperity from the Barents to the Black Sea*. London/New York: Macmillan, 1999, p. 55.

a *frame of reference* for action. Territorial flexibility was instrumental in construing relations between variegated types of actors and at different layers of society. Once the Cold War overlay shuttered, older maps resurfaced. A different historical cartography of borders and connections in most walks of life was brought up.

A Plurality of Actors

The regional formation took strength from the synergetic effects of many decentralized efforts, collaborating institutions and networks. In the economic sphere, the Chambers of Commerce network guided and stimulated enterprises and companies in their search for new economic partners and projects. The early story of contemporary Baltic Sea co-operation is filled with entrepreneurial spirit and direct people-to-people networking. Popular movements and associations, local communities and civic interests both stimulated the growth of the region and gave shape to some of its institutional and substantive innovations.

The many initial initiatives and projects were often short-lived but covered broad grounds. Much direct support was given to democratic development and the strengthening of public law and judicial system, economic development and banking, commerce and transportation, environmental problems and sustainable development, energy and nuclear safety, physical planning and small enterprises, cultural exchange, research and education. Gradually the ensuing pattern of bottom up-processes was overtaken by formal decision-making and planning. International and national assistance programs provided new incentives for many societal actors to solidify their contacts. They incited many national authorities, public agencies and MNCs to open 'regional windows' and to establish a presence.

The tilt was perhaps even more drastic in the peripheral High North on the 'Skull-cap' of the Baltic. A sub-regional process between Nordic countries and Russia was initiated for mitigating threats stemming from the legacy of nuclear infrastructures and cross-border ills. If Baltic Sea regionalism was inspired by and profited from the Hansa metaphor, so in the Barents Sea the impetus to convert barriers into bridges was found in old Pomor trading routes and sea-lanes for transport. Obviously, the appeals for regionalism fell onto fertile ground when changing cultural, social and political needs coincided and interacted with natural and physical environments.

Common Interest

Shifting answers have been given to the question as to what factors were conducive to region-building. A very modest degree of regional cooperation emerged only early in the 1970s as a rational response to a shared problem. Two conventions were then signed, one on the management of fisheries and one on environmental protection of the Baltic Sea. These two Baltic Sea Conventions were among the few instruments and relations that were not affected by negative spill-over from worsened political and military relations in the early 1980s. Evidently they embodied both a symbolic and substantial value, although within limited fields.

It is further noteworthy how national cultural institutions and educational grant schemes were turned into diplomatic assets in the early years of cooperation with new neighbours. A Finnish estimate of a decade of allocations to political and economic change in Central and East Europe claims that more than 600 million Euros were spent on grants only.[7] A former Director of the Danish Cultural Institute has confirmed that his institute turned into an asset and foreign policy tool in the late 1980s. The foreign minister personally suggested a quick expansion of means available to a scholarly and cultural exchange program and the quick establishment of information centres in the newborn polities.

Second to culture was the concern for the environment. The securitization of the environment mirrored the gravity of the situation but also resonated well with public opinion and donor countries' willingness to assist. Sometimes the many projects also corresponded to the recipient's concerns. Not least, after the Chernobyl nuclear catastrophe and Gorbachev's Murmansk speech in 1987, the notion 'comprehensive environmental security' legitimized direct and decentralized cooperation. Securitization of life-sustaining processes and alarming conditions in ailing industries and chemical-intensive agricultural practices made 'comprehensive environmental security' a shared objective for foreign assistance. Not least Poland became a favoured target.

In fact, a widely shared perception of environmental deterioration interacted with political developments and precipitated a number of decisive turning points. In the struggle for Baltic independence, resistance against Moscow-directed projects with negative environmental consequences mobilized public opinion behind the banners of National fronts. Oil spills and an infectious disease among seals effectively brought home the message of the common Baltic Sea as a shared responsibility. Moreover, such issues induced the Swedish and Polish Prime Ministers jointly to arrange a first post-Cold War conference that reflected new realities and a different political geography in the region. A meeting in Ronneby, Sweden in September 1990 gathered mixed participants for the framing of an action program. Not only the riparian states but also part-states, international organizations, and international banks, NGOs and functionally related observer states were present.[8] The inclusive representation settled a management example for other issue areas in regional cooperation.

Environment protection received the lion's share of assistance money and technical assistance. A calculation of total transfer of European assistance aid shows moreover that a higher proportion of the projects were justified by environmental

---

7   'From Support to Partnership', Finland's Strategy for Cooperation in its Neighbouring Areas. Helsinki: Ministry of Foreign Affairs, 2004.

8   When commenting on his life-long political carrier, former Swedish Prime Minister Ingvar Carlsson mentioned the meeting as a primary achievement – i.e. more important than Swedish EU membership.

arguments in the Baltic Sea region 1988-96 than in central or southern Europe.[9] It took some time before loans; grants and corporate FDI's were coordinated and geared to costly infrastructural projects and commercial investments.

Security Downplayed

Certainly security concerns were prominent. Gradually they changed from preoccupations with the strategic balance to a widened understanding of what was at stake. Instead of fearing Russian expansionism, an image of a new environment descending into instability took over. Two kinds of fears and challenges made inroads on the regional agenda: civic security risks yielded by intensified exchanges and trans-boundary effects, and common problems stemming from the socialist legacy and societal turbulence.[10]

An assertion in small state theory claims, that when great-power alliances and the international environment is 'fixed', small states have a great amount of security, but little freedom of action. When, on the other hand, the system collapses, breaks up, changes its character, then there is considerable freedom of movement, but many uncertainties for the small states. It so seems in retrospect that in the 1990s a combination of freedom and security prevailed. The small Nordic grouping had a considerable room of manoeuvre to sustain regionalization. Nordic ideology and modes of cooperation were projected onto the emerging networks and proliferating trans-local contacts.[11] Bo Huldt even claims that the coincidence might be not only a unique period in the history of the region-and also, essentially a unique event in small state history.[12]

A side effect was a certain distance to the main transatlantic institutions. The role played by the Nordic countries in inventing *institutional responses* at the sub-regional level is noteworthy. The Barents Euro-Arctic Council, the Arctic Council and the later EU Northern Dimension proposal have such roots. The proposal to establish the Council of Baltic Sea States (CBSS) was made jointly by the Danish and German Foreign Minister. The Nordic and Baltic Councils in combination with their associated networks have also impacted on the shape of political landscapes. Despite individual priorities in national foreign policies to become members within or to develop special relations with NATO and EU,

---

9   Bergh, R., *Environmental Cooperation with the Baltic States*. Stockholm: Swedish Environment Protection Agency, 1996.

10   Moroff, H. (ed.) *European Soft Security Policies: The Northern Dimension*. Programme on the Northern Dimension of the CFSP, FIIA Helsinki and IEP, Berlin, 2002.

11   Waewer, O., 'From Nordism to Baltism' in Jervell (ed.) *The Baltic Sea Area: A Region in the Making*. Karlskrona: Baltic Sea Institute, 1992.

12   Huldt, B., 'The Post-Cold War Transition in the Baltic Sea Region: A Decade of Small State Activism' in *International Security in a Time of Change: Threats, Concepts, Institutions*. Festschrift für Daniel Adam Rotfeld, Serie Demokratie, Sicherheit, Frieden No. 164. Baden-Baden: Nomos, 2004.

it took almost a decade before the two main collective organizations prevailed also in a regional perspective.

The tendency to base cooperative proposals on a security-conscious strategy while excluding them from the explicit mandate of regional bodies managing cooperation reflects an old Nordic tradition. The Nordic Council itself only accepted security as a proper topic for cooperation with the demise of the Cold War. When the five heads of governments concluded in 1991 'on the interests and needs of their citizens, the Nordic countries must try to influence developments in Europe and among their neighbours', requiring a renewal of Nordic international consultations, they carefully circumscribed the mandate of the emerging new bodies.[13]

Neither was security not a proper object for the CBSS to handle although members could introduce 'other matters or possible subjects for cooperation should they so decide'.[14] A similar duality was glaringly expressed in the Finnish proposal for a EU Northern Dimension initiative. It was feared that the inclusion of such questions would impede rather than facilitate any progress. Moreover, they might elevate the dimension to a purely intergovernmental mode of foreign policy decision-making rather than staying within the confines of the Union's 'external relations' and having recourse to the Commission's expenditures. Also, the Barents Council stayed away from bones of high political contention. Perhaps one can say that should the need arise such issues could then be raised on the sidelines of meetings, without any pressures to reach agreement and with negligible repercussions on other items.

Regionalization cum Laboratory

So, by happenstance and calculation, a number of different organizing principles and institutions have both created and integrated a system of co-operative multilevel relations among public and private actors. From a theoretical point of view a number of interpretative designations have been proposed for describing and characterizing the ensuing Baltic Sea formation. A significant number of studies concur in their view on the significance of bottom-up processes in fostering a regional perspective. However, the exact nature of the Baltic Sea constellation defies a simple classification. It clearly differs from the Nordic community of small states based on homogenous civic values and similar institutions. Regional cooperation flourished thanks to rather than despite heterogeneous background factors, divided histories and a diversity of actors.

At the same time, the nature of the constellation is an argument for caution. The Baltic Sea area is a peripheral sub-region, linking peoples and authorities in Europe's key regions, the EU, Nordic non-EU states, and Russia. To no surprise,

---

13   Nordic Council report from the 42nd session, Stockholm, 1992.
14   Declaration, Foreign Ministers of the Baltic Sea States, Copenhagen, 5-6 March 1992.

relations encompass many contradictions between and across the countries. Regionalization and decentralized cooperation unfolds as part of government strategy among Nordic states or as a consequence of a basic political trait in German political culture. In Russian politics, this trait is rather seen by many as a policy of default, or as a token of weakness and incapacity of state authority. Politics and the policies pursued by Putin have steered Russia away from the turbulent years of early system change and the battle of laws between the centre and the regions. Russia's good economic record for a number of consecutive years has facilitated national consolidation. Administrative reforms impacting on internal centre-periphery relations have halted a further decentralization of foreign relations but also given certain established cross-border contacts a more solid basis.

A neo-liberal argument about conditions for stability and order probably summarizes the essentials of 'the Baltic Sea laboratory'. Ideas about the virtues of pluralism are transferred to the international realm. Overlapping authorities and competing organizational solutions to different concerns are said to be underpinning stability. Fuzzy borders of competence are depicted as frontiers and meeting grounds for win-win games while clear demarcations and exclusions might only reach sub-optimal gains. Not least, cities and local municipal co-operation functioned as inroads into transnational networking and region-building. With the risk of oversimplification, a vibrant civil society going transnational epitomizes much of the social science discourses about Baltic Sea regional cooperation. This neo-medieval or post-modern vision is different from a modern order of sovereign states and clear delineations of self-controlled national spaces.

This portrait entails a positive appreciation of popular mobilization, and 'recourse to several sources of national and international' funding opportunities. Once established, many transnational contacts and cooperation between functional authorities, private corporations and NGOs were self-sustained. Baltic Sea regionalization rests on a solid material foundation. Different indicators for trading patterns, economic relations, investments, transport and communication all bear witness to the extent with which the Baltic Sea Basin countries and Norway and Iceland are interacting with each other, and have become interdependent in many walks of life. Not the least, large region-based international companies and financial institutions have invested heavily and expanded their activities by FDI: s, mergers and acquisitions of new plants.

Stabilization

Bringing States In

Regional dynamics was conducive for the establishment of a pattern, but not for its transformation. As noted, politics have rather been framed on the logic of *a dual agenda*. A different type of game and strategic calculations guided national governments when new options were opened by reforms in European and Atlantic institutions and the gradual opening of doors. In setting national objectives, and while adjusting to accelerating changes, the distinction between high and low politics impacted on the appreciation of the nature of the European strategic environment. The core question – conditions for inclusion in Euro-transatlantic structures – added diplomatic heterogeneity to the Baltic constellation. Not least the Nordic states have been and remain divided. Different formal affiliations did not, however, impede these five countries – and a number of interested outsiders as well – from engaging in 'competitive cooperation' in cultivating links with new democracies and neighbours. As multilateral negotiations and national preparations for membership either in the EU or NATO dragged on, more pressing threats made inroads on the regional agenda. The new challenges were mainly of two kinds: civic security risks yielded by intensified exchanges and trans-boundary effects, and common problems stemming from the socialist legacy.[15]

So, with the demise of Cold War confrontation and the advent of conflicts rooted in internal situations, the security spectrum of contingencies widened. Potential threats suggested a rethinking of national security problems to include other violent disruptions and societal vulnerabilities to non-military challenges. To mitigate and tackle such threats, according to Anders Bjurner,[16] not only inter-governmental actions were called for but even more '*trans-state*' actions. Upon this conflation of security and stability, Baltic Sea national governments embarked on a course where soft security measures were accepted as a main line of action. Broad co-operation and the provision of targeted support to the transition process in individual countries were adopted as instruments of international and national security and stability policies. Uncertainties in institutional capacity and order-maintaining functions prompted concrete assistance, training and cooperation in enhancing skills and advice and dialogue aiming at the improvement of legal norms and rules. Reform advice and assistance was not only confined to MoD and the military sector but broader state functions were targeted. Institution-building and enhanced capacities comprised border guards, customs, legal training, the judiciary and police and rescue services despite varying administrative solutions. Liaison officers were exchanged between twin authorities, and some spectacular law enforcement operations were synchronized.

Low politics and soft security implies costly action beyond conditional intention. Policies of this kind differ from national positioning and declarative policy in dialogues between governments – increasingly framed and implemented in negotiated bilateral and multilateral programs. The interaction between ideas, decisions and institutions has a particular import for making policies succeed. It

---

15   Hubel, H. and Gänzle, S., 'The Soft Security Agenda at the Sub-Regional Level: Policy Responses of the Council of Baltic Sea States' in Moroff (ed.) *European Soft Security Policies*. The Northern Dimension, Helsinki and Berlin, FIIA and Institut für Europäische Politik, 2002.

16   Bjurner, A., 'European Security at the End of the Twentieth Century: The Sub-regional Contribution' in Cottey, ibid., p. 9.

engages partners and structures across states and nations. It is a quality embedded in state structures and civil society. Neither is the assessment of how to enhance conditions for security tied to the idea of security and protection as an indivisible good. To mitigate and defuse latent conflict, much assistance has been targeted to integration of the Russian speaking minorities 'in the Baltic states' via language training courses for non-citizens.

At the same time, improvements in security, protection measures, and capacity to cope with different sorts of crises, are at the mercy of budget lines, programme conditions and application procedures. Shifting priorities between successive tenders might also inhibit lasting projects. The framing and realization of the Northern Dimension revealed the problems in coordinating the many funds and instruments of the European Commission. Some of these instruments, action plans and stock of experience were transferred into EU programs once Sweden and Finland joined. Not few of the ideas and proposals first probed by regional bodies have been emulated to or been deliberately transferred to the EU level. Despite commitments to the contrary by EU civil servants in connection with the Northern Dimension, the Commission seems to have downplayed the utility of sub regional institutions as initiators or executers of policy. The inherent trade offs between substantive areas of cooperation for many partners and individual country strategies were acknowledged when it was decided to phase out national development programs in view of EU enlargement.[17] In preparing for membership and a later adoption of the Schengen regime, heavy investments were made in Poland and the Baltic States as regards border protection, crossing stations and safety surveillance.

Improvements in civil security and less threatening military contingencies notwithstanding, they were kept apart from strategic disputes and diplomatic battles. A widely shared appreciation of the vulnerable situation of the three small Baltic States prompted many donor governments also to assist in the build–up of their military security. But the main political question hovered around the reconciliation of NATO expansion and regional stability. The Swedish Prime Minister scored some points when he announced in 1996 that the Baltic States' own decision should be respected. While Poland's prospective membership in 1999 was met with fierce resistance in Russian campaigns, the inclusion of former Soviet territory was claimed to be inadmissible. There was also hesitation among many allies, bar Denmark, before the Bush administration decided to go along with a Big Bang expansion of the Alliance. More secure Baltic States no longer caught in grey zones might also give comfort to Russia. Also Finnish politicians aired many concerns until membership was the least guarded secret of 2002.

At that time American policy in the aftermath of 9/11 had upset the global agenda. Putin's Russia lowered the fierce resistance campaigns against Baltic

---

17 'Att Utveckla Samarbetet med Central och Östeuropa' ('Enhancing Cooperation with Central and Eastern Europe'), Swedish Ministry of Foreign Affairs (2000), SOU 2000, 122, p. 101.

NATO membership by admitting that the step would not be a tragedy for Russia, although it would not do any good to a Baltic state. NATO-Russian relations were placed on a firmer footing by the creation of the NATO-Russia Council already before the Prague summit, in Reykjavik in May 2002. Although alliance membership signified a triumph for the three small ex-Soviet republics, it occurred under radically altered transatlantic and global conditions. Russia has noted that the NRC could be a diplomatic asset in monitoring the evolution of NATO, including the policies pursued by its Baltic neighbours. The more so, as the non-article 5 new threats include the Global War on Terrorism – in which Russia is a privileged partner – and that this threat image also pervades members' domestic security preparations.

Normalization: Steps into Different Games?

Again: the year 2004 marked a watershed. Not the least political discourses and national strategies changed with EU enlargement and NATO expansion. The intense Russian advocacy against new NATO members in 1996-99 succeeded in postponing the complete opening of the door to the former Baltic Republics.

Russia's many alternative proposals on security arrangements and guarantees, backed up by visible measures and conditions were however all dismissed. NATO members' own wish to develop good relations with Russia probably acted as a restraint on the Baltic States' relations with Russia. Potential entrants had to digest the Membership Action Plans where a number of political and military conditions were laid down; for instance that they should settle ethnic and territorial disputes by peaceful means.

Domestic reforms during the pre-membership period profoundly reshaped the social and economic fabric of new members. The Baltic States, like Poland, have accomplished their foreign policy objectives. Their security concerns have been salved. Their economic, legal and administrative progress has been sanctioned by EU accession. Supported by the Nordics and Germany, and with Russia acquiescing to the new European realities of the post cold-war period, *normalization* is a catchword for the new rules of the game. Thus on a visit to Finland in September 2001, President Putin found enlargement useless since nobody threatened anyone in Europe. He nevertheless declared that Russia would not start 'a hysterical campaign' against the Baltic States.

Much restraint and caution characterized the military and deployment aspects of alliance extension. Already in 1997, with the signing of the Founding Act on Mutual Relations, Cooperation and Security with Russia, NATO gave reassurances that it had 'no intention, no plan and no reason to deploy nuclear weapons on the territory of new members'.[18] Baltic politicians have also in various statements signalled their reluctance for establishing new and foreign bases on their soil. Actual deployments have also been modest in volume. One exceptional issue is the demonstrative air policing tours undertaken by Belgian pilots in NATO aircraft on the eve of formal membership in April 2004.

So, the master notion of the previous decade – transition – is out. Neither is the language of donor and recipient adequate any longer. With the provision of foreign professional assistance, the frequent misuse of donor-country consultants in well paid but not always accurate advice positions have left scars behind.

Some conceivable consequences for security, welfare and regional cooperation follow:

Security: The emergence of new global threats and the war on terrorism diverted attention to other more distant unruly areas and hot spots. The assertive American policy on Europe 'old and new' split Baltic Sea countries as well.

Via the logic of collective diplomacy, former Eastern European countries meet Russia as a strategic partner, be it in matters of security or economy. Baltic accession left Finland and Sweden in a shrinking camp of partners in PfP exercises and activities. Their previously not insignificant security-enhancing support for the Baltic States left a legacy of Nordic total defence thinking and preparations for territorial defence. But these policies were easily dismissed as the new members were assigned to quite different roles and missions within the alliance. Reorienting the strategic nexus from homeland guarantees and security receiver to out-of-area operations is in tune with the international agenda, but it is a costly exercise for a would-be security provider. As an Estonian official maintained, 'in joint operations small states have the possibility of providing small but effective niche-capacities, both independently as well as in cooperation with other nations of a similar size'.[19]

However, hard choices might be in the cards for small countries that have secured double entries. In general they have seen NATO as the main security provider. The hope for a good NATO-EU partnership in the aftermath of 'Berlin-plus' and a concurrent view on the division of labour, might be upset if there are more than operation that require a contribution and the same national asset is committed to more than one register. In the built up of EU crisis management capacity new external options have emerged for members: A free choice of partners in European battle groups. It is note-worthy that Estonia is aligned with the Nordic Battle Group, led by Sweden while Latvia and Lithuania have chosen continental partners. Emerging foot-loose threats also challenges old thinking. The

---

18   A new situation emerged when the US (but not NATO) entered a new bilateral arrangement with two European allies. The forward anti missile defence should shield against possible enemy attacks from new global adversaries.

19   Tiido, H., *Estonia Anchoring Itself in the Euro-Atlantic Security Structures.* Tallinn: Estonian Ministry of Foreign Affairs Yearbook, 2002.

solidarity clause and the commitment for EU members to assist in case of natural disasters or terrorism open up new prospects for cooperation in the civilian field and with regard to functional security. In the latter field, Baltic Sea cooperation has already a good record, and appears as a possible stepping-stone when building up multinational support teams.

The expanded Union will face many different foreign endowments. The centre of gravity in the stabilization policies pursued by NATO and EU, respectively, has moved to the new eastern members. In this sense, non-alignment entails a political marginalization dilemma rather than a security problem for Finland and Sweden. Norway and Iceland face the reverse situation with regard to EU decision-making.

In this situation, new Baltic Sea EU members have also taken a lead in *cultivating stability into the new neighbourhoods*. Polish activism and pivotal position within the EU was put to a test early in connection with the disputed presidential election in Ukraine in November 2004. Baltic state activism in Caucasus and in West Balkan states also reveals similar concerns. Having successfully experienced the hardships and joy of transition, they are well placed to advice prospective listeners.

The next set of states further to the East and in the Caucasus is a new testing ground for European security and stability. Russia is most reserved and is vehemently resisting certain EU policies in the post-Soviet space. The Union is criticized for its unilateral framing of policies and a 'conceptual deficiency' in making the new neighbours and Russia 'objects' of policies.[20]

What will other Baltic Sea countries do? Is there enough domestic popular engagement? The Baltic experience suggests that links between civil society associations facilitate and propel formal cooperation. But conditions apparently differ between these proto-democracies of today and the freedom of action that the demise of totalitarianism and socialism entailed fifteen years ago. There is apparently less certainty about the stakes and forces at play. Popular mobilization is likely to follow the lead of public policy rather than the other way around.

Welfare: European governance is up for a profound transformation. A Union of 27 is different from one of only 15 members. Membership will impact on a wide array of policies not only in the domestic field. Just to pinpoint the obvious, it has left Russia as the only Central and East European partner in the Northern Dimension revising it into a four party arrangement.[21]

Although economic cooperation and trade questions are important in Baltic Sea cooperation, it is not a system for legal integration and regulation. Baltic Sea countries will in certain matters become a regional intergovernmental lobby within a much more complicated system for shaping decisions.

---

20   Emerson, M., *The Wider Europe Matrix*. Brussels: CEPS, 2004.

21   Iceland, Norway, Russian Federation and the EU agreed on new terms of reference and action programme. Finnish MFA, 24 November 2006.

Baltic Sea cooperation in the perspective of EU-Europeanization is quite institutionalized; a habit which could be an advantage but not sufficient. Former Swedish Prime Minister made strong efforts to orchestrate a unity of views among the new members before meetings in the Council of Ministers. The EU Baltic-Nordic group is recognized as 3 + 3. The need to secure support from Poland and Germany is also mentioned, but institutionalized forms are said to be absent.[22]

However, decision rules in the final test complicate matters. In majority voting the eight-member state caucus will neither be strong enough to bloc a proposal nor to secure its acceptance. The assessment is true both for decisions taken according to Nice rules and the simplified and revised 'constitutional treaty (Lisbon)' regulations.

Regionalization Reappraised? The Prospects of Normalization

A few indications from 2004-05 suggest that Baltic Sea regionalization has lost much popular appeal and political zeal. Ministers meet less often. The frequently heard argument that this is a place where the inclusion of Russia is realized makes less sense if a centralized Russia pursues strategic dialogues with Brussels over the heads of regional stakeholders. Conversely, Russian quarrels with individual countries – like the outdrawn meat embargo against Polish exports – that for a period put EC cohesion to test. In areas where there is little consensus- the energy security field domes to mind- Russia is playing with a strong hand and pits new members against old ones also within the Baltic Sea region. Support for some of national, local and specialized Baltic Sea secretariats for regional cooperation has disappeared or the functions have merged with other public tasks.

In Sweden the high tide of a decade of Baltic Sea activism were marked by three consecutive billions, 1996-2000, spent in extraordinary procedures.[23] But these expenditures and other national programs for vicinity areas have been phased out. One example: funding for the Estonian language-training programme for the Russian speaking minority has ceased 'although the salience of the objective was reactivated in the aftermath of the Geogian crises in August 2008'.

It has been argued that a dense network of civil society contacts and city and county twinning sustains the regional pattern. This is well supported and published figures reveal the many interconnections and city-chains created.[24] However, people-to-people contacts seem to have reached a saturation point.

---

22 'Finland's Security and Defence Policy'. Helsinki: Prime Minister's Office, 2004.

23 The observation conforms with the theory of securitization – that the extraordinary defines the national interest, i.e. essential values are taken care of in non-normal procedures, within a institutionalized setting it means that these means but not the yearly defence budget allocated to a subordinated military authority with its task to prepare for the worst-case contingency of an armed attack – was handed directly by central ministries.

24 Data from the Baltic Sea international city twinning is provided by the Swedish Association of Municipalities, international activities branch.

Although there are renewals and changes, the list of Baltic Sea secretariats, NGOs and action groups remain constant since their founding a decade ago. Creation of new region-specific NGO networks and twinned sister institutions is rather due to organizational fusions and administrative reorganizations than innovations.

When promoting cooperation, solidarity and friendship motives have been overtaken by questions about utility and return. It is likely that some sister city-relations will contract as new generations of decision-makers come into power and the initial zeal is lost. Likely winners are those that occupy hub positions within regional and European networks. Cities and municipalities that diversified contacts and engaged a broader section of municipal services and private interests in sustained economic exchanges with regional partners are also likely to stay in place.

So, to conclude, Baltic Sea developments are still likely to be influenced by different categories of actors. The passage of time reflects different discourses and reassessment of motives and interests. A dialogue between *donors and receivers* supported the rise of participatory transboundary regionalism. *Partnerships* created under normal conditions suggest a more utilitarian and rational pursuit of interests between corporate business, bureaucracies and political authorities. In normalized but institutionalized settings for taking decisions governmental *parties* become preeminent players. They resume their formal roles but at a risk of getting bogged down in diplomatic battles and formal subtleties about rules.

More significant is the changed nature of stakes. To a certain extent they have moved beyond internal regional preoccupations to external threats, concerns and interrelations. A much less pronounced image of Russia as a tacit enemy has lessened the motives for Nordic security assistance. Normalization might render the Baltic Sea region a less distinct profile in a wider Europe. Certain latent flash points are nevertheless conceivable in bilateral relations that could ignite crises. The nature of conflict however, is apparently rather related to the exploitation of technological and economic interdependencies. The close down of Estonia's communication net and international Internet connections when massively attacked by foreign hackers in May 2007 epitomizes a new type of incident and vulnerability.

Institutional factors in Europe are likely to redefine interests in tactical games. As the rift over the Iraqi war in major international institutions 'demonstrated', much discord within cooperative organizations and political and military alliances are part and parcel of normalization. Such conditions together with centralized and long-term bureaucratic planning might despite good intentions slow down and impede issue-based networking and financially dependent but routinized and local cross-regional cooperation. If it turns out that the different corners of Europe are reconstituted as rather fixed alliances in outdrawn distributive negotiations, stalemate might result. If quick action is required, flexible frameworks have to be designed. In such a situation, Baltic-Nordic cooperation has a good record of reasserting itself and of working together at all levels of governance. This is true above all for all the diverse and security-related items that gave shape to the present Baltic Sea Region and that nowadays increasingly are conceptualized as SSR.

References

'Att Utveckla Samarbetet med Central och Östeuropa' ('Enhancing cooperation with Central and Eastern Europe'), Swedish Ministry of Foreign Affairs (2000), SOU 2000, 122.

Auffermann, B. and Visuri, P., *Nordeuropa und die Deutsche Herausforderung*. Baden-Baden: Nomos Verlag, 1995.

Bergh, R., *Environmental Cooperation with the Baltic States*. Stockholm: Swedish Environment Protection Agency, 1996.

Emerson, M., *The Wider Europe Matrix*. Brussels: CEPS, 2004.

'Finland's Security and Defence Policy'. Helsinki: Prime Minister's Office, 2004.

'From Support to Partnership', Finland's Strategy for Cooperation in its Neighbouring Areas. Helsinki: Ministry of Foreign Affairs, 2004.

Hubel, H., 'The Baltic Dimension of European Unification' in Lahteenmäki (ed.) *Dimensions of Conflict and Cooperation in the Baltic Sea Rim*. Tampere: TAPRI Research Report No. 58, 1994, pp. 283-98.

Hubel, H. and Gänzle, S., 'The Soft Security Agenda at the Sub-regional Level: Policy Responses of the Council of Baltic Sea States' in Moroff (ed.) *European Soft Security Policies*. The Northern Dimension, Helsinki and Berlin, FIIA and Institut für Europäische Politik, 2002.

Huldt, B., 'The Post-Cold War Transition in the Baltic Sea Region: A Decade of Small State Activism' in *International Security in a Time of Change: Threats, Concepts, Institutions*. Festschrift für Daniel Adam Rotfeld, Serie Demokratie, Sicherheit, Frieden No. 164. Baden-Baden: Nomos, 2004.

Moroff, H. (ed.) *European Soft Security Policies: The Northern Dimension*. Programme on the Northern Dimension of the CFSP, FIIA Helsinki and IEP, Berlin, 2002.

Stålvant, C.-E., *Actors around the Baltic Sea: An Inventory*. Stockholm: Ministry for Foreign Affairs, 1996.

Stålvant, C.-E., 'The Council of Baltic Sea States' in Cottey (ed.) *Sub-Regional Cooperation in the New Europe: Building Security, Prosperity from the Barents to the Black Sea*. London/New York: Macmillan, 1999.

Tassinari, F., *Mare Europaeum*. Copenhagen: Department of Political Science, 2004.

Tiido, H., *Estonia Anchoring Itself in the Euro-Atlantic Security Structures*. Tallinn: Estonian Ministry of Foreign Affairs Yearbook, 2002.

Waewer, O., 'From Nordism to Baltism' in Jervell (ed.) *The Baltic Sea Area: A Region in the Making*. Karlskrona: Baltic Sea Institute, 1992.

Chapter 3

Searching for Homeostasis in the Security Domain: The Polish Experience

Witold M. Patoka

Introduction

The ultimate goal of modern transformations in the security domain is to accomplish homeostasis between army, military industry, crisis management system, on one hand, and national security priorities and feasible resources, on the second one. However, neither national security priorities are formed *ex nihilo*, nor they are constant. In ideal terms, security policy priorities ought to be a function of threat assessment, human and material assets and reliability, or trust, in military alliance. In practice however, a formation of national security priorities is a process that brings together strategic, political and institutional rationales.[1] Hence, this chapter maps and analyses interactions between strategic, political and institutional forces that drew security sector reforms in Poland 1989-2009 in the three distinct domains: armed forces, military industry and crisis management system. The ambition is to answer the key questions how strategic developments trigger political and organizational processes within army, military industry and crisis management system and how these processes interact in shaping changes in these three distinct domains.

A great challenge is to redesign national security system during fundamental or paradigmatic shifts on security arena. That is exactly what has happened in Central and East Europe when the fall of Berlin Wall, in 1989, caused a rapid dysfunction, and then collapse of the Warsaw Treaty Organization, in 1991. In the aftermath, Central and East Europe quite rapidly became a security gray zone. Poland, a pivotal country in that region, initially had no choice but had to respond with policy of self-sufficiency in security matters. A utopian policy that was in power until the country became a member of the North Atlantic Treaty Organization, in 1999. Now, the country is one of NATO's leading nations and an active participant in missions conducted by the alliance. Does it mean that during the past two decades Poland has successfully accomplished reforms of security domain and

---

1 See Patoka, W., *Poland Under Pressure 1980-81. Crisis Management in State-Society Conflict.* Umeå: Umeå University, 2001 (ISBN 91-7305-041-5). Also, Allison, G., 'Conceptual Models and the Cuban Missiles Crisis', *American Political Science Review* LXIII(3), 1969, pp. 689-718.

achieved homeostasis between its core components: army, military industry and crisis management system?

Pursuing radical transformations of the security domain politicians face three fundamental choices. They may strive to adapt existing means toward new objectives, emulate reforms that elsewhere proved to be effective or introduce innovative solutions. The first path, an adaptation of existing means towards new objectives, is considered as a cost-effective approach but not always efficient. In essence, this path requires just minor upgrades of hardware and organizational procedures. Reforms through emulation are a more demanding process. Inevitably, this path involves substantial changes of organizational structures, establishment procedures and introduction of hardware that match new structure, routines and goals. Most challenging however are innovative reforms. As a rule, innovative changes are triggered by emergence of new security paradigm, which substantially diminish value or even make valueless the existing military apparatus, or by an introduction of *revolutionary* technologies, which fundamentally change security arena. What path of reforms has Poland followed? How have the introduced changes affected national security domain and its core components: army, military industry and crisis management system? Are accomplished transformations consistent with national goals and priorities?

Security Domain First Component: The Army

The Polish Army in 2010 consists of 100,000 professional soldiers and 10,000 reservists, contracted to serve in the National Reserve Forces. The core of the army is made up by the Land Forces, structured around one division of tanks and three divisions of mobile infantry. The core of the equipment is quite modern. It includes Lockheed F-16 multirole jet fighter aircraft, German 'Leopard 2' tanks, and the armoured fighting vehicle 'Wolverine', produced in Poland in cooperation with Finish 'Patria' and Italian 'Otomelare'. At present, the Land Forces provide contingents of 2,000 troops to ISAF forces in Afghanistan and to European Union humanitarian operation in Chad. To these tasks, best units were chosen from 11th Lubuska Armoured Cavalry Division, Gliwice Special Unit of Military Police, Air Component of 25th Air Cavalry Brigade, 10th Opole Logistic Brigade and 2nd Mazovian Sapper Brigade of Kazun.

The core units of Air Forces represent high value. Three squadron of Lockheed F-16 Fighting Falcon are supported by Mig-29 Fulcrum and SU-22 Fitter aircrafts upgraded to NATO's standards. What's more, modern transport planes, C-130 Hercules and CASA C-295 M, assure satisfactory airlift capabilities to out-of-area operations. That was an imperative step, as Special Forces to expeditionary missions become the Polish speciality. At present, the country has the capabilities to deploy five combat units of Special Forces and plans to double such capabilities by 2018.

Regrettably, the Navy is not in good shape. Just 6 percent of the defence budget is assigned to the Navy. In the past, a few good deals were made for four refurbished *Kobben* class submarines, *Hazard Perry* class frigate, two rocket frigates and a desperately needed logistics ship, the 'Xawery Czernicki'. Nevertheless, that was a temporary solution made a few years ago and all these ships ought to be replaced until 2015. Original plans assumed that the Navy would get by the end of 2006 two new corvettes, *Gavron* class, and a few new supporting ships. That did not happen. The present schedule assumes a delivery of a single corvette *Gavron* in 2012. Even if that happened, is highly likely that the Navy would lose roughly 75 percent of operational capabilities within next five years.

The creation of National Reserve Forces was a just in time decision. The out-fashioned Territorial Defence Forces badly needed to be replaced by modern multifunctional reserve forces created as a component of modern crisis management system as well as forces capable to secure host nation capabilities and, when needed, to support core operational forces. The timetable assumes that the National Reserve Forces would double its capabilities within next two years.

Certainly, that is a potent professional army capable to participate in out-of-area missions under the flag of the North Atlantic Treaty Organization and the European Union. Without doubt, that is an impressive achievement if we recall that twenty years earlier, in 1989, the entire security system in Poland was over-stretched. Then, the 500,000 men strong army was in very bad shape. The hardware was mainly Russian, robust but non-modern offensive weaponry with an enormous surplus of tanks, aged air forces and bulky ships for landing operations. The forces were based on conscripts, but a number of officers were relatively high to assure smooth mass mobilization.

In Poland, the entire security system became obsolete as early as the summer of 1989, despite that the Warsaw Treaty Organization was officially dissolved in July 1991.[2] The army was huge, roughly 500,000 troops, but only 10 percent of the forces had garrisons on the right side of the country, dubbed by Polish strategists as the 'Eastern Wall'.[3] In the autumn, the first democratically elected cabinet concluded that the posture of the military forces were unsuitable for the new geopolitical situation in Europe. As a first step, the legacy political structures, within the army, were dissolved and top military commanders swiftly replaced.[4]

---

2   It is worth to stress that Warsaw had to act prudently in choosing the proper time to declare a radical revision of security policy, due to the fact that the Kremlin delayed the withdrawal of troops from Germany and Poland for four long years. Finally, on 18 September 1993, the last Russian troops left Poland for good.

3   See Balcerowicz B., 'Dylematy Polski w okresie przejsciowym' ('Strategic dilemmas of the army in transition') in *Mysli Wojskowa*, No. 3, 1997, Warsaw.

4   On 4 September 1989, all key commanders were replaced. General Z. Zalewski became the new commander of the Pomeranian Military District, General T. Wilecki in the Silesian Military District, and General Z. Stelmaszczuk in the Warsaw Military District. General J. Gotowala became the new commander of the Air Force. General H. Szumski, General E. Bolociuch and General F. Puchala assumed key posts in the General Staff.

Then, to strengthen the democratic control over armed forces, two civilian deputies were appointed to the Minister of National Defence.[5] However, in practice all efforts were focused on re-positioning of military forces from western borders to the 'Eastern Wall'.

A new security doctrine of self-sufficiency was approved on 2 November 1992.[6] It declared that the country intends to strengthen links with NATO and West European Union, but in essence, it expressed a belief that Central and East Europe had become a 'gray zone' of security.[7] Looking at western patterns, the new doctrine postulated a reduction of conscripts and an increasing professionalization of forces. In practice however, the lack of capabilities to secure the 'Eastern Wall' was the key dilemma. It was nearly impossible, due to lack of adequate infrastructure, to relocate troops from west to the eastern frontiers. Disbanding western garrisons was also out of the question as such step would substantially impair the capabilities of the armed forces and make further reforms even more difficult. Hence, the reduction of the troops was stopped at the level of 250,000 men.

Paradoxically, the new security doctrine of 1992 effectively disabled further reforms. It introduced an ambiguous division of authority between the iconic President Lech Walesa and the prime minister, as it was constructed around the assumption that the ultimate power in national security matters ought to be held by the president and that the role of a prime minister was to execute the presidential policy. In consequence, the 'dual chain of command' caused permanent tensions and stalemates, between the President and succeeding prime ministers, as well as between the Chief of the General Staff, who was nominated by the President, and the Minister of National Defence, who was appointed by prime minister.

The new President, A. Kwasniewski, renounced the vague prerogative to control the army, which had been extensively exploited by his predecessor. What's more, the ambiguous distribution of power between the Minister of National Defence and the General Staff was brought to an end by a new 'Decree about the Minister of National Defence', adopted by the new parliament on 14 December 1995. These changes came just in time. The dynamic development of the Partnership for Peace, and corresponding changes of NATO's policy, meant that Poland could abandon the utopian policy of self-sufficiency in security matters.

In fact, Yanayev's *coup d'état* of 1991, in Moscow, plainly exposed that the policy of self-sufficiency in security matters is an utopian concept and Poland

---

5   See Rozkaz Nr. Pf 63/org z dnia 19 Czerwca 1990 w sprawie wprowadzenia stanowisk wice-ministrow obrony narodowej oraz nadania im ramowych zakresow dzialan (Ministry of National Defence, Order No. 63, 19 June 1990).

6   The entire military doctrine of 1992 contained two documents: 'Zalozenia Polskiej Polityki Bezpieczenstwa' ('Assumption of national security policy'); and 'Polityka Bezpieczenstwa i Strategia Obronna Rzeczypospolitej Polskiej' ('Security policy and Poland's defensive strategy'). They were signed by President L. Walesa on 2 November 1992.

7   See 'Przeglad Rzadowy' ('Governmental review'), Nr. 12, 1992, Warsaw.

has no choice but to strive to join NATO. On 10 February 1992, the Minister of National Defence J. Parys publicly declared that the country intends to seek membership in NATO, but pragmatic diplomats regarded such statement as a premature one. The NATO summit in London on 6-7 July 1990 did not open any doors and the final communiqué contained only a vague promise of cooperation with new democracies in Eastern and Central Europe.

A real chance emerged when the Pentagon established a military mission in Warsaw, on 11 March 1993.[8] As time would show, this mission heralded the Partnership for Peace, which Poland joined on 11 January 1994. National media dubbed the Partnership for Peace as a 'stopper to NATO', a move designed to avoid NATO enlargement. Nonetheless, military commanders cautiously exploited this initiative to transfer 'Stang' planning documents and initiated remodelling of forces and procedures in accordance with NATO's standards.

Poland received a formal invitation to join the alliance at the NATO Summit in Madrid, on 8 July 1997. Accessing requirements defined that one-third of the Polish Army had to achieve inter-operability by 1999, and that the country had to develop capabilities needed to act as host nation for two to three divisions and for five to ten wings of tactical air forces. It was agreed too that three Polish units will operate as part of a multinational corps and one rapid reaction division would be kept on high readiness, on three to seven days notice.[9] Furthermore, NATO standards required a new territorial division of the country into two military districts: North-Pomeranian Military District and South-Silesian Military District.

The new model of army assumed that Land Forces ought to be 118,000 men, the Air Force was to have 37,800 men and the Navy 12,600 of men. The military education system was to be reduced to 9,000 men and employment in central institutions was set at 1,800. The mobilization plans called for a 500,000-man army, with 360,000 land forces, 50,000 air force, 20,000 navy, 50,000 territorial defence and 20,000 troops assigned to the General Staff. Military experts however were critical of the size territorial defence forces, arguing that they are the most effective in terms of cost-performance and might even be able to assist core operational forces. In essence, the model of forces was based on the central premise that the entire security system ought to be constructed as an integral component of NATO.[10] Then, it had been planned that the restructuring of core forces would be completed by 1999. Unfortunately, that did not happen.

---

8   See Ministry of National Defence, Rozkaz Nr. 15, 11 Marzec 1993 (Ministry of National Defence, Order No. 15, 11 March 1993).

9   See Col. Ryszard Warszewski, 'Aspekty wewnetrzne przystapienia Polski do NATO' ('Domestic aspects of Polish accession to NATO') in *Mysl Wojskowa*, Nr. 2-1999, Warsaw 1999. Also, Col. Dr. Jozef Garbach, 'Wojsko Polskie u progu NATO' ('Polish army's accessing NATO') in *Zeszyty Naukowe WSP 'Poglady i Doswiadczenia'*, Nr. 1-111-1999, Poznan 1999.

10   It seems that such pattern of integration with NATO was an outcome of negotiations with the SHAPE, conducted between 16 September and 23 October 1997, than a genuine product of Polish military thought.

A new model of armed forces, drawn up by the 'Programme of transformation and modernization of the armed forces 2001-2006', was developed after it was determined that the previous blueprint of army was constructed on erroneous premises, foremost on overly optimistic assumptions about available resources. Hence, the new plan for 2001-2006, as well as its update for 2003-2008, was designed to eliminate the false optimism and create a balance between available resources and NATO requirements, paying particular attention to modernization of infrastructure and acquisition of new equipment for the core forces.

In essence, the programme of transformation and modernizing of the armed forces 2001-2006/2003-2008 aimed to accomplish the promised but delayed inter-operability of roughly one-third of total forces with NATO's core forces.[11] The basic goal was to reduce the share of budget devoted to personnel costs from 66 to 52 percent and to devote 32 percent of resources to investments and hardware acquisition.[12] Consequently, to match these constraints, the programme for 2001-2006/2003-2008 called for a semi-professional army of 150,000 men and women.

The initial years of programme implementation showed that old deficiencies had not been eliminated. In 2001, the armed forces did not get a needed 1,1 billion zlotys, which significantly affected the new weapons procurement and slowed down structural conversion.[13] However, the ministry muddled through in an admirable fashion and managed to cut annual fixed costs by 2,5 billion zlotys. First, it got rid of the superfluous weapons and recycled 2,142 artillery pieces, 815 tanks, 159 planes, 23 ships and 82,704 rifles. Second, it repositioned troops to larger cost-effective garrisons and closed down 51 garrisons. What is even more important, the ministry made some good deals for refurbished weaponry from other NATO countries. It purchased 116 refurbished 'Leopard 2A4' tanks and 23 'Mig-29' combat aircraft from the German army. The Navy also made quite a few good deals for refurbished vessels. It bought four 'Kobben' submarines, two rocket frigates and a desperately needed logistics ship, the 'Xawery Czernicki'. Furthermore, the air forces got three squadrons of F-16 combat aircrafts and land troops got modern armed mobile vehicles 'Wolverine'. Unexpectedly, due to post-11 September 2001, shifts in NATO's priorities, the army acquired substantial airlift capabilities, including transport aircraft C-130 'Hercules' and CASA 295M.

---

11   In accordance with NATO's standards, Poland uses progressive planning, which assumes a major update each second year.

12   See 'Ustawa o przebudowie i modernizacji technicznej oraz finansowaniu Sil Zbrojnych RP 2001-2006' ('The decree about transformation and technical modernization of the Polish army 2001-2006'), Druk Sejmowy Nr. 2746, Warsaw 2001.

13   See Council of Ministers, 'Informacja Rady Ministrow RP o realizacji programu przebudowy i modernizacji Sil Zbrojnych w latach 2001-2003' ('The information about the implementation of the programme for 2001-2003'), Warsaw, 30 September 2003. Also, Council of Ministers, 'Informacja Rady Ministrow RP o realizacji programu przebudowy i modernizacji Sil Zbrojnych w latach 2001-2006' ('The information about the implementation of the programme for 2001-2006'), Warsaw, 30 September 2003.

As a result, the 2001-2008 were exceptionally good years as regards the technical modernization of the armed forces.

The progress of technical modernization and experiences from the missions in Iraq, Afghanistan and Chad proved that only fully professional forces are capable to fulfil complex tasks in multinational missions. Hence, on 5 August 2008, the government took decision to transform the army into a fully professional force by 2010.[14] Now, the process is successfully completed. The Polish Army of 2010 consists of 100,000 professional solders.

Does it mean that the armed forces are 100,000 men strong? In fact, it does not. A few factors mean that a high operational value has roughly 1/10 of the total forces, 10,000 troops, including five operational units of Special Forces. In direct terms, the growing gap is a synergetic outcome of the optimistic construction of the national defence budget, on one side, and rather unsteady NATO's preference, on the other side. In theory, the national defence has 1.95 percent of GNP to its disposal. In practice however, the national defence is highly vulnerable to governmental 'savings programmes'. For instance, in 2008 it did not get 21 percent of promised funds. In other words, it got just 1.64 percent of GNP, instead of legally guaranteed 1.96 percent of GNP. In practice, the top priorities are assigned to the Special Forces, units selected to the Multinational Corps North-East and other units that were chosen to participate in international operations. Nevertheless, this phenomenon is rather common for nearly all armies although disproportions are much smaller.

Security Domain Second Component: The Military Industry

The military industry, with 13,000 employees in 33 enterprises, is consolidated into a single holding 'BUMAR'. This could be considered as being a success, if we recall that this sector initiated reforms with 180,000 man and women employed in 128 enterprises. A positive effect, especially through introduction of new advanced technologies, brought contracts and offset programmes with Lockheed Martin Corporation, for jetfighter F-16, with Raphael, Israel, for guided missiles 'Spike', with NAMO, Norway, for ammunition and explosives, with Patria, Finland, and Otomelare, Italy, for armoured vehicle 'Wolverine'. Further positive effects are expected from strategic cooperation with such international giants such as Sagem, Nitro and MBDA. On negative side is a lack of competitive products for foreign markets. That cause that consider as an optimum 50/50 balances between export and domestic orders is still a remote goal. Just now, 21.5 percent of production goes to foreign markets.

---

14   See Council of Ministers, 'Program profesjonalizacji Sił Zbrojnych Rzeczypospolitej Polskiej na lata 2008-2010' ('The programme of professionalization of the Polish armed forces for 2008-2010'), RM, 5 August 2008, Warsaw 2008.

To improve the ratio between export and domestic orders, the BUMAR pursue a marketing strategy that focus on small and mid-sized contracts on traditional 'Polish' markets: Asia, Middle East, South America, Bulgaria and Hungary. However, the nature of major hindrances did not change a much since the departure from planed economy. First, the portfolio of domestic orders quite frequently suffers from 'unforeseen' budget cuts. For instance, in 2008, domestic orders were cuts by 40 percent and payments for delivered hardware were postponed to next budget years. Second, succeeding governmental programmes for reforms of military industry suffer from unrealistic financial assumptions. Third, complex ownership and legal status of some enterprises could be considered too as one of major factors negatively affecting the pace of reforms, especially privatization of enterprises.

Market forces alone rarely drive a military industry. In the case of Poland, the country's membership in the Warsaw Treaty Organization guaranteed full portfolio of orders and preferential treatment, such as low-cost credits, easy access to raw materials and far-reaching reduction of taxes. In 1989, 128 enterprises had enjoyed the privileged status of special production enterprises. A part of them, 89 enterprises, had dual-use capabilities but the top 39 factories had a 'purely' military profile and were specialized in the production of armoured vehicles, self-propelled howitzers, anti-aircraft guns, helicopters and light aircraft, landing ships, minesweepers, anti-aircraft missiles launchers, anti-tank guided launchers and radars.

The fall of the Berlin Wall, in 1989, radically changed rules of the game. Then, the portfolio of 'special' orders became a liability rather than an asset, due to the simultaneous collapse of the military alliance and its economic device known as the Council for Mutual Economic Assistance. What is worse, the military industry was left without 'shock-absorbers', when the state decides to conduct a 'single leap' switch from planned to market economy. Then, a consolidation of military industry into four industrial holding was seen as best solution to optimize manufacturing costs and assure cost-effective research, development and implementation of new projects and technologies. To translate this approach into practice, an Industrial Development Agency was created to stimulate financial restructuring of military industry by means of such instruments as refunding of debts, guaranteed loans and credits. The ultimate goal was a transformation of military industry enterprises into stock companies with control-package of shares belonging to the State Treasury.

These ambitious goals were never achieved, at least not until 1996. The six initial years, 1989-1995, were bad for the military industry in Poland, The portfolio of defence orders went down by 80 percent, and that meant that 'special' production lines were using only 20 percent of its capacity, predominantly for the domestic market. A rapidly shrinking demand from the traditional foreign markets, a substantial reduction of the national armed forces, surplus of weaponry and difficulties in conversion, due to specific nature of the military enterprises, are seen as the key reasons for the failure but the nature of forces driving the process is more complex than that. The positive assumption about a quick privatization of the military industry was the gravest error when the Polish capital markets were still underdeveloped and foreign investors did not consider the military industry as an attractive investment in low-demand times. Certainly, the creation of four holding groups had economic rationale but this move stimulated a reactivation of the branch's interest group. This resulted, for instance, in growing pressure to invalidate growing debts. An unstable legal system, especially in respect to executive acts, can be seen as an ordinary factor during times where political cabinets had a short life expectancy.

The new 'Programme of Military Industry Restructuring for 1996-2010' was designed as a remedy for these deficiencies, especially as an antidote for the unsuccessful privatization of the military industry enterprises.[15] Hence, the core of the programme was a suite of executive measures, which included the postulate to ground two economic instruments: 'National Military Industry Investment Fund' and 'Fund for Restructuring of Military and Aviation Industry'. Nevertheless, the ambitious programme was slaughtered in political wrestles between the Ministry of Industry and Trade and the State Treasury, which did oppose the creation of both funds. Without them, the programme became an archival file.

Its successor, the 'Programme of Restructuring Military Industry for Technical Modernization of Armed Forces' aimed to create stable conditions allowing for a smooth integration of national military forces with NATO.[16] This programme tended to avoid past deficiencies and clearly drew associated financial requirements. Nevertheless, its assumptions were unrealistic in all other aspects. Firstly, it assumed that the restructuring of military industry would be driven by policy of debt reduction and successful privatization. Secondly, it took for granted that the process of integration with NATO will cause a boost of new orders from the national armed forces and that, in turn, will lead to an introduction of new products and technologies. The third assumption was a logical conclusion from previous one. Namely, that the introduction of new products will bring about a boost to exports. Consequently, the programme postulated establishment of a 'financial consortium to support the export of military materials'.

The real life soon proved that all these assumptions were overly optimistic. Initially, the process of integration with NATO caused a reduction of domestic orders, instead of the assumed increase. In turn, that caused that the production costs grow from 92 percent in 1996 to 116 percent, in 2002. The conducted debt reduction brought no effects either and the total debt of the defence industry rose from 1.5 billion in 1996 to 1.65 billion zlotys in 2002. The privatization of

---

15   See Council of Ministers, 'Program Restrukturyzacji Sektora Przemyslu Obronnegi i Lotniczego na lata 1996-2010' ('The programme of military industry reforms for 1996-2010'), RM, 10 April 1996, Warsaw 1996.

16   See Council of Ministers, 'Program Restrukturyzacji Przemyslu Obronnego i Wsparcia w Zakresie Modernizacji Technicznej Sil Zbrojnych RP' ('The programme of reforms in military industry and support for technical modernization of the armed forces'), RM, 2 February 1999, Warsaw 1999.

military industry was a big fiasco, only two enterprises were found attractive by foreign strategic investors, from 26 factories that were for sale. The Treasury got 320 million zlotys from both sales, but this capital was not used to support the conversion of military industry, due to lack of executive legal acts. The assumed boost to exports never did happen. The industry did not have 'hits' in its product catalogue, neither did the Treasury succeeded to establish the promised 'financial consortium to support export of military materials'.

The continued existence of the national military industry is threatened, concluded the government in 2002. The export of military materials collapsed quite rapidly from 382.2 million zlotys, in 2001, to 181.6 million zlotys in 2002, and the remaining orders were mainly for maintenance and spare parts. A prospect for the future was equally dark, 776 million zlotys invested in development of new products and technologies were spending on redundant projects that brought no effects. In response, the government decided to act radically and came forth with 'Strategy for Structural Transformation of Industrial Defence Potential in Years 2002-2005' to rescue the entire military industry sector, which then consisted of 38 'special production' enterprises, 12 enterprises managed by the Ministry of National Defence, 10 research and development centres and 3 centres responsible for foreign trade.[17]

The 'Strategy for Structural Transformation of Defence Industry Potential in Years 2002-2005' diagnosed that further reforms of the military industry ought to be constructed on clearly formulated criteria from the Ministry of National Defence, allowing for long-term planning, the development of financial instruments guaranteeing the realization of export orders and development of new world-class products for international markets.[18] A consolidation of military industry into two holdings was seen as the only feasible solution to form capital strong actors capable of rationalizing production, management and marketing as well as to develop new products.

The first holding *Bumar* consolidated 15 enterprises producing equipment for the Land Forces, the core of the second holding was Foreign Trade Corporation 'Cenzin' that consolidate five enterprises from aviation and electronics sector. A further, 15 enterprises were not included in any holdings as they were found in need of serious restructuring.

The strategy brought some positive effects. First, military industry enterprises got long-term domestic orders. That was an optimistic sign that the Ministry of National Defence managed to set up its long-term priorities. The portfolio of export orders looked better too. The Bumar collected export orders worth in excess of

---

17   See Council of Ministers, 'Strategia przeksztalcen strukturalnych przemyslowego potencialu obronnego w latach 2002-2005' ('The strategy of structural reforms in military industry for 2002-2005'), RM, 14 May 2002, Warsaw 2002.

18   See Council of Ministers, 'Strategia przeksztalcen strukturalnych przemyslowego potencialu obronnego w latach 2002-2005' ('The strategy of structural reforms in military industry for 2002-2005'), RM, 14 May 2002, Warsaw 2002.

one-billion dollars.[19] In overall terms, the Bumar doubled value of orders, from 1.7 million zlotys in 2002 to 3.300 million zlotys in 2005. The second holding, lead by the Foreign Trade Corporation 'Cenzin', improved its order portfolio too, from 500 million zlotys, in 2002 to 700 million in 2005. For the Treasury, the primary owner of the military industry enterprises, the real success story was a transformation of a 150 million zloty deficit into a 130 million zloty profit. Nevertheless, the privatization of the enterprises was a story of failure.

The military industry entered 2006 on an optimistic note. The priority list of the Ministry of National Defence included a few long-term deals, including a contract for 48 multi-purpose aircraft F-16, armoured fighting vehicle 'Wolverine', anti-tanks guided missiles 'Spike', satellite communication systems, 3D radar systems and RPS Mk III water-water missiles. For the military industry, it has been important that associated offset programmes promised the transfer of technology and profitable new contracts. The contract with the Lockheed, USA, included offset projects worth roughly 9.8 billion dollars, and that included 900 million dollars in transfer of technology and 1.3-1.4 billion dollars of direct investments in the military industry.[20] The contract with Raphael, Israel, for anti-tank guided missiles 'Spike', secured existence of the ZM Mesko. The contract with Patria, Finland, and Otomelare, Italy, for the armoured fighting vehicle 'Wolverine' it was worth 790 million Euros for Bumar-Siemianowice, Bumar-Stalowa Wola, Radmor-Gdynia, Obrum-Gliwiece and Stomil-Poznan. The contract with CASA, Spain, for the CASA C295 M transport aircrafts, brought another 212 million dollars in offsets.

On the bad side, non-export contracts were signed during 2006 and 2007. That was hardly a surprise. For many years, export portfolio had no sales hits as research and development brought no fruits. It was expected that involvement of Polish troops in Iraq will brings a billion dollars export contracts but that did not happen. In 2007, politicians concluded that a fusion of military industry into a single holding BUMAR is the most appropriate solution to consolidate capital as well as to boost R&D, marketing and export. That is the central assumption of the new 'Consolidation and support strategy for development of the Polish military industry for 2007-2012'.[21] The executive scheme postulated a need for organizational and technological consolidation until 2010, capital consolidation by the end of 2011 and introduction on Stack Exchange in 2012.

---

19   The export is concentrated on markets in Asia, Middle East and Africa. Especially to India, Venezuela, Indonesia. These countries bought PT 91 tanks, radar systems, 'Grom' guided missiles, service vehicles.

20   Lockheed Corporation estimates that the offset contracts are worth roughly 9.8 billion dollars. However, Polish experts consider that their value is approximately 6.028 billion dollars.

21   See Council of Ministers, 'Strategia Konsolidacji i Wspierania Rozwoju Polskiego Przemyslu Obronnego w latach 2007-2012' ('The strategy for consolidation and development of the Polish military industry for 2007-2012'), RM, 31 August 2007, Warsaw 2007.

Until now, there are no indications that the new strategy for 2007-2012 put paid to the overly optimistic assumptions of the previous measures aiming to cure weaknesses of the Polish military industry. First, the strategy assumes internal generation of required funds. For instance, the boost of R&D is to be achieved through cooperation between the industry, the Ministry of National Defence and the Ministry of Science and Education. Similarly, the strategy did not solve the problem of capital for realization of long-terms export contracts. Second, the strategy assumes coordination and synchronization with the army's programme of technical modernization for 2007-2012.[22] However, the army is vulnerable to budget cuts and the current crisis causes delay of payments and matching cuts of domestic orders. Third, the strategy assumes generation of imperative funds through privatization of redundant enterprises. Privatization of military industry never was a success story in low-demands times. In the past, underdeveloped capital market in Poland was seen as a factor-limiting pace of privatization. Now, this limitation is gone. Unfortunately, for investors, the military industry is less attractive today that it was 20 years ego. In addition, the legal status of enterprises is still complex, including split ownership between Ministry of Treasury, Ministry of National Defence, and Agency of Industrial Development.

The core factor stimulating reforms of the military industry in Poland is the governmental procurement programme, with associated offset contracts. These programmes, especially offset contracts, secure a minimal portfolio of domestic contracts and make possible a further functioning of key enterprises. Equally important is that these offset contracts are the only instances of the transfer of modern military technology to Poland.

Unfortunately, succeeding programmes of reforms did not solve the most elementary obstacles. During the twenty years of reforms, Polish military industry neither was capable to develop attractive portfolio of competitive products for foreign markets, nor to overcome the *ad hoc* mode of cooperation with national armed forces and impose long-term planning and coordination. The most serious obstacle however, is a fact that the hopeful planning of the state budget means that the succeeding strategies and programmes of reforms never were designed in coherent fashion.

Security Domain Third Component: The Crisis Management System

The crisis management system was, and in some way still is, an *Achilles' heel* of the national security system in Poland. In the old epoch, prior to the Velvet Revolution of 1989, the country had a rigidly centralized national security system,

---

22   See Council of Ministers, 'Strategia Konsolidacji i Wspierania Rozwoju Polskiego Przemyslu Obronnego w latach 2007-2012' ('The strategy for consolidation and development of the Polish military industry for 2007-2012'), RM, 31 August 2007, Warsaw 2007.

submitting in crises and emergencies non-military actors to supervision by 'total defence' authorities. Then, the Committee of Homeland Defence acted as the most powerful institutional actor responsible for coordination and supervision of all activities roughly interpreted as being security matters. Nevertheless, such model of crisis management system was of no use for a country initiating democratic reforms.

Regrettably, the domain of civil protection and crisis management was rather 'forgotten' in the initial phase of the reforms, at least until 2008. From necessity, due to lack of legal and procedural norms, actors involved in crisis management acted on basis of the parliamentary act about disasters of 2002, which did not regulate such key issues as national system of coordination and command, civil-military cooperation, integrated procedures or planning and interoperability in accordance to NATO's directives and EU Ministerial Guidance for Civil Emergency Planning. That unfavourable situation changed with the establishment of the Governmental Centre of Security on 2 August 2008, and its integral part, the Governmental Unit for Crisis Management.

The idea to establish Governmental Centre of Security was not a novel one. On 26 April 2005, the government sent to the parliament a draft of legal act proposing to create Governmental Centre of Security, a new national body responsible for crisis management. Then, the parliamentary majority was in favour of the functioning status quo, despite its deficiencies in matters other than natural disasters, where civil protection and crisis management lay on State Fire Service. Then the State Fire Service was the only institution capable of coping with national emergencies in coordinated fashion. In fact, the Commander in Chief of the State Fire Service succeeded to establish National Coordination Centre of Civil Protection and Rescue Operation, which led and coordinated planning, carried out education and training and systematically conducted post-crisis evaluations. What is even more important, the State Fire Service succeeded in creating a coherent system of crisis management centres in each region, with quite well functioning coordination and communication between units.[23] In practice, the State Fire Service, and its National Coordination Centre of Civil Protection and Rescue Operation, acted as the key executive body for the Committee for Crisis Management of the Council of Ministers. Legally, the State Fire Service did not have such competencies, but in praxis, it was the only organization capable to fulfil such functions.

According to an old Polish saying it is '*better something than nothing*'. Prior to that, the situation was much worse. The field of civil protection and crisis management was 'forgotten' until it surfaced to light during accession to NATO in 1996. On 1 January 1997, the domain of civil defence, which included civil

---

23   The Head of the Fire Department, Gen. Zbigniew Meres became a new Chief of Civil Defence on 22 March 2000. Since then, the HQ of the Fire Department functioned simultaneously as the 'Office of the Chief of Civil Defence'. On 15 April 2000, the minister shut down the Department of Crisis Management and Civil Protection but left without changes all regional and local cells.

protection and crisis management, was transferred from the Ministry of National Defence to the Ministry of Interior and Administration. That was a troublesome inheritance for the Ministry of Interior and Administration. *De jure*, still in power was the old security doctrine that contemplated nature of threats in terms of tensions between East and West. What's more, since 1993 the old set of laws of 1984 was abolished but no new rules were created to replace the old ones. Thus, since 1993, the domain of civil protection and crisis management existed in legal vacuum.

Dealing with such constraints, the Ministry of Interior and Administration needed several months to establish the National Centre for Coordination of Rescue Operation.[24] The situation was even much worse in other governmental institutions. For instance, the Ministry of Health and Social Welfare and Ministry of Economy did not prioritize activities in the 'forgotten' domain and until the end of 1998 did not establish contingencies and routines of actions under crisis circumstances. The ability to conduct coordinated operations on regional and local levels was also rather questionable as actors involved in crisis management were equipped in non-compatible means of communication. Under such conditions, the Superior Chamber of Control concluded its 1998 control of civil protection structures with a phrase stressing that '*deficiencies in organizational structures on central level and half-done realization of tasks deferred adaptation of organizational structure toward new tasks*'.[25]

Gradually, the State Fire Service, existing within organizational structures of the Ministry of Interior and Administration, consolidated its position as the best performing actor in the crisis management and the only actor capable of coping with national emergencies in a coordinated mode.[26] Then in 2004, the parliament considered that *de jure* recognition of the existing status quo is a best way out from the problematic legal vacuum. On 30 April 2004, parliament proposed the legal decree, 'Decree about civil protection and crisis management', acknowledging the legal recognition of the status quo, despite its faults in civil protection fields

---

24   See Naczelna Izba Kontroli. Department Obronny Noarodowej i Bezpieczenstwa Wewnetrznego: 'Informacja o wynikach kontroli organizacji i funkcjonolopwania obrony ciwilnej' (The Supreme Chamber of Control. Department of National Defence and Domestic Security: 'Information about organization and functioning of the civil defence'), Control No. 2009/98/P/97/074/DON, Warszawa, 1998.

25   In Naczelna Izba Kontroli. Department Obronny Noarodowej i Bezpieczenstwa Wewnetrznego: 'Informacja o wynikach kontroli organizacji i funkcjonolopwania obrony ciwilnej' (The Supreme Chamber of Control. Department of National Defence and Domestic Security: 'Information about organization and functioning of the civil defence'), Control No. 2009/98/P/97/074/DON, Warszawa, 1998.

26   As a matter of facts, the State Fire Service was quite effective instrument in handling small and mid-sized catastrophes and natural disasters but has no capabilities to conduct large-scale coordinated actions, involving cooperation with others governmental agencies. Such inadequacy was for instance revealed during large-scale international exercises conducted in Poland, in 2002 and 2004.

other than natural disasters.[27] A year later, on 26 April 2005, the government issued counter-proposals, submitted to parliament as the 'Act about crisis management', aiming to redress executive power in these matters to the Council of Ministers. In essence, the government proposed to establish Governmental Security Centre and Governmental Centre for Crisis Management, bodies directly submitted to the Council of Ministers.[28]

Certainly, both projects were not free from deficiencies. The parliamentary proposals did not provide a satisfactory solution to the problem of nationwide coordination and did not address requirements related to NATO's directives and EU's Ministerial Guidance for Civil Emergency Planning. In fact, the parliamentary proposals were tailored towards the management of catastrophes and natural disasters and did not aim to address other challenges, such as the protection of critical infrastructure or from asymmetric threats.[29] In contrast, the governmental proposals included the postulate to create national bodies capable to address the broad spectrum of contemporary challenges, including these arising from asymmetric threats. Fortunately, the prolonged parliamentary debate was settled in favour of the governmental proposals. At last, on 2 August 2008, has been established the Governmental Centre of Security and its integral part, the Governmental Unit for Crisis Management.[30]

In essence, the Governmental Centre of Security is designed as the brain of the National Crisis Response System as well as an integral component of the NATO's Crisis Response System.[31] At the initial stage, the main task of the body is to establish and implement uniform standards and procedures for all national actors involved in civil protection and crisis management and assure compatibility of standards and procedures with NATO's Crisis Response Guidance and EU's Ministerial Guidance for Civil Emergency Planning. In praxis, the first task is to install and put into operation 'SI PEM HEART', NATO's system of information transmission. Then, the centre has to develop catalogue of threats and database of

---

27 See Parliament, 'Poselski Projekt Ustawy o Bezpieczenstwie Obywateli i Zarzadzaniu Krysysowym' ('Decree about civil protection and crisis management. Parliamentarian Project'), Parliament, Print No. 2953, 26 April 2004, Warsaw 2004.

28 See Parliament, 'Rzadowy Projekt Ustawy o Zarzadzaniu Kryzysowym' ('Act about crisis management. Governmental Project'), Print No. 3973, 30 April 2005, Warsaw, 2005.

29 See Parliament, 'Poselski Projekt Ustawy o Bezpieczenstwie Obywateli i Zarzadzaniu Krysysowym' ('Decree about civil protection and crisis management. Parliamentarian Project'), Parliament, Print No. 2953, 26 April 2004, Warsaw 2004. Also, see Parliament, 'Rzadowy Projekt Ustawy o Zarzadzaniu Kryzysowym' ('Act about crisis management. Governmental Project'), Print No. 3973, 30 April 2005, Warsaw 2005.

30 Assessment of health systems' crisis preparedness: Poland, Copenhagen, World Health Organisation Europe, October 2009, http://www.euro.who.int/__data/assets/pdf_file/0007/112201/E93850.pdf, p.21.

31 In the present shape, the crisis management system in Poland operates in accordance with 'Ustawa z dnia 26 kwietnia 2007 r. o zarządzaniu kryzysowym' ('Act about crisis management'), 26 April 2007, Warsaw 2007.

experts, develop relevant procedures and contingency plans and set up interface making possible smooth cooperation between civilian and military components. Now, it is too early to appraise progress that the centre made but it is certain that the establishment of the Governmental Centre of Security and its integral part, the Governmental Unit for Crisis Management, is the first mature attempt to create over-ministerial institution capable to fulfil the functional vacuum that arose after the dissolution of the Committee of Homeland Defence.

Searching for Homeostasis in the Security Domain

Poland responded to the shift of security paradigm in Central and East Europe, due to Velvet Revolution of 1989, with the policy of self-sufficiency in security matters. That was hardly the best security policy for a mid-sized country sharing land borders with two continental major powers, Russia and Germany. For the country however, that was the only feasible policy option during transitory period when Central and Eastern Europe was a security gray zone and Poland neither was a member of a reliable military alliance, nor could count on support from other countries. Under such circumstances, Warsaw had no choice but have to use existing assets and means to cope with the new geostrategic situation in Central and Eastern Europe. In practice, the top priority was to relocate military forces from western borders to 'Eastern Wall', to secure the exposed and vulnerable frontiers with disintegrating Soviet Union.

Ultimately, the strategy of adoption of existing means towards new geostrategic situation in Europe slowed down the pace of transformations in the entire security domain. For military industry, as well as for associated lobbies, that was a rationale to justify a preservation of the *status quo ante*. After all, the policy of self-sufficiency in security matters was a circumstantial 'shock absorber', at least for the military industry. However, the most decisive factor negatively affecting, and ultimately disabling, transformation of the security domain was the unfortunate constitutional 'dual chain of command' between the President Lech Walesa and succeeding prime ministers.

The accession to NATO has been a turning point. Since then, Warsaw pursues reforms emulating 'NATO model'. Initially, in accordance with international practices, particular efforts were placed to achieve interoperability of 1/3 of forces but a post-11 September 2001, shift in NATO's preferences caused a top priority in assigning 1/10 of the forces designated to participate in expeditionary missions under the flag of the alliance. Furthermore, a special preference has been assigned to Special Forces. Warsaw consider that partaking in the initial 'combat' phase of an expeditionary mission is the best way to strengthen direct link with Washington as well as to build up the country position as USA key ally in Europe, or at least as the key ally in Central and Eastern Europe. In other words, Special Forces are seen by Warsaw as a particularly effective mean of political leverage.

The focus on such an understood 'NATO model', in its post-11 September 2001 appearance, generates an inharmonious development of other components of the security domain. The crisis management system remained 'forgotten' until the issue emerged as a top agenda on NATO, European Union and NATO forums, due to growing risks of asymmetric threats. In respect to military industry, the 'NATO model' has dual impact. On the bright side, the governmental armament programmes, with related offsets, are the only instances of modern technology transfer that resulted in a development of new products. On the down side, the priorities assigned to the 'NATO model', especially focus on development of capabilities to expeditionary missions causes the relocation of resources. In turn, that negatively affects the portfolio of domestic orders, especially during low conjuncture periods. The optimistic construction of the national defence budgets however is the most destructive factor for the military industry. Ultimately, it paralyses long-term Research & Development projects and creates conditions making impossible long term planning. For many years, it is common practice that most domestic orders are placed 6-12 months prior to the required delivery. In other words, from the angle of the military industry, NATO requirements have a positive function in the short-term, although they destabilize the industry in the long-run. National authorities however, are capable to reduce the negative impact of NATO requirements by improving the budget process thus making possible for the Ministry of National Defence to place long-term domestic orders.

Despite significant achievements, the security domain in Poland still cannot be considered as balanced one, as a one that achieved a homeostasis between its core components: the armed forces, the military industry and the crisis management system. Firstly, needed reforms were slowed down by the strategy of adoption existing means towards new objectives. Then, the authorities had no other choices but have to adopt such response due to dynamic changes, and even instability, in Central and Eastern Europe. The accession to NATO, and a switch towards reforms emulating 'NATO model', stimulate developments of selected components, especially Special Forces and top 1/10 of the armed forces, on behalf of the other 9/10 of forces, the military industry and the crisis management system. In praxis, further improvements of such unbalanced prioritizing can be achieved by tailoring the posture of the armed forces to feasible resources, primarily by improving the budget discipline as well as by changing pattern of resources distribution. Present range of these constrains indicate that a homeostasis in the security domain would require further reduction of the armed forces from 100,000 to roughly 60,000 professional troops, extending the multifunctional National Reserve Forces from 10,000 to 30,000 contracted reservists, and relocate a substantial part of feasible resources to build up durable crisis management system. The size of the National Reserve Forces is motivated by their multifunctional character as forces capable to cope with asymmetric threats, secure host nation capabilities, support operational units in defensive operations as well as to take part in crisis management.

References

Academy of National Defence, 'Przygotowanie i prowadzenie wojny obronnej przez Polske po roku 2000. KAPPA. Gotowasc obronna panstwa w warunkach sytuacji kryzysowych' ('Conduct of defensive war in Poland, after 2000. Project KAPPA. National capabilities in crisis situations'), Warsaw 1997.

Allison, G., 'Conceptual Models and the Cuban Missiles Crisis', *American Political Science Review* LXIII(3), 1969, pp. 689-718.

Balcerowicz, B., 'Dylematy strategiczne Polski w okresie przejsciowym' ('Strategic dilemmas of the army in transition') in *Mysl Wojskowa*, No. 3-1997, Warsaw 1997.

Balcerowicz, B., Pawlowski, J., Marczak, J., 'Podstawowe Zalozenia Strategii Obronny Polski' ('Basic principles of national defence strategy') in *Mysl Wojskowa*, No. 6-1991, Warsaw 1991.

Bearne, S., Oliker, O., O'Brien, K. and Rathmell, A., *National Security Decision-Making Structures and Security Sector Reform*. RAND Europe, 2005.

Biuro Bezpieczenstwa Narodowego, 'Strategiczny Przeglad Obronny. Konferencja' ('Strategic review of defensive capabilities. Conference Report'), Warsaw 2007.

Council of Ministers, 'Program Restrukturyzacji Sektora Przemyslu Obronnegi i Lotniczego na lata 1996-2010' ('The programme of military industry reforms for 1996-2010'), 10 April 1996, Warsaw 1996.

Council of Ministers, 'Programme of Military Industry Restructuralization for 1996-2010', Warsaw 1996.

Council of Ministers, 'Governmental Programme of Army Modernization for 1998-2012', Warsaw 1998.

Council of Ministers, 'Programme of Integration with NATO and Modernization of Armed Forces 1998-2012', Warsaw 1998.

Council of Ministers, 'Program Restrukturyzacji Przemyslu Obronnego i Wsparcia w Zakresie Modernizacji Technicznej Sil Zbrojnych RP' ('The programme of reforms in military industry and support for technical modernization of the armed forces'), 2 February 1999, Warsaw 1999.

Council of Ministers, 'Programme of transformation and modernization of the armed forces 2001-2006', Warsaw 2001.

Council of Ministers, 'Dekret o katastrofach' ('The decree about natural disasters'), RM, 18 April 2002, Warsaw 2002.

Council of Ministers, 'Strategia przeksztalcen strukturalnych przemyslowego potencialu obronnego w latach 2002-2005' ('The strategy of structural reforms in military industry for 2002-2005'), 14 May 2002, Warsaw 2002.

Council of Ministers, 'Informacja Rady Ministrow RP o realizacji programu przebudowy i modernizacji Sil Zbrojnych w latach 2001-2006' ('The information about the implementation of the programme for 2001-2006'), 30 September 2003, Warsaw 2003.

Council of Ministers, 'Informacja o dzialaniu rzadu na rzecz zapewnienia bezpieczenstwa panstwa i obywateli na wypadek kleski powodzi oraz przeciwdzialania jej skutkom' ('Information about readiness to secure state and citizens in the case of massive water floods'), 12 April 2007, Warsaw 2007.

Council of Ministers, 'Strategia konsolidacji i wspierania rozwoju przemyslu obronnego w latach 2007-2012' ('Strategy of consolidation and support for defence industry 2007-1012'), Warsaw 2007.

Council of Ministers, 'Ustawa z dnia 26 kwietnia 2007 r. o zarządzaniu kryzysowym' ('Act about crisis management'), 26 April 2007, Warsaw 2007.

Council of Ministers, 'Program profesjonalizacji Sił Zbrojnych Rzeczypospolitej Polskiej na lata 2008-2010' ('The programme of professionalization of the Polish Armed Forces for 2008-2010'), 5 August 2008, Warsaw 2008.

Czaputowicz, J., 'Bezpieczenstwo Europejskie. Koncepcje, instytucje, implikacje dla Polski' ('European security. Conceptions, institutions and the implications for Poland'), Warsaw 1997.

Daniluk, M. (ed.) 'Analiza sektorowa konwersji przemyslu zbrojeniowego w Polsce w okresie transformacji na system rynkowy. Lata 1989-1997' ('Analysis of military industry conversion 1989-1997'), Warsaw 1999.

Garbach, J., 'Wojsko Polskie u progu NATO' ('The Polish army accessing NATO'), Zeszyty Naukowe WSP 'Poglady and Doswiadczenia', No. 1-111-1999, Wroclaw 1999.

Golebiewski, J., 'Zarzadzanie kryzysowe a standardy bezpieczenstwa' ('Crisis management and national security standards') in *Bellona*, No. 1/2007, Warsaw 2007.

Jarmoszko, J., 'Przemiany w silach zbrojnych RP pierwszej dekady transformacji ustrojowej' ('The changes in armed forces during the first decade of political transformations'), Akadmia Obrony Narodowej, Warsaw 2000.

Jedrzejko, M., 'Armie w dobie przemian' ('Armies in transition'), Warsaw 1997.

Karkoszka, A., 'Dylematy Partnerstwa dla Pokoju' ('Dilemmas of the Partnership for Peace') in *Sprawy Miedzynarodowe*, No. 2-1994, Warsaw 1994.

Koziej, S., 'Doktryna obronnosci Rzeczypospolitej Polskiej. Zarys projektu' ('Poland's security doctrine. A draw of project'), Akademia Obrony Narodowej, Warsaw 1992.

Koziej, S., 'Szkic do dyskusji o przyszlej strategii poszerzonego NATO. Spojrzenie z polskiej perspektywy' ('A voice to discussion about the strategy of an enlarged future NATO. Poland's view'), Warsaw 1998.

Kulczycki, R. and Dworecki, S., 'O Zagrozeniach Bezpieczenstwa Polski' ('National security threats') in *Mysl Wojskowa*, No. 1-1994, Warsaw 1994.

Kupicki, R., 'NATO a terrorism. Nowy etap transformacji Sojuszu' ('NATO and terrorism. A new stage of transforming the Alliance') in *Sprawy Miedzynarodowe*, No. 3/2001, Warsaw 2001.

Kuszak, W., Baran, S., Szymanski, M. (eds) 'Zarzadzanie Kryzysowe w Wojewodztwie Swietokrzyskim. Zarzadzanie Kryzysow. Doswiadczenia i Wnioski' ('Regional crisis management in Swietokrzyskie. Experiences and conclusions'), Swietokrzyski Urzad Wojewdzki, Rzeszow 2005.

Kuzniar, R. (ed.) 'Miedzy polityka a strategia' ('Between politics and strategy'), Warsaw 1994.

Kuzniara, R. (ed.) 'Polska polityka bezpieczenstwa 1989-2000' ('Polish security policy 1989-2000'), Warsaw 2001.

Naczelna Izba Kontroli, Department Obronny Narodowej i Bezpieczenstwa Wewnetrznego, 'Informacja o wynikach kontroli organizacji i funkcjonolopwania obrony ciwilnej' ('Information about organization and functioning of the civil defence'), Control No. 2009/98/P/97/074/DON, Warsaw 1998.

Naczelna Izba Kontrol, 'Informacja o wynikach kontroli organizacji i funkcjonowania obrony ciwilnej' ('Information about organization and functioning of the civil defence'), Control No. 2009/98/P/97/074/DON, Warszawa, Wrzesien 1998, Warsaw 1998.

Naczelna Izba Kontrol, 'Informacja o wynikach kontrol przygotowania administracji zespolonej do dzialan w sytuacjach kryzysowych' ('Information about readiness for crisis management'), P/02/074, Warsaw 2003.

Naczelna Izba Kontrol, 'Informacja o wynikach kontrol restrukturyzacji sektora obronnego' ('The information about reforms of the defence sector'), P2/02/056, Warsaw 2004.

Onyszkiewicz, J., Olaf Osica, 'Towards a New NATO', Center for International Relations, Research Paper No. 2/02, Warsaw 2002.

Parliament, 'Komisja d/s Obronny Narodowej. Biuletyn 1996-2010' ('The Commission of National Defence. Minutes 1996-2010'), Warsaw 1996-2007.

Parliament, 'Ustawa o przebudowie i modernizacji technicznej oraz finansowaniu Sil Zbrojnych RP 2001-2006' ('The decree about transformation and technical modernization of the Polish Army 2001-2006'), Print No. 2746, 12 March 2001, Warsaw 2001.

Parliament, 'Program Wyposazenia Sil Zbrojnych RP w samoloty multi-funkcyjne' ('The programme of acquisition of multifunctional aircrafts'), Print No. 29111, 2 May 2001, Warsaw 2001.

Parliament, 'Poselski Projekt Ustawy o Bezpieczenstwie Obywateli i Zarzadzaniu Krysysowym' ('Decree about civil protection and crisis management. Parliamentarian Project'), Print No. 2953, 26 April 2004, Warsaw 2004.

Parliament, 'Rzadowy Projekt Ustawy o Zarzadzaniu Kryzysowym' ('Act about crisis management Governmental Project'), Print No. 3973, 30 April 2005, Warsaw 2005.

Patoka, W., *Poland Under Pressure 1980-81. Crisis Management in State-Society Conflict.* Umeå: Umeå University, 2001.

Prezydent, R.P., 'Polityka Bezpieczenstwa i Strategia Obronna Rzeczypospolitej Polskiej' ('Security policy and Poland's defensive strategy'), Warsaw 1992.

Prezydent, R.P., Zalozenia Polskiej Polityki Bezpieczenstwa ('Assumption of national security policy'), Warsaw 1992.

Stefanowicz, J., 'Rzeczypospolitej pole bezpieczenstwa' ('Poland's areas of security'), Warsaw 1993.

Stus, M., 'Krotka historia zarzadzania kryzysowego w Polsce po roku 1997' ('Crisis management in Poland 1997-2005. A concise information'), Stencil, Ministerstwo Spraw Wewnterznych i Administracji, Departament Bezpieczenstwa i Porzadku Publicznego, Warsaw 2005.

Warszewski, W., 'Aspekty wewnetrzne przystapienia Polski do NATO' ('Domestic aspects of Polish accession to NATO') in Mysl Wojskowa, Nr. 2-1999, Warsaw 1999.

Wieczorek, P. and Zukrowska, K., *Conversion in Poland: The Defence Industry and Base Redevelopment*, BICC International Centre for Conversion, Bonn 1996.

Zebrowski, A., 'Kontrola cywilna nad silami zbrojnymi Rzeczypospolitej Polskiej' ('Democratic control over armed forces'), Warsaw 1998.

PART II
EU Policies

Chapter 4

The Quest for an EU Approach for Security Sector Reform

Alyson J.K. Bailes[1]

Security Sector Reform has come full circle in the two decades since the Berlin Wall fell, which coincidentally also cover the most intensive development of the EU's Common Foreign and Security Policy.[2] Before 1990, SSR was a concept most used in the field of development aid policy, designed as an extra tool to promote good governance in less developed countries so that assistance would not be misapplied *inter alia* through excessive military spending. From 1990 onwards, it became a very important aspect of transformation, partnership, and enlargement policy in Europe, and the most prominent laboratories of SSR became the former Communist countries that sought to renew their defence and security policies so as to qualify for membership of NATO and – to a lesser extent – the EU.[3] This gave a significant twist to the concept. Reform in the context of future Alliance membership clearly did not mean reducing the national defence effort, but in some cases actually increasing it,[4] while making it less 'national' in the sense both

---

1   This chapter is updated and adapted, with thanks and acknowledgement, from the version published in   Spence, D. and Fluri, P. (eds) *The European Union and Security Sector Reform*. London: John Harper Publishing for the Geneva Centre for Democratic Control of Armed Forces (DCAF), 2008.

2   The term Common Foreign and Security Policy (CFSP) was coined in the 1992 Treaty of Maastricht, or Treaty on the European Union (TEU) – which entered into force in November 1993 – to codify and strengthen former work in the EC/EU framework on external political cooperation. This Treaty stated i.a. that 'the CFSP should include all questions relating to the security of the Union, including the eventual framing of a defence policy, which might in time lead to a common defence'. However, an EU Security and Defence Policy allowing the direct use of military instruments (for crisis management) was not incorporated into CFSP until the Helsinki European Council decisions of December 1999.

3   See Caparini, M., 'Security Sector Reform and NATO and EU Enlargement' in *SIPRI Yearbook 2003: Armaments, Disarmament and International Security*. Oxford: Oxford University Press, 2003; text also available at: http://www.sipri.org.

4   During the NATO accession process, for instance, applicants were encouraged to set a goal for their defence spending of around 2 percent of GDP, which is more than a number of existing members currently achieve.

of entering into collective guarantees and of shifting the focus rapidly towards engagement in multilateral operations abroad.

Nowadays, with NATO and the EU enlarged to cover practically the whole of traditional Europe, SSR experts are returning to the wider world scene for the bulk of their current tasks – but with some significant differences from the 1980s. One obvious change is that the present targets for concerted international efforts at SSR are often *post-conflict* states or, in some cases, governments struggling for 'normality' in the sense of being able to control their whole territory: witness Afghanistan, the Congo, Georgia and Moldova, entities of contestable status like the Palestinian territories and Kosovo, and (in its own special way) Iraq. Two more subtle differences may be seen in the total geographical range of SSR, and in the range of those who are offering to help promote it. First, the continuing impact of the events of 1989-90 can be seen in the fact that western states can offer to support defence reform in societies that used to be deeply under Soviet control, like the Central Asians: though these countries are clearly harder nuts to crack than the Central Europeans, and few are bold enough to talk of SSR for Russia itself.

Secondly, promoting and supporting SSR is not now, and in this author's view should not be, the monopoly of a few strong Western countries that happen also to be major aid donors. Nations who experienced SSR in the 1990s can pass on their experience to others in the 2000s, as happens for instance when new members of NATO and the EU join in programmes and missions aimed at the Western Balkans and the Eastern neighbourhood zone. Increasingly, processes that equate to SSR (even if they are not always called that) are also developing *between* countries in non-European regions, such as parts of Africa,[5] Latin America and the Caribbean. Finally, in all regions and contexts there is stronger pressure than ever for both local governments and their external partners to design their SSR programmes, not in isolation, but within a properly coordinated institutional or at least multilateral framework and to use standards that are as transparent and as universally accessible as possible.

Any policy field with such a tangled history is liable to suffer from complications, ranging from identity confusion to contradictions between differing motives, methods and interests and perhaps even some questioning of legitimacy. The present chapter is designed to highlight a number of broader issues of this sort, not for the sake of accentuating the negative, but because they raise questions that seem important and may help illuminate challenges of present-day security and politics ranging well beyond SSR itself. Further, by examining the agenda with specific reference to and in the framework of the European Union as a global security actor, the aim will be to draw out some typical dilemmas or ambiguities of Europe's place in global security governance today. The EU has greatly sharpened and increased its focus on SSR as part of its external tool-

---

5   For the role of the African Union in developing a local, UN-backed SSR concept see the speech of Commissioner for Peace and Security Ramtane Lamamra at a workshop in March 2009 at Addis Ababa, available through http://www.africa-union.org.

box since the early 2000s – perhaps not coincidentally, as NATO's corresponding work (with applicant states in the Partnership for Peace framework) has narrowed in scope and salience.[6] In a Council of Ministers decision of 12 June 2006,[7] the EU adopted a 'Policy framework for Security Sector Reform' that aimed to pull together the European Commission's related activities and doctrines with the military route now available to execute and support SSR through the European Security and Defence Policy (ESDP).[8] At the time of writing in autumn 2009, of 12 ongoing ESDP missions around the world, three mention security reform in the core language of their mandates[9] and at least five others are *de facto* situated in the SSR field – three of them with a specific emphasis on Rule of Law.[10] An ample literature is springing up on the analysis of these missions,[11] alongside other works that dissect the experience of the UN and other SSR providers. The more micro-analysis is accumulated, however, the more relevant it becomes also to make sure that the macro-questions are not simply taken for granted.

Such questions set the agenda for the present text, and logically the first must be: are we sure we know what SSR is and what it covers? The second question is, why are we so sure that 'we' (meaning here the members and supporting partners of the EU, and other 'Westerners') are the right people to help with it, and that we

---

6   For detailed institutional comparisons see Law, D. (ed.) 'Intergovernmental organizations and Security Sector Reform', DCAF Yearbook 2007. Available at: http://www.dcaf.ch/publications/kms/details.cfm?lng=en&id=44888&nav1=4.

7   2736th General Affairs Council meeting Conclusions, Luxembourg, 12 June 2006. Full texts of this and other EU documents referred to are usefully included as annexes in Spence, D. and Fluri, P. (eds) *The European Union and Security Sector Reform*. London: John Harper Publishing for the Geneva Centre for Democratic Control of Armed Forces (DCAF), 2008.

8   See 'A Concept for European Community Support for Security Sector Reform', Communication from the Commission to the Council and the European Parliament, COM(2006) 253 final of 24 May 2006, and 'EU Concept for ESDP Support to Security Sector Reform', Council Doc. 12566/4/05 of 13 October 2005.

9   All three are in West Africa i.e. EU SSR Guinea Bissau, EUSEC RD Congo and EUPOL DR Congo. Available at: http://www.consilium.europa.eu/showPage.aspx?id=268&lang=EN.

10   Namely the Rule of Law missions in Iraq and Afghanistan, EULEX Kosovo, and the police missions in Bosnia-Herzegovina and the Palestinian territories. The tally could be extended by including some missions already completed. For source and details see note 9 above.

11   See for example Gross, E., 'Security Sector Reform in Afghanistan: The EU's Contribution', EU Institute of Security Studies Occasional Paper 78, April 2009. Available at: http://iss.europa.eu; and for a similar critique of UN missions, Hanggi, H. and Scherrer, V. (eds) *Security Sector Reform and UN Integrated Missions: Experience from Burundi, the Democratic Republic of Congo, Haiti, and Kosovo* (DCAF 2008). Rich quarries for such literature are the DCAF website at http://www.dcaf.ch, and the UK-based Global Facilitation Network for Security Sector Reform (GFN-SSR) at: http://www.ssrnetwork.net/.

have the means to succeed? The third question concerns how to reconcile SSR with other aims and processes of security and/or governance that certain actors and schools of thought see as being in contradiction to it, or that have been found to cut across it in practice. Here such issues are pertinent as the distinctions between SSR and DDR (Disarmament, Demobilization and Reintegration), or the broader issue of security and development, SSR and the post-9/11 slogan of democracy promotion, or for that matter SSR and the arms trade – all issues on which the EU has become irretrievably, if not always transparently and decisively, engaged in recent years.

What is SSR?

It should always be remembered that SSR started as a tool of 'good governance' policies. Even if it has grown a long way since then, it will start to lose its distinctness and credibility if it ever loses contact with such fundamental goals and values as pluralistic democracy and democratic control (including the role of parliaments), transparency, honesty and humanity. More specifically, the common ground among authoritative general statements on what constitutes 'good governance' in general includes the notions of a voice for the people and accountability for the government: political stability and non-violence; government effectiveness, regulatory quality and the rule of law; and last but not least, proper resource management and the control of corruption.[12]

There is nothing in any of these facets of 'good governance' that conflicts *a priori* with 'good defence' in such incarnations as legitimate self-defence, minimum adequacy, loyalty to allies or the conduct of international missions. There is thus no need to baulk immediately at the idea that SSR can and should also promote defence modernization and efficiency: above all when the focus includes interoperability, and thus creates new capacities for cooperative international peace missions. However, any would-be SSR provider that finds itself promoting an efficient, modern defence (with or without exportable capacities) in a given country without doing anything to democratize the process will not only risk failing in the prime purpose of SSR but will also possibly be wasting its time. The current literature emphasizes the importance of 'ownership' by the local authorities who are the proximate partners in implementing such programmes; but if ownership and the acceptance of legitimacy and equity do not extend further into the national polity, the progress made will be weakly anchored and will be open to reversal if either the people get more power or the rulers change their minds. This objection can arguably be directed at much of the USA's terrorism-

---

12   A good collection and comparison of such definitions is provided by the World Bank at http://web.worldbank.org/WBSITE/EXTERNAL/COUNTRIES/MENAEXT/EXT MNAREGTOPGOVERNANCE/0,,contentMDK:20513159~pagePK:34004173~piPK: 34003707~theSitePK:497024,00.html.

related security assistance after the events of 11 September 2001 (e.g. Azerbaijan, Kazakhstan, Uzbekistan for a while, Pakistan, Colombia, etc.).[13] Without room to develop that argument fully here, it can surely be concluded that an entity like the EU cannot afford to make such misjudgements, if it wants both to use its limited resources productively and to keep its still relatively 'clean', benign and peaceful international image.

In fact, if the EU (and *mutatis mutandis* NATO) are ever tempted to cut corners on the more high-minded aspects of SSR, it would most likely happen in the context of preparations for enlargement where SSR is only one of many drivers, and where some might feel that the complete experience of EU entry would be the final catalyst needed to shift national habits and mentalities.[14] SSR-related efforts in the EU's own 'near abroad', such as the Middle East, North Africa and the former Soviet space, may also fall victim to the overall confusion and inconsistency in European policy between whether promoting security and stability, or championing democratic change with all its risks, is more important. A detailed study carried out within the EUROMESCO collaborative research network on experiences in Turkey and the Palestinian territories concluded simply, but damningly, that 'the EU emphasizes democracy or security depending on the respective circumstantial differences'.[15]

Outside Europe, on the other hand, it is hard to see a scenario where the relevant decision-makers and experts in Brussels would start building up a set of military satellites and collaborators for the EU without proper regard for their democratic record – if only because there could be no consensus on such a line among member

---

13   The chapter 'Military Expenditure' by Elisabeth Sköns, Wuyi Omytoogun, Catalina Perdomo and Petter Stålenheim in *SIPRI Yearbook 2005: Armaments, Disarmament and International Security* includes an interesting comparison of the impact of external security influences in Colombia and Sierra Leone respectively during this period. Available at: http://yearbook2005.sipri.org/ch8/ch8.

14   Cf. the arguments at the time of Bulgarian and Romanian entry about governance standards in the areas of crime and corruption. In the next test-cases of Western Balkan states' EU applications, the most widely advertised governance stumbling-blocks have been attitudes in places like Serbia and Croatia to surrendering war criminals; but questions could be asked also about the course, speed and depth of wider security reform in almost any state of the region (including Kosovo). See for instance the ongoing critical studies of Serbian progress being carried out by the Centre for Civil-Military relations at Belgrade, http://www.ccmr-bg.org/.

15   Collantes-Celador, G. et al., 'Fostering an EU Strategy for Security Sector Reform in the Mediterranean: Learning from Turkish and Palestinian Police Reform Experiences', EUROMESCO Paper No. 66, January 2008. Available at: http://www.eurom esco.net/2.0//index.php?option=com_content&task=view&id=691&Itemid=48&lan g=en. See also Hänggi, H. and Tanner, F., 'Promoting Security Sector Governance in the EU's Neighbourhood'. Chaillot Paper No. 80, July 2005, EU Institute of Security Studies, Paris. Available at: http://www.iss.europa.eu/index.php?id=18&no_cache=1&tx_ ttnews[cat]=21&tx_ttnews[pS]=1104534000&tx_ttnews[pL]=31535999&tx_ ttnews[arc]=1&tx_ttnews[tt_news]=191&tx_ttnews[backPid]=143&cHash=490d85d625.

states 'at 27'. Yet the reminder of the West's more self-serving motives for working with military clients suggests a need to look carefully, both at the interaction between an EU SSR programme and what EU nations do *individually* in their defence or security-related assistance contacts with some of the same countries; and at what the designers of ESDP as it evolves might be planning with them for the purposes of purely military cooperation (bases, logistics etc.).[16] Europe, as a whole, may otherwise potentially end up sending mixed messages. Conversely, the image and coherence of the operational side of ESDP could be much helped by considering a possible SSR dimension and/or follow-on programme for *every* ESDP conflict management operation or, at least, making sure that any defence training and transformational services delivered by the EU in the process can be fitted into a larger, coherent, SSR network. As things stand, studies have found that a combination of EU inexperience with the notoriously fragmented ownership and control of practical inputs between Council and Commission, different bits of the Commission, civilians and military etc has resulted in emphases within individual SSR actions that are not only partial and unbalanced, but inconsistent from place to place.[17]

A related point on the *nature* of SSR concerns its overall functional scope, and here it is hard to disagree with the interpretation held by the EU[18] (and the OECD-DAC[19]) that it covers far more than traditional military organs and activities. What might be called the vertical expansion of the concept, to cover everything from heads of government down to the roles of private companies, NGOs and individual citizens, has been accompanied over the last decade by a horizontal expansion to cover (at the least) border and customs authorities, any other paramilitary forces, the police, the law and justice system, especially as it relates to public order, the

---

16   An example that one already sees debated is the EU's habit of borrowing transport aircraft for its missions from Ukraine and even Russia – nations that might be hard pressed themselves to show compliance with the SSR goals that the relevant missions profess.

17   Derks, M. and More, S., *The EU and Internal Challenges for Effectively Supporting Security Sector Reform*. The Hague: Clingendael Institute, June 2009. Available at: http://www.clingendael.nl/cscp/publications/2009/. The authors find that despite the comprehensive nature of the EU SSR concept, missions in practice tend to single out just one or two of the following: military arrangements, police, justice or border control; and that aspects of local consultation, democratic control and transparency, and resource management are most commonly overlooked.

18   The EU document on ESDP support for SSR (note 7 above) identifies four very broadly drawn target areas and sets of actors: 'core security actors' (including customs, border guards and militias), 'security management and oversight bodies' including NGOs, 'justice and law enforcement institutions', and 'non-statutory security forces' including guerrilla groups, private militias and private military/security companies.

19   The OECD's Development Assistance Committee plays an important role in deciding what security-related activities may be claimed by the donors as falling within the scope of development aid. It has more recently engaged directly in setting standards for SSR as shown by its handbook on SSR: 'Supporting Security and Justice'. Available at: http://www.oecd.org/document/6/0,3343,en_2649_33693550_37417926_1_1_1_1,00.html.

work of intelligence agencies, and the oversight, funding, and grievance-handling procedures associated with all of these. In the present author's view, however, there is a strong case for stretching the concept even further to take account of the 'defence economy': including not just armaments production and trade but the handling of industries with dual-use nuclear, chemical or biomedical capacities that are important for non-proliferation policy, and the many aspects of critical infrastructure and civil emergency management. Including this set of issues would also open up, in a wider and more balanced way than can the much-hyped issue of private security providers (PMCs/PSCs), the little-researched and generally under-regulated area of relationships between the public authorities and the entire private business sector in tackling security challenges.[20]

Of course, no-one would think it realistic for current providers of SSR, including the EU, to offer detailed reform prescriptions for these last areas – and still less for other new and fashionable dimensions of security like energy and the environment – not least because not many countries within Europe have got a proper grip on them yet.[21] But when talking to the central actors in traditional security work and helping them to start designing their overall security concepts, plans and coordination structures, donors surely need at least to ask them how they intend to handle these less traditional areas and in general, how they see the proper distribution of resources and bureaucratic efforts between military defence – including external missions – and the other areas more relevant to internal, societal and individual human security. It is a cliché nowadays to recognize that armed forces as such are of very limited use in tackling even 'new threats' of human origin like terrorism or proliferation. The most perfect military reform is of very little help to a society facing mass deaths from bird or swine 'flu, AIDS or starvation. Even more to the point in the normative framework of SSR, the rights and welfare of parliaments, of civil society and of individuals can be just as much damaged by misconduct of police, border and intelligence personnel, by private security companies, or by companies that cause massive environmental pollution and careless accidents, as they can by the ravages of uncontrolled military forces.

---

20   For an attempt to widen as well as explore this agenda see Bailes, A.J.K. and Frommelt, I., *Business and Security: Public-Private Security Relationships in a New Environment*. Oxford: Oxford University Press, 2005; and Bailes, A.J.K. 'A "New Deal" between State and Market' in Østerud and Matláry, *Denationalisation and Internationalisation of European Defence*. Aldershot: Ashgate, 2007. Many relevant titles on PMCs/PSCs will be found at the sources recommended in note 11 above.

21   See for instance Bailes, A.J.K. 'What Role for the Private Sector in "Societal Security?"', European Policy Centre Issue Paper No. 56, 2008, EPC Brussels. Available at: http://www.epc.eu.

SSR and Other Objectives

What of the broader interface between SSR and other tools and policies designed to build security and good governance? First, what is the relationship between Disarmament, Demobilization and Reintegration (DDR)[22] and SSR in post-conflict cases? While SSR can also and should also be applied as a conflict prevention measure, or as part of governance reform and regime transition in states not facing conflict (including those which suppress disorder through dictatorship), it clearly or even primarily has a place when security has broken down including in the case of open armed violence. In such settings it should not be seen as a rival or enemy to DDR, but rather as a complementary tool or even a guarantee of the correct wider framework in which DDR should be carried out. Even if there seems to be a *prima facie* tension between reducing military activity and nurturing it in the proper forms – and if relations can sometimes be strained between the proponents of each – the two are hard to separate not only in post-conflict settings, but in just about any country's experience. It is clear that most conflicts, also among 'strong' states, see an over-large proportion of the population resorting to arms, and that early action to disarm and reintegrate many of them is crucial: but it is hard to think of a case where it is right or practical to leave a nation with no army at all. Redesigning the national forces and other crucial parts of the security sector then becomes a proper task for SSR and ought to start in parallel with DDR. Otherwise there is a risk of an unclear and inappropriate framework for any remaining armed forces on the one hand (including the risk of rival militias), and on the other the possibility of a security vacuum, exploitation by neighbours, and/or a demand for the indefinite presence of foreign forces – all of which variations have recently been seen in Iraq.[23]

A similar answer may be given on the broader issue of how to reconcile security and development policies.[24] It has long been obvious that good, sustainable development is unlikely to work in countries that spend too much on the military, or where the military and other security actors have excessive rights compared with the rest of the population. But recent experience has made abundantly plain that unless lasting external and internal security can be provided – or restored – to a weak and troubled state, it has no real hope of succeeding in peaceful development either. It is more likely in such circumstances that all external aid poured into the country (including humanitarian aid) will end up wasted or having perverse effects. A very useful tool of policy in such cases – as recognized above all by

---

22   For the EU's definition of, and policy on this see the 'EU Concept for Support to DDR', Council Document 1637/06 of 6 December 2006, also available in Spence and Fluri, *The European Union and Security Sector Reform* (as note 7 above).

23   For more by the present author on these themes see Bailes, A.J.K. and Nord, D., 'Non-State Actors in Conflict: A Challenge for Policy and for Law' in Mulaj (ed.) *Violent Non-State Actors in World Politics*. London: C Hurst, 2010.

24   This also is covered at the World Bank site referred to in note 12 above.

the EU with its doctrines of 'effective multilateralism' and of redemption through integration[25] – may be to encourage the growth of regional communities with direct or indirect security agendas that can surround and support the suffering state and hopefully release it sooner from the need to depend for its security and welfare on intervening states from thousands of miles away. If Europe's own history teaches anything it is, surely, that building good security and good SSR is much easier when it can be done across a whole region than if results are sought through a privileged relationship with isolated protégé states, still stuck in the midst of a backward and predominantly hostile environment. The application of such lessons to the Middle East, to West Asia and to Afghanistan and its neighbours is one of the toughest, most elusive and yet vital challenges for Western security policy in the next decades.

This provides the opening for a short remark on SSR and the more ideological agenda of 'democracy promotion' that has been a significant sub-theme in US global security policies since 9/11 – even if a little less was heard of it during President George W. Bush's second term. In the post-Cold War as in the Cold War period, the states that the USA has singled out both as its favoured democratic partners and as its targets for regime change have often had one thing in common, namely that they were somewhat isolated in their regions and had unstable relations with the dominant local powers – Israel with the Arab states, Azerbaijan with Moscow, Taiwan with China and so on. It is *prima facie* difficult to teach a partner state SSR as part of democratic reform while at the same time giving it massive military aid, perhaps much more than it can sensibly and transparently use, to build it up against its neighbours as a kind of strategic proxy. It is even clearer that the most propitious environment for SSR is not created by forcibly invading a state and compelling it to change its regime. The coercive agent's unlawful use of force may be the problem in some such cases, by sending double messages; but more often the problem is that the implied 'hostile takeover' makes it even more complicated for the affected state to live at peace with its neighbours, thus creating a climate in which its future defence spending is likely to be either excessive or insufficient or both. This is one reason why the EU could, paradoxically, turn out to be a rather good carrier of the SSR message: precisely because it is not (yet) playing its own military strategic game in most parts of the world, and would genuinely like to see local states getting on well with each other rather than picking up military proxies and protégés for itself.

Last and not least, should arms sales by partners in reform to the reforming nation always be seen as a complication for SSR, and as inevitably conveying double standards and mixed messages? That judgement has not been made in Europe's own context, since – as noted at the outset – the EU and NATO in their respective efforts to promote military modernization and interoperability

---

25 These are key concepts of the European Security Strategy, 'A Secure Europe in a Better World', adopted by the European Council in December 2003. Available at: http://www.consilium.europa.eu/cms3_fo/showPage.ASP?id=266&lang=EN&mode=g.

have urged their existing and new members explicitly to buy more state-of-the-art defence equipment of more compatible kinds. If it was a moral or practical mistake to foster such rearmament then, to put it plainly, the whole of Central Europe's SSR experience would have no legitimacy at all. Through the European Defence Agency (EDA) the EU is now actively promoting the joint production, and potentially joint marketing of such items, including outside the European area.[26] On the other side, the EU has a state-of-the-art code of conduct to prevent the irresponsible export of conventional arms to the wrong people by any of its members: though it is widely, and correctly, felt that the code would be much more effective and convincing if it could be put in legally binding form.[27]

If only to avoid accusations of hypocrisy and *suppressio veri*, therefore, there is much to be said for bringing the question of equipment procurement explicitly into European SSR dialogues with other countries. Much as with the gross level of defence spending, the obvious way to square the ethical circle is to suggest to them that it is not armaments as such that are wrong, but illogical, non-transparent and corrupt methods of choosing, acquiring and using them – as well, of course, as infringements of humanitarian, arms-control and terrorism-related international obligations. On this last point, it would seem not only logical but rather simple for the EU organs to include adequate teaching and clear norms in their SSR packages regarding the universal limitations on armaments that all good states should respect, covering not just the technical nature of obligations but ways of translating them both into local law and effective action (national and international, in both the public and the private sectors).[28]

Who Should do SSR, and Why Europe?

There remains the core question of why the EU or European countries individually should think they are qualified to help other countries with security sector reform, using the definitions and against the background laid out above. In actuality, the very modern, typically broad and multifunctional European vision of security is both a major asset and a potential handicap. Generally speaking, European states

---

26   The EDA was created in 2004 as part of a post-Iraq surge of consolidation in EU defence work. It analyses requirements, fosters joint projects relevant to EU missions and works for a more open and competitive European defence market, but does not itself own or export arms. Export control work is still handled separately in the EU system by the Commission and the Council of Ministers depending on the class of products. Available at: http://www.eda.europa.eu.

27   'EU Code of Conduct on Arms Exports', adopted by the Council of Ministers in 1998. Available at: http://www.consilium.europa.eu/uedocs/cmsUpload/08675r2en8.pdf.

28   The EU has already carried out a lot of such activity in the narrower field of strategic export controls, where both Council officials and the Commission (through a series of 'Pilot Projects') have helped a range of applicant and partner states to adopt both state-of-the-art legislation and effective systems for information, training and enforcement.

that belong to the EU or NATO or both do not design their own defences today on the assumption of a military attack. They may keep some elements of territorial defence as it were in reserve, particularly in Northern Europe, but they more and more design, train and equip the cream of their forces to take part in multilateral military interventions far away from the homeland. In many countries, homeland security against the so-called 'new threats' has also been defined as an important task of armed forces, and new ways have been explored for the military and police and various civilian actors to work together for those kinds of scenarios and also in natural disasters affecting their own territory.[29] In Central Europe, where most Western states gained their main experience of promoting SSR in the 1990s, what happened was basically an uncritical export of these same concepts from West to East: the aim both of enlargement talks and of technical assistance (provided through NATO's Partnership for Peace as well as by nations severally) was simultaneously to make Central European forces more interoperable for EU- and NATO-led missions, and to encourage them to toughen up their civilian defences. The 'hardening' and professionalization of border control in particular was a *sine qua non* of entry to the EU and to its Schengen system of movement control.[30]

Now, this kind of modern or even post-modern, internationalized or 'sublimated' military profile may make perfect sense in the integrated European environment – even if many Central and Northern Europeans in particular are not entirely happy with how far it has been pushed and how fast.[31] But there are very few if any other regions of the world that enjoy a similar local and external strategic environment. Even the non-European countries that contribute the highest numbers of UN peacekeepers – Bangladesh, India and Pakistan – have very real military threats to contend with in their own region, mainly from each other. The same goes for countries as close to the European Union as Georgia, Moldova and Azerbaijan, which find themselves in a quite different security world from mainland Europe, with barely frozen conflicts, internal insurgencies and in Georgia's case open war affecting their own territories. Even countries recovering from conflict in regions like Africa, where on the face of it Europe makes a real difference to multifunctional peace-building, may need to be rebuilt first as 'strong(er) states' – with strong *territorial* defence policies, probably including a fair and universal system of conscription – in order to reaffirm the government's authority, unity and control of its territory, before it makes sense to embark on helping with other

---

29 Well-developed examples of such approaches would be the UK, Denmark, Italy (with the inclusion of paramilitary forces) and increasingly France.

30 See Caparini, M., op. cit. note 3 above, for some queries that might be raised about the compatibility of these institutional demands with the broader values of democracy and SSR.

31 A rare high-level expression of this concern was the open letter to US President Obama signed by 22 thought leaders of Central Europe in July 2009 which called i.a. for more attention to Europe's own physical security and a tougher stance on Russia, available at: http://www.opendemocracy.net/article/east-central-europe-to-barack-obama-an-open-letter.

people's crises or even 'professionalizing' defence in general. A study carried out by the Stockholm International Peace Research Institute (SIPRI) in the early 2000s of defence spending in a wide range of African states, including such tragic cases of conflict as the Congo and Sierra Leone, showed rather unexpectedly that the outside world would often do better to help such states spend more, not less, on defence as they start on the road to recovery.[32] As in other fields of public business, an initial injection of resources is often unavoidable to kick-start reforms that will provide more security at hopefully decreasing cost in the longer term.

All this leads to a rather obvious conclusion, namely that Europeans' credentials for offering other people a model of SSR do not lie in the present-day European model of defence and security policy as such. Indeed, the EU or its nations could be making a big mistake by trying to impose that model on many of the countries outside Europe who require and will accept European help. The way out of this apparent conundrum is to return to the point made earlier above, that SSR must be about the defence *process* or the *way* of designing and running defence forces, rather than about precisely what size and sort of forces any given country should have. SIPRI's African study just cited (which was carried out almost exclusively by Africans themselves) concluded that certain techniques of rational threat assessment, defence prioritization, transparency and honesty in the allocation and use of military funding would help all the countries under examination, regardless of their widely varying substantial needs. Surely, Europeans should be both well qualified, and have some historical and ethical justification, to set about teaching others this democratic *way* of defence?

Well, yes and no. Standards of defence and security governance in the whole of Europe are probably superior on average to those of any other continent of similar size, but national practices are not particularly consistent in terms of democratic process and control, any more than all European defence forces yet share the same national defence philosophy and force profile. This in turn reflects the reality that NATO actually exercised very little homogenizing influence in its first 50 years,[33] while the EU's ESDP – with, at least potentially, more resources and harmonizing experience behind it – still stops short of the 'real' defence competence that would allow Brussels to adjudicate on nations' total defences. At the level of policy and values, meanwhile, the episode of the Iraq war shows how widely national views can differ even on basics like the legitimate use of force and the acceptability of pre-emption. Systemically, different EU and NATO countries' constitutions vary

---

32   See Hutchful, E. and Omitoogun, W., *Budgeting for the Military Sector in Africa: The Processes and Mechanisms of Control*. Oxford: Oxford University Press, 2006.

33   The Alliance's traditional focus on territorial defence, and the logic thereof in face of Soviet numerical superiority, to an extent imposed diversity since forces stationed abroad and reinforcements would be drawn only from the more capable countries, peripheral nations would focus almost exclusively on their own defence, and so on. As one crude measure of resulting diversity, in 2007 the US was spending 4 percent of its GDP on defence, Greece 3.3 percent, Spain 1.2 percent and Belgium 1.1 percent (NATO figures).

widely in terms of how far parliaments can control the act of going to war, how much information governments have to release to their parliaments and peoples, who controls the money-bags and so forth. Looking at the broader security sector would reveal a similar variety in the degree of democratic control over intelligence agencies, or over the rights of ethnic groups *vis-à-vis* military service and the police, or over the nature of police forces themselves[34] – countries like Britain feeling that a permanent armed police force would be an offence to the constitution, whereas in Italy the armed Carabinieri enjoy not only acceptance but considerable legitimacy, and so on. Conversely, the use of the uniformed military to deal with internal emergencies is usually popular in the UK or Denmark, and in Central Europe for such clearly 'civil' disasters as floods, but remains subject to a strong taboo in Sweden.

Thus, even if a European SSR policy for the wider world may be properly focussed upon democratic and efficient *process* rather than on specifics, exactly what country's version of those things is the EU supposed to teach? Must all nations and all the official and non-state personnel involved agree on some harmonized or average EU 'standard' in all these matters, before the EU as an institution can go out and conduct SSR programmes? Or should Europe try to make a virtue precisely out of the fact that it has a wide range of acceptable national models to offer – but then, how to avoid making it too confusing and complicated for the countries receiving help? (Another pertinent question is whether a clearer collective European norm might challenge and detract from the standards being developed in wider frameworks like the UN, the OECD or the relevant CSCE/OSCE *acquis* – all of these being frames in which European countries also carry on SSR or SSR-equivalent work.)

Last but not least under the heading of European qualifications, some sober questions need to be asked about the resources and the leverage Europe can muster to succeed in the goal of SSR, which is nothing less than to persuade countries to make possibly sweeping changes in precisely the areas of government that are considered most vital for national security and most sensitive for national sovereignty. Again, the experience of reform in the Central European nations now belonging to the EU and NATO, or even in the Western Balkans, may not be a good guide because the 'old' EU frankly had an easy ride. Individual nations and programmes like Partnership for Peace did provide some concepts, some training and some equipment to guide and support the process, although usually at commercial prices for the larger armaments. But all the really hard choices and sacrifices were made and are still being made by the candidate countries themselves, under the pressure of their driving will to get into both NATO and the EU as soon as possible. That is not an incentive that the integrated Europe can currently offer with any confidence even to a country already belonging to NATO like Turkey, let alone to other Eastern or Southern Mediterranean neighbours.

---

34   Publications on all the areas of governance variation mentioned in this paragraph will be found at the DCAF website, http://www.dcaf.ch.

And that particular kind of leverage is clearly irrelevant to cases in Africa, Latin America, Central Asia, or perhaps even the South Caucasus region in the nearer term (after the setbacks related to Georgia).

Europe's security sector reformers are thus standing on a weaker base of leverage and motivation than before, exactly when they have to start tackling cases that are tougher than before – because the target nations/territories have less rational defence systems and more conflict damage to start with, less democratic approaches to governance in general, or both. How for instance does the EU propose to pursue SSR in a Central Asian or North African country where one man, the monarch or the president, ultimately makes all defence decisions? Even if Europeans can skilfully adapt their own ideas and experiences to such environments, where are the sticks and carrots to drive the lessons home? Would the EU, collectively, ever go so far as to make progress in SSR an actual condition for receiving other kinds of benefits from the EU, as it did with the 'non-proliferation clause' on Weapons of Mass Destruction (WMD) policy a couple of years ago?[35] Can countries be warned that their SSR performance will, more specifically, determine the EU's treatment of them in terms of defence assistance, or the licensing of arms sales? But the EU does not actually have a defence assistance programme, and those particular carrots are still held in the hands of European nations who are not very likely – as hinted above – to let their bilateral assistance or arms supply relationships be steered *positively* from Brussels in the name of a collective SSR policy, even if they accept some collective judgements on whom we should *not* sell to. All these issues exist independently of such practical headaches as the question of who in the EU's central mechanisms should fund and execute such a 'linkage' policy, and how the information needed to assess relevant performance would be found and judged. Even if Brussels could address that question for once without silly institutional jealousies, the fact would remain that a good SSR programme needs a combination of military, police, civilian, financial, hardware and development aid competences that at the moment are scattered between a number of different staffs and organs in Brussels, let alone in national capitals. Implementation of the Lisbon Treaty[36] will collapse most of the problematic divisions between Council and Commission, between military and civilian staffs and between related funds within the EU's 'second pillar' of foreign, security and defence affairs, but it offers no direct solutions for combining tools, expertise and leverage from this pillar with resources held in the first and the third (i.e. traditional Community business including aid and economic relations, and internal security questions respectively).

---

35   The 'non-proliferation clause' is an innovation arising from the EU's WMD strategy of December 2003: states concluding an economic cooperation agreement or similar with the EU are now required to adopt this clause pledging themselves i.a. to more effective export control measures. For details see Kile, S.N. (ed.) *Europe and Iran: Perspectives on Non-Proliferation.* Oxford: Oxford University Press, 2005.

36   Available at: http://europa.eu/lisbon_treaty/full_text/index_en.htm.

One last generalization may be suggested: the European Union is in several ways one of the *best* potential agents to carry out a modern-day, wide-reaching SSR programme; but it is very far from being the *easiest* choice. This author would strongly contend that it is worth making the effort to overcome the many challenges, and not only because SSR is a worthy and worthwhile goal in itself. If the EU's nations, organs and staffs can face up to the task of designing a European SSR programme clearly and convincingly, and operating it coherently and professionally, that process could also throw a clearer – and ethically informed! – light on many of the larger unsolved issues hanging over the European defence and security personality today.

References

Bailes, A.J.K., 'A "New Deal" between State and Market' in Ø. Østerud and J.H. Matláry, *Denationalisation and Internationalisation of European Defence*. Aldershot: Ashgate, 2007.

Bailes, A.J.K. and Frommelt, I., *Business and Security: Public-Private Security Relationships in a New Environment*. Oxford: Oxford University Press, 2005.

Caparini, M., 'Security Sector Reform and NATO and EU Enlargement' in *SIPRI Yearbook 2003: Armaments, Disarmament and International Security*. Oxford: Oxford University Press, 2003.

Derks, M. and More, S., *The EU and Internal Challenges for Effectively Supporting Security Sector Reform*. The Hague: Clingendael Institute, June 2009.

Gross, E., 'Security Sector Reform in Afghanistan: The EU's Contribution'. EU Institute of Security Studies, Occasional Paper 78, April 2009. Available at: http://iss.europa.eu.

Hänggi, H. and Tanner, F., 'Promoting Security Sector Governance in the EU's Neighbourhood'. Chaillot Paper No. 80, Paris, EU Institute of Security Studies, July 2005.

Hänggi, H. and Scherrer, V. (eds) *Security Sector Reform and UN Integrated Missions: Experience from Burundi, the Democratic Republic of Congo, Haiti, and Kosovo*. Geneva: Democratic Control of Armed Forces (DCAF), 2008.

Hutchful, E. and Omitoogun, W., *Budgeting for the Military Sector in Africa: The Processes and Mechanisms of Control*. Oxford: Oxford University Press, 2006.

Law, D. (ed.) *Intergovernmental Organizations and Security Sector Reform*. Geneva: DCAF Yearbook, 2007.

Sköns, E., Omytoogun, W., Perdomo, C. and Stålenheim, P., 'Military Expenditure' in *SIPRI Yearbook 2005*. Stockholm: SIPRI, 2005.

Spence, D. and Fluri, P. (eds) *The European Union and Security Sector Reform*. London: John Harper Publishing, 2008.

Chapter 5

The EU's View on Security Sector Reform

Malena Britz

Introduction

The political emphasis on security sector reform (SSR) as an important activity for the international community has increased both on a global level in the UN, on a regional level in the EU and on national levels. This emphasis is shown in a number of documents. One example is within the framework of the OECD Development Assistance Committee (DAC), where both the European Commission and EU member states have participated in the development of guidelines for the support to SSR (OECD 2004). OECD DAC has also developed a Handbook on SSR.

The EU refers to SSR in a number of policy documents. The European Security Strategy from 2003 mentioned SSR; and both the Council and the Commission have presented proposals for the development of SSR in the two documents 'EU Concept for ESDP Support to Security Sector Reform (SSR)' (Council 2005) and 'A Concept for European Community Support for Security Sector Reform' (Commission 2006a). The political attention to the SSR concept also has practical consequences. In the EU, documents on a more operational level such as the (military) 'Headline Goal 2010' and the 'Civilian Headline Goal 2008', mention SSR as an important area of activity. The EU has also named two of its CSDP operations as SSR-operations.

In general, the EU documents that are analysed in this chapter emphasize that the Union already has a number of instruments, and is involved in a number of activities, that *can* be part of SSR. However, these instruments and activities are not formulated as one coherent package or as a coherent policy, but exist both in the Common Security and Defence Policy (CSDP, formerly European Security and Defence Policy – ESDP[1]) and in Community activity. This was also pointed out in the Council Conclusions on a Policy framework for Security Sector Reform from June 2006, which stated that: '[t]he EU has a broad range of civilian and military instruments which are able to support SSR activities' (Council 2006) and it continued by saying that activities can be carried out through CSDP or Community action or through a combination of these actions.

---

1   In this chapter, the term CSDP will be used for reasons of consistency, even though the documents analysed themselves use the older term ESDP because the policy was called ESDP at the time when they were written. Obviously this does not apply to quotes, which will use the exact term used in the original text.

The two concept papers presented by the Council and the Commission will in this chapter be referred to as the Council Concept and the Commission Concept, respectively. In the introduction of the Council Concept it was stated that the 'purpose of this paper is to provide a concept for ESDP support to Security Sector Reform in partner countries' (Council 2005: 5). It was pointed out that EU's civilian and military instruments can be used to support SSR activities, and that it can take both CFSP/CSDP action or Community action or combine these.

SSR is a concept under development, and therefore the Council Concept also stated that the concept presented should be broad not to constrain future activities. In the Commission Concept, the relationship between CSDP and Community activities was mentioned when it was stated that the early stages of SSR in a crisis or post-crisis situation often involve CSDP missions, especially in areas such as military and intelligence reform. Here greater coordination both between Community and bilateral member state support, and Community and CSDP action was asked for. As stated by Sheriff (2007) such demands also occur in most reports and analyses of EU SSR. This is something of which the EU is aware, as is shown in the two concept papers.

Despite the awareness on the EU's side of problems of coherence, progress to solve this conundrum has not been easily achieved. Some of the changes brought by the Lisbon Treaty that came into effect in late 2009 are meant to create a greater coherence. The new External action service, bringing together large parts of the Council Secretariat with the Commission's Directorate-General for External relations and the Directorate-General for Development (Presidency 2010), might be of particular relevance for the development of EU SSR. However, at the time of writing this chapter it is too early to make any judgements on the practical effect of the Lisbon Treaty on EU SSR.

This chapter analyses the two SSR Concept papers produced by the Commission and the Council. It goes through how the two concept papers deal with the following questions:

- What is the Security Sector and Security Sector Reform?
- What activities are included in SSR?
- When and where does the EU engage in SSR?
- What resources are needed for SSR?

In addition, the latter three questions also study EU SSR in practice. An analysis is made of the CSDP operations that the EU itself has named SSR-operations. The chapter then analyses what view on security is manifested in the Concept papers, it also takes into the analysis EU SSR practice as shown in the CSDP operations. The view on security is important because it has consequences for EU's SSR activities and for what is required from EU's member states when they want to engage in SSR. One important aspect of the CSDP is that the capacities that the EU has to engage in crisis management in fact belong to the member states. The EU is not the owner of these kinds of capacities, which means that member state resources are very important when it comes to EU's possibility to actively participate in activities that are part of SSR.

What is the Security Sector and What is Security Sector Reform?

The security sector was in the Council Concept paper defined on the basis of the OECD DAC guidelines as a system that includes:

- core security actors (different kinds of state actors e.g. the armed forces, the police, intelligence services and coast guards);
- security management and oversight bodies (state bodies such as security and economy related ministries and authorities, but also civil society organizations);
- justice and law enforcement institutions; and
- non-statutory security forces with whom donors rarely engage (private actors or irregular armies).

The Commission Concept paper referred to the same OECD-DAC definition of the security sector as the Council concept paper referred to. In the Community concept paper the role and strength of Community support for SSR, the added value that can be provided by the EU, was discussed. It was stated that the added value was based on the supranational nature of the Commission and its previous experiences, the global reach of activities, the long term presence, and the great number of instruments that the Community has as SSR is part of regional external assistance.

Some other strengths of Community action were also pointed out. One was the commitment to policy coherence for development; another was the experiences of SSR among the member states that the EU can draw from (especially in the new member states, which have experiences of their own of such activities). A third strength was the potential the Community has to co-ordinate and harmonize EU actions by complementing these with CFSP/CSDP actions, member states, or other regional and multilateral organizations and local civil society.

Further, the Commission Concept on SSR stated that 'SSR concerns reform of both the bodies which provide security to citizens and the state institutions responsible for management and oversight of those bodies ...' and that it '... focuses on the overall functioning of the security system as part of a governance reform policy and strategy of the public sector' (Commission 2006a: 3). It stated that security for the EC not only is limited to territorial security but 'includes both the external and internal security of a state and its people.' In addition it was stated that '[c]itizens should be able to expect the state to be capable of maintaining peace and guaranteeing the strategic security interests of the country, as well as ensuring that their lives, property, and political, economic and social rights are safeguarded. The state has to be able to protect citizens from the threats of insecurity, including violent conflict and terrorism, while protecting rights and institutions from being undermined by these threats' (Commission 2006a: 4).

In the Council Concept it was stated that '[s]ecurity sector reform seeks to increase the ability of a state to meet the range of both internal and external security needs in a manner consistent with democratic norms and sound principles of good governance, human rights, transparency and the rule of law. It concerns not only state stability and regime security of nations but also the safety and well-being of their people' (Council 2005: 9). It was further stated that '[s]ecurity sector reform will contribute to an accountable, effective and efficient security system, operation under civilian control consistent with democratic norms and principles of good governance, transparency and the rule of law, and acting according to international standards and respecting human rights, which can be a force for peace and stability, fostering democracy and promoting local and regional stability' (Council 2005: 4).

What Activities are Included in SSR?

In the Council Concept paper it was pointed out that the CSDP (with its dimensions of civilian and military crisis management and the prevention of conflict) can offer 'an integrated as well as focused approach to SSR'. The concept should complement existing concepts for crisis management missions in the field of Rule of Law and Civilian Administration. It was stated that the CSDP support to SSR usually would take the form of advice and assistance to local authorities such as the executive, the legislature and the judiciary.

It was also stated that EU has the possibility to support reform of the defence sector, the police sector, justice/Rule of Law elements, border and customs sector, and financial and budgetary aspects of the security sector. In addition it was pointed out that concepts for activities that aim to strengthen or reorganize particular agencies or institutions already have been developed in the CSDP framework and therefore can contribute to SSR.

In general, Council activities to support SSR are the same kind of activities as are undertaken as civilian and military crisis management. Civilian crisis management within the CSDP has been specified in four priority areas: police, rule of law, civilian administration and civil protection, but since these priority areas were specified monitoring missions have also become important. When it comes to civilian capabilities within the CSDP, personnel from the member states are generally civil servants. For military crisis management military officers are of course the most important category of personnel (Boin et al. 2005, Annex, p. 44, 56; Gourlay 2004: 413-14).

In the Council Concept paper it was also emphasized that long term activities should be locally owned and build on national ownership and partnership. Further, it was stated that these activities generally are 'undertaken in close co-operation with the work of other International Community actors' (Council 2005: 9), both

NGOs and INGOs, but particularly the UN were mentioned. It was also pointed out that the integrated civilian-military approach that was being developed for the CSDP should be taken also for CSDP actions in support of SSR.

Community support in the area of SSR is by nature civilian. The activities undertaken by the Commission that relate to civilian crisis management mainly 'relate to provision of humanitarian assistance, through the European Community Humanitarian Office (ECHO) or the provision of longer-term technical assistance and aid for institution-building and post conflict reconstruction efforts' (Gourlay 2004: 406).

The Commission is also involved in pre-crisis, conflict prevention activities such as human rights monitoring, and democracy and human rights programmes. These activities are typically implemented by international organizations (e.g. the UN or the OSCE) or non-governmental organizations (Gourlay 2004: 415-16).

SSR-Operations

In spite of the concept papers, and the fact that many EU operations are efforts to support competence-building in different areas of the security sector (such as police or rule of law), the EU itself has so far only named two of its operations explicitly as Security Sector Reform-operations. These are the EUSEC DR CONGO and EU SSR Guinea Bissau. EUSEC DR CONGO started in 2005 with the task to contribute to the integration of the Congolese army and help improving the salary system. It has since then been expanded to more areas such as administration, the use of IT, human resources, training and logistics within the armed forces. The objective of the operation is to support the rebuilding of the army so that it can guarantee security, and make economic and social development possible (Council 2010). The operation EU SSR Guinea Bissau is more comprehensive and aims at supporting the authorities to implement the National SSR Strategy Document that was approved by Guinea Bissau's National Assembly in January 2008. An important task is to downsize and restructure the Armed Forces and the Security Forces encompassing all sectors defence, police and justice. The EU operation thus consists of both military and civilian advisors and has resulted in a new legislative package as well as other regulative documents such as codes of conduct to be adopted by the national legislators and authorities (Council 2009).

When and Where does the EU Engage in SSR?

In a background paper to the Commission Concept, examples of EC support undertaken in the years 2003-2005 were given (Commission 2006b). These examples show that Community support was given in regions all over the world: Africa, the Caribbean, the Pacific, Western Balkans, Eastern Europe and Central Asia, the Mediterranean, the Middle East, Asia and Latin America. In addition to this geographical engagement, the Commission Concept paper pointed out a number of existing Community policies and strategies that are relevant for support to SSR. The examples given are: the enlargement policy, The European Neighbourhood Policy (the ENP), the EU Development Policy, Conflict prevention and crisis management, Human rights and democracy policy, and the external dimension of the EU policy of freedom, security and justice.

In the Commission Concept paper *four different situations* where the Commission has already given support to SSR were pointed out. These were: conflict or immediate post-conflict countries; in countries with medium to long term post-conflict situations or countries with simmering tensions; in countries in transition; and in more stable environments undergoing reform as part of long term democratization and development process.

In the Council Concept, in the section of 'core requirements and modalities' of the document it was stated that '[t]he legal basis for an EU action should be either a UNSCR or an invitation by a host partner state or International/Regional/Sub-Regional Organization, bearing in mind that proposals for EU action in support of SSR in a partner state can be initiated by EU Member states or the Commission' (Council 2005: 17). When it comes to the preparation and planning of an SSR mission it was stated in the Council Concept that a fact-finding mission could be launched in consultation with the partner government in order to collect facts for the preparation of the mission. In such missions the Head of Mission should participate and they should be carried out in association with the Commission. A general concept of a CSDP action would then need to be developed on the basis of these findings. The concept will set out the general framework for action and be approved by the Council.

In the Council Concept paper, *three scenarios* in which CSDP could be involved in SSR activities were foreseen. The *first scenario* foresaw an immediate post conflict situation in which disarmament and demobilization were given as examples of activities that the EU could engage in. It was also pointed out that as part of a whole 'DDR package' the capacities of the Commission would be given special attention in the field of reintegration. External military or police presence would ensure the security situation. The *second scenario* dealt with a transition and stabilization phase where the environment was expected to be more stable with local political authorities in place at least on a temporary basis. The *third scenario* regarded an environment that was assessed as stable and where no return to significant conflict is to be expected, and CSDP action would in such a scenario assist the on-going development of democratic institutions and be closely related to other governance reforms and complement Community assistance. This also means that civilian activities would be shared with the Commission.

SSR-Operations

As discussed in the previous section, the only two EU operations that so far have been called SSR-operations have taken place in Africa in environments that perhaps are most similar to the second scenario referred to above, a transition and stabilization phase. However, as is evident in both DR Congo and in Guinea Bissau, the different phases that these three scenarios represent are not always as clear cut in practice as their ideal types suggest. In addition, the possibility of the EU to assist in achieving SSR can also be limited due to changes in the local political environment that makes levels of tension increase or escalates conflict. If encompassing EU SSR activities to other military operations, police missions, and rule of law missions, it is clear that the EU has experience of all three scenarios.

What Resources are Needed for SSR?

In the Council Concept it was stated that both well-trained and well-equipped personnel were needed to carry out SSR. Teams of experts need to be made available by member states on a voluntary basis. It was pointed out that EU personnel should have correct professional and region-specific knowledge, and courses offered through the EU training programme should be taken into account. In order to provide with both appropriate personnel and equipment that can be deployed quickly, mechanisms of logistics, of effective planning capability, and of financial procurement were pointed out as necessary.

Expertise was also emphasized in the Commission Concept where it was stated that: '[e]ffective support needs exchanges of expertise and a broader base of experts in the Member States who can be deployed in the different aspects of SSR' (Commission 2006a: 9). It was also stated that the expertise, including pool of experts of field missions and programmes, needed to be expanded. Here the effective mobilizations of human resources were in need of appropriate modalities, and specific SSR-training should be developed in order to broaden the expertise in both EU and member state institutions.

One instrument that the Commission has had in situations of crisis was the Rapid Reaction Mechanism that enabled it to mobilize funds quickly (Boin et al., 2005, Annex, p. 48). From 1 January 2007 the Rapid Reaction Mechanism was replaced by a new Instrument for Stability. This Instrument builds on the Rapid Reaction Mechanism and can be used either in 'a situation of crisis or emerging crisis' or 'in the context of stable conditions for the implementation of Community cooperation policies in third countries' (Commission 2006c: 2). According to the Regulation establishing this Instrument, the Commission shall keep the Council regularly informed about the planning of its crisis (or emerging crisis) assistance.

SSR-Operations

As the two EU SSR operations in DR Congo and Guinea Bissau exemplify, EU operations are often not very big. These two operations both consist of around 50 (or just fewer than 50) people. This means that the possibility for the EU to post experts in these different areas of defence, police and judiciary reform becomes crucial for its activities in SSR. An interesting aspect here that would merit further study is the role that international NGOs could play in providing expertise and contribute to the assessment of progress.

The View on Security in the Two Concept Papers

The emphasis in the Concept papers on both state security and on individual security illustrates the changed view of the security concept that has taken place among some scholars since the end of the cold war. One example is Bigo (2000) who speaks of a conceptually blurred distinction between internal and external security in the European states today. The fact that this blurred distinction is pointed out in the Council Concept paper show that the 'post cold war' scholarly way of thinking about security also is present when political efforts are made to think about how security could be created for others (in this case non-EU members in post conflict or transition countries). In addition, the security and safety of humans have received increased attention, the state is not considered to be secure unless its citizens are safe and secure. Both Concept papers emphasize that security not only is sought for the state but also for its citizens.

The diminished importance of territorial borders, in combination with the increased emphasis on the safety and security of humans, erases a conventional division between first and second order security. First order security is closely thought of in relation to the territory and indivisible values: control over external borders, monopoly of violence in the territory, political sovereignty and (in the case of the European states) by safeguarding democratic rule. Second order security is then concerned with internal security, with the safety of people. The development towards an erased division between first and second order security is particularly visible in the European states (both EU members and states in the Union's neighbourhood).

The erased division of first and second order security means that security concerns stem from threats to *societal security*, which comprises aspects of both first and second order security. This means that when the importance of the border between the national and the international diminishes, threats to the state are not only expected to have their origin externally of the state, but might also have their origin in events internally. For example, a situation where there is a demand for measures of civil protection (making sure that citizens are safe), primarily a second order security problem, might lead to a first order security problem, i.e. difficulties in securing the state, if the effort to provide necessary means fails. Such a situation is bad for a stable state but could be fatal to a more instable state.

This situation might be most easily pinpointed in post conflict states or states in transition, but increased interdependencies in an internationalized society also make the statement true for more stable states. The diminished importance of territorial borders not only erases the conventional division between first and second order security, it also creates a new political space – an intermestic space (Sundelius 2005) – which partially is domestic, and partially is international. Interdependencies of basic infrastructures such as electricity means that second order security problems might spread between states, creating political challenges that need to be dealt with in common.

This might also mean that there is a similarity between the kind of security problems that more stable developed states (such as the EU member states) have, and the kind of security problems that less developed states have. Here it might be possible to argue that the security problems are similar in kind, but differ in degree. One important aspect of the differences in degree is of course that democratic western states for a long time have worked to create a political system that can act as a buffer between second and first order security problems, whereas more instable and less democratic states do not have such a buffer.

Going back to the activities that are to be undertaken in support of SSR, the two EU concept papers show a tension between activities that are to be undertaken rapidly and more long term activities to support SSR. This could be seen as two lines of thinking about this concept, one is to think about it as crisis management, and the other is to think of it more in terms of general efforts to create 'good governance', but with a special focus on the security sector. Good governance is one of the areas where SSR meets the development agenda, a cross-road that in general has not been unproblematic (cf. Ta Thi 2006). This can bee seen in the Council Concept paper when stating that a 'well organized and controlled security system that is managed in accordance with democratic norms and principles of accountability, transparance and good governance' is needed to create durable stability and development (Council 2005: 10). This possible dichotomy draws the attention to the issue of policy (and activity) coherence. One aspect of this is the relationship between Community activities and CFSP/CSDP activities in support of SSR. The EU operations referred to in this chapter could perhaps be thought of as medium term. They are not operations that manage the most acute phase of a situation but rather part of efforts to make a transition phase stable.

Consequences for Member States

At least two consequences for EU member states when considering the development of SSR activities are possible to discern from the analysis of the EU documents presented here. Interestingly, both of these have to do with member state resources and how they are dealt with. First, it is clear in both the Commission and the

Council Concepts on SSR that the activities needed in order to help countries outside the EU to increase their societal security to a great extent relies on the interest and capacities of the member states. Looking at the activities, they are activities that not only demand financial support but also human resources in order to spread knowledge and experiences. How the human resources that are necessary in order for the member states to be able to send out personnel in support for SSR activities are to be made available, is something that the EU member states struggle with. One way to create access to human resources is to create pools of experts, one example of this is the Civilian Response Team concept that has been created as a part of the CSDP, and another example is a Norwegian proposal to create a Nordic pool of SSR experts. However, at least in the Nordic states, the political ambition to create possibilities to send out personnel is not yet mirrored in the administrative structures and the difficulties of finding the right human resources have not been resolved.

The coherence issue discussed above brings us to the second consequence for member states. It raises the issue of whether the EU and its member states should aim for a clearer division of roles between the Commission and the Council in SSR activities. This division is important because it affects how member states allocate their own resources. As one Danish civil servant has pointed out '[m]ost national administrations tend to organize its work in relation to the EU on the pillar structure, meaning that different ministries and departments work with different pillars and policy areas' (Interview, Copenhagen March 2006). This also shows that the relationship between Council activities and Commission activities (the issue of coherence), in the absence of clear roles between the Council and the Commission might develop into a question of resources for the member states. The reason for this is that different parts of the same national administration might undertake similar tasks but in relation to different kinds of EU measures. The creation of the European External Action Service, might bring changes here in the relationship between the EU and the member states in that it might provide a clearer focal point for the member states in developing SSR. Related to this last issue is the fact that EU member states need to consider how SSR-related activities that take place outside the EU context, for example their bilateral activities, take place in relation to the activities that are undertaken through the EU.

References

Bigo, D., 'When Two become One: Internal and External Securitisations in Europe' in Kelstrup and Williams (eds) *International Relations and the Politics of European Integration: Power, Security and Community*. London: Routledge, 2000.

Boin, A., Ekengren, M. and Rhinard, M., 'Functional Security and Crisis Management Capacity in the European Union: Setting the Research Agenda'. Draft Report, February 2005.

'Civilian Headline Goal 2008', 15863/04, Brussels, Council of the European Union, 7 December 2004.

Commission (2006a), Communication from the Commission to the Council and the European Parliament, 'A Concept for European Community Support for Security Sector Reform', COM(2006) 253 final, Brussels, 24 May 2006.

Commission (2006b), Commission Staff Working Document, Annexes to the Communication from the Commission to the Council and the European Parliament, 'A Concept for European Community Support for Security Sector Reform', COM(2006) 253 final.

Commission (2006c), Regulation (EC) No. 1717/2006.

Council (2005), Note from the Secretariat to the Political and Security Committee on the Subject: 'EU Concept for CSDP Support to Security Sector Reform (SSR)', 12566/4/05, Brussels, 13 October 2005.

Council (2006), 'Council Conclusions on a Policy Framework for Security Sector Reform', 2736th General Affairs Council meeting – Luxembourg, 12 June 2006.

Council (2009), 'EU mission in support of security sector reform in the Republic of Guniea-Bissau (EU SSR GUINEA_BISSAU)'. Updated November 2009.

Council (2010), 'EU Mission to Provide Advice and Assistance for Security Sector Reform in the Democratic Republic of Congo (EUSEC DR CONGO)'. Updated April 2010.

European Security Strategy, 'A Secure Europe in a Better World. European Security Strategy', Brussels, 12 December 2003.

Gourlay, C., 'European Union Procedures and Resources for Crisis Management' in *International Peacekeeping* 11(3), Autumn 2004, pp. 404-21.

'Headline Goal 2010', approved by General Affairs and External Relations Council on 17 May 2004, endorsed by the European Council of 17 and 18 June 2004.

Interview, Civil Servant at the Danish Ministry for Foreign Affairs, Copenhagen, March 2006.

OECD 2004, Security Sector Reform and Governance, Policy and Practice, DAC Guidelines and Reference Series. Paris: OECD, 2004.

Presidency, Note from the Presidency to the Council on the subject: 'Proposal for a Council Decision Establishing the Organisation and Functioning of the European External Action Service – Presidency Compromise', Brussels, 23 April 2010.

Sheriff, A., 'Security Sector Reform and EU Norm Implementation' in Law (ed.) *Intergovernmental Organisations and Security Sector Reform*. Yearbook Geneva Centre for Democratic Control of the Armed Forces, LIT Verlag, 2007.

Sundelius, B., 'Disruptions – Functional Security for the EU' in Elbe, Luterbacher Missiroli, Sundelius and Zupi (eds) 'Disasters, Diseases, Disruptions: A New D-Drive for the EU'. Chaillot Paper No. 83, September 2005.

Ta Thi, H., 'Post-Cold War Security Sector Reform (SSR): New ODA Instrument for Peace and Stability?' in Chetail, van der Poel, Ramel and Schwok (eds) *Prévention, gestion et sortie des conflits*. Institut européen de l'Université de Genève, 2006.

Chapter 6

Prospects and Advantages of EU Security Sector Reform

David Spence

Introduction

More than any other concept in the EU's considerable foreign policy arsenal, Security Sector Reform sits at the centre of Europe's foreign, security and development policies. At the same time, as a policy area it epitomizes European integration. It does this through its situation – part national, part national interest even; but actually part of a wider concept – security policy itself – which is transnational in implication, and which calls for a regional/European response for which EU institutions and policy-making mentalities are so far ill-primed – so where there is a strong case for further integration.

In this chapter I argue that Security Sector Reform is an area which illustrates three key themes. It is interesting in itself to those of us concerned on a day to day basis with security issues. It goes without saying. But it is also:

a. key to understanding the potential of the EU's role as an international actor;
b. fundamental to an assessment of how its overall approach to international relations is unique;
c. a pointer to a more far reaching debate about the norms and values of the EU as a growingly important political and security actor.

Behind this chapter lies the premise that Europe has a chance to represent something new and worthwhile in international relations, providing its individual policy stances are melded into a coherent, pragmatic and democratic whole.

Advantages of a Shared EU Stance on SSR

Of course, the emergence of the EU security agenda is undoubtedly attributable to such factors as the evolution of the EU as a political actor, its status as the world's largest market, and its key position as an aid and trade actor. All these features explain, in turn, the emergence of the EU's international identity itself. And they also explain the fact that it now has interests to defend and consequently policies to advocate worldwide. But these are points that have frequently been made before, and there is no point in dwelling on them here.

What is worth dwelling on, however, is a concomitant feature in the EU's political make-up, namely the inability of single countries to tackle today's complex security problems on their own, whether in Europe's immediate neighbourhood or further afield. This is also a frequently made point, but it does underline the whole rationale for European integration itself, and oblige us to consider why and how the European Union can share responsibility for SSR with member states' own independent action as part of their bilateral relations with countries outside the EU.

What is interesting is that the 'Europe' we increasingly call 'a global actor' remains, at the same time, a conglomerate of 27 national actors, each with varying attributes and capabilities internationally. Some of these attributes reflect highly integrated segments of policy – international trade policy is the prime example of this, for some 95 percent of trade policy issues are no longer national, but European. But other individual national attributes and capabilities can and are put to work in the national interests of the individual states. And the action of these individual states may never be conceived of as 'European Action' in the EU sense – take Security Sector Reform in Sierra Leone, undertaken by the British, for example, or the less far-reaching in Disarmament Demobilisation Reintegration (DDR) efforts of France together with UN forces in the Côte d'Ivoire. But, the individual policies and actions of EU member states nevertheless form part of the total of security outputs of Europe. And just as environmental policy 30 years ago was purely national, despite its European ramifications and implications, so security policies, such as Security Sector Reform, are today still decided nationally, though they simultaneously demonstrate potential to be part of a future overarching European Security Strategy. It is a question of bringing together diverse national elements, with diverse national justifications and creating a European conceptual whole out of them. And this, I would argue, is the policy process you see before you in the EU today, with regard to Security Sector Reform and its sister concept DDR.

The most salient point to retain, however, is that once these numerous national policy approaches are melded into a European policy stance, 'national' interests in outcomes diminish – or, more correctly, perhaps, are themselves melded into a wider European interest. And the interesting fact here is that the process implies a shedding of national interest in outcomes. European interest is about assisting other countries evolve into models we feel comfortable with, not about the more sordid, calculable interests of a donor state with a political or economic national axe to grind. While I would not be so naïve as to argue that European security policy is free of self-interest – somehow a value-free contribution to overall peace and security – what is clear is that European level policy and action sets itself apart from accusations of 'national interest', imperialism, neo-colonialism etc. So my first argument is that the EU's stance on Security Sector Reform is novel and, in terms of norms and values, rather more healthy than a purely national policy could be. It may therefore prove more effective in the long run, but that cannot be judged in advance.

But, that is not the whole story. It is also about the maturing of a concept. Security Sector Reform has been bandied about by various policy actors for some 20 years. In one sense I liked it more under its old-fashioned definition as reform of armies and police, and nothing more. Then, it was limited in focus, easy to grasp and not subject to interminable debates about values. The old-fashioned version of SSR was limited in scope, but was not limited in implications, however. By restricting the policy discussion to issues of human resource management and efficiency of armed forces and police alone, security sector reform ran the risk of blanketing out real concerns about democratic control per se and the democratic legitimacy not only of the security sector but of the whole process of governance itself.

Recently we were unfortunately confused about what was happening in Turkey. So to say that blanketing out democracy and legitimacy was part of a restrictive notion of security sector reform is ironic. In the spring of 2007 we found an army threatening to intervene in the political process. We cannot caution such action if we are supporters of the security sector finding its rightful place in the hierarchy of politics. Yet, here we have an army ready to intervene to uphold a key feature of the Turkish constitution we all presumably actually like – secular politics is 'a good thing'. And the more so in a world where fundamentalism has been proved 'a bad thing' when it gets near to government. But, we don't like an army intervening in politics even if we applaud its reasoning! There is a parallel here with our work on security sector reform. Our assumption in having an SSR policy for relations with our international partners is that a reformed security sector automatically means less corruption, less strife, more development and more democracy. This is reflected in key policy documents such as 'The European Consensus on Development' (adopted in November 2005) and the 'European Security Strategy' (adopted in December 2003).[1] As the Commission's (2006) Concept for European Community Support for Security Sector Reform put it:

> The European Union's external action underlines its identity as a global player and partner working to promote its common values, namely respect for human rights, fundamental freedoms, peace, democracy, good governance, gender equality, the rule of law, and solidarity and justice, including in the area of security sector reform.

So, the modern concept of SSR goes far beyond a mere focus on armies and police, and their efficiency in terms of resource management. It is a wider concept addressing the whole gamut of actors in state security and democracy.

---

1   European Commission (2006) 'A Concept for European Community Support for Security Sector Reform', Brussels, 24 May 2006, COM(2006) 253F. http://eur-lex.europa.eu/LexUriServ/site/en/com/2006/com2006_0253en01.pdf.

A Widening SSR Concept

Today, the EU notion of SSR includes all state institutions formally committed to the security of the state and its people, and it is less concerned with purely military implications. The Commission analyses and funds SSR within a framework inspired by post-conflict peace building and the quest for good governance. The sources for this can be found in development policies governing the European Development Fund, in particularly the governance sections of the Lomé and Cotonou Agreements.[2] This conception of SSR makes more sense in terms of Peace building than a purely military perspective, such as the earlier NATO concept.

At a logically prior level the EU conception of SSR relie on a political (even moral) commitment to democratic governance and legitimacy.[3] Its use of the term 'Security' in SSR is not restricted to a conception based on territorial security or the security of a particular regime. In expanding the concept to cover human security,[4] and thus covering freedom from want, freedom from fear and freedom to take action on one's own behalf, the EU clearly puts the security of citizens at the heart of its policy preoccupations, rather than restricting its policy framework and funding mechanisms to an approach focussed primarily on state security and military/police institutional parameters. The EU point of departure is the hypothesis that citizens rightfully expect the state to maintain peace and to guarantee the strategic security interests of the country, yet at the same time to provide a secure environment for human lives and property on the one hand and political, economic and social rights on the other.

The EC Communication on Security Sector Reform outlines how the human security concept is useful not only in defining the relationship between citizens' needs and the state's responsibilities (including the state's ability to maintain peace and guarantee the citizen's security of life, property, political, economic and social rights), but in understanding the interlinkage and differences between external and internal security needs. It thereby helps to clarify the separation of tasks between the different institutions and bodies constituting the security system.[5] The traditional view of the European Commission has ceded place to a view of SSR that encompasses the responsibilities of other law enforcement institutions than the military and police, such as border guards and customs authorities. In the new approach to SSR, the security system also covers the wider justice system (the judiciary, prisons, prosecution services, human rights commissions

---

2   Cotonou reference: http://www.acpsec.org/en/conventions/cotonou/cotonou_revised _e.pdf.

3   See Spence, D., 'EU Governance and Global Governance: New Roles for EU Diplomats' in Cooper, Hocking and Maley (eds) *Global Governance and Diplomacy: Worlds Apart?* Basingstoke: Palgrave, 2008.

4   Kaldor, M., *Human Security.* Cambridge: Polity Press, 2007.

5   See Ekengren's analysis of the practical implications for EU policies and institutions in Chapter 7.

and ombudsmen functions) as well as security management and oversight bodies (the legislature, executive, traditional authorities and civil society). Democratic oversight is vital. The Commission has defined its SSR concept to cover 'those aspects which are designed to contribute to peace, the protection of life and limb, and to ensure the upholding of the law and oversight through the justice system and democratic institutions of the relevant executive bodies'.[6]

The Making of EU SSR Policies

There have been many divergences of view on where overall responsibility for SSR should lie. By and large, this has depended on the particular aspects of SSR actors have wished to pursue. The rapid development since the late 1990s, and especially after 2001, of strengthened EU capacity and objectives in the areas of conflict prevention and crisis management have had a significant impact on the way the Union currently approaches SSR, both in policy and operational terms. SSR can be covered by specific projects financed under country programmes or specific financing facilities. Between 2002 and 2006, the Rapid Reaction Mechanism allowed the Commission to respond urgently to the needs of countries threatened by serious political instability or suffering from the effects of an industrial or natural disaster. On 1 January 2007 the Instrument for Stability (IfS) replaced both the Rapid Reaction Mechanism and several other funding instruments in the fields of drugs, mines, displaced people, crisis management, rehabilitation and reconstruction, allowing, for example, support to the United Nations Interim Mission in Kosovo and the office of the High Representative in Bosnia and Herzegovina. In general, however, SSR related activities are integrated into country strategies within the framework of wider development and external cooperation.

ESDP missions, the Community's Rapid Reaction Mechanism, and now the Instrument for Stability, have covered a number of SSR related activities, especially in post-conflict settings. They complement SSR support under long-term community instruments and include both civilian aspects of SSR and more recently defence reform such as that of EUSEC Congo (2005). The DRC was the test case for the EU in SSR, following the achievement in 2006 of the overarching EU policy framework. Civil-military coordination, cross-pillar coordination, sequencing of short and long term instruments and EU coordination and cooperation with national and international actors have been carefully honed. EUSEC Congo was the first time the EU engaged in defence reform, undertaking police and justice reform at the same time. It seems unlikely that there will be another case on the same scale and level of political commitment for some years. In most geographical locations the main focus of EU support is likely to continue

---

6   Commission Communication on SSR, pp. 4-5.

to be on civilian aspects of SSR. The EU is starting to take a more holistic and coordinated approach to SSR, as in Kosovo, Afghanistan or Guinea Bissau.

Competence debates between Commission and Council were frequent until the European Court of Justice (ECJ) ruled in 2009 that EU support in certain security-related areas such as small arms and light weapons control (SALW), SSR, border management and the rule of law, may be legally pursued under either EC external assistance instruments or through CFSP/ESDP missions.[7] It also clarified that if an action can be adopted legally under the Community pillar, it may not be adopted in the framework of CFSP/ESDP, thus confirming the Commission's view on the primacy of the first (EC) pillar as the legal basis for EU support in these areas. The ECJ verdict stated that the 'aim and content' of action should determine the framework for EU intervention and that if goals pertaining to development, rule of law or good governance are the objectives pursued, an EC legal basis is necessary. By contrast, if a purely security goal is pursued, such as resolving issues pertaining to state failure, creating institutions from 'scratch' or military intervention, then a CFSP/ESDP legal basis is required. Importantly, if the thrust of an action can be considered as pursuing both objectives, an EC legal basis should be used.

The Commission has long and extensive experience in SSR. Just as Monsieur Jourdain was delighted to hear that he had been speaking 'prose' throughout his life, so the Commission has, in a sense, been content to realize that it had long been promoting SSR through its efforts in democracy, human rights and good governance. Indeed, if 'SSR' is relatively new, it is not a new area of engagement for the EC. It is an integral part of its enlargement and development policies in partner countries and regions across the world and this in a wide range of policy areas. Policy coherence for development is enshrined in the EU Treaties and the link between security, development and governance has become recognized as crucial. The EC increasingly combines technical and financial support with structured political dialogue and this contributes significantly to the promotion of legal and institutional reforms necessary to SSR. Since the Commission is considered by most governments as a neutral rather than a self-interested partner, this clearly contributes to the creation of trust necessary for effective cooperation on sensitive issues raised by SSR. The Commission's global reach and long term presence on the ground through its wide network of Delegations is a prime facilitator of efforts to build trust as a key to successful SSR support. SSR is a long term process requiring cultural, legal, institutional and organizational change. EC external assistance instruments, most of which also focus on long term developmental processes, are thus well adapted to respond to these needs, as opposed to a more specific (and today outmoded) focus on military structures alone.

---

7   ECJ ruling of 20 May 2008 on Case C-91/05 (ECOWAS). For a brief overview of the issues see Spence, D., 'The Commission and CFSP' in Spence, D. (ed.) *The European Commission*. London: John Harper, 2006.

In 2009 the Council argued for a single focal point for the SSR in the framework of ESDP to be established in the Council Secretariat. The point was to reflect the development on the UN side, where a core expert capacity for SSR was created in the newly established Office for the Rule of Law and Security institutions in DPKO in 2008. In addition a UN Inter-Agency Task Force on SSR was set up with the aim of enhancing coordination among the various UN actors. The proposal was then made to establish a coordination mechanism involving all the EU actors responsible for the SSR-related agenda in different EU areas. DPKO then appointed a permanent high level liaison officer in Brussels, to enhance practical EU-UN co-operation and the related institutional arrangements. The relevance and importance of coordination and common approaches with other donors in addition to training and tools for implementation is underlined by the fact that many partner countries lack comprehensive SSR analyses and there is a need to prioritize a limited number of areas, with most strategies focusing on one or two sub-sectors.

Conclusion

In Molière's famous play, Le Bourgeois Gentilhomme, the fatuous Monsieur Jourdain, striving to punch above his social and intellectual weight, discovers the word 'prose' as opposed to poetry. He is sad not to be a poet, but overjoyed to realize that he does pronounce prose:

> Heavens, he says, "I have been speaking prose for the last forty years without knowing it ... thank you for teaching me that ... prose is all I need ... made fashionable and arranged just right, of course ..."[8]

So it is with the EU and Security Sector Reform. SSR is not a new area of work for the EU. Through Community instruments the EU has supported different aspects of security sector reform for many years, even if they have not systematically been labelled Security Sector Reform, but came under headings of Rule of Law/Public Administration Reform/Justice and Home Affairs/Human Rights etc. Our work in SSR has taken the form of both direct and indirect support through a wide range of instruments and policy areas. EC support to SSR has been carried out under the strategic umbrella of good governance, civilian control, transparency and rule of law. Importantly, until ESDP was developed, the Commission's efforts in Security Sector Reform focussed on those parts of the security system outside the traditional notion of military reform. This was largely left to NATO. Yet today the EU is becoming more and more involved in the traditional areas.

8　'Par ma foi! Il y a plus de quarante ans que je dis de la prose sans que je susse rien, et je vous suis le plus obligé du monde de m'avoir appris cela ... je ne veux que ces seules paroles là, mais tournées à la mode, bien arrangées comme il le faut'.

Significantly, although we had been doing SSR for a long time, we hadn't called it that. The same goes for a few other concepts in the book. Five years ago the discussion in the EU on the relations between internal and external security had not really begun. Fifteen years ago, when Europe wanted to get involved in Bosnia we had no experience in military issues, though individual member states of course did, and there were only 12 of them then.

The next step was a new reflection on security and external relations, in particular development which, with trade, had been one of the mainstays of Community activity from the beginning. Security is now everywhere – ours (which we attempt to manage through a multitude of counter terrorism activities) and the security of those parts of the world where we have opted for a leadership role as a donor of aid and technical assistance.

It is a long road from national policy with restricted international impact to international policy with potential for enormous positive impact throughout the world. Security Sector Reform is not only part of our security policy as European nations, but part of our conception of development priorities, democracy, legitimacy and good governance. Not surprisingly, as the concept has evolved, it has become infinitely more complex, harder to grasp, no longer the restricted terrain of security experts but part of the decentralized ownership of a variety of political actors, governmental, intergovernmental and non-governmental. If the EU can make sense of the new maze so much the better.

References

Cotonou Agreements, ACP/CE/2005/en 1, 23 June 2000, http://www.acpsec.org/en/conventions/cotonou/cotonou_revised_e.pdf.

European Commission, 'A Concept for European Community Support for Security Sector Reform', Brussels, COM(2006) 253 final, 24 May 2006, http://eur-lex.europa.eu/LexUriserv/site/en/com/2006/com2006_0253en01.pdf.

Kaldor, M., *Human Security*. Cambridge: Polity Press, 2007.

Lomé IV Convention, ACP-CE 2163/95, 4 November 1995, http://www.acpsec.org/en/conventions/lome4_bis_e.htm.

Poquelin, J.-B. (known by his stage name Molière), 'Le Bourgeois gentilhomme' ('The Bourgeois Gentlemen'), first presented 14 October 1670.

Spence, D., 'The Commission and CFSP' in Spence and Edwards (ed.) *The European Commission*, 3rd edition. London: John Harper, 2006.

Spence, D., 'EU Governance and Global Governance: New Roles for EU Diplomats' in Cooper, Hocking and Maley (eds) *Global Governance and Diplomacy: Worlds Apart?* Basingstoke: Palgrave, 2008.

Chapter 7

The Challenge of a Broadening Security Agenda for EU Security Sector Reform

Magnus Ekengren

Introduction

The European Union has in itself always essentially been a project of security sector reform (SSR) built on broad transformation of national government including security and defence structures. For the first forty years of the Union's existence, it promoted economic integration and an institutionalized system of networks that aimed at peaceful development, democratization and inter-state state security in Europe. The result was that external security relations among states were turned into 'domestic' European politics. War among the EU member states became 'unthinkable' and national defence was adapted in line with this new situation. A European security community was created. The challenge for the Union's global role became to create inter-state security also in other parts of the world through the support of similar reforms.

Today's broadening of the security concept beyond the threat of inter-state conflicts has led the Union to develop new methods and instruments that implies a widening also of the EU's global reform agenda. In only a few years the EU has established a Common Security and Defence Policy (CSDP),[1] internal safety and emergency measures, a security strategy and a Solidarity Clause for the protection against terrorism and natural disasters. The Union is taking on a new proactive responsibility through its peace keeping missions for human security and safeguarding of EU citizens from natural disasters, pandemics, terrorism and international crime. The question is what this deepening of the European security community means for the EU's support of SSR in post-conflict reconstruction and failing and developing states.

An increasing number of observers are recognizing possible tensions between the extension of the classical 'non-war' security community through trade and aid and the support of reform for explicit security objectives. In many of the chapters in this book, the authors refer to various aspects of the EU's widening security

---

1 Technically speaking, the Common Security and Defence Policy only exists since the entering into force of the Lisbon Treaty 1 December 2009. In this article I take into account the history of the European Security and Defence Policy (which began in 1999) as well when referring to CSDP.

tasks in their analyses of the potential but also possible constraints for SSR. In their analysis of the Western Balkans Collantes-Celador and Juncos (Chapter 8) point to the risk of 'securitizing' SSR as a result of prioritizing short term goals such as support of counter-terrorism capacity at the expense of assistance for long-term development and democratization. Britz shows how the EU will increasingly rely on the interests and capacities of the EU member states when strengthening its focus on human and societal security in SSR support (Chapter 5). This particular development risks weakening the role of the supranational organs, such as the European Commission, which traditionally have been the driving force for the security community.

In their ground-breaking book from 2008 Philipp Fluri and David Spence argued for a shift from an EU SSR focus on the armed forces and territorial defence – that has characterized many national policies – to universal 'human security' (Spence and Fluri 2008). Fluri and Spence suggest that a clear distinction, a new conceptual start, needs to be made not least to avoid the risk of pursuing a widened EU SSR checklist for desirable policies for other governments that EU member states would have difficulties to implement domestically. They also underline the importance to remember that the European Commission for many years have carried out broad security sector reform in Europe and beyond without calling it SSR. The European Commission emphasizes that citizens should be able to expect the state to be capable of maintaining inter-state peace *and* ensuring that their lives, property, rights are safeguarded (European Commission 2006).

However, there are still very few comprehensive examinations of how the broader agenda affects the principles and prospects of Union SSR in practice. The purpose of this chapter is to analyse SSR implications of the EU's new policy objective to protect 'humans', 'citizens' and 'society' as expressed in policies such as CSDP and the Solidarity Clause of the Lisbon Treaty.

How will the broadened agenda affect the Union's ability to manage the three p's – policy, policies and practices – the politics of SSR? The question for policy is: *what* is EU SSR in an era of human and societal security? For policies the key issue is: *who* will do SSR in the EU? Will the Union be able to reform its policies and institutions and overcome the constraints of sector divides and the external – internal security division for coherent SSR? Are the EU member states ready to break up corresponding domestic barriers and be able to provide the resources needed for broad SSR support to other parts of the world? With regard to the third p: *how* will the Union manage to 'export' the EU styled agenda beyond its borders? It is in answers to questions such as these that an understanding of the prospects for implementing Union SSR will grow. Before examining policy objectives, policies and how they are put into practice the chapter begins with a theoretical background to these questions. It ends by recommendations for EU SSR in the light of tentative answers.

Theoretical Background:
Extending Security and Reform Beyond EU Borders

There are very few theoretically informed works on the Union's global SSR role. Instead we need to draw on more general discussions related to EU governance and security over and beyond Union borders (Schimmelfenning and Wagner 2004; Webber et al. 2004; Kirchner and Sperling 2008).

The more specific reason that can explain today's growing theoretical interest in the projection of security beyond Union borders is two-fold. Firstly, the question concerned to what extent the Union extended 'soft-security' through the enlargement process when the EU candidate states were woven into the European fabric (Friis and Murphy 1999; Filtenborg et al. 2002). This focus was only strengthened after 2004 when the Union no longer offers a membership perspective to its neighbours at the same time as security and good governance in 'the near abroad' remain a strong goal. The issue is here in what way the Union can compensate for the weaker institutional embeddedness and reform incentives in wider Europe through new policies (Schimmelfennig and Sedelmeier 2004; Scott 2005; Preston 2008). Through the European Neighbourhood Policy (2004) and the extension of the *acquis communautaire* to non-member states in areas such as justice and home affairs, energy and environment, the EU tries to minimize the soft-security risks and the difference between insiders and outsiders (Lavenex 2004). The Union is said to externalize its internal security success – the security community – through the exercise of normative powers in the world (Manners 2002).

Secondly, the projection of EU security has been increasingly debated also as a result of the development of the CSDP (Howorth 2007; Kirchner and Sperling 2008; Grevi, Helly and Keohane 2009). The consequences are today discussed in terms of whether the Union still could be seen as a civilian power given the new military means. The question is whether its internal 'civilized' way of creating security is a guarantee for 'peaceful' security projection externally (Sjursen, 2007). The discussion focuses on whether the Union can be the benevolent world power it purports to be through the European Security Strategy of 2003 (Council of the European Union 2003; Biscop and Andersson 2007). The implications of the EU's internal security tools have so far been analysed mainly from a constitutional perspective including issues such as to what degree the Solidarity Clause is legally binding for the member states (de Wijk 2004; Ekengren 2007; Boin and Ekengren 2009).

Thus, there is a growing literature on the philosophical, normative and legal consequences of the EU's broader security ambitions. Unfortunately, the more concrete implications and requirements for the EU's practical implementation of these policies – through EU institutions and national administration as well as in 'receiving' states – have not been given the same attention. This is surprising when considering how the question of how to rethink security policy and design institutions in an era of transboundary threats has placed policy-makers within the Union at perhaps the same fundamental crossroads they faced 50 years ago.

Projecting EU security, e.g. through SSR, today probably puts just as great demands on visionary leadership, new thinking and scientific analysis, as did the formation of the Union. Some examples of the magnitude of the challenges: Lavenex has pointed to the basic tension between the expansion of the 'legal boundary' to neighbouring states without extension of the 'institutional boundary' which risks the 'politics of exclusion'. In turn this could lead to *weakened* EU security as a result of more instability and aversion *vis-à-vis* the Union due to unpopular national adaptation to the conditional EU export of norms, rules and resources. There is also a great risk of conflicting strategic interests with both the closest neighbours and Russia (Lavenex 2004; Lavenex and Wichmann 2009). Consequently, there is an urgent need for the Union to place its security sector reform efforts in the broader framework of development cooperation, democracy and human rights promotion (Hänggi and Tanner 2005). Duke and Ojanen have explained the need for fundamentally new institutional links between the EU policy sectors for more efficient CSDP reform and good governance missions around the globe (Duke and Ojanen 2006; The Security & Defence Agenda 2006). Kirchner has emphasized the great coordination needs between EU institutions and member states and between security functions such as conflict resolution and development cooperation. He calls for more in-depth empirical studies of management problems for EU security policy (Kirchner 2006: 963-65).

The Widening Agenda: Evolving Goals and Means

Policy Objectives

Over the years, the objectives for EU security have evolved incrementally within the Union as a result of its growing field of competences. Since the 1950s the Union has provided for inter-state security, i.e. external security for its member states.[2] But, owing to the gradual expansion of tasks of EU institutions, namely the Commission, those institutions have also been forced to take on a growing responsibility for safeguarding and protecting the EU functions and 'systems' when new policy competences have been created. In the 1970s and 1980s, economic welfare and stability came to be perceived as a critically important object for EU members to secure jointly. A crisis for the functioning of the common market and the institutional and legal measures taken to uphold the 'four freedoms' of intra-European exchange became an EU crisis (Boin, Ekengren, and Rhinard 2006a). By focusing on safeguarding the vital flow of resources for the welfare and identity of EU member states, the Union in effect took steps towards transnational *societal* security (Buzan, Waever, and de Wilde 1998; Møller 2001). In the 1990s, the outbreak of war and violence in the Balkans also forced EU leaders

---

2   Technically speaking, the European Union only exists since 1992. I take the history of the EEC (which began in the late 1950s) into account as well.

to define this crisis as a crisis for the Union. The value of peace and stability in the neighbourhood – the 'near abroad' – was added to the EU's security goals. The objective of protecting civilians was no longer limited to EU member states. Consequently, the reference object for the Union's endeavours became the same within and outside its borders: to secure states or individuals (or groups) against each other. Today, the new capacities of the CSDP have meant that a threat or event that undermines peace and stability not only in wider Europe but globally presents a potential crisis for the EU. In this way the concept of *human security* (Paris 2001) could be added as a label for characterizing the aim of European security. This development was further underlined in subsequent years when natural disasters increasingly became defined as EU crises. The Commission and its Directorate-General (DG) for Humanitarian Aid (ECHO) gave a high priority to helping Turkey when the country was hit by two earthquakes in 1999 (Ekengren and Ramberg 2003). EU security has increasingly come to refer to all humans in grave international crises.[3]

The 1990s saw further developments towards the EU objective of securing citizens and individuals. The so called 'Mad Cow Disease' crisis in 1996 was a serious threat to the common market but at the same time to the safety of European consumers (Grönvall 2000: 89). The events of 11 September 2001 started a chain of policy responses that have clearly expressed 'EU citizens' as an object of EU security. The Solidarity Clause constitutes the next step by declaring that the EU aims should be to 'protect democratic institutions and the civilian population' not only from terrorist attack but also in the event of natural or man-made disasters (Article 222 of the Lisbon Treaty). Therefore, the referent object of security is not just a matter of individuals, but also concerns their ability to govern society and to articulate political goals – the vital functions of society. The security aim of the Union has been characterized as functional rather than territorial integrity (Sundelius 2005).

In sum, today the Union's more or less explicit aim is to protect certain fundamental values such as peace and stability (both within the EU and outside), the European economy (in a globalized world) and the safety of people and society (wherever under threat). In other words, the Union has developed a security policy for the twenty-first century which it is currently attempting to achieve with policies and institutions that were basically created for inter-state peace of the last century (Boin, Ekengren and Rhinard 2006b). The practical implications must be considerable.

Policies

The Union's policies have had a hard time to keep up with the demands stemming from the many new security objectives. One explanation is that the many tragic

---

3   It is perhaps significant that 'A Human Security Doctrine for Europe' was proposed as a doctrine for Europe's security capabilities (Kaldor 2004).

events since the beginning of the 1990s early forced the EU onto the defensive. The development of the EU's security instruments has so far been a reaction triggered by conspicuous events.

- Experiences from the Balkan wars resulted in the formation of CSDP for external crises;
- '9/11' led to the intensification of EU internal security efforts. Currently almost every area of Union cooperation has a security plan, a security committee and a network for rapid communication and reaction;
- The events in Madrid on 11 March 2004 led to the EU adopting the 'Solidarity Declaration'[4] that was later codified in the Lisbon treaty as the Solidarity Clause;
- The Asian tsunami disaster in 2004 resulted in closer consular EU cooperation and the establishment of civilian teams for international rescue missions;
- The bomb attacks in London in the summer of 2005 have led to closer EU cooperation on intelligence and discussions of a Programme for the protection of critical infrastructure in Europe;[5]
- The disaster at Haiti in January 2010 was the first test for the objectives and institutions of the Lisbon treaty and will most probably result in policies for better EU coordination of humanitarian and security forces assistance.[6]

Thus, despite its innovative and transnational roots the Union has tended to fall into the same traps as the nation states; i.e. basing its policies on the last crisis (or war) and making a strong distinction between internal and external security. This has caused many problems. In fact, most of the recent external actions were forced to be carried out by EU instruments that were initially created for 'internal' crisis management (Ekengren, Matzén, Rhinard, and Svantesson 2006).[7] The 2003 European Security Strategy declares that 'internal and external aspects are indissolubly linked'.[8] However, the implications of this merger are not (yet) reflected in the analysis and making of Union policies, institutions and operational planning.

At the same time the EU's fast growing tools for the protection of citizens, society and human rights are probably the best example of a security concept that has broadened beyond territorial defence and military power (Buzan, Waever, de Wilde 1998). This development only reflects the changed threat picture in the world where the size and scope of international terrorist and criminal networks have grown to historically unprecedented levels (Eilstrup-Sangiovanni 2005). The

---

4   European Council (2004).
5   European Commission (2005).
6   Rhinard, M. and Boin, A. (2010).
7   In this regard, however, the EU displayed a similar pattern as some member states.
8   Council of the European Union (2003), p. 2.

Union's focus is increasingly put on 'security governance' for new global risks rather than military defence averting existential threats to states (Kirchner 2006; Cottey 2007). In contrast to the six (as of March 2010) rather limited military CSDP missions, there are today no less than 25 to 30 systems led by the Commission and Council Secretariat in Brussels for information, early warning, rapid reaction, coordination and mutual support covering rescue service, the spread of infectious diseases, natural catastrophes and preventive measures in the area of combating terrorism (Boin, Ekengren and Rhinard 2006a). The total EU regulatory output in the fields of civil protection, health security, and anti-terrorism policies for the period 1992-2007 amounted to 4126 items[9] which has lead to an increasingly institutionalized 'protection policy space' in the Union (Boin, Ekengren, Rhinard 2008). Common security thinking is streamlined into almost all of the EU's policies and institutions, compared to the approximately only 200 officials that are 'doing' CSDP in the EU Council secretariat (Howorth 2007: 4). In many respects the EU's widening security and safety work both reflects and pushes the national reforms that since 9/11 are involving an increasingly broader spectrum of national administration (Zimmermann and Wenger 2006).

What is clear is that the current scope and depth of EU policies show how existing studies of SSR might risk putting the light on issues that *used* to constitute key elements of the Union's global impact and potential, leaving the new security agenda and its implications in the dark. Thereby it underestimates important areas of change that can point in the direction of new types of challenges for EU SSR as a consequence of the Union's growing responsibility for 'the safety of the people', seen by Thomas Hobbes as the 'supreme law' for sovereigns and nation-states to uphold.[10]

Practice

EU member states and institutions are increasingly carrying out broad security and crisis management activities together, at home as well as internationally. To mention a few examples: the EU responded promptly after the Haiti disaster by sending civil protection experts and money for immediate needs and reconstruction. It has provided assistance to those affected by the floods in Central Europe, supported American federal authorities during the Katrina disaster, coordinated aid packages and consular support to those affected by the Asian tsunami, water-carrying aircraft to fight forest fires in Southern Europe, rescue teams in Turkey and Morocco after earthquakes and the cleaning-up of oil-spill in the north Atlantic. The Union has taken measures to prevent the further spread of avian and swine influenza and coordinated EU member states efforts in patrolling Union

---

9   Including regulations, directives, decisions, 'other acts', commission proposals and communications. Divided in the following way: civil protection (1857), health security (1566), and anti-terrorism (703).

10   Hobbes, T., *On the Citizens*.

borders and in bringing home thousands of refugees after the war in Lebanon in the summer 2006. More than twenty military and civilian missions within the Common Security and Defence Policy (CSDP) have been or are being carried out around the globe, ranging from border control in Gaza to peace keeping missions in the Democratic Republic of Congo (DRC) and police training programmes in Kosovo and Afghanistan.[11] '9/11' intensified EU internal anti-terrorist efforts. The bomb attacks in London in July 2005 led to closer EU cooperation on intelligence to give practical implementation to the programme for the protection of critical infrastructure in Europe.[12] There are growing demands from the European public, as codified in the Lisbon Treaty,[13] that 'Europe should do more' in the area.[14] All of these actions are important evidence of the broad security experiences that now will affect Union support to the building of military, police, civil protection, border and crisis management capacity in the other parts of the world.

Implications for EU SSR

Implications of CSDP

The first SSR missions within CSDP – in Congo 2005-10[15] and Guinea-Bissau 2008 (Chapter 14 by Bahnson in this book) – have given rise to fundamental discussions about how to develop the EU SSR concept. In general, the CSDP missions have started a process which has led the EU to rethink its previous demarcation lines between trade, aid, diplomacy and the civilian and military crisis management capacities. Discussions on whether or not to include the capacities of the EU's cooperation in Justice and Home Affairs – for example, in the areas of personnel and threat identification – early signalled a development towards a broad security approach to the CSDP. Many observers have argued that there is an urgent need for better coordination between non-military CSDP activities, work within the Justice and Home Affairs area and the European Commission. It has often been suggested that security thinking should be 'mainstreamed' into other areas of EU cooperation as well (Dwan 2003). However, many of the issues still remain to be solved as of writing (2010).

It is widely acknowledged that the Union's strength as an international SSR actor lies, above all, in the possibility of gathering together the full range of instruments that it has acquired over the years. However, there are also many implications of a more integrated approach. Just as it will be difficult to separate internal security policy aspects from the external ones, it will probably be difficult to separate

---

11   http://www.consilium.europa.eu/showPage.aspx?id=268&lang=en.
12   European Commission (2005).
13   The Treaty includes several new articles in the field.
14   European Commission (2009).
15   EUSEC RD Congo.

non-political aid instruments – humanitarian and development assistance – from activities with a security-political dimension. Therefore, to be really successful, the EU SSR must find ways to bridge the divides between these policies, which currently militates against effective coordination of the various resources that the Union has at its disposal. The question is to what extent the EU's new External Action Service will manage to do so.

The challenge of different principles for decision-making in each area of the external role – EU organs are more independent in humanitarian aid action than CSDP military mission – will, however, remain. Some analysts predict CSDP in the long run will remain intergovernmental due to weak incentives for member states to delegate to supranational institutions (Wagner 2003). Other, in contrast, show how the institutionalization of EU security policies over time is leading to more supranational solutions (Boin, Ekengren, Rhinard 2007).

Generally, the CSDP is to a large extent dependent on the capacities and will of the EU member states. Thus to a greater degree than EU level coordination, effective SSR within CSDP depends on EU member states being prepared to break up or redefine corresponding barriers on the home front: barriers between internal vulnerability and external defence, between defence and police forces, military and civilian intelligence agencies, between defence, justice and foreign ministries, and between defence policy, emergency planning and rescue agencies (Sundelius 2005). National ability is not just about having material resources to hand; it is also – as in the 1950s when the European Community was created – about being ready to think in new ways and with new priorities. Current SSR capability will most likely not be greater than the contributions by member states. For example, to what extent EU SSR policy is intertwined with national security is largely a national question. One reason that the EU Police Mission (EUPM) for reform in Bosnia (starting 2003) initially did not receive a strong response to its request for national experts in organized crime was a reluctance amongst justice ministries and police forces in member states to send away expertise that was considered to be needed at home. Not until after a couple of months they understood that drug smuggling and crime syndicates, which threaten the EU's major cities, are best countered by being on the spot in the Balkans (Dwan 2003). These experiences led the Union to strengthen its capacity through the creation of deployable European expert teams including national officials familiar with SSR problems (Council of the European Union 2008). The political question is how much security the member states achieve at home for money invested in reforms abroad through the EU, and how well national policy-makers manage to explain this link to domestic public opinions.

Member states have differing views about certain issues in joint operations, which are of central importance to the breaking up of divisions between policy areas and competences and thus for the provision of SSR resources to CSDP. For example, there are ongoing discussions about to what extent there should be strict demarcation between military and police tasks in CSDP operations. As many chapters in this book have made clear the EU will be seen as an actor only with a well-coordinated contribution.

Certain countries have made moves seeking to place the EU Commission under the authority of CSDP. Others have maintained that the objective of the Union has always been to turn European security policy into a matter of EU domestic policy; therefore, they have resisted any attempts to subordinate what they see as the engine for the whole process – the EU Commission – under the infrastructure for Union foreign policy. One of the key tasks for the EU's High Representative – which now presides over both CSDP and Commission structures – is to lead this discussion. The outcome will be of central importance for the generation of resources for EU SSR (cf. chapters by Britz (5) and Spence (6) in this book).

Implications of the Solidarity Clause

The Solidarity Clause of the Lisbon Treaty (article 222) states that 'The Union shall mobilizes all the instruments at its disposal, including the military resources made available by the Member States, to:

- prevent the terrorist threat in the territory of the Member States;
- protect democratic institutions and the civilian population from any terrorist attack;
- assist a Member State in its territory, at the request of its political authorities, in the event of a terrorist attack;
- assist a Member State in its territory, at the request of its political authorities, in the event of a natural or man-made disaster.'

The Clause will have important practical SSR implications. It emphasizes the need for capabilities embracing all sectors. The thinking is that, in the long term, member states should move in the same direction in their security and defence policy. The assumption is that, today, member states are converging in terms of values and have reached a sufficient degree of integration in terms of cooperative networks. Another condition for the Clause to be successful is that preventive measures and national infrastructures are coordinated to the point that member states can act jointly at times of crisis. This readiness to act can most probably not be legislated for through the EU, but must be based on a long-term common viewpoint and, perhaps, on the development of new forms of cooperation within the EU.

Earlier studies show how the handling of the broader security agenda of the Clause is built on lower-level units of national government such as rescue and emergency management services. Specialized domestic officials and agencies operate in a highly informal and decentralized fashion that draws on earlier contact and experiences of working together, not only in the EU but with NATO, UN, OSCE, Council of Europe (Ekengren, Matzén and Svantesson 2006). Indeed, many facts indicate that crucial dynamics of internal security cooperation take place within European *transgovernmental* networks. EU SSR will increasingly have to include support for the fostering of security, defence and emergency management structures in receiving states that are able to work within these evolving global networks (Slaughter 2004 and 2009; Sabel and Zeitlin 2008).

But earlier research has also discovered clear indications of a weak national implementation of EU rules and agreements and voluntary – ad hoc styled – participation in Union networks and that the power to decide when and how EU capacities should be used very much remains in national government. In the 'terrorism' sector many EU directives and guidelines are still not transformed into national rule (Rhinard 2008; cf. Bossong 2008), in the health sector institutional change for truly joint management of major diseases seems very distant (Matzén 2008), and in civil protection there is strong resistance from many member states to further institutionalization in the form of EU capacities and funding (Ekengren 2008).

Moreover, the comparisons of national systems have given evidence of great variety between the EU member states with regard to overall structures and practices. There is little convergence with regard to how responsibilities are divided within government (between elected politicians and officials) or between levels of administration. Terrorism and disaster response is primarily decentralized in the member states. The management structure for epidemics is highly centralized. Belgium, Bulgaria, Czech Republic, Estonia, Germany and Sweden have established general EU 'contact points' for disaster management in their national structures (Kuipers and Matzén 2008).

The challenge for EU SSR is to include these experiences and new demands on national administration in the international support of security and defence structure reform. This will be key not least in neighbouring areas, because the requirements of making the Clause work in practice reach beyond borders. The Clause points in the direction of an EU SRR increasingly focused on immigration and border issues, counter-terrorism capacity, cross-border crime and the protection of critical infrastructure. Most probably the EU will together with NATO be one of the most important actors in this support.

An EU SSR based on the principles of the Clause is more easily reconciled with European integration's traditional role of creating a long-term zone of peace and security community, in contrast to the defence of territory for its own sake. The latter is more closely associated with traditional military instruments of power, which could be detrimental to relations with certain third countries and to the image of the EU as a security model. Through the Solidarity Clause the EU could thus strengthen its own security and develop its SSR while simultaneously avoiding a new and potentially destabilizing clash of strategic interests and balance-of-power relationship with neighbouring regions. EU SSR should help the EU candidate states to be involved in the 'solidarity' structures at an early stage of the accession process, and neighbouring and other states would be allowed to participate as far as possible. The Clause could be a step that, with time, might be a model also for other parts of the world. Perhaps Europe could be linked together with similar regional systems into a global security network for the combating of today's network-based global terrorism. Practical requirements for the new agenda include new transnational, cross-sector infrastructures of 'working networks' between countries around the globe. This will have to include national public administrations as well as the civilian community, private business and voluntary organizations, the military, police forces, the judiciary and intelligence agencies.

Implications of Battle Groups and Counter Terrorism

As mentioned, the ability of the EU member states to provide for capacities adapted to the needs of the CSDP and the Solidarity Clause will be crucial also for the EU's possibilities to achieve its SSR aims.

A central component of the CSDP is the EU battle group concept that was decided by the European Council in 2004, as part of the Headline Goal 2010. The background was the early CSDP missions such as the one in the Democratic Republic of Congo in 2003 where EU member states experienced the need for quicker availability of forces and transport facilities ('deployability'). The goal was to create multinational standby forces for EU missions ready for use from 2007 onwards.[16] The generation of national force contributions to these forces was guided by three framework objectives; 'interoperability', 'deployability' and 'sustainability'. Criteria were also set for 'evaluation and certification'. The 'Interoperability' section prescribed the standards that have to be met by member states in order to make their forces able to communicate and operate with each other in joint air, sea and maritime operations. Standards ranges from weapon and communication techniques over headquarter procedures to training. The 'Deployability' part sets quantitative benchmarks and criteria for strategic airlift and other 'enablers' in order to meet the goal of battle groups to be in the hot spots within 10 days. 'Sustainability' referred to the member states' capacity to stay on the ground for up to 120 days. Those member states that are not able to contribute to a battle group are given the possibility to provide 'niche capabilities' to battle groups, such as medical teams. As a way to facilitate interoperability and joint pre-deployment training it was early decided that battle groups should be based on smaller homogeneous groups of member states.[17]

---

16   The battle groups are based on agreements and close contacts between the Armed Forces of the countries taking part. In practice two to four member states stand by in joint battle groups for six months on a rotating scheme. The group exercises and prepares together and is ready for deployment as soon as the EU so decides. Possible tasks are predicted to be separation of parties by force, conflict prevention, evacuation operations, assistance to humanitarian operations.

17   Council of the European Union: *Declaration on European Military Capabilities* (2004).

In 2008, Ukraine declared that it wants to join the EU military battle groups within the CSDP.[18] The country has consulted Poland, Hungary, Czech Republic and Slovakia on the possible inclusion in a battle group planned to be formed by these EU countries. Ukraine's cooperation with EU member states will be intense and involve close cooperation for reforms that will facilitate the on-going work of increasing the flexibility and usability of the battle groups.[19]

In the EU Strategy for Africa (2007) one of the key policies is to provide Union support to the AU's building of capacity for conflict prevention, management and resolution. The objective is 'An African Peace and Security Architecture' (APSA), including the development of an African Standby Force (ASF) towards 2010, a Continental Early Warning System and Security Sector Reform.[20] The support builds on the CSDP 'Action Plan for Africa' and includes military and civilian elements. The goal is to make the AU able to plan and conduct peace support operations autonomously. A 'Common African Defence and Security Policy' (CADSP) was adopted in 2004, only four years after the establishment of the CSDP.

The framework objectives for the ASF commitments by 2010 are in practice set jointly by the AU and the EU and are very similar to the Union's Headline Goals. At the AU (Commission) level the goal is one continental planning element and one continental military logistic depot. The Situation Centre (intelligence function) in the CSDP has participated in the implementation of the 'road maps' for strengthening the AU Situation room and Joint Operations Centres. For each of the selected five African sub-regional organizations (the sub-regional organizations are a key component of APSA) the objective is one permanent brigade headquarters and one standby brigade (3,000). The objectives corresponds closely to the 13 EU battle groups with the important difference that these are aimed for operations outside Europe while ASF is for use on the African continent. The goal for civilian capabilities of the ASF are set to be 'at least 240 police officers' for each region to be deployed on a 14-day notice, two stand-by police units at company level deployable in 90 days, and rosters of mission administration and civilian experts (human rights and humanitarian law, governance, DDR, reconstruction) (cf. the EU civilian Headline Goals). Also the scenarios laying the ground for these framework objectives are very similar to the ones of EU Headline Goals. Ministerial troika and senior officials meeting monitor the process.[21]

The EU offers support in the field of training, technical assistance, and funding of African personnel. It also supports the AU in specific operations such as AMIS in Darfur (since 2004). The EU is contributing with doctrine and standing operating procedures to the ASF. This includes participation of military and civilian expertise from the General Secretariat of the Council. The EU

---

18 *European Voice* (2008).
19 Council of the European Union (2009).
20 Council of the European Union (2007).
21 Lindstrom (2007: 23).

Military Staff is closely involved in the joint workshops and the Secretariat has contributed to the development of concepts for police, rule of law and civilian administration. The EU is funding many of these workshops and has a military liaison officer and police representative at the Commission delegation in the AU 'capital' Addis Ababa. The AU and its predecessor OAU has been involved in the following peace support operations: Rwanda (2003), Burundi (1993), DRC (1999), Ethiopia-Eritrea (2000), Burundi (2003), Sudan (AMIS 2004-), Central African Republic (FOMUC), Comors (AMISEC). Through the so called Peace Facility (established 2004, in total EUR 250 million), the EU has helped to fund many of these operations (except weapons and ammunitions) in addition to the continuous support of the capacity building of the AU.[22] EUR 92 million has been used to the support of AMIS. One of the key goals of the EU's support of reform in Africa is to make the AU to adhere to international security standards in the field of counter-terrorism, proliferation of WMD, the fight against mercenary activities, and submission of the parties to the Statute of the International Criminal Court (Kingah 2006).

With regard to the resources requested for the EU's counter-terrorism policies, governments have started to fundamentally rethink traditional division of roles such as the one between the *police* and the *military*. The emerging new domestic role of the armed forces and the converging roles of the police and the military in international missions is a significant example of the national reforms that increasingly will affect the EU's SSR focus.

The EU member states have adopted many different solutions for providing and regulating these functions. For instance, the French Gendarmerie Nationale is made up of paramilitary forces and is organized under the Ministry of the Interior. Austria, Belgium, Greece (to a certain extent), Italy and Luxembourg have similar forces. All these forces are specialized in terms of training, equipment (often comprising heavy weaponry, armed vehicles, etc.) and lines of command for tasks that straddle the border between internal order and external security. The Italian Arma dei Carabinieri is responsible for certain military operations as well as for 'internal' civilian tasks, such as maintaining order. In some countries the forces are under the control of the defence ministry, in others, of the interior ministry. In some states (e.g., Italy) the authority, chain of command and rules of engagement change depending on the particular task (Benyon 1994; Stålvant 2004).

In all of the Nordic countries there has historically been a strict division between the military's defence of the state border and national security and the maintenance of order by the police. In the aftermath of September 2001, however, the Nordic governments have begun to re-examine their legal frameworks with regard to the use of military assistance to combat terrorist attacks on their territory.

The Finnish police can now ask the Ministry of the Interior to request assistance from the Ministry of Defence. The two ministers together decide whether this type

---

22   Council of the European Union (2006a), Council of the European Union (2006b), European Commission (2007).

of assistance ought to be provided. The naval and air force units of the defence forces can be put at the disposal of the police if the nature of the terrorist threat calls for these resources (Finnish Prime Minister's Office 2004: 127-128). In emergency situations when there is a 'serious' and 'direct' threat to 'particularly important' functions of society, the police force's request for assistance can be made directly to the top military command (Republic of Finland, Government proposition 2004). In the Finnish Government's strategy for national preparedness, the basic functions of society are defined as 'state leadership, external capacity to act, the nation's military defence, internal security, functioning of the economy and society, securing the livelihood of the population and its capacity to act, and their ability to tolerate a crisis' (Finnish Ministry of Defence 2003: 5).

The Swedish Ministry of Justice has proposed that, on the request of the police or coastguard, the armed forces could intervene against non-state actors with the degree of force necessary to avert immediate danger to the safety of the state or to human life or to prevent extensive destruction of property. It is suggested that this condition should also apply in the event of large-scale terrorist attacks (Swedish 11 September Commission 2003: 24-25). In the framework of the EU Solidarity Clause on terrorism, the Swedish Government predicts that military support for civilian crisis management, including the police, will most likely concern the provision of nuclear, biological and chemical expertise, logistics and command resources (Bjurner 2004: 10).

Conclusion: Broadened SSR for Deepened Security Community

What is EU SSR?

By analysing the CSDP, the Solidarity Clause, battle groups and counter terrorism, this chapter has put emphasis on the broad spectrum of security sector reforms that could be expected from the EU side in the years ahead. In this way it has shown the on-going shift towards transboundary rather than inter-state threats as a basis for Union SSR in the world. It has also pointed out the very demanding implications of EU SSR defined as 'a holistic, multi-sector, and long term process encompassing the overall functioning of the security system as part of governance reforms' (Council of the European Union 2006b).

The increasingly important role of SSR in CSDP is naturally resulting from the Union's overall aim and strength in providing long term support for stability and development. Military and civilian crisis management missions should be transformed into longer term SSR engagements whenever possible. One of the EU's overall aim in supporting SSR is to enhance receiving countries' capabilities to handle threats to the external *as well as* internal security in a way that is consistent with democratic norms and good governance.

At the same time, as Alyson Bailes emphasizes in Chapter 4, the EU can probably not simply externalize its broadened agenda to the rest of the world.

Many countries are faced with traditional, territorial military threats where defence reform for post-national relations and international humanitarian missions will not be the most needed for the time being. On the other hand, the EU *does* need to preserve the image stemming from its internal life of being strict on good governance and democracy as a prerequisite for support of SSR in any country or region of the world.

What will be very crucial is to keep the discussion alive on what the EU is supposed to help to safeguard by its SSR support and what should be the deciding factor in mobilizing this assistance. In the light of the results of this chapter the longer term aim of EU SSR would be to help states integrate regionally towards a point where they trust that disputes are settled peacefully (security community) and would act jointly against enemies attacking their territorial borders and in cases of large scale disasters (mutual defence and assistance in the spirit of art 42 and 222 of the Lisbon treaty) and would be in agreement on a common strategic culture backed up with capacities for the protection human security around the globe (CSDP type missions). The goal would be that receiving states and regions should move in similar direction in the streamlining of security thinking into broad sectors of public administration, civil society and business in order to meet threats such as cross-border crime, terrorism, failing states and natural disasters.

Who Does EU SSR?

Who are we talking about when referring to the 'actors' who are supposed to provide resources for and carry out EU SSR? The EU's 'export' of the classical security community is focused on members of a potentially emerging security community in other parts of the world, thought of as high-level policy-makers at ministries of defence and foreign affairs. The aim is to support a reform process of integrating these people regionally to a point where they are convinced that neighbouring countries would settle disputes by non-violent means.

For decades this support to other regions has been led by the EU-Commission whose aim is to help to foster economic development and integration and build common institutions. Today security support is also carried out by the CSDP where the EU has chosen to pool military and civilian means with the help of mainly intergovernmental, diplomatic coordination of member state resources and personnel.

This chapter has shown that the broadening of the security agenda puts emphasis on the need for reforms embracing nearly all sectors of society. This will widen the circles of helping EU experts as well as partners at the receiving end. These groups will include not only central government officials of traditional military and civilian defence sectors but transgovernmental (lower units of government) and transnational actors (business, civil society, NGOs) in sectors ranging from the police to epidemiological monitoring. New concepts such as security governance is already recognizing the multitude of actors, rules and layers (Kirchner and Sperling 2008).

EU SSR: How and Where?

The EU is aware of the fact that the readiness to act and provide resources and personnel, to a limited extent, can be legislated for through the EU, but must be based on a long-term common viewpoint and, perhaps, on the development of new forms of cooperation within the EU. Current national strategies and voluntary pooling of personnel for the European expert teams (Council of the European Union 2008) is a first step towards a more capable and prepared EU. The next step could be the establishment of 'EU SSR Guidelines' that member states should have to fulfil through 'National Action Plans' and that would be evaluated on a yearly basis jointly by the Council and the EU-Commission (Ekengren 2006). Other far-reaching questions are how EU candidate countries and neighbouring countries can best be involved in this process, and what links there should be between the EU and the NATO, the UN, USA and Russia in these matters.

In view of the earlier EU reform aid and the Baltic experience described by Stålvant (Chapter 2) – it is essential that EU SSR is carried out in close dialogue with the partners and through networks at all levels, engaging civil society and private actors. There is an urgent need to find forms for truly joint projects on the basis of EU normative and institutional foundations. The programming dialogue must probably at a very early stage involve partner countries in need. Their participation should also be ensured at some point in the EU Country and Regional Strategy papers and Actions plans. Also planning should allow for 'associating' receiving states, perhaps in similar forms to today's EU association agreements for neighbouring states. All this in order to avoid that a 'post-modern' organization with a broadened security agenda goes wrong in its aid to pre-modern and modern states and regions. Still, irrespective of the specific demands of reform aid, the EU should in the dialogue always infuse as much as possible of its post-national/ modern philosophy of regional solutions. It is a fact that regional solutions are in demand. The African Union, ASEAN, MERCOSUR and sub-regional fora such as Black Sea Cooperation are watching the Union closely and inter-regional cooperation is rapidly growing not least between the AU and the EU with regard to Sudan and other problem areas. The EU should make the most of this in its export of SSR, which should be shaped by the strategic goal of promoting regional security solutions. But the question remains: Could the Union's efforts to help creating regional security community through economic integration be hampered by the more explicit security objectives of broad SSR (defence reform, counter-terrorism etc.) that by nature is politically more sensitive?

The EU member states and receiving states need to find formulas that all of them can agree upon. But here again, there is a strong need for visionary thinking on which to base long term EU strategies and programmes for SSR. There is probably no other solution for the EU than to build on European lessons. Not in substance but in philosophy and process. In this way the Union can provide a clear added value in SSR.

Without drawing on qualities of its internal dimension of being a security community it can never play the 'normative' role that is perhaps its great assets and source of legitimacy in world affairs. Without a close link between the internal and external life of the Union it is perhaps doubtful whether the Union will be an efficient – or even a requested SSR actor – around the globe. One of these qualities is to build on the Union's tradition of creating regional communities that can surround and bind in the state in need when shaping an EU SSR policy. Indeed, the future implementation of SSR constitutes a crucial test for the Union's ability to retake the initiative internationally when it comes to shaping international security in an innovative and strategic manner.

The fact that EU SSR should be 'holistic, multi-sector, and long term' evokes the question of priority. To a much larger extent than before, the Union might need to point out specific regions where it wants to take a really strong pull in order to get all its instruments to work in parallel for success. In this way the Union will be able to build more clearly on its regional, cross-sectoral experience and at the same time decrease the risk of many but less successful projects due to European SSR 'over-stretch'. We could here for example think of Europe creating 'twin regions' with East Africa and Central Asia. In this perspective, the Union should perhaps sharpen its SSR focus on its neighbourhood, where its internal success most easily can be projected externally and where its comparative advantages best can play out. To a much larger extent than hitherto the EU will have to compensate for the lost leverage of a membership perspective for states that are being pushed to reform. It will have to realize that the conditions for successful SSR in many parts of the world will involve economic carrots and a readiness to engage in the partner country for a longer period of time. To what extent will harder regional priorities be politically possible?

Final Words

Viewed over the last five decades, the projection and extension of EU 'security sector reforms' into increasingly wider geographical areas is nothing new. In the 1950s Western Europe emerged as a security community: defined by Karl Deutsch as a group of people integrated to the point where there is a 'real assurance that the members of that community will not fight each other physically, but will settle their disputes in some other ways' (Deutsch et al. 1957: 6). For the policies promoting the European security community, there was no sharp boundary where the community was supposed to end. Fifty years later the challenge is to try to make the most of European innovative thinking on the broadening security agenda and the reforms needed to meet it, at home as well as abroad. This chapter examines some of the clearest and most visible signs of this development. It also shows that much remain to be done to make this new era of SSR successful.

CSDP, the Solidarity Clause and EU SSR might together with enlargements and neighbourhood policies – provide the EU with an opportunity to take the lead again in innovative solutions for international security. The EU SSR should be used for nation building around the globe – a nation building geared towards regional cooperation and security community. The question raised in this chapter is whether the EU will manage to export also its solutions for the broadening security agenda – a deepened security community. The way the EU shapes its SSR will be crucial for whether the Union will be successful in this task. It is in this perspective the challenges and requirements for EU SSR should be assessed.

References

Benyon, J., *Police Forces in the European Union.* University of Leicester, Leicester, Centre for the Study of Public Order, 1994.

Biscop, S. and Andersson, J.J. (eds) *The EU and the European Security Strategy – Forging a Global Europe.* London: Routledge, 2007.

Bjurner, A., 'The Development of the European Security and Defence Policy', Statement in the Committee on Foreign Affairs, Swedish Parliament, 20 April 2004.

Boin, A., Ekengren, M. and Rhinard, M., 'The Commission and Crisis Management' in Spence (ed.) *The European Commission.* London: John Harper Publishing, 2006a, pp. 481-501.

Boin, A., Ekengren, M. and Rhinard, M. (eds) 'Special Issue: Protecting the Union: The Emergence of a New Policy Space', *Journal of European Integration* 28(5), 2006b, pp. 405-21.

Boin, A., Ekengren, M. and Rhinard, M. (eds) *Protecting the European Union – Policies, Sectors and Institutional Solutions.* Report No. B 38, ACTA-Series, Stockholm: National Defence College, 2007.

Boin, A., Ekengren, M. and Rhinard, M. (eds) *Security in Transition – Towards a New Paradigm for the European Union.* Report No. B 41, Stockholm: National Defence College, 2008.

Boin, A. and Ekengren, M., 'Preparing for the World Risk Society: Towards a New Security Paradigm for the European Union', *Journal of Contingencies and Crisis Management* 17(4), 2009, pp. 285-94.

Bossong, R., 'The Action Plan on Combating Terrorism: A Flawed Instrument of EU Security Governance', *Journal of Common Market Studies* 46(1), 2008, pp. 27-48.

Buzan, B., Wæver, O. and de Wilde, J., *Security: A New Framework for Analysis.* London: Lynne Rienner, 1998.

Cottey, D., *Security in the New Europe.* New York: Palgrave Macmillan, 2007.

Council of the European Union, *A Secure Europe in a Better World: European Security Strategy*, Brussels, 12 December 2003, http://ue.eu.int/cms3_fo/showPage.ASP?id=266.

Council of the European Union, 'Declaration on European Military Capabilities', November 2004, www.consilium.europa.eu/./MILITARY%20CAPABILITY %20COMMITMENT%20CONFER.

Council of the European Union, 'European Union concept for Strengthening African Capabilities for the Prevention, Management and Resolution of Conflicts', Brussels, 11316/06, 7 July 2006a.

Council of the European Union, 'Council Conclusions on a Policy Framework for Security Sector Reform', 2736th General Affairs Council Meeting – Luxembourg, 12 June 2006b.

Council of the European Union, 'The Africa-EU Strategic Partnership – A Joint Africa-EU Strategy', 16344/07 (Presse 291), www.consilium.europa.eu/ Newsroom, Lisbon, 9 December 2007.

Council of the European Union, 'Security Sector Reform – Draft Document on Deployable European Expert Teams', doc 14576/1/08 REV1, Brussels, 21 October 2008.

Council of the European Union, 'Increasing the Flexibility and Usability of the EU Battlegroups', ESDP/PESD Secretariat, 14036/1/09, Brussels, 29 October 2009.

de Wijk, R., 'Civil Defence and Solidarity Clause: EU Homeland Defence', Paper prepared for the Directorate-General for Research of the European Parliament, Brussels, 5 January 2004.

Deutsch, K.W. et al., *Political Community and the North Atlantic Area: International Organization in the Light of Historical Experience.* Princeton, NJ: Princeton University Press, 1957.

Duke, S. and Ojanen, H., 'Bridging Internal and External Security: Lessons from the European Security and Defence Policy', *Journal of European Integration* 28(5), 2006, pp. 477-94.

Dwan, R., 'Capabilities in the Civilian Field', Speech at the Conference on the European Union Security Strategy: Coherence and Capabilities, Working Group 2, Capabilities, Swedish Institute of International Affairs, Stockholm, 20 October 2003, http://www.sipri.org/contents/conflict/nonmilitary.htm.

Eilstrup-Sangiovanni, M., 'Transnational Networks and New Security Threats', *Cambridge Review of International Affairs* 18(1), 2005, pp. 7-13.

Ekengren, M., 'New Security Challenges and the Need for New Forms of EU Co-operation – the Solidarity Clause and the Open Method of Coordination', *European Security* 15(1), 2006, pp. 89-111.

Ekengren, M., 'The Internal-External Security Challenge for the EU', *Studia Diplomatica* LX(1), 2007, pp. 81-106.

Ekengren, M., 'EU Civil Protection – an Ascending Sector' in Boin, Ekengren, Rhinard (eds) *Security in Transition – Towards a New Paradigm for the European Union.* Report No. B 41, Stockholm: National Defence College, 2008, pp. 47-61.

Ekengren, M., and Ramberg, B., 'EU Practices and European Structure of Crisis Management: A Bourdieuian Perspective on EU Foreign Policy – the Cases of

Earthquakes in Turkey and Reconstruction of Kosovo, 1999', Paper presented at ECPR Conference, Canterbury, UK, September 2003.

Ekengren, M., Matzén, N. and Svantesson, M., 'The New Security Role of the European Union – Transnational Crisis Management and the Protection of Union Citizens'. Report No. B 35, ACTA-Series, Stockholm: National Defence College, 2006.

Ekengren, M., Matzén, N., Rhinard, M. and Svantesson, M., 'Solidarity or Sovereignty? EU Cooperation in Civil Protection', *Journal of European Integration* 28(5), 2006, pp. 457-76.

European Commission, 'Green Paper on a European Programme for Critical Infrastructure Protection', COM(2005) 576 final, Brussels, 17 November 2005.

European Commission, 'A Concept for European Community Support for Security Sector Reform, Brussels', COM(2006) 253 final, 24 May 2006.

European Commission, Commission/Council Secretariat Joint Papers, 'Beyond Lisbon. Making the EU-Africa Strategic Partnership Work', press release, COM(2007) 357 final, Brussels, SEC 856, 27 June 2007.

European Commission, 'Special Eurobarometer 328: Civil Protection', 2009.

European Council, 'Declaration on Combating Terrorism', Brussels, 25 March 2004, http://ue.eu.int/ueDocs/cmsUpload/79635.pdf.

European Voice, 'Ukraine Wants to Join EU Battle Groups', 31 October 2008, www.europeanvoice.com/article/2008/10/ukraine-wants-to-join-eu-battle-group.

Filtenborg, M.S., Gänzle, S. and Johansson, E., 'An Alternative Theoretical Approach to EU Foreign Policy. "Network Governance" and the Case of the Northern Dimension Initiative', *Cooperation and Conflict* 37(4), 2002, pp. 387-407.

Finnish Ministry of Defence, 'Government Resolution on Securing the Functions Vital to Society and Strategy for Securing the Functions Vital to Society', Helsinki, 27 November 2003.

Finnish Prime Minister's Office, 'Finnish Security and Defence Policy 2004'. Government Report No. 6/2004, Prime Minister's Office: Helsinki, 2004, pp. 127-28. http://www.vnk.fi/vn/liston/vnk.lsp?r=88862&k=en.

Friis, L. and Murphy, A., 'The European Union and Central and Eastern Europe: Governance and Boundaries', *Journal of Common Market Studies* 37(2), 1999, pp. 211-32.

Grevi, G., Helly, D. and Keohane, D. (eds) *European Security and Defence Policy: The First 10 Years (1999-2009)*. Paris: Institute for Security Studies, 2009.

Grönvall, J., *Managing Crisis in the European Union: The Commission and 'Mad Cow' Disease*. Stockholm: CRISMART/Swedish National Defence College, 2000.

Hobbes, T. *On the Citizens* (1651), in R. Tuck and M. Silverthorne (eds) *Cambridge Texts in the History of Political Thought*. Cambridge: Cambridge University Press, 1998.

Howorth, J., *Security and Defence Policy in the European Union*. Basingstoke: Palgrave Macmillan, 2007.

Hänggi, H. and Tanner, F., *Promoting Security Sector Governance in the EU's Neighbourhood*. Paris: EU Institute for Security Studies, 2005.

Kaldor, M., 'A Human Security Doctrine for Europe, the Barcelona Report of the Study Group on European Security'. Presented 10 November 2004, led by Professor Mary Kaldor at the request of EU Secretary-General Javier Solana. Available at: http://www.lse.ac.uk/Depts/global/, accessed 6 October 2005.

Kingah, S., 'The European Union's New Africa Strategy: Grounds for Cautious Optimism', *European Foreign Affairs Review* 11, 2006, pp. 527-53.

Kirchner, E., 'The Challenge of European Union Security Governance', *Journal of Common Market Studies* 44(5), 2006, pp. 947-68.

Kirchner, E. and Sperling, J., *EU Security Governance*. Manchester: Manchester University Press, 2008.

Kuipers, S. and Matzén, N., 'Do Birds of a Feather Flock Together? – Variation in Crisis Management Capacity Amongst EU Member States' in Boin, Ekengren, Rhinard (eds) *Security in Transition – Towards a New Paradigm for the European Union*. Report No. B 41. Stockholm: National Defence College, 2008.

Lavenex, S., 'EU External Governance in "Wider Europe"', *Journal of European Public Policy* 11(4), 2004, pp. 680-700.

Lavenex, S. and Wichmann, N., 'The External Governance of EU Internal Security', *European Integration* 31(1), January 2009, pp. 83-102.

Lindstrom, G., 'Enter the EU Battle Groups'. Chaillot Paper No. 97, February 2007.

Manners, I., 'Normative Power Europe: A Contradiction in Terms?', *Journal of Common Market Studies* 40(2), 2002, pp. 235-58.

Matzén, N., 'EU Health Security Sector: An Ascending Sector' in Boin, Ekengren, Rhinard (eds) *Security in Transition – Towards a New Paradigm for the European Union*. Report No. B 41. Stockholm: National Defence College, 2008, pp. 63-77.

Møller, B., 'Global, National, Societal and Human Security, a General Discussion with a Case Study from the Middle East'. Paper presented at the *4th Pan-European Conference*, at the University of Kent at Canterbury, UK, 8-10 September 2001.

Paris, R., 'Human Security: Paradigm Shift or Hot Air?', *International Security* 26(2), 2001, pp. 87-102.

Preston, C., 'Obstacles to EU Enlargement: The Classical Community Method and the Prospects for a Wider Europe', *Journal of Common Market Studies* 33(3), 2008, pp. 451-63.

Republic of Finland, 'Hallituksen esitys Eduskunnalle laiksi puolustusvoimien virka-avusta poliisille annetun' ('Government proposition to parliament concerning amendment of the act on the provision of assistance by the defence forces to the police'), Government Proposition to Parliament No. 187/2004, 8 October 2004, http://www.finlex.fi/linkit/hepdf/20040187/.

Rhinard, M., 'EU Counter Terrorism: An Ascending Sector' in Boin, Ekengren, Rhinard (eds) *Security in Transition – Towards a New Paradigm for the European Union*. Report No. B 41. Stockholm: National Defence College, 2008, pp. 79-87.

Rhinard, M. and Boin, A., 'Relief Effort Reveals Some Uncomfortable Truths', *European Voice*, Brussels, 28 January 2010.

Sabel, C. and Zeitlin, J., 'Learning from Difference: The New Architecture of Experimentalist Governance in the EU', *European Law Journal* 14(3), May 2008, pp. 271-327.

Schimmelfennig, F. and Sedelmeier, U., 'Governance by Conditionality: EU Rule Transfer to the Candidate Countries of Central and Eastern Europe', *Journal of European Public Policy* 11(4), 2004, pp. 661-79.

Schimmelfenning, F. and Wagner, W., 'Preface: External Governance in the European Union', *Journal of European Public Policy* 11(4), 2004, pp. 657-60.

Scott, J.W., 'The EU and "Wider Europe": Toward an Alternative Geopolitics of Regional Cooperation?', *Geopolitics* 10(3), October 2005, pp. 429-54.

Sjursen, H. (ed.) *Civilian or Military Power? – European Foreign Policy in Perspective*. Abingdon: Routledge, 2007.

Slaughter, A.-M., *A New World Order*. Princeton: Princeton University Press, 2004.

Slaughter, A.-M., 'America's Edge: Power in the Networked Century', *Foreign Affairs* 88(1), Jan/Feb 2009, pp. 94-113.

Spence, D. and Fluri, P. (eds) *The European Union and Security Sector Reform*. London: John Harper Publishing, 2008.

Stålvant, C.-E., 'Questioning the Roles of the Military and Police in Coping with Functional Security: Some Assertions about National Variations and their Impacts'. Paper presented at the *Second Pan-European Conference on EU Politics of the ECPR Standing Group on European Union Politics*, Bologna, Italy, 24-26 June 2004.

Sundelius, B., 'Disruptions – Functional Security for the EU' in Elbe, Luterbacher, Missiroli, Sundelius and Zupi (eds) 'Disasters, Diseases, Disruptions: A New D-Drive for the EU'. Chaillot Paper No. 83, September 2005, pp. 59-68.

Swedish 11 September Commission, 'Vår beredskap efter den 11 September' ('Our preparedness after 11 September'), Statens Offentliga Utredningar No. 2003: 32, Stockholm: Swedish Ministry of Justice, 2003, http://www.regeringen.se/sb/d/108/a/424.

The Security & Defence Agenda, 'Protecting Europe – Policies for Enhancing Security in the EU'. International conference organized by The Security & Defence Agenda, 'Session Four: Is Europe Getting the Politics of Security Right?', Brussels, 30 May 2006.

Wagner, W., 'Why the EU's Common Foreign and Security Policy Will Remain Intergovernmental: A Rationalist Institutional Choice Analysis of European

Crisis Management Policy', *Journal of European Public Policy* 10(4), 2003, pp. 576-95.

Webber, M., Crift, S., Howorth, J., Terriff, T. and Krahmann, E., 'The Governance of European Security', *Review of International Studies* 30(1), 2004, pp. 3-26.

Zimmermann, D. and Wenger, A. (eds) *How States Fight Terrorism*. Boulder, CO: Lynne Rienner, 2006.

PART III
Case Studies of
SSR Politics in Practice

Chapter 8

Security Sector Reform in the Western Balkans: The Challenge of Coherence and Effectiveness

Gemma Collantes-Celador and Ana E. Juncos[1]

Introduction

Security Sector Reform (SSR) is an intrinsic part of the international strategy for democratization and long-term development in the Western Balkans.[2] It has entailed a considerable investment of time and resources (human and financial) from a wide range of international organizations and individual governments to change security agencies that, as a result of the communist era and the wars of the 1990s, were fragmented, politicized along ethnic lines, corrupted, underdeveloped and guilty of some of the worst war crimes. It has also been treated as a testing ground for the EU, as part of a learning process that culminated in the two SSR concept documents of 2005 and 2006.

Much has been achieved, but equally much remains to be done. The failure to apprehend Ratko Mladić, the role of organized crime and corruption, the ongoing Kosovo question (despite independence) and the economic precariousness of the region are some of the clearest illustrations of the outstanding issues. This chapter seeks to contribute to a better understanding of the threats and opportunities facing SSR in the Western Balkans by providing an overview of what has been done in the last fifteen years and what remains to be introduced to ensure the good governance of what is a set of *key* actors in the development of stability at the regional level. The argument presented here will illustrate that SSR has not always been treated as a long-term issue, leading to a number of shortcomings in the programmes introduced. These problems – that have come to the fore during the implementation phase – have in many instances been the product of inappropriate coordination arrangements among international actors, and a lack of proper consideration of a

1 We gratefully acknowledge the assistance provided by the editors of this volume when preparing this chapter as well as the help of all those international and local experts in Brussels and the Western Balkans that gave up their time to talk to us about the issues explored here.
2 For a definition see the Council and Commission SSR concepts, mentioned later in the analysis.

number of endogenous and exogenous factors pertinent to any assessment of the effectiveness of these reforms in bringing out change in the right direction.

The chapter will begin by providing a detailed overview of the security, political and economic challenges still facing the Western Balkans. These have an impact that goes beyond the region, as illustrated by their importance in the EU's consideration of its internal security needs. A brief overview of the opportunities offered by EU and NATO membership in the face of these challenges, and the SSR responses formulated by the international community will follow as a prelude to a more detailed analysis of the main shortcomings, in terms of coordination and effectiveness, of the international SSR strategy. This chapter will provide a synopsis of the most important trends, notwithstanding that the situation on the ground in the Western Balkans varies enormously form country to country.[3]

Challenges: The Security, Political and Economic Situation in the Region

Drafted under the responsibility of the former EU High Representative Javier Solana, and approved by the European Council held in Brussels on 12 December 2003, the 'European Security Strategy' provides a comprehensive overview of the contemporary security environment, strategic objectives and policy implications facing the EU. In terms of the security environment, this strategic document identifies five 'key threats':

- Terrorism, with Europe considered not only as a target but also as a base for terrorist actions/groups linked to violent religious extremism;
- Proliferation of weapons of mass destruction, possibly the greatest threat to the Union, particularly if terrorist groups acquire them;
- Regional conflicts, particularly in terms of the opportunities this context of insecurity (that can also result from state failure) offers for the development of the other four threats, and the impact other threats – namely organized crime – can have in the perpetuation of conflicts or weak/failing states;
- State failure; and
- Organized crime, defined to include by and large cross-border trafficking in drugs, women, illegal migrants and weapons, with possible links to terrorism.[4]

Moreover, this strategic document specifies that, due to the interdependence generated by a globalized world, the EU is also vulnerable to the implications

---

3   The 'Western Balkans' includes Albania, Bosnia and Herzegovina (hereinafter Bosnia or BiH), Croatia, Serbia, Kosovo, Montenegro and the former Yugoslav Republic of Macedonia (hereinafter Macedonia).

4   Council of the EU, 'A Secure Europe in a Better World: European Security Strategy', Brussels, 12 December 2003, pp. 3-5.

arising from poverty, disease, competition for scarce resources, global warming and migratory movements. These phenomena are often linked to, or have the potential to lead to, political problems and violent conflict.[5]

Among the strategic objectives listed in the 'European Security Strategy' to deal with the threats facing the EU, one can find the goal of building political, economic, cultural and security partnerships in the neighbourhood:

> Neighbours who are engaged in violent conflict, weak states where organized crime flourishes, dysfunctional societies or exploding population growth on our borders all pose problems for Europe.[6]

Needless to say, one of the most obvious 'neighbours' is the Western Balkans, which even before 2003 was considered crucial to European security: '[t]he outbreak of conflict in the Balkans was a reminder that war [had] not disappeared from our continent'.[7] This region is often portrayed as a clear representation of the 'cycle of conflict, insecurity and poverty' that the 'European Security Strategy' identified as affecting a number of regions and countries around the world. This understanding of security is based on the conviction that security is a precondition for economic and social development.[8]

Three types of challenges are discernable in the Western Balkans: security challenges, political challenges and economic challenges that, within the context of the 'European Security Strategy', have reinforced the priority status of this region in the face of the EU's internal security needs. The rest of this section will treat each of these in more detail.

Security Challenges

The security challenges that have affected the Western Balkans include those arising strictly from the need to complete the post-conflict stabilization of these societies (from ethnic tensions to the presence of non-state armed formations, large amounts of small arms and light weapons, and the war crimes legacy) to other 'larger' phenomena that have emanated from, or been accentuated by, the legacies of the wars of the 1990s: organized crime and the perceived threat of Islamic terrorism.

---

5   A report on the implementation of the 'European Security Strategy', adopted in December 2008, stated that these five threats 'have not gone away' and focused on terrorism, weapons of mass destruction and organized crime. European Council, 'Report on the Implementation of the European Security Strategy – Providing Security in a Changing World', S407/08, Brussels, 11 December 2008, p. 3.

6   Council of the EU, 'European Security Strategy', op. cit. p. 7.

7   Ibid., p. 1.

8   Ibid., p. 2.

Ethnic tensions and violence have continued to prevail in the Western Balkans, albeit to a much lesser extent than during the wars of the 1990s (including the 2001 events in Macedonia) and the immediate post-conflict phase. In Bosnia ethnic-motivated crimes are no longer considered as a pressing issue.[9] However, they are not entirely ruled out, particularly against the context of the political crisis that has gradually developed since 2006. Tim Donais' words remain very pertinent: 'Bosnians of different ethnicities may once again be able to live together, but they have neither forgotten nor forgiven, and the deferred nature of the country's reconciliation process continues to provide traction for nationalist politics and politicians.'[10] Similarly, international observers have recorded incidents of ethnically-motivated violence and harassment in both Croatia (against Croatian Serb returnees) and Serbia (in the Vojvodina against members of minority groups).[11] Finally, the violent clashes that took place in Kosovo in March 2004 provide another example of how important the ethnic factor remains when judging security levels in the Western Balkans. Churches and monasteries have since also been the target of attacks and freedom of movement for minorities continues to be a problem, especially after the declaration of independence.

The Kosovo example is interesting because the causes of the March 2004 clashes are to be found, among other things, in the reluctance of the Kosovo Albanian leadership to cooperate with the International Criminal Tribunal for the former Yugoslavia (ICTY).[12] As judged by events in Serbia, Croatia and Bosnia, the war crimes legacy also has serious political and economic repercussions when their leadership proves unwilling to cooperate in meeting the membership conditionality required by the EU and NATO.

The issue of weapons in the possession of citizens has been an ongoing problem throughout the Western Balkans. As concluded by a study carried in 2004 by *Saferworld*, they are often a contributing factor – and at times the direct cause – in civilian injuries and deaths, sluggish social and economic development, distrustful ethnic and social tensions and the ongoing criminalization of these societies.[13]

---

9   Interviews with EU officials in Sarajevo, 2009.

10   Donais, T., 'A Tale of Two Towns: Human Security and the Limits of Post-War Normalization in Bosnia-Herzegovina', *Journal of Southern Europe and the Balkans* 7(1), April 2005, p. 31.

11   See, for example, Bieber, F. and Wintergahen, J., 'Ethnic Violence in Vojvodina: Glitch or Harbinger of Conflicts to Come?' Working Paper No. 27, European Centre for Minority Issues, Flensburg, April 2006, www.ecmi.de/download/working_paper_27.pdf, accessed 28 April 2010; Ivanisevic, B., 'Croatia: A Decade of Disappointment – Continuing Obstacles to the Reintegration of Serb Returnees'. Report 18(7) (D), Human Rights Watch, London, September 2006, pp. 10-16, http://hrw.org/reports/2006/croatia0906/, accessed 28 April 2010.

12   Gow, J., 'Security in South Eastern Europe: The War Crimes Legacy', *Southeast European and Black Sea Studies* 5(1), January 2005, pp. 9-20.

13   SEESAC, 'A Fragile Peace: Guns and Security in Post-Conflict Macedonia', London, January 2004, p. 1.

But these problems in turn reinforce citizens' hold onto their illegally owned weapons as a means to protect themselves, especially in those contexts where state institutions are considered unreliable (particularly the police and courts) or where the future of the territory is uncertain due to ongoing political tensions. Both Macedonia and Kosovo provide clear illustrations of these patterns.[14]

Interestingly, the 2006 security report by the Bosnian Ministry of Security, that detailed events during 2005, made a direct link between the availability of illegal arms in large quantities, Islamic terrorism and organized crime:

> As participator in operation "Iraq Freedom" BiH becomes potential target of possible terrorist attacks. We should take into account that large quantities of illegal arms and military equipment are still in BiH and illegal trafficking of arms represents serious security problem in the sense of possible arming of potential terrorist groups.[15]

A similar relationship between small arms and organized crime was the subject of a 2007 article in *Jane's Intelligence Review*, where it was argued that Albania had become a centre for the illegal trafficking of weapons both as a source country and a transit country.[16]

In the post-9/11 context the fear of radical Wahhabism taking root and Islamic terrorism using the Western Balkans as a base for its operations in Europe seems to have influenced some perceptions of the region.[17] The West's insistence (mainly US-driven) on de-nationalizing many of those citizens that arrived in Bosnia during the war to fight on the Bosnian Muslim side results from this trend.[18] Serbia's Sandžak region (mainly Muslim-Slav, bordering Montenegro, Kosovo and Bosnia) and Kosovo are similarly under scrutiny. This fear is nevertheless not shared by everyone, at least in the exaggerated form it is often presented, in part because of what is considered as a rather 'relaxed observance' of moderate versions of Islam throughout the region. Keeping this issue in perspective is of utmost importance to ensure stable inter-ethnic relations. Indeed, in 2001 it led to a wave of anti-Muslim opinion and propaganda in Serbia, Macedonia and Bosnian Serb areas. If treated carelessly, this issue can also have a negative impact on the image of the Western Balkan countries abroad at a time when they still need the

---

14   See Hislope, R., 'Crime and Honor in a Weak State: Paramilitary Forces and Violence in Macedonia', *Problems of Post-Communism* 51(3), May-June 2004, pp. 35-44.

15   Bosnian Ministry of Security, 'Information on the Security Situation in Bosnia and Herzegovina in 2005', Sarajevo, April 2006, p. 35.

16   'Small-Arms, Big Problem – Light Weapons Trafficking in Albania', Jane's Intelligence Review, 14 September 2007.

17   Interviews with EU officials in Sarajevo, 2006 and 2009.

18   Anes Alic and Damir Kaletovic have covered this topic in various *ISN Security Watch* articles, http://www.isn.ethz.ch/isn/Current-Affairs/Security-Watch, accessed 28 April 2010.

international community's support to complete their post-conflict stabilization, development and integration into the world community.

Unlike the terrorist threat, there seems to be an overwhelming agreement among both scholars and practitioners over the fact that the post-conflict stabilization of the Western Balkans has turned into an even more difficult problem due to the growing presence of organized crime (cross-border trafficking in drugs, people and weapons; racketeering; tax, custom and privatization fraud; capital flight). The extent of the problem is clearly appreciated in the following passage of the 'European Security Strategy': '90 percent of the heroin in Europe comes from poppies grown in Afghanistan ... Most of it is distributed through Balkan criminal networks which are also responsible for some 200,000 of the 700,000 women victims of the sex trade world wide.'[19]

In fact, the role played by organized crime within the Western Balkans illustrates single-handedly the complexity and interconnectedness of the security challenges in the region. Combined with high corruption levels, it reinforces the fragility of states that are unable to fight it effectively. At the same time, organized crime has thrived in the region because, as many scholars would argue, parts of the Western Balkan states collude with organized crime rings. Macedonia, Kosovo and Montenegro are typical examples, the latter known for the 'cigarette transit business' and money laundering during Milo Đukanović's administration. The links between state authorities and organized crime groups date back to the communist period when leaders in the republics of the former Yugoslavia made use of it to control ideological opponents. This practice was reinforced during the wars of the 1990s, as the example of Arkan's Tigers at the service of Belgrade's ethnic cleansing campaigns in Croatia and Bosnia illustrate.[20] The relations consolidated – or newly created – during the wars explain the close associations existing nowadays in the region between organized crime rings and war criminals.

A similar self-perpetuating relationship can be observed between organized crime and inter-ethnic relations.[21] On the one hand, the persistence of organized crime in the Western Balkans endangers inter-ethnic relations since, as illustrated by the cases of Kosovo and Macedonia, police actions against Albanian criminals have in the past led the latter into instigating inter-ethnic violence as a retaliatory

---

19   Council of the EU, 'European Security Strategy', op. cit., p. 5. For a more detailed description of the situation see European Commission and Council of Europe, 'Update of the 2006 Situation Report on Organised and Economic Crime in South-eastern Europe', No.PC-TC(2007)6, CARPO Regional Project, Strasbourg, June 2007, http://www.coe.int/carpo/, accessed 28 April 2010.

20   For a detailed account of this relationship, including a historical overview, see Andreas, P., 'The Clandestine Political Economy of War and Peace in Bosnia and Herzegovina', *International Studies Quarterly* 48(1), March 2004, pp. 29-51; Kostovicova, D., 'Old and New Insecurity in the Balkans: Lessons from the EU's Involvement in Macedonia' in Glasius and Kaldor (eds) *A Human Security Doctrine for Europe: Project, Principles, Practicalities.* Abingdon: Routledge, 2006, pp. 48-50.

21   Kostovicova, D., 'Old and New Insecurity in the Balkans', op. cit., p. 49.

measure. This is a very powerful tool in the hands of criminals given that, through the manipulation of ethnic relations, not only in Macedonia and Kosovo but also in the rest of the Western Balkans, criminal networks became an important contributing factor throughout the wars. At the same time, organized crime in the Western Balkans has thrived, at least partly, on the basis of inter-ethnic criminal cooperation as amply documented during the war and post-war periods.

Political and Economic Challenges

The security challenges facing the Western Balkans do not only have implications for the EU's internal security needs but, as already alluded to, also feed into (and profit from) the serious political and economic challenges facing the region. At a political level, the greatest danger has come from the unsettled nature of the geographical map. This has led to the ongoing politicization of some borders, as illustrated by the Piran Bay dispute – under international arbitration at the time of writing – which Slovenia used to block Croatia's EU accession process between 2008-2009.[22] In Bosnia, where the identity of the state was the subject of the war, over a decade of international intervention has not led to a solution accepted by the three main ethnic groups, as illustrated by the ongoing constitutional talks, the 'failed' police restructuring process, and repeated calls for a referendum on independence in Republika Srpska. The failure of Kosovo's talks and the unilateral declaration of independence by Kosovo Albanians in February 2008 are additional reminders of fundamental disagreements over borders in the region.

The contentious nature of some borders accentuates the internal political and economic problems faced by the Western Balkan countries in their two-fold transition from war to peace and from communism to liberal democracy. In economic terms these transitions have so far not been easy if judged by the difficulties facing the populations in parts of the region, with persistent high levels of unemployment and poverty,[23] and the ongoing heavy reliance in some countries on external funds for reconstruction, which aggravates what is already a well-developed 'dependency syndrome'. The global financial crisis that began in 2007 has only added to these problems, as judged by the violent clashes in Sarajevo on 21 April 2010 between members of war veterans' organizations and Bosnian police in protest for the Federation government's attempt to cut their welfare benefits as part of the conditionality linked to IMF loans.[24] This example illustrates that economic

---

22 Background information on this border dispute is available at the European Stability Initiative website: http://www.esiweb.org/enlargement/?cat=15#awp::?cat=15, accessed 28 April 2010.

23 See the European Commission Enlargement Strategy and Progress Reports 2009, http://ec.europa.eu/enlargement/press_corner/key-documents/reports_oct_2009_en.htm, accessed 28 April 2010.

24 *Balkan Insight*, 'Bosnian War Veterans in Violent Clashes with Police', Sarajevo, 21 April 2010.

precariousness can have a very significant impact on the trust of the population on their own nascent democratic institutions, something that is not beneficial for the long-term stability of the region.

Opportunities: EU and NATO Membership

Despite the challenges the Western Balkans might face, one cannot forget the opportunities provided by the perspective of membership into the Euro-Atlantic structures. A credible membership perspective appears as one of the strongest incentives for reform in pre-accession countries.[25] Within this context, membership conditionality has become the cornerstone of EU and NATO's policies in the region.

The origins of the EU's engagement in the Western Balkans can be found in the mid-1990s as a response to the conflict in Bosnia. Following the signing of the Dayton Peace Agreement, the EU assumed responsibility for helping post-conflict reconstruction in the region. Through various initiatives (the Royaumont Process, the Stability Pact), the EU introduced for the first time political and economic conditionality. In other words, economic assistance would be provided on condition that the recipients respected, *inter alia*, human rights, democracy, and the rule of law. The instruments used for the promotion of the *acquis communautaire* have been primarily economic in nature (economic, humanitarian and technical assistance), but in the last few years the EU has also deployed several European Security and Defence Policy (ESDP) – now Common Security and Defence Policy (CSDP) – operations, including both police and military operations. Currently, the Stabilisation and Association Process constitutes the main platform for the institutionalization of relations between the EU and the Western Balkans, with membership as the end goal.[26] While Croatia and Macedonia have already been granted candidate status, Albania, Montenegro and Serbia had at the time of writing applied for membership. In its October 2009 Annual Report, the Commission published a study on Kosovo that recommended several initiatives to improve the political and socio-economic situation in the territory, in particular, through visa liberalization and trade agreements, once the requirements were met.[27] In Bosnia, which signed a Stabilisation and Association Agreement in June 2008,

---

25   Schimmelfennig, F. and Sedelmeier, U., 'Governance by Conditionality: EU Rule Transfer to the Candidate Countries of Central and Eastern Europe', *Journal of European Public Policy* 11(4), 2004, pp. 661-79.

26   The Thessaloniki European Council affirmed the perspective of integration and EU membership for the Western Balkan countries. See EU-Western Balkans Summit – Thessaloniki, 21 June 2003 – Declaration, No. 10229/03 (Press 163).

27   European Commission, 'Communication from the Commission to the European Parliament and the Council. Kosovo – Fulfilling its European Perspective', COM(2009) 5343, Brussels, 14 October 2009.

disagreement between the main groups on the organization of the state remains a stumbling block for progress towards EU membership.

EU policies in the region have emphasized the importance of SSR issues; however, there is no section in the *acquis communautaire* that refers to SSR as such. On the contrary, SSR aspects appear scattered in the relevant EU criteria that refer to democracy, rule of law, human rights and respect for and protection of minorities; the so-called Copenhagen criteria. In the Commission's reports, progress on SSR is usually assessed with regards to the implementation of political criteria and European standards in the area of freedom, justice and security. With the development of the EU's SSR concepts, closer attention has been paid to these issues,[28] although no specific criteria has been added to the current conditionality.

NATO has remained committed to the region since its early intervention during the Bosnian war. The first NATO contingent, IFOR, was deployed in Bosnia in December 1995 to implement the Dayton Agreement, and was followed by another Alliance operation, SFOR, that remained in the country until 2004. NATO also led the 1999 bombings in Kosovo and it is still responsible for the peace-keeping mission in that country (KFOR). In Macedonia, NATO's Operation Allied Harmony helped to prevent a resumption of hostilities among parties to the conflict before handing the mission to the EU. NATO's support to the region has not been limited to the provision of troops. It has also provided technical assistance, particularly in the area of defence reform, through the Partnership for Peace Programme (PfP) and the Membership Action Plan (MAP). Moreover, it is committed to integrating the region into the Alliance through membership, which it granted to Croatia and Albania in April 2009 while Montenegro and Bosnia have been invited to join the Membership Action Plan (in December 2009 and April 2010 respectively). At the time of writing, Serbia is still a PfP member and for Macedonia the dispute with Greece over the name of the country continues to jeopardize its chances of membership.

In July 2003, the EU and NATO agreed on a 'concerted approach' for the Western Balkan region. Their common vision included the establishment of 'self-sustaining stability based on democratic and effective government structures and a viable free market economy, leading to further rapprochement towards European and Euro-Atlantic structures'.[29] This approach acknowledges an implicit division of labour between the two organizations when it comes to SSR activities. While the EU concentrates on 'police reform and governance issues', NATO's activities through the Partnership for Peace and Membership Action Plan focus on defence reform. The two organizations also insisted that they would 'continue to work

---

28   Collantes-Celador, G., 'The EU and its Policy Towards Security Sector Reform: a New Example of the "Conceptual-Contextual" Divide?' in Soler and Carbonell (eds) *6th International Seminar on Security and Defence in the Mediterranean*. Barcelona: Edicions Bellaterra, 2008, pp. 153-63.

29   'EU and NATO Concerted Approach for the Western Balkans', No. 11605/03, Brussels, 29 July 2003, p. 1.

together in developing relevant new activities to meet the region's needs'.[30] The 'joint strategic approach' sketched in this document has however been difficult to implement due to strained relations at the political level as a consequence of the Turkish-Cypriot conflict. On the other hand, as illustrated later in the chapter, cooperation on the ground has been smoother.[31]

Main Focus Areas

To date, SSR activities in the Western Balkans have concentrated primarily on three main areas: border management, defence and police reform. The effective control of borders in the region has increasingly turned into a priority for international donors. Emphasis has been placed on promoting comprehensive approaches, inter-agency, regional and international cooperation, and de-militarization. One of the most significant initiatives has been the Ohrid Process (2003-2008) that, under the umbrella of the then Stability Pact, brought together the three main international organizations (OSCE, NATO and EU) and the five countries of the region at the time (Macedonia, Serbia and Montenegro, Bosnia, Croatia, Albania) to search for common solutions. The Ohrid Process achieved progress in the demilitarization of borders and the introduction of national border strategies. However, among its main shortcomings was the prioritization of technical aspects of border management despite the fact that it was initially conceived, at least partly, as a political process to foster regional stability.

The EU has gradually adopted a more prominent role in border issues in the Western Balkans, on the basis of a range of goals brought together under the framework of the Integrated Border Management Strategy. In other words, ensuring the existence of secure and effective borders that contain the security challenges emanating from within the region while, at the same time, enabling its economic, political and social development. However, these two set of goals have at times become incompatible, as illustrated later in the chapter with the example of visa regimes.[32]

In spite the legacies of the war in the region (oversized and ethnic-based armies), defence reform constitutes one of the sectors where most progress has been achieved in the last few years. In this respect, it is worth mentioning NATO's strong engagement, as well as the role played by private companies like the US

---

30   Ibid., p. 3.

31   Interviews with EU officials in Sarajevo and Brussels, 2006-2007.

32   The analysis of border management is based on Collantes-Celador, G. and Juncos, A.E., 'The Reform of Border Management in the Western Balkans: Safeguarding EU External Borders or Preparing for European Integration?' in Ekengren et al. (eds) 'Challenges and Prospects for Nordic-Baltic Security Sector Reform – the Western Balkans, Ukraine, Afghanistan and Sub-Saharan Africa'. Research Report. Stockholm: Swedish National Defence College, 2007, pp. 173-205.

defence contractor MPRI. A significant effort has been made in recent years to downsize, professionalize and restructure armed forces. Yet, modernization has been hampered by limited economic resources. Here the situation has differed between those countries that have had difficulties to increase their small defence budgets, like Albania;[33] and those that have struggled to do the opposite, i.e. to reduce an oversized army and budget without putting at risk the reforms recommended by NATO (such as Bosnia).[34]

Politicization and corruption have affected the armed forces of the region,[35] although international pressure has been successful in bringing about reforms. For instance, the Defence Reform Commission established by the High Representative in Bosnia and assisted by the NATO Headquarters in Sarajevo succeeded in setting up a new State-level Ministry of Defence, surmounting early opposition by Bosnian Serbs. For its part, in Serbia, defence reform suffered from obstruction by military ranks loyal to the Milošević regime and was also slowed down during the State Union period due to political uncertainty. A first stage of reforms was led by the Minister of Defence Boris Tadić in 2003 culminating with the White Paper on Defence in 2005.[36] Nevertheless, judging by the pace of developments not only in Serbia and Bosnia but also in Montenegro and Croatia, international support remains crucial to the sustainability of defence reform in the Western Balkans.

Police reform has understandably become one of the most important intervention areas for the international community in the Western Balkans. The UN police missions in Bosnia (IPTF) and Kosovo (UNMIK-Police), as well as the EU operations in Bosnia (EUPM), Macedonia (Proxima, EUPAT) and Kosovo (EULEX) best exemplify this trend. Although initially with more interventionist roles, international police missions have gradually limited their functions to monitoring, mentoring and providing expertise to the local police forces. Together with short term interventions, there have also been long-term programmes that have offered technical assistance, training and new infrastructure with funding

---

33   Dowling, A. 'EU Conditionality and Security Sector Reform in the Western Balkans' in Fluri and Spence (eds) *The European Union and Security Sector Reform*. London: John Harper Publishing, 2008, p. 178.

34   In Bosnia, the defence budget reached at one point 5 percent of GDP. Caparini, M., 'Security Sector Reform and Post-Conflict Stabilization: The Case of the Western Balkans' in Bryden and Hänggi (eds) *Reform and Reconstruction of the Security Sector*. Geneva: DCAF, 2004, p. 10.

35   For instance, in Bosnia the so-called ORAO affair, involving illegal arms transfers to Iraq, evidenced the weaknesses of the Republika Srpska Army. Vetschera, H. and Damian, M., 'Security Sector Reform in Bosnia and Herzegovina: The Role of the International Community', *International Peacekeeping* 13(1), 2006, pp. 32-33.

36   Dowling, A. 'EU Conditionality and Security Sector Reform in the Western Balkans', op. cit., pp. 183-86.

from, among others, the European Commission, OSCE, ICITAP,[37] the Council of Europe and bilateral donors. In this regard, it is worth mentioning the EU's Police Assistance Mission (PAMECA) to Albania, under the Commission's responsibility, and the OSCE assistance to police reform in Serbia and Montenegro. However, police forces still suffer – to varying degrees – from operational problems due to corruption (often linked to low salaries), inadequate training, poor infrastructure and lack of inter-agency cooperation.[38]

Reform in the judicial, penitentiary and intelligence sectors, although as important as the aforementioned areas, has tended to be relegated in the agendas of external donors. Some funding has nevertheless been directed to these sectors. In the area of prison reform examples include projects by the Swedish International Development Agency (SIDA) and the European Commission/Council of Europe Joint Programme. The goal of the latter, supported with CARDS funding,[39] was to enhance the legal systems and penitentiary practices of the countries of the region according to European standards, as well as fostering regional cooperation.[40] Moreover, a recent trend in CSDP/ESDP operations has been to link police reform to reform in other rule of law sectors (prisons, prosecution, and judiciary).

Even when reforms in these sectors have taken place, the results have not always been optimal. In Serbia for instance, the Law on Security Services adopted in 2002 only brought minimal changes and as late as 2006, the European Commission highlighted as problematic the enduring links between security services and war criminals, especially in the Army ranks.[41] The same can be noted in the case of Croatia,[42] even if the 2006 Law on Intelligence and Security Services was intended to improve the performance and civilian oversight of Croatian intelligence services. Progress in intelligence reform in Bosnia might be an exception here because of

---

37   ICITAP (or International Criminal Investigative Training Assistance Program) is a US Department of Justice agency responsible for the provision of advice and technical support to law enforcement agencies worldwide.

38   Caparini, M., 'Security Sector Reform and Post-Conflict Stabilization: The Case of the Western Balkans', op. cit., p. 15; Dowling, A., 'EU Conditionality and Security Sector Reform in the Western Balkans', op. cit.

39   Since 1 January 2007 CARDS has been replaced by the new Instrument for Pre-Accession (IPA). Information on financial assistance to the Western Balkans can be found at the European Commission's website: http://ec.europa.eu/enlargement/how-does-it-work/financial-assistance/index_en.htm, accessed 28 April 2010.

40   CARDS Regional Prison Project (Council of Europe/European Commission Joint Programme), http://www.coe.int/t/e/legal_affairs/legal_co-operation/prisons_and_alternatives/technical_co-operation/cards_regional_prison_project/Western%20Balkans%20summary.asp, accessed 28 April 2010; SIDA, 'Guidelines for Swedish Bilateral Support within the Sector of Justice and Home Affairs for the Western Balkans', Stockholm, July 2003, p. 17.

41   See European Commission, 'Serbia 2006 Progress Report', No. COM(2006) 649 final, Brussels, 8 November 2006, p. 9.

42   Caparini, M., 'Security Sector Reform and Post-Conflict Stabilisation: The Case of the Western Balkans', op. cit., p. 14.

the role played by the High Representative who established an Intelligence Reform Commission in 2003. The outcome was the creation of a state-level Intelligence and Security Agency (OSA), although the ownership of the process was compromised by the strong interventionism of the High Representative.[43]

Judicial systems in the region continue to suffer from politicization, inadequate legislation, lack of appropriate training and resources. This is particularly the case in Albania, but also Serbia, Bosnia, Kosovo and Montenegro suffer from serious problems that affect their capacity to fight organized crime, among other things.[44] As a result of the problems faced with the last enlargement to Romania and Bulgaria, conditionality in this area has become stricter and the European Commission is carefully monitoring progress on issues related to the rule of law, including the presence of an independent and functioning judicial system and the fight against corruption and organized crime.[45]

Much more disappointing is the progress regarding the democratic dimension of SSR: democratic oversight by national parliaments, an active participation by civil society and local media. This aspect has not featured among the top priorities in the projects of international organizations dealing with SSR in the Western Balkans. This is surprising given that, at least in paper, everyone seems to acknowledge the importance of this dimension in ensuring sustainability of the reforms.[46] Having said that, certainly the Commission reports, by outlining these problems, have put pressure on the governments of the region to empower civil society and to guarantee media freedom.[47] Oversight by national parliaments has been ensured by the establishment of appropriate legislation and the creation of specialist parliamentarian committees. Nevertheless, it is often hampered by the lack of expertise, the links between the executive and the legislative branches and the absence of independent external supervisory bodies. In many cases, the media remains politicized and/or ethnically divided, necessitating further reform. In Bosnia one of the EU conditions to sign an SAA was the adoption of new broadcasting legislation. In other cases, there has been some progress in the adoption of the necessary legal provisions. However, it remains to be seen how that legislation is then translated into day-to-day practices.

---

43   Ibid., p. 11.

44   See the European Commission Enlargement Strategy and Progress Reports 2009 (for both candidate countries and potential candidates), http://ec.europa.eu/enlargement/press_corner/key-documents/reports_oct_2009_en.htm, accessed 28 April 2010.

45   See, for instance, 'Seminar on Lessons Learned of the Fifth Enlargement in the Field of Justice and Home Affairs', http://ec.europa.eu/enlargement/5th_enlargement/key_recommendations_en.htm, accessed 28 April 2010.

46   See European Commission, 'A Concept for European Community Support for Security Sector Reform', No. COM(2006) 253 final, Brussels, 24 May 2006, p. 5.

47   In the case of Albania, see European Commission, 'Albania 2006 Progress Report', COM(2006) 649 final, Brussels, 8 November 2006.

The Challenge of Coherence

The broad range of activities under the umbrella of the SSR label means that coordination between different instruments and actors constitutes a key issue in any given intervention. Typically in post-conflict situations one can witness a multiplication of the actors present on the ground. Military organizations might be involved in tasks of defence reform and ordnance control, while civilian actors often concentrate on monitoring activities, police reform, institution-building or support to civil society. In this context, the activities of the different organizations involved in SSR may affect each other at the strategic, operational and tactical level, and even, in some instances, have a negative impact. Hence the importance of establishing appropriate coordinating arrangements.

If complexity is characteristic of international SSR assistance, the Western Balkans is paramount to the density of the network of actors involved in this field. Only as an example, one can mention the following international organizations that have undertaken SSR projects in the region at some point since the mid-1990s: the EU, NATO, OSCE, the Council of Europe, ICITAP, DFID,[48] DCAF[49] and SECI.[50] To this jungle of acronyms, one can add a vast number of non-governmental organizations and other bilateral donors (e.g. the EU Member States). Some of these actors have a multi-sectoral approach to SSR (such as the EU); others focus on specific activities (such as NATO). What is evident is that very often these activities are motivated by different rationales and have been launched at different stages, complicating overall coordination efforts.

While problems of coherence have impinged upon the efforts of every international organization and country involved in SSR, in the case of the EU internal coherence represents a specific challenge. For this reason, this section will pay particular attention to this issue. Different factors explain why coherence is such a mounting task for the EU: the pillar division, the complexity of procedures and the number of actors involved both in the decision-making and the implementation process. Coherence needs to be ensured across EU policies and between EU and Member States policies, Council and Commission activities and military and civilian instruments. The development of CSDP/ESDP capabilities has increased the EU's ability to play a significant role in the world, but it has also made coordination within the EU more difficult. The lack of a comprehensive planning strategy and appropriate coordinating mechanisms have caused some

---

48   The UK Department for International Development (DFID) manages Britain's external aid, including assistance to SSR.

49   DCAF established an *International Security Advisory Board (ISAB) for SEE Countries* to review the progress of security sector reform in South-Eastern European countries and offer expert advice to governments on different SSR policies.

50   More information on the Southeast Europe Cooperative Initiative (SECI) can be found at http://www.secinet.info/, accessed 28 April 2010.

problems and prevented the implementation of a coherent and effective external action in the field of SSR.

The overall system is complicated by the fragmentation of the EU's presence on the ground. The EU SSR activities in Bosnia (particularly since 2003) provide a good illustration of the situation. The Commission Delegation's programmes in the field of SSR have concentrated on institution-building, economic assistance and training through twinning programmes. The EU Special Representative (EUSR) has also played an important political role by pressuring the local authorities to carry out reforms in the areas of police and rule of law, if necessary resorting to the use of the High Representative's resources (including the Bonn powers) and credibility. The EU Police Mission (EUPM) is the leading organization in supporting the policing aspects of SSR, while the EU military force (EUFOR Althea) has played a role in the fight against organized crime. Other EU bodies such as Europol are involved in SSR activities in the areas of intelligence reform and the fight against organized crime.

The need for a more coherent approach is acknowledged both at the political and operational levels. For instance, the *EU Concept for ESDP Support to Security Sector Reform* affirms that '[d]uring the preparation, planning and conduct of the EU action by the appropriate Council bodies, the comprehensive integration of civilian and military aspects will, as appropriate, need to be ensured'.[51] However, the fact is that the EU is still far from using all its instruments in a coherent way. For the purpose of clarity, the following sub-sections will focus on three different types of coordination: (1) mil-mil coordination; (2) civ-mil coordination; and (3) civ-civ coordination. Some examples will be provided to illustrate the state of affairs in each of these issue-areas.

Mil-Mil Coordination

NATO has traditionally been the main actor dealing with defence reform in the region. First, through its military operations in the region, NATO played an important role in disarmament, demobilization and re-integration of former combatants. Furthermore, through the PfP, NATO has led the reform process of the armed forces of these countries by providing advice on legislation, capabilities and training in order to bring them closer to the Alliance standards. The build-up of military capabilities has increased the capacity of the EU to play a more important role in maintaining security and stability in the region, but it has logically increased the potential for tensions between the two organizations.

As mentioned before, the 2003 agreement between the EU and NATO on a common strategic approach towards the region recognized an implicit division

---

51   Council of the EU, 'EU Concept for ESDP Support to Security Sector Reform (SSR)', No. 12566/4/05, Brussels, 13 October 2005, p. 10. See also General Affairs and External Relations Council, 'GAERC Conclusions', No. 9946/06 (Presse 161), Brussels, 12 June 2006, p. 20.

of labour: police reform and good governance for the EU, defence reform for NATO. This distribution of tasks was followed in both Macedonia and Bosnia. In Macedonia, the EU took over from NATO, first deployed in 2001, the task of monitoring the security situation and overseeing the implementation of the reforms included in the Ohrid Peace Agreement. The role of the remaining NATO presence (NATO HQ Skopje) became supporting defence reform. Moreover, the Concordia Operation, the first ever EU military operation, was also the first one to resort to Berlin Plus arrangements, serving as a 'test-case' for EU-NATO cooperation. In Bosnia, the much larger EU military operation (EUFOR Althea) depended for its success on cooperation with NATO as the latter could fall back on years of experience in the country. NATO HQ Sarajevo was also tasked with defence reform, counter-terrorism and the detention of persons indicted by the ICTY.

However, despite this division of labour between NATO and the EU in Bosnia, concerns were raised by the existence of some grey areas, in particular in the fields of counter-terrorism and war crimes. Very often these problems were solved in an ad-hoc manner on the ground due to 'frozen' relations among the two organizations at the political level. The fact that both organizations shared the same installations at Camp Butmir as well as co-location at the operational level also increased linkages and cooperation among them. All the interviewees from NATO and EUFOR Althea Headquarters agreed that possible overlaps of competences between the EUFOR and NATO missions were not likely to occur as cooperation took place on a daily basis.[52] Moreover, an informal agreement between the NATO and EUFOR Commanders was achieved by which they agreed to share the authority to vet senior Bosnian officers and to authorize the movement of weapons in the country. They also agreed that each organization had to notify the other of their planned operations against persons indicted for war crimes and it was also implicitly agreed that NATO would take the lead in defence reform.

Civ-Mil Coordination

The deployment of 7,000 EU troops in Bosnia by 2004 entailed not only an important challenge in terms of planning and conducting a large scale operation, but also required a co-ordinated approach involving all relevant EU actors participating in SSR activities. However, from the outset, there were some problems, a case in point being coordination between the police and the military mission in the fight against organized crime. In theory, the mandates of the two missions did not clash. The role of EUPM was to monitor, mentor and inspect at the medium and senior level, assisting in the building of the capabilities of the Bosnian police forces.[53] EUFOR Althea was to provide a safe and secure environment, and to implement

52   Interviews with NATO and EUFOR officials, 2005-2006.

53   Council of the EU, 'Council Joint Action 2002/210/CFSP of 11 March 2002 on the European Union Police Mission', *Official Journal of the European Communities* L(70), 13 March 2002, pp. 1-6.

other aspects of ANNEX 1A and 2 of the Dayton Agreement.[54] Whereas, the EUPM's mandate aimed at the long-term capacity-building of the police forces, EUFOR focused on the short term (deterrence). The first had a non-executive mandate (monitor, mentor and inspect); the latter had an executive mandate, i.e. it could resort to the use of force if necessary. In spite of the different mandates and approaches, during EUFOR's first year of mandate tensions arose between the two missions due to overlapping tasks, especially in the fight against organized crime.

EUPM provided expert advice and monitored the creation and strengthening of various state institutions (the Ministry of Security, the State Investigation and Protection Agency, the BiH Border Police) to increase the local capacity to fight organized crime. The role of EUFOR Althea was rather different. Having been identified as one of the supporting tasks of EUFOR's mandate, the then EUFOR Commander General Leakey expressed his personal commitment to play a significant role in this issue. Since December 2004, several operations were launched to support local law enforcement agencies in fighting illegal activities such as weapons smuggling, drug trafficking and illegal logging. Although EUFOR officials stressed that these operations were not meant to usurp local efforts, the Mission's assertive approach generated some criticism amongst EUPM and other EU officials for exceeding its mandate and undermining EUPM's objective of promoting long-term capacity-building and ownership of the reforms.

However, soon EU actors realized the need for better co-ordinating arrangements. In September 2005, the representatives of EUPM, EUFOR and the EUSR agreed on *Seven Principles for Coordination* and on *General Guidelines for Increasing Cooperation between EUPM-EUFOR and EUSR*.[55] According to the *Seven Principles*, EUPM would take the lead in the policing aspects of ESDP, supporting efforts in tackling organized crime and assisting the local authorities by mentoring and monitoring the planning of these operations, while EUFOR would provide the operational capabilities to these operations, all under the political coordination of the EUSR. This agreement was later developed into Operational Guidelines that specified the new 'adjusted roles' of EUPM and EUFOR in supporting Bosnian law enforcement agencies in fighting organized crime and corruption. The implementation of these guidelines led to EUFOR progressively reducing its role in the fight against organized crime and transferring these tasks to the Bosnian police forces. At the same time, since 2006 EUPM has had a stronger, more pro-active role in the fight against organized crime, assisting the local

54 Council of the EU, 'Council Joint Action 2004/569/CFSP of 12 July 2004 on the European Union military operation in Bosnia and Herzegovina', *Official Journal of the European Union* L(252), 28 July 2004, pp. 10-14.

55 EUPM, EUFOR, EUSR, 'Guidelines for Increasing Co-operation between EUPM-EUFOR and the EUSR', Sarajevo, 2005.

authorities in planning and conducting investigations.[56] In sum, Bosnia provides some interesting lessons on how civil-military coordination in SSR activities can be worked out.

Civ-Civ Coordination

Coordination between civilian actors has also encountered some problems. Here, the focus is on coordination between the European Commission activities and the EU police missions in the region.[57] In general, these problems have been of an institutional nature. As mentioned by Annika Hansen, missions in the field of policing were conceived from a different perspective according to which pillar was involved: for the first pillar (European Commission), they were a long-term tool to support development projects; for the second pillar (Common Foreign and Security Policy – CFSP), police missions were considered a short term instrument of security; for the third pillar (Justice and Home Affairs – JHA), police missions were a preventive instrument to fight organized crime and secure EU borders.[58] Police operations like EUPM were designed by the Council structures to tackle the urgent needs of police forces, whereas the Commission designed its own long term institution-building projects which did not always follow the same logic. One of the main challenges referred to the difficulties to establish a precise division between short (the focus of CSDP/ESDP operations) and long-term needs (the focus of the Commission). As witnessed in the cases of Bosnia and Macedonia, CSDP/ESDP missions ended up stepping on the Commission's territory and carrying out institution-building activities, as well as operational management. The abolition of the pillar structure, the establishment of the new double-hatted High Representative for Foreign Affairs and Security Policy and the creation of the External Action Service foreseen in the Lisbon Treaty might go some way in addressing these problems.

In Bosnia, coordination between the Commission and EUPM has been facilitated by an informal Joint Coordination Group. Moreover, a small CARDS team has been co-located at the EUPM Headquarters. Although coordination with the Commission has worked fairly well,[59] some difficulties are worth noting. The lack of appropriate funding procedures has generated some troubles for EUPM, having to apply for CARDS funding in order to launch new projects or seek

---

56   Council of the EU, 'Council Joint Action 2005/824/CFSP of 24 November 2005 on the European Union Police Mission (EUPM) in Bosnia and Herzegovina (BiH)', *Official Journal of the European Union* L(307), 25 November 2005, pp. 55-58.

57   For more information see Gourlay, C., 'Civil-Civil Co-ordination in EU Crisis Management' in Nowak, A. (ed.) 'Civilian Crisis Management: The EU Way'. Chaillot Paper No. 90, June 2006, pp. 103-22.

58   Hansen, A., 'Security and Defence: The EU Police Mission in Bosnia-Herzegovina' in Carlsnaes, Sjursen and White (eds) *Contemporary European Foreign Policy*. London: Sage, 2004, p. 181.

59   Interviews with EUPM and Commission officials, Sarajevo, 2005-2006.

funding through the Member States' embassies.[60] Moreover, there has not always been full cooperation in harmonizing the projects launched by the Commission and EUPM, leading for example to the duplication at times of advisors to some Bosnian institutions, with one co-located police officer coming from EUPM and one advisor from the Commission's twinning projects.[61] This duplication has caused confusion among local stakeholders and undermined the consistency of the SSR policies in the country.

Compared to the situation in Macedonia, coordination in Bosnia has nevertheless been a 'happy' story. In Bosnia, police aid was mainly undertaken by the UN mission (UNMIBH/IPTF, 1995-2002) and then handed over to the EUPM, with the Commission only playing a complementary role. In Macedonia, however, from the outset, the Commission had a significant role to play in police reform and saw the arrival of the EU police mission Proxima as interfering in its area of activities. Moreover, the situation was complicated by the fact that another EU actor, the European Agency for Reconstruction (AER), also had projects in the field of policing.[62] Following increasing tensions between all these actors, EU Member States agreed on a drastic solution: to appoint the first ever double-hatted EUSR, i.e. acting at the same time as Head of the Commission Delegation and as EUSR to Macedonia.

Most of the problems in civ-civ coordination resulted from the fact that Proxima was launched in what was already a very 'crowded' scenario.[63] Only in the policing sector one could identify the following actors involved from 2001 in the reform of the police: the OSCE, providing training in the Macedonian police academy and advice regarding community policing and minority recruitment, among others; the US, through ICITAP, running training programmes and supporting capacity-building for the Ministry of Interior; the UK assisting in public order and crowd control; and France providing training and technical assistance on crime investigation.[64] In this overcrowded context, tensions did not take time to materialize, in particular, between the newcomer Proxima and other international actors, like the OSCE, which had been present in the country for much longer and who – just like the European Commission Delegation – saw Proxima as an unwelcomed intruder in their areas of activity.[65] Problems in Macedonia illustrate the need for a more comprehensive international strategy on SSR.

---

60   Interviews with EUPM officials, Sarajevo, 2005-2006.

61   Ibid.

62   For more information see Ioannides, I. 'EU Police Mission *Proxima*: Testing the "European" Approach to Building Peace' in Nowak, A. (ed.) 'Civilian Crisis Management: The EU Way', op. cit., pp. 69-86; and Merlingen, M. and Ostrauskaite, R., *European Union Peacebuilding and Policing*. London: Routledge, 2006.

63   Merlingen, M. and Ostrauskaite, R., *European Union Peacebuilding and Policing*, op. cit., p. 85.

64   Ibid., pp. 84-85.

65   Ibid., p. 91.

The Challenge of Effectiveness

The term effectiveness is commonly defined as productive or capable of producing the intended result. From previous sections one can begin to discern that the reform of the security sector in the countries of the Western Balkans has in some ways been limited in its capacity to achieved the intended results, understood in this chapter as the use of SSR to help improve people's lives and to strengthen the political, economic and social development of these countries. There is a variety of reasons for this conclusion, including limited human and material resources, inadequate training and legislation, high corruption levels, opposition from some powerful local stakeholders, poor inter-agency cooperation among international donors, and a mismatch between the needs of these countries and the agendas of external actors. This section will expand on some of these issues and bring into the discussion others that are crucial when making sense of the complex panorama that has developed in the Western Balkans after over a decade of post-conflict SSR involvement. In fact, the SSR initiatives in the Western Balkans can be evaluated, in terms of effectiveness, from two perspectives: endogenous and exogenous explanations. The former looks into the internal making and implementation of SSR initiatives or missions, and the latter takes into account (local) contextual factors that have a bearing in the design and implementation of those SSR efforts.

Endogenous Explanations

One of the main objectives of the SSR process in the Western Balkans has been the introduction of 'the highest democratic standards of security sector governance'.[66] In this respect, the missions on the ground as well as other SSR initiatives have sought to act as transmission mechanisms of the best democratic values, embodied in concepts such as 'democratic policing', 'community policing' or 'European best police practices'. Despite their appealing nature, these police concepts are rather elusive in nature and thus, can lead to a range of problems both during the design and implementation of mission mandates. There have been attempts to codify them, as exemplified by the international standards for policing prepared by the UN Crime Prevention and Criminal Justice Division, the OSCE or the Council of Europe. However, as summarized by Alice Hills, 'such guidelines are essentially descriptive or normative, so working definitions of effective policing must be extracted from specific projects'.[67] In the case of the Western Balkans, this situation has in fact led to a nationality or personality-driven application of police standards.[68] This can

---

66   Dowling, A., 'EU Conditionality and Security Sector Reform in the Western Balkans', op. cit., p. 193.

67   Hills, A., 'The Possibility of Transnational Policing', *Policing and Society* 19(3), 2009, p. 304.

68   For an illustration see Collantes-Celador, G., 'The EU's Capacity to Engage in Security Sector Reform: Lessons from Police Reform in Bosnia and Herzegovina' in *The*

result in operational problems due to the different legal and social backgrounds of international police officers, with different occupational cultures and attitudes to social authority. For EU police missions the disparities have never been as great as within UN missions but, nevertheless, there is an increasing realization that operationally so-called 'European police practices' are very difficult to pin down. In this regard the views of Roland Zinzius, at the time Deputy Head of the Civ/Mil Cell at the EU Military Staff, become rather interesting. He described the EU as embarked in a 'soul searching process', which might explain, at least partially, the essence of this problem.[69]

These difficulties have led at times to a lack of legitimacy in the face of the local population, particularly when mission personnel or mission mandates have not adhered to the same norms being conveyed on local stakeholders. Examples range from the lack of an appropriate gender representation and consensus over certain police practices (e.g. community policing) among EUPM ranks, to the international response to the post-UN police certification problems in Bosnia, the relationship between peacekeepers and the proliferation of prostitution and human trafficking activities in the region, and the April 2004 shoot-out in a UN detention centre in Mitrovica (Kosovo) among UN police officers over a quarrel about the war in Iraq. Given that international missions like EUPM rely heavily on their co-location programmes to help the Bosnian police solve its structural and behavioural problems, legitimacy is of utmost importance. A similar lesson can be drawn from looking at the police restructuring process in Bosnia, which was based on certain EU conditions that not all Member States would meet. In other words, as put by Gergana Noutcheva, the normative and moral arguments used by the EU to justify its policy of conditionality in the region lack at times the necessary authority to ensure compliance.[70]

More realistic parameters to measure progress could perhaps help solve or attenuate some of these difficulties. So far each organization has applied its own method. This reality also applies to EU actions given that neither the Copenhagen criteria nor the *acquis communautaire* seem by themselves able to provide a workable approach to assess SSR effectiveness. The most common strategy has often consisted in contrasting objectives in the mandate against actual results, habitually presented as number of specific programmes accomplished or numbers of trained security actors or number of weapons bought. One obvious problem with this self-made solution is that mandates are the product of negotiations

---

European Union and Security Sector Reform. Workshop Report, Swedish National Defence College. Research Report Series Acta B, 2008.

69   'European Union Presidency Seminar on Security Sector Reform (SSR) in the Western Balkans', Vienna, 13-14 February 2006, p. 4, http://www.bmlv.at/pdf_pool/publikationen/19_conference_2006.pdf, accessed 28 April 2010.

70   Noutcheva, G., 'Fake, Partial and Imposed Compliance: The Limits of the EU's Normative Power in the Western Balkans'. CEPS Working Paper, No. 274, Brussels, July 2007.

and thus, tend to be shaped by the needs and interests of contributing countries. Consequently, there is an inbuilt limitation in measuring results against mandate objectives when determining effectiveness levels. Another complication has often been the overtly technical nature of benchmarking systems, at the expenses of wider questions in security sector reform.[71] EUPM initially introduced implementation and assessment criteria for its programmes that proved too complex to be applied and that by including too many projects lost the capacity to prioritize the real needs of the country. This methodology was amended during the Mission's second mandate (2006-2007).[72]

Another structural difficulty generally encountered by SSR efforts in the Western Balkans has been the tendency to 'securitize security sector reform'.[73] In other words, the propensity to prioritize tactical short-term objectives (capacity-building, investment on resources and personnel) in the fields of counter-terrorism, the fight against organized crime and corruption, and the maintenance of order in society. This has often come at the expense of strategic long-term objectives more concerned with the governance side of the security sector (including issues of accountability, legitimacy, transparency, democratization of institutions and attitudes). This situation can only bring long-term negative repercussions for the region since without the governance side the sustainability of SSR – as conceived of by the international community – is questionable. This trend underpins the writings of those scholars that criticize the EU's investment patterns in recent years, characterized by an emphasis on justice and home affairs-related issues at the expense of other security needs of the region,[74] and regardless of the limited absorption capacity of security agencies in the Western Balkans. Similarly, these priority patterns have in occasions led to the export rather than adaptation of external security models, for the sake of expediency but at the expense of local ownership and suitability.

A visible effect of this short term vs. long-term imbalance is the mixed progress in linking security sector reform to wider reform processes in the countries of the Western Balkans. Throughout the 1990s there has been a growing realization

---

71   For example, one of the usual benchmarks followed has been the 10 percent female ratio within police ranks, often presented as a European best practice. However, even if 10 percent of the local police are made up by women this does not always mean that wider questions related to gender awareness have been answered.

72   Collantes-Celador, G., 'The EU's Capacity to Engage in Security Sector Reform', op. cit.

73   This term is borrowed from Sedra, M., 'Security Sector Reform in Afghanistan: An Instrument of the State-Building Project' in Andersen and Møller and Stepputat, *Fragile States and Insecure People? Violence, Security, and Statehood in the Twenty-First Century.* Houndmills: Palgrave Macmillan, 2007, pp. 14, 151-76.

74   Juncos, A.E., 'Of Cops and Robbers: European Union Policy and the Problem of Organized Crime in Bosnia Herzegovina' in Balamir-Coskun and Demirtas-Coskun (eds) *Neighborhood Challenge: The European Union and its Neighbors.* Boca Raton: Universal Publishers, 2009, pp. 47-68.

that security and development are interdependent and consequently, measures that do not take into account the root causes of security problems (often to be socio-economic and political) are bound to have only a cosmetic impact. A case in point is the approach so far adopted in the Western Balkans by the EU to fight organized crime.[75] An effective policy in this field requires military, police and border control measures but these do little if unaccompanied by greater socio-economic development efforts. In other words, SSR by itself cannot solve problems that have arisen and prospered on the basis of serious economic and social precariousness and that, therefore, require as much as anything else greater economic assistance and a more relaxed visa regime.[76] Adopting this approach requires good intra-EU cooperation as well as cooperation between the Union and other actors on the ground. It is also dependent on Member States' political will to make sacrifices at home given that some of the necessary measures will not be popular among certain European constituent groups.

Exogenous Explanations

Local ownership is of utmost importance to ensure that the reforms introduced are politically, economically and socially sustainable and thus, not perceived as imposed from the outside. The problem faced by the international community in the Western Balkans has often been a lack of cooperation or willingness to cooperate from some key local stakeholders. This situation should not come as a surprise given that SSR is not a technical issue alone, but also a political reform that entails redistributing power in societies that by and large continue to be deeply divided. It could be argued that SSR has not been a priority for certain key actors in the region, at least not until it was clearly linked to NATO and EU conditionality and even then, with mixed results (as illustrated by the police restructuring process in Bosnia). The argument is that these actors are 'caught between acrimony, which is an inevitable legacy of past conflicts, and a deep-rooted nationalism that places the military in a pedestal and, even at times, makes heroes of indicted criminals'.[77]

Operating in the complex political contexts of the Western Balkans also makes it difficult to reconcile local and international approaches to SSR. In the words of Jean-Christian Cady, at the time Deputy Special Representative

---

75   Ibid.

76   The situation improved in 2009 when the EU included Macedonia, Serbia and Montenegro in its visa-free regime. Bosnia and Albania have since made substantial progress in meeting the requirements for visa liberalization. The European Commission proposed visa-free travel for Bosnian and Albanian citizens in May 2010. For Bosnia it is expected that the Council will adopt this proposal in November 2010, after the country's general elections. Information found in the European Stability Initiative's 'The Schengen White List Project', http://www.esiweb.org/index.php?lang=en&id=353, accessed 28 April 2010.

77   Montanaro-Jankovski, L., 'Security Sector Reform in the Balkans: A Key to Ending Conflict'. Policy Brief, European Policy Centre, Brussels, June 2006, p. 2.

of the UN Secretary-General for Police and Justice in Kosovo (UNMIK), '[l]locals have a tendency to underestimate difficulties and wish to have a quick and quasi immediate hand-over of powers. Internationals are more aware of the shortcomings in competencies but are often too reluctant to let go'.[78] This situation is not limited to Kosovo. In Bosnia the differences in opinion among local stakeholders and internationals on the perception and understanding of organized crime have revolved around the relevance of linking security measures to larger structural economic and social reforms (as claimed by local stakeholders). This lack of mutual understanding has led to 'a blame game ... in which each side blames uneven successes on the other'.[79]

The lack of (local) cooperation or willingness to cooperate has resulted at times in imposed reforms, with the two extremes cases being the 'protectorates' – as many would argue – in Bosnia and Kosovo. Imposition leads to a range of problems in terms of setting 'hand over' processes and minimizing the development of the so-called dependency syndrome of local decision-makers on the international community to make the tough decisions on their behalf. Controlling the effects of this syndrome is of utmost importance if we take into account that the legacy of one-party political systems and ideological control during the Cold War, exacerbated by the wars of the 1990s, has meant that societies in the Western Balkans have been slow at developing a political culture that endorses the democratic and governance-related concepts embedded in SSR initiatives. The different tactics employed by the High Representative Paddy Ashdown and his successor, Christian Schwarz-Schilling, in Bosnia exemplify the conundrum of local ownership in the Western Balkans. The former used a heavy-handed approach that through imposition achieved many important reforms. The latter tried to operate through local ownership and achieved almost no reforms, leading to his early departure from office. The question is therefore whether in such a context Bosnia's defence, intelligence and police reforms can endure without the international community pushing the process at all times, as clearly illustrated by the outcome of the police restructuring process in 2008. This is a crucial question if we take into account that EU membership for the Western Balkans countries is premised on the basis of reforms being introduced by local consensus, not imposition.

---

78   Cady, J.C., 'The United Nations and Security Sector Reform in Kosovo' in UNOG and DCAF, *Security Sector Reform: Its Relevance for Conflict Prevention, Peace Building and Development*, Geneva, January 2003, p. 96.

79   Corpora, C.A., 'Framing the Gap between International and Local Perspectives on Addressing Local Organised Crime and Corruption in Bosnia and Herzegovina', *East European Studies News*, March-April 2005, pp. 9-11.

Conclusion

Although no one neglects the importance of short-term interventions in conflict situations, in general SSR is best seen as a long-term effort. It is a demanding process in terms of material and human resources. It requires a comprehensive perspective that takes into account all the different SSR components, but, at the same time, only a focused and intensive intervention can bring about results. Notwithstanding these factors, the SSR balance sheet in the Western Balkans is mixed. The international community, including the EU, has somewhat managed to stabilize the region but has not freed it from a number of security, political and economic problems that continue to challenge regional progress as well as the internal security of the EU.

Coordination across the broad range of SSR areas and donors remains one of the main problems influencing the effectiveness of those reforms in tackling the real needs of the region. A concerted effort to streamline international SSR activities from the planning to the implementation stages is needed in order to ensure complementarity rather than duplication. A more coordinated approach among the various organizations present in the region would have led to a more fruitful set of reform efforts, rather that what often ended up being 'laundry-list' approaches to reform, as exemplified by events in Macedonia.[80] Ideally this concerted approach should be complemented by a needs-assessment exercise that allows countries in the region to have a greater say on what they need, rather than choosing from what is offered by the international community. However, as illustrated in this chapter, one needs to be aware that due to the fragility of some of these societies as an enduring legacy from the wars of the 1990s, these greater levels of ownership might not always be possible, particularly on the political aspects of SSR.

Implementation remains a real challenge. Successful SSR requires more than changes in the current legislation. It needs to be followed by changes in the political culture, something that cannot be expected from one day to the other. In this regard, the endeavour has been complicated by the presence of a number of endogenous and exogenous factors that have played a role in slowing down the effectiveness of the SSR initiatives introduced. In terms of issues embedded in the SSR policies, one should highlight the tactical vs. strategic objectives dilemma, the ideational problems embedded in police missions and related donors' activities, and the lack of clear criteria to determine effectiveness.

SSR activities in the Western Balkans have also been hostage to a set of factors arising from the complex political, economic and social regional context that has resulted from the communist period and the wars of the 1990s. The lack of cooperation, or will to cooperate, from stakeholders that are key entry points to develop reforms that are politically acceptable to the locals and economically and

---

80   Merlingen, M. and Ostrauskaite, R., *European Union Peacebuilding and Policing*, op. cit., pp. 90-91.

socially sustainable by existing structures, is an ongoing challenge for the international community. It has put to the test the attractiveness of EU membership and the effectiveness of its conditionality, at a time when EU membership fatigue leads to fears that some of the Western Balkan countries might have to wait longer than expected to reach the desired end goal of belonging to this European club. Within such context, the stringent conditionality becomes a source of frustration among local stakeholders as well as the populations that increasingly regard their leaders as accountable and responsive to the international community, not to the electorates.

References

Andreas, P., 'The Clandestine Political Economy of War and Peace in Bosnia and Herzegovina', *International Studies Quarterly* 48(1), March 2004.

Balkan Insight, 'Bosnian War Veterans in Violent Clashes with Police', Sarajevo, 21 April 2010.

Bieber, F. and Wintergahen, J., 'Ethnic Violence in Vojvodina: Glitch or Harbinger of Conflicts to Come?' Working Paper No. 27, European Centre for Minority Issues, Flensburg, April 2006.

Bosnian Ministry of Security, 'Information on the Security Situation in Bosnia and Herzegovina in 2005', Sarajevo, April 2006.

Cady, J.C., 'The United Nations and Security Sector Reform in Kosovo' in UNOG and DCAF, 'Security Sector Reform: Its Relevance for Conflict Prevention, Peace Building and Development', Geneva, January 2003.

Caparini, M., 'Security Sector Reform and Post-Conflict Stabilization: The Case of the Western Balkans' in Bryden and Hänggi (eds) Reform and Reconstruction of the Security Sector. Geneva: DCAF, 2004.

Collantes-Celador, G., 'The EU's Capacity to Engage in Security Sector Reform: Lessons from Police Reform in Bosnia and Herzegovina' in *The European Union and Security Sector Reform*. Workshop Report, Swedish National Defence College. Research Report Series Acta B, 2008.

Collantes-Celador, G., 'The EU and its Policy Towards Security Sector Reform: A New Example of the "Conceptual-Contextual" Divide?' in Soler and Carbonell (eds) *6th International Seminar on Security and Defence in the Mediterranean*. Barcelona: Edicions Bellaterra, 2008.

Collantes-Celador, G. and Juncos, A.E., 'The Reform of Border Management in the Western Balkans: Safeguarding EU External Borders or Preparing for European Integration?' in Ekengren et al. (eds) 'Challenges and Prospects for Nordic-Baltic Security Sector Reform – the Western Balkans, Ukraine, Afghanistan and Sub-Saharan Africa'. Research Report. Stockholm: Swedish National Defence College, 2007, pp. 173-205.

Corpora, C.A., 'Framing the Gap between International and Local Perspectives on Addressing Local Organised Crime and Corruption in Bosnia and Herzegovina', *East European Studies News*, March-April 2005.

Council of the EU, 'Council Joint Action 2002/210/CFSP of 11 March 2002 on the European Union Police Mission', *Official Journal of the European Communities* L(70), 13 March 2002.

Council of the EU, 'A Secure Europe in a Better World: European Security Strategy', Brussels, 12 December 2003.

Council of the EU, 'Council Joint Action 2004/569/CFSP of 12 July 2004 on the European Union Military Operation in Bosnia and Herzegovina', *Official Journal of the European Union* L(252), 28 July 2004.

Council of the EU, 'EU Concept for ESDP Support to Security Sector Reform (SSR)', No. 12566/4/05, Brussels, 13 October 2005.

Council of the EU, 'Council Joint Action 2005/824/CFSP of 24 November 2005 on the European Union Police Mission (EUPM) in Bosnia and Herzegovina (BiH)', *Official Journal of the European Union* L(307), 25 November 2005.

Donais, T., 'A Tale of Two Towns: Human Security and the Limits of Post-War Normalization in Bosnia-Herzegovina', *Journal of Southern Europe and the Balkans* 7(1), April 2005.

Dowling, A. 'EU Conditionality and Security Sector Reform in the Western Balkans' in Fluri and Spence (eds) *The European Union and Security Sector Reform.* London: John Harper Publishing, 2008.

'EU and NATO Concerted Approach for the Western Balkans', No. 11605/03, Brussels, 29 July 2003

EU-Western Balkans Summit – Thessaloniki, Declaration, No. 10229/03 (Press 163), 21 June 2003.

EUPM, EUFOR, EUSR, 'Guidelines for Increasing Co-operation between EUPM-EUFOR and the EUSR', Sarajevo, 2005.

European Commission, 'A Concept for European Community Support for Security Sector Reform', No. COM(2006) 253 final, Brussels, 24 May 2006.

European Commission, 'Albania 2006 Progress Report', No. COM(2006) 649 final, Brussels, 8 November 2006.

European Commission, 'Serbia 2006 Progress Report', No. COM(2006) 649 final, Brussels, 8 November 2006.

European Commission, 'Communication from the Commission to the European Parliament and the Council. Kosovo – Fulfilling its European Perspective', No. COM(2009) 5343, Brussels, 14 October 2009.

European Council. 'Report on the Implementation of the European Security Strategy: Providing Security in a Changing World', S407/08, Brussels, 11 December 2008.

European Commission and Council of Europe. 'Update of the 2006 Situation Report on Organised and Economic Crime in South-eastern Europe', No. PC-TC(2007)6, CARPO Regional Project, Strasbourg, June 2007.

General Affairs and External Relations Council, 'GAERC Conclusions', No. 9946/06 (Presse 161), Brussels, 12 June 2006.

Gourlay, C., 'Civil-Civil Co-ordination in EU Crisis Management' in Nowak (ed.) 'Civilian Crisis Management: The EU Way'. Chaillot Paper No. 90, June 2006.

Gow, J., 'Security in South Eastern Europe: The War Crimes Legacy', *Southeast European and Black Sea Studies* 5(1), January 2005.

Hansen, A., 'Security and Defence: The EU Police Mission in Bosnia-Herzegovina' in Carlsnaes, Sjursen and White (eds) *Contemporary European Foreign Policy*. London: Sage, 2004.

Hills, A. 'The Possibility of Transnational Policing', *Policing and Society* 19(3), 2009.

Hislope, R., 'Crime and Honor in a Weak State: Paramilitary Forces and Violence in Macedonia', *Problems of Post-Communism* 51(3), May-June 2004.

Ioannides, I. 'EU Police Mission *Proxima*: Testing the "European" Approach to Building Peace' in Nowak (ed.) 'Civilian Crisis Management: The EU Way'. Chaillot Paper No. 90, June 2006.

Ivanisevic, B., 'Croatia: A Decade of Disappointment – Continuing Obstacles to the Reintegration of Serb Returnees'. Report 18(7) (D), Human Rights Watch, London, September 2006, pp. 10-16.

Jane's Intelligence Review, 'Small Arms, Big Problem – Light Weapons Trafficking in Albania', 14 September 2007.

Juncos, A.E., 'Of Cops and Robbers: European Union Policy and the Problem of Organized Crime in Bosnia Herzegovina' in Balamir-Coskun and Demirtas-Coskun (eds) *Neighborhood Challenge: The European Union and its Neighbors*. Boca Raton: Universal Publishers, 2009.

Kostovicova, D., 'Old and New Insecurity in the Balkans: Lessons from the EU's Involvement in Macedonia' in Glasius, M. and Kaldor, M. (eds) *A Human Security Doctrine for Europe: Project, Principles, Practicalities*. Abingdon: Routledge, 2006.

Merlingen, M. and Ostrauskaite, R., *European Union Peacebuilding and Policing*. London: Routledge, 2006.

Montanaro-Jankovski, L., 'Security Sector Reform in the Balkans: A Key to Ending Conflict'. Policy Brief, European Policy Centre, Brussels, June 2006.

Noutcheva, G., 'Fake, Partial and Imposed Compliance: The Limits of the EU's Normative Power in the Western Balkans'. CEPS Working Paper, No. 274, Brussels, July 2007.

Schimmelfennig, F. and Sedelmeier, U., 'Governance by Conditionality: EU Rule Transfer to the Candidate Countries of Central and Eastern Europe', *Journal of European Public Policy* 11(4), 2004.

Sedra, M., 'Security Sector Reform in Afghanistan: An Instrument of the State-Building Project' in Andersen and Møller and Stepputat, *Fragile States and Insecure People? Violence, Security, and Statehood in the Twenty-First Century*. Houndmills: Palgrave Macmillan, 2007.

SEESAC, 'A Fragile Peace: Guns and Security in Post-Conflict Macedonia', London, January 2004.

SIDA, 'Guidelines for Swedish Bilateral Support within the Sector of Justice and Home Affairs for the Western Balkans', Stockholm, July 2003.

Vetschera, H. and Damian, M., 'Security Sector Reform in Bosnia and Herzegovina: The Role of the International Community', *International Peacekeeping* 13(1), 2006.

Chapter 9

Ukrainian Security Identity and NATO Generated SSR

Fredrik Bynander

The Security Identity of Ukraine

In the process that led to the collapse of the Soviet Union, Ukraine's drive for independence was pivotal to force the events of 1991. The new state, however, in electing the former ideological secretary of Ukraine's Communist Party, Leonid Kravchuk, as its first president and Leonid Kuchma (who headed the Soviet Union's largest missile factory) as his successor, has straddled the divide between Russia and the West with some unease. The presidential election of 2004, and the 'Orange revolution' that it triggered, brought the domestic tensions concerning this divide to the fore. Turmoil has characterized domestic politics ever since, and only with the 2010 exit of Viktor Yushchenko from the Mariyinsky Palace soon to be followed by former partner Yulia Timoshenko from the prime minister's office, has the power struggle been decided. The political comeback of the other Viktor – Yanukovich – has meant a rapprochement to Russia, symbolized by the Black Sea Fleet agreement of April 2010, and the denouncement of NATO membership aspirations in May. Today's Ukraine continues to be torn between the Russian influence and the frustrating integration processes with the EU and NATO. This chapter will be concerned mainly with the relationship to NATO and its repercussions for Ukrainian security sector reform (SSR), leaving the EU process for Greg Simons's chapter that follows.

As an illustration of the centrality of foreign and security policy to Ukraine's domestic politics, consider then Prime Minister Yanukovich's call for a referendum on NATO membership in the run up to the September 2007 election. President Yushchenko had declared his ambition that Ukraine should apply for NATO membership before the end of his term in 2009. Yanukovich reaped the dual benefits of extra incentive for his Russian-speaking powerbase to cast their vote against the orange parties, and to expose the weak position of the president in the NATO issue as most experts agree that a referendum would reject the idea (Fawkes 2007).

The September election was the result of the May crisis in which the president and prime minister battled out a fierce power struggle on the streets of Kiev. The president was already weakened after the breakdown of Yulia Timoshenko's orange coalition government, the return of Viktor Yanukovich as Prime Minister, and the president's dissolution of the Verkhovna Rada (parliament) in April of 2007. The close results of the election further emphasized the internal conflict over the direction that Ukrainian foreign policy should take and which relations should be prioritized. At issue is the *security identity* of the nation and the repercussions that the articulation of such an entity can have. In no uncertain way, the outcome of this conflict strongly impacts the prerequisites for achieving SSR, as well as the goals that such a process should realize.

The term security identity refers to the embedded priorities of a nation as expressed by its lawful government, and entails all aspects of its security policies. It is not, as realism would have it, directly derived from material interests that constitute a state's power base. Rather, it relates strongly to a collective perception of the state and its place in the world. Security identity contains historical ideas of what the state should be and which role it should play. It is a reasonable assumption that the official version of such an identity can only survive in a democratic or semi-democratic system of government if it attracts a reasonable amount of electoral support, or is uncontroversial enough not to cause great voter dissatisfaction. In most mature democracies the security identities are sufficiently consolidated not to cause political turmoil except under special circumstances such as the growth of an external threat or the rise of internal differences in perceptions of important international relationships. There the main characteristic of a security identity takes the form of an operative consensus on which security elites have compromised to obtain a political balance. In the typical transitional state, however, the security identity regularly causes severe conflicts in the formation of new political structures. The strategic options are often much more polarized and the societal stakes for loosing are higher. The security identity thus becomes heavily politicized as a tool for redefining the state in terms that aims to foster long term dominance for the respective political elites.

Leonid Kuchma's declaration in 2002 that Ukraine aimed for full membership in NATO was such a powerful move in the contest for security identity, that it reset the game board dramatically and impacted on the primary relationships of the state.[1] It also set in motion the huge western apparatus of institutional change that will coax and entice the national security structures to conform to NATO interoperability standards, a new security concept and military doctrine (Kuzio 2007). Interestingly, political integration was rapid with Ukraine supporting a number of NATO missions even when they drew heavy Russian opposition. The headway made in this strategic relationship is seriously pushing the boundaries of what Ukraine's security identity can stomach.

In the case of Ukraine the struggle over its security identity has been evident since the birth of the state and often taken the form of internal elite debates over

---

1   Although Ukraine had been member of Partnership for Peace since 1994, and had signed the *Charter on a Distinctive Partnership* in 1997, it was the membership card that altered the political approach of Ukrainian political elites along with the NATO-Ukraine Action plan that came with it.

the ties to Russia, e.g. concerning the abandonment of its nuclear arms in 1996, the conflict over the Tuzla dam construction in 2003 as well as the reaction to the Georgian war in 2008. In terms of domestic politics, the issue of which horse to bet on in the race to guarantee Ukraine's security has serious ideological overtones, and the issue of *identity* lies behind the conclusions that are made. Clearly, the foundations of SSR are promoted to a larger extent by cooperative arrangements with the EU and NATO than by rapprochement to Russia, which makes security identity a relevant starting point when studying Ukraine's recent choices in the policy arena.

Security Identity Related to NATO and the EU

'Western values' do have basic traits in common that applies to security, especially when it comes to SSR – both the EU and NATO adhere to a number of distinctly compatible principles for controlling and structuring the security sector. Nevertheless, an EU/NATO institutional divide exists, and it is especially troublesome for states who seek to integrate with both organizations (Bynander 2006). For the accession states of the first and second rounds of enlargement, a very concrete issue where they came to consider themselves between a rock and a hard place was the strong conflict between NATO's calls for higher defence expenditure and EU's demands for budget deficit reductions. In the Czech Republic and other accession states during the late nineties, this caused severe criticism from NATO, as the government cut the defence budget in nominal terms, partly as a result of commitments in the EU accession process. Pressure in the security sector usually emanates bilaterally from the US, but the repercussions for accession states in their process to become members were institutional, as their bargaining positions were generally weak and they were in need of flexibility from both organizations to be considered in accordance with their respective central regulations. For Ukraine, this logic is troubling, as the domestic friction to SSR measures is bad enough, and tension between EU and NATO standards adds to the burden.

In addition, there is a distinct difference of institutional political logic between the two organizations. NATO is a military alliance created at the dawn of the Cold War to counter the Soviet threat, now transforming to meet new threats, but essentially geared to foster effective military cooperation and resolve hard security problems. The EU approached the continent's age-old security dilemma from another direction by founding the Coal and Steel Union on cooperation outside the core of national security, hoping that collaborative solutions would spill over and tie the European states into a strong institutional framework of cooperation. The EU thus became an 'issue magnet' ever incorporating new policy areas into its sphere of regulation, whereas NATO's military security core was diligently protected from dilution by its largest power, the United States.

As NATO has for some time looked beyond a major war as its principal contingency, considering the threat of global terrorism and potentially other major cross-boundary sources of instability and with France and others pushing for a higher security profile for the EU, clashes are inevitable. The EU tends to agree generally on and announce grand ambitions first, and only then starting to worry about how to realize them. NATO usually works by different standards. The Cold War lesson of guarantees for member states to deliver its required resources has produced strong pressure and strict codes to ensure the performance of its member states, although the end of the Cold War led to large cuts in defence expenditure. In SSR terms this produces expectations that NATO is more likely to focus on traditional core security sector issues. The EU's ambitions as security actor are viewed with more scepticism, and SSR commitments partly suffer from this weak link to *core security*. However, the structure of EU commitments in this area is changing, and the strengths of the Union in other areas may make it an increasingly attractive partner also for the fundamentals of comprehensive security sector reform.

NATO demands that SSR is carried out according to Euro-Atlantic standards, especially regarding civilian control of military and security organs. In the case of Ukraine this approach especially targets reform of the Ministry of Defence, administrative boards of investigation, the Internal Forces, Security Service, External Investigation Service and the State Border Service.

So far, this has meant a number of concrete, but modest measures:

- Defence analysis of the armed forces, including proposed new armed force levels;
- Potential security threat analysis up to 2015;
- Creation of defence budget indicators up to 2015;
- List of reform tasks to be conducted by the armed forces and a proposed armed forces structural re-organization; and
- Training of the armed forces on armed forces restructuring (Horbulin, Fluri and Pirozhkov 2007).

Security Identity and Security Sector Reform under Yushchenko

Ukraine's security sector of the early 1990s was characterized by the effort to regain the capacity of the soviet times by the means of the soviet times. A major surge of funds was directed towards the institutions that were vital for internal control of the state, the Ministry for internal affairs and the Security Service of Ukraine (SBU), whereas the Armed Forces (UAF) were reduced in similar proportions. Defence reform has therefore taken a different route than that of the internal security sector which has successfully resisted any push for delimitations in mandate or increased oversight (Kozlovska 2006). The neglect that has characterized the situation for Ukraine's Armed Forces has caused a growing political debate not only concerning its ability to protect national security, but even safety within the services, which is evident by a steep rise in accidents and fatalities involving the military (Melnyk and Polyakov 2004).

In domestic politics, the relation to NATO was not as big a party divider as it may seem. In fact, the first Yanukovich government supported president Kuchma declaration of Ukraine's intention to join NATO. It sponsored a number of joint NATO exercises on Ukrainian soil, as well as the second round of NATO enlargements staunchly opposed by Russia. After the return to power and the formation of the second Yanukovich government, the support for close cooperation continued (Perepelitsya 2004). However, as part of the struggle for votes, Yanukovich's Party of Regions has consistently played the anti-NATO card and painted the alliance as hostile towards Ukrainian national interests. In September, 2006 Viktor Yanukovich visited NATO headquarters and declared a 'pause' in the country's NATO Membership Action Plan. Apart from the fact that it is not Ukraine's position to request or pause the request for such a plan, NATO had already halted the process in which the Yushchenko/Timoshenko leadership had looked favoured by major NATO states to become an enlargement candidate with a Membership Action plan (*BBC News*, 14 September 2006).

The Party of Regions and its ally, the Social Democratic United Party (SDPUo) initiated preparations for a referendum on NATO membership as early as 2004 following their election victory and government formation. SDPUo's leader at the time was Viktor Medvedchuk who was Kutchma's chief of staff in 2002-04 when the official policy of Ukraine was to seek membership in NATO (See Kuzio 2007). The simple truth is that there are too many votes to be counted on an anti-NATO platform in eastern and southern Ukraine for these actors to pass over the opportunity. On the other hand, the foreign policy realities forced the hand of responsible heads of government to remain in the fold of western security cooperation. The fears of a security vacuum speak for keeping these ties alive, and the policy options open.[2]

Ukraine was increasingly involved in active cooperation with NATO including participation in all of the NATO sponsored international missions. In Former Yugoslavia, Ukraine has contributed an infantry battalion, a mechanized infantry battalion and a helicopter squadron to the NATO-led peacekeeping force in Bosnia and Herzegovina, and in Kosovo Ukraine has deployed a helicopter squadron and a substantial contribution to the joint Polish-Ukrainian battalion (Sherr 2004). In line with NATO's policies on international stability and the fight against terrorism, Ukraine is providing over-flight clearance for forces deployed in Afghanistan as part of the NATO-led International Security Assistance Force (ISAF) or as part of the coalition forces under US-led 'Operation Enduring Freedom'. Ukraine provided 1600 troops to the Polish-led multinational force in the US led mission in Iraq. These missions have impacted SSR, as NATO doctrine and operational guidelines has become mandatory for the UAF.

---

2 See 'European Integration of Ukraine: Public Opinion', *National Security and Defence* 89(5), 2007, pp. 51-60.

A memorandum of understanding on Host Nation Support, ratified in March 2004, raised the bar further for NATO-Ukraine operational cooperation. This agreement provides a legal framework for the provision of civil and military assistance by Ukraine to Allied forces located on, or in transit through, its territory in peacetime, crisis or war. Moreover, a memorandum of understanding on Strategic Airlift permits Ukraine to make a substantial contribution to NATO's capability to move outsized cargo. These are concrete and politically significant areas for cooperation that carries consequences in terms of investments and long-term commitments.

The major source of reform in the military sector has been the annual Ukraine-NATO Target Plan first signed in 2002 that includes specific provisions for SSR. In addition, they call for: 'comprehensive overall review of the national security sector in accordance with NATO standards. In this context, Ukraine will adapt its law-enforcement authorities to European standards: a fundamental reform of the Ministry of the Interior will seek to clarify the status, tasks and missions of the Interior Troops, to ensure that their basic mission will be to protect the fundamental rights of citizens by contributing to the maintenance of law and order within the society' (NATO 2006). It is however in the area of defence sector reform that headway has been made, although the extent of which is a matter of some controversy. Official Ukrainian estimations shows that out of 409 actions provided for in the 2006 target plan, 297 actions were carried out in full, 82 in part, and 24 not at all (Ministry for Foreign Affairs 2007). These figures seem a little optimistic in view of the still meagre political control and funding practices in place. The UAF is developing a two-tier structure, where one portion is set up to meet NATO standards featuring a second level of contract personnel on petty officer level, and the other retaining the conscript system as basis for a large scale territorial defence apparatus (The Bonn International Centre for Conversion 2006).

The NATO influence on the military side of the security sector has been significant, partly due to the institutional cooperation, but also via bilateral cooperation with the United States and as a result of the several international missions that UAF is (and has been) involved in: NATO-led operations in the Balkans, the Polish-Ukrainian Battalion in Iraq to name two. The immediate effect of this collaboration is the development of interoperability on the ground, but long-term effects ran deeper than that. The adaptation of the Ukrainian officer corps to NATO practices extends back to national structures and potentially carries seeds for change. To argue that this has provided SSR per se is, however, stretching the argument a bit too far.

Twists and Turns

The repeated political failures of the Yushchenko presidency weakened Ukraine's strategic position, and as NATO-Russia rapprochement made Ukrainian membership more distant in 2007-08 the situation became increasingly problematic. Repeated gas delivery disputes between Russia and Ukraine illustrated Ukrainian exposed position, especially with an ongoing rift between the President and Prime Minister Timoshenko. Yanukovich's (second) return to the premiership practically ended membership aspirations, as the lack of popular support for continued integration became evident.

The real game changer was, however, the Russian invasion of Georgia in August of 2008, and the uncoordinated response to the event by Ukraine's leadership. Russia's justifications for it actions – the protection of ethnic Russians abroad – is a direct analogy to the Crimea and Sevastopol situation for the Ukrainians (Kuzio 2009). Moscow put pressure on Kyiv by accusing Ukraine of supplying 'weapons, mercenaries and diplomacy' (German 2009). The lack of support to Georgia from NATO members and the quick normalization of relations with Russia by key European states spelled out the *de facto* end to membership aspirations for CIS states and forced a fundamental revaluation of the strategic options for these states. It is too early to say how SSR will be affected, but it is not far fetched to suggest that the pace will be significantly halted or reversed.

For Ukrainian NATO membership advocates this undermined their position and the momentum was now clearly with Yanukovich's coalition. When Viktor Yanukovich won the Presidency in February 2010, he rapidly went about improving the relations to Russia, negotiating the deal for the Black Sea Fleet which gives Russia access to Sevastopol until 2042 in April and ruling out NATO membership for Ukraine in May. Yanukovich has made a point of not recognizing the independence of Abkhazia and South Ossetia (nor Kosovo) in order to defend the Ukrainian position regarding separatist regions and Russian policies towards them (*Moscow Times*, 6 June 2010). Obviously, the balancing act a Ukrainian president has to conduct is as challenging for Yanukovich as it was for his predecessor.

Conclusions

Ukraine's situation of political and economic vulnerability causes its security identity to be a seed for continued contention. Receptive to pressure both from Russia and the West, striking a 'balance of belonging' is hard for (more or less) democratic actors on the national political scene, and the swing of the electoral pendulum will cause further ruptures in the path to a stable security identity. Nevertheless, the institutional overbuild of the NATO-Ukraine Action/Target plans and other formalized modes of cooperation has impacted the Ukrainian security sectors and could have a lasting effect on the way that future governments can pursue security policy. The weakness, as has been broadly noted for the NATO partnership especially, but also that with the EU, lies in the poor penetration to internally focused structures of the security sector, such as the SBU and Ministry of Interior.

The removal of NATO membership from the political agenda has drastically weakened pressure for further reform. The recent deal making with Russia, especially regarding the Sevastopol base, illustrates simultaneously the balancing necessary to decrease pressure in the Crimea and the weak position Ukraine is in when asserting its foreign policy towards Russia. Financial woes further undercut the ability of the government to act independently of Russian interests in the energy sector that seem to loom even larger in the region in lean economic circumstances.

The unsurprising conclusion of this state of affairs is that SSR is heavily contingent on the wider process of democratic transition and consolidation. Only a Ukrainian leadership that can aspire to speak both for the east and west of the country will be able to firmly express on behalf of the state a security identity that can be used for long-term commitments to integration with the west, or for a more autonomous position *vis-à-vis* Russia. In the mean time security sector reform will be on the backburner, not only insufficient to be efficient and legitimate in the engagement with international security structures, but also to support the development of a mature democratic system that does not use security means to achieve domestic political ends. However, and regardless of which side of the relentless domestic power struggles in Ukraine that are currently in charge, a way forward on internal SSR can be politically viable as it would increase medium term political stability as well as the likelihood of better managed transitions of political power. Ukraine could use both.

References

BBC News, 'Ukraine "Not Ready" to Join NATO', http://news.bbc.co.uk/1/hi/ world/europe/5345406.stm, 14 September 2006.

BBC News, 'Orange Bloc Wins Ukraine Ballot', http://news.bbc.co.uk/2/hi/ europe/7031018.stm, 5 October 2007.

'European Integration of Ukraine: Public Opinion', *National Security and Defence* (Ukrainian Centre for Economic and Political Studies named after Olexander Razumkov) 89(5), 2007, pp. 51-60.

Fawkes, H., 'Ukraine Vote Threatens More Turmoil', *BBC News*, http://news.bbc. co.uk/2/hi/europe/7016827.stm, 28 September 2007.

German, T., 'David and Goliath: Georgia and Russia's Coercive Diplomacy', *Defence Studies* 9(2), 2009, pp. 224-41.

Horbulin, V.P., Fluri, P.H. and Pirozhkov, S.I., *Perspectives on Ukrainian Security Sector Reform*. DCAF & Valentin Ramirovich Suvaldo, Bern, 2007.

'Inventory of Security Sector Reform (SSR) Efforts in Partner Countries of German Development Assistance: Ukraine', The Bonn International Centre for Conversion, http://www.bicc.de/ssr_gtz/pdf/ukraine.pdf, 2006.

Kozlovska, O., 'A Roadmap for Ukraine's Integration into Transatlantic Structures'. NDC Occasional Paper, NATO Defence College, 2006.

Kuzio, T., 'Indecision and Opportunism Derail NATO in Ukraine', *The Ukrainian Observer*, Issue 224, http://www.ukraine-observer.com/articles/224/933, 2007.

Kuzio, T., 'Strident, Ambiguous and Duplicitous: Ukraine and the 2008 Russia-Georgia War', *Demokratizatsiya* 19(4), 2009, pp. 350-72.

Melnyk, O. and Polyakov, L., 'Ukraine: The Armed Forces and Beyond' in *Security-Sector Reform and Transparency-Building: Needs and Options for Ukraine and Moldova*. Centre of European Security Studies, http://www.cess.org/publications/harmoniepapers/pdfs/harmoniepaper-17.pdf, 2004.

Ministry of Foreign Affairs of Ukraine, 'Information Material about the Results of Activity of the Ministry for Foreign Affairs in 2006 and Urgent Issues in the Sphere of Foreign Policy of Ukraine', 2007.

Moscow Times, 'Yanukovych Defends Closer Ties With Russia', http://www.themoscowtimes.com/news/article/yanukovych-defends-closer-ties-with-russia/407625.html, 6 June 2010.

National Centre of Euro-Atlantic Integration of Ukraine, 'NATO-Ukraine Annual Target Plan for the Year 2006', www.nceai.gov.ua/download.php?1fb3eceece4897a0328826d7306dc1c4&target=1.

NATO, 'NATO-Ukraine Annual Target Plan for the Year 2007', www.nato.int/docu/basictxt/b070618atp-e.pdf.

Perepelitsya, G., 'Ukraine: Reform Issues and Democratic Control', in *Security-Sector Reform and Transparency-Building: Needs and Options for Ukraine and Moldova*. Centre of European Security Studies, http://www.cess.org/publications/harmoniepapers/pdfs/harmoniepaper-17.pdf, 2004.

Sherr, J., 'Ukraine's Reform Accomplishments and Challenges', in *Security-Sector Reform and Transparency-Building: Needs and Options for Ukraine and Moldova*. Centre of European Security Studies, http://www.cess.org/publications/harmoniepapers/pdfs/harmoniepaper-17.pdf, 2004.

Chapter 10

The Politics of Borders and Nationalities in Ukraine: Impacts Upon Security Sector Reform

Greg Simons

Introduction

According to Bruce Parrott from Johns Hopkins University, there are certain countries, such as Czech Republic, Poland and Ukraine, that try to make up for their historical past.

> But even in nations such as these, a strong popular aversion to decades of communist oppression may compensate for the absence of "usable" democratic past. Due to the exceptional severity of most communist regimes, this kind of negative learning may be considerably stronger in post-communist countries than in non-communist countries that aspire to democratise.[1]

In 1654 Cossack leader Bohdan Khmelnytsky, who sought to create an independent Cossack state signed the Treaty of Pereyaslav between Russia and Ukraine, which eventually led to the loss of independence for Ukraine.[2] The past plays a significant impact upon Ukraine, with powerful negative memories (such as what is termed the Great Famine that was brought about by the collectivization of farmland resulting in the deaths of millions of Ukrainians). This also to some extent ensures that antagonisms remain in Ukraine's relations with her neighbours, Russia in particular. A flow on effect is created, resulting in a freeze on various sensitive issues affecting these nations, such as border delimitation for example. A factor that has an impact upon politics in Ukraine is the presence of a reasonably large ethnic Russian minority.

This work shall look at issues that affect Security Sector Reform in Ukraine during the present day. As explained the past has a significant impact upon how events in the present are perceived and managed. The first thing that is needed is

---

1   Dawisha, K. and Parrott, B. (eds) *The Consolidation of Democracy in East-Central Europe*. Cambridge: Cambridge University Press, 1997, p. 12.

2   Butkevych, V.G., 'Who Has a Right to Crimea', http://infoukes.com/history/crimea/page-12.html, 1997.

the clarification of the term Security Sector Reform, and what it means for society. Who are the key stakeholders and actors in the process? External actors must be aware and take into account, the at times, complex and seemingly contradictory currents at play in a country, especially a complex history and social dynamics such as Ukraine's. The politics of today are often a reflection or reaction to an event in the past. An example of this is the strong Ukrainianization theme of the Orange Coalition. Thus an external actor could get unwittingly embroiled in an ethnic conflict should they be seen to be taking the side of a particular group in a forming conflict.

The next question to be tackled is the problem of boundaries and nationalities in Ukraine, but rooted in a historical setting, which is necessary to give meaning to the present day situation. The impact of the Soviet Union upon a number of contemporary problems is assessed. A number of issues are raised within this category including; ethnic mobilization and the tense situation with the Autonomous Republic of Crimea. One of the rising issues is that of ethnic mobilization, especially in Crimea and potentially in eastern parts of Ukraine, where other ethnic groups (than Ukrainians) tend to dominate.

Focus then shifts to the issue of national borders; those who guard them, the problems associated with the protection of borders, and problems and events on the setting of state borders. The section begins with a description of the meaning of borders, which is important insofar as it makes some of the problems in border delineation more understandable. A comprehensive description on the characteristics of the Ukrainian state border is also given. Then State Border Guard Service of Ukraine, their size, functions and problems are given.

The problem of Russian military presence and the NATO question are raised. Both of these questions are extremely divisive in Ukrainian society. At times the differences begin to surface in a most public manner, such as the differences on NATO entry as stated by the President and the Prime Minister. A number of protests occurred in Crimea in 2006, which links this section to previous material raised on the issue of ethnic mobilization, forcing the Ukrainian authorities, on this occasion, to back down. Russian military presence in the area is another thorny issue, and for some, perhaps a reminder of the years of the Soviet Union.

In the last section of this paper, the issue of political stability, on the national level, is raised. Political instability in contemporary Ukraine threatens to cause a number of problems, potentially in the worst case scenario the possibility of open political violence and the issue of territorial integrity is raised. There appeared to be little prospect of resolving the political tension as no one side is able to gain a significant advantage over the other and little prospect for compromise or reconciliation exists. However, the rise to power of Viktor Yanukovich in the 2010 presidential elections, in spite of much criticism, may potentially offer some opportunities.

Defining Security Sector Reform

As an initial step in this chapter, it is necessary to clarify some theoretical understandings and definitions in order to make sense of some of the following empirical material. One of these steps is to define the term Security Sector Reform; who are the actors involved, what are their overall goals? When this is defined, it shall provide a theoretical framework on which to hang a varied mass of empirical material from the contemporary situation in the Republic of Ukraine.

The United Nations Security Council defines a broad collection of actors involved in the Security Sector Reform process:

- *Core security actors* – Armed forces; police; gendarmeries; paramilitary forces; presidential guards, intelligence and security services (both military and civilian); coast guards; border guards; customs authorities; reserve or local security units (civil defence forces, national guards, militias);
- *Security management and oversight bodies* – The Executive; national security advisory bodies; legislature and legislative select committees; ministries of defence, internal affairs, foreign affairs; customary and traditional authorities; financial management bodies (finance ministries, budget offices, financial audit and planning units); and civil society organizations (civil review boards and public complaints commissions);
- *Justice and law enforcement institutions* – Judiciary; justice ministries; prisons; criminal investigation and prosecution services; human rights commissions and ombudsmen; customary and traditional justice systems;
- *Non-statutory security forces* – Liberation armies; guerrilla armies; private body-guard units; private security companies; political party militias.[3]

This represents a broad range of actors involved in the process of Security Sector Reform. For the purposes of this particular work though, interest and consideration shall be given to the government (President and government), border guards and minority groups living in Ukraine that exert an impact upon the political landscape. There are other actors in existence too, such as the Ukrainian National Security and Defence Council, the SBU (former KGB) and the Ministries of Interior and Defence. In the last regard, the Tartar peoples of Crimea and ethnic Russians are of the greatest interest due to a certain level of political mobilization.

These different actors that have a stake in the SSR process in Ukraine have diverse aims and demands. President Viktor Yushchenko for instance has announced a positive attitude towards NATO and the EU. Viktor Yanukovich, then the Prime Minister on the other hand has altered his originally negative view (during the Orange Revolution) to a more cautious and 'let us not be too hasty' approach to these organizations. Yanukovich still wants to retain some ties with Russia, for a

---

3   'Update Report on Security Sector Reform 14 February 2007', UN Security Council, www.securitycouncilreport.org, 12 August 2007.

number of reasons, such as historical and economic. Joining NATO may very well endanger Ukraine's ability to foster close relations with Russia. There are also a number of ethnically based NGOs in existence, especially in Crimea. The Russian NGOs tend to take a negative stance on closer relations with NATO, as evidenced by protests during joint exercises with NATO.

Security Sector Reform has a number of important considerations to take into account to be truly effective and have an impact upon society. The primary consideration and end goal of Security Sector Reform being the physical security of a population through a number of reforms and measures designed to enhance their protection and welfare.

> Security Sector Reform must account for the overall security context and address the fundamentals as well as the specifics. Effective management, transparency and accountability of the security sector is just as necessary as with any other part of the public sector.[4]

To sum up this section, Security Sector Reform is about providing a physical and psychological security to the population of a state. One of the constituent parts in the process is the process of nation-building, which is about the process of bringing about the physical and psychological conditions in the formation of a state. Some of the acts are symbolic, such as a common currency, language, armed forces and state symbols (national anthem, national parliament) as well as more practical (but at the same time symbolic) aspects such as the creation of state borders. These all represent the trappings of a modern and independent state. This is important for Ukraine, which ceased to exist as an independent state for some 300 years.

EU and NATO in Ukraine

Ukrainian political elite, depending on their particular orientation (such as those of the Orange Coalition), tend to support the idea of joining EU and NATO. Both of these organizations have been engaged in the country for some years now, in a number of capacities. This section is intended to give a very brief insight into some of the projects that have, and are taking place.

NATO in Ukraine

In the wake of independence, Ukraine joined the North Atlantic Cooperation Council (renamed Euro-Atlantic Partnership Council) in 1991. Then in 1994 Ukraine joined the Partnership for Peace (PfP) programme, and was the first

---

4   Roth, C. (ed.) *Understanding and Supporting Security Sector Reform.* London: Department for International Development, 1997, p. 7.

Commonwealth of Independent States to do so.[5] On 9 July 1997 the NATO-Ukraine Charter of cooperation was formalized. In practical terms, this cooperation is especially geared towards the reform of the defence and security area. Issues such as the restructuring and management of personnel and equipment from the old Soviet system to one that is compatible with NATO standards. There has also been active participation from the Ukrainian side in this issue too, such as the opening of Ukrainian airspace and the use of Ukrainian military transport for the NATO operation in Afghanistan. Ukraine has also supplied troops for peace keeping operations, such as those attached to the Polish-Ukrainian brigade in Kosovo.[6]

As part of the NATO membership requirements, Ukraine needs to prove sufficient reform and meeting targets in the spheres of: internal political issues; foreign and security policy; defence and security sector reform; public information; economic and legal reform; and information security.[7] Ukraine has been slowly building up the level of cooperation with NATO over a number of years and there appears to be a good level of communication on a national political level.

The road to joining NATO is very long and complicated. At first, the arguments for joining NATO shall be presented, then the counter arguments will be given. In December 2006 President Yushchenko stated 'our strategic aim is membership' but he added, in response to the claim that there was low support, 'people don't support the idea because they know nothing about NATO and its goals. People still have in mind the terrible myths of the 1950s (when NATO was created as a defensive bloc against the Soviet Union)'. In order to prepare and persuade the public to be more receptive to the idea of joining NATO an 'awareness' campaign has been mooted by the President. 'We will start a special programme aimed to inform society about what NATO is, its history and activities next year. Ukraine is part of Europe. We have a lot of common interests and values. Thus, we must have a common system of protection.'[8] A plan of action between Ukraine and NATO appeared in 2003, but for some reason the government did not make it

---

5   'NATO-Ukraine Relations', Topics: North Atlantic Treaty Organisation, NATO, www.nato.int/issues/nato-ukraine/index.html, updated 19 September 2007, accessed 28 September 2007.

6   'Meeting of the NATO-Ukraine Commission in Defence Ministers' Session', Statement, NATO, www.nato.int/docu/pr/2002/p02-075e.htm, 7 June 2002, accessed 28 September 2007.

7   Orlova, D., 'Kyiv Committed to NATO Bid', *Kyiv Post*, www.kyivpost.com/nation/29072, 5 June 2008.

8   'Ukrainian President Vows to Continue Push for EU, NATO Entry', Official Website of President of Ukraine, http://ww7.president.gov.ua/en/news/data/print/12348.html, 6 December 2006, accessed 19 June 2007; 'Ukraine Unwavering About Joining NATO', *RBC News*, www.rbcnews.com/free/20070613162612.shtml, 13 June 2007. Yushchenko stated that he would like to see Ukraine enter NATO before the expiry of his term in office, which is in 2009.

known to the public for some two months.[9] This demonstrated that there was some reservation about the public's response to such a document and its implications by keeping it secret for two months.

In June 2007 the Ukrainian government approved a plan of cooperation with NATO for the year. It is the 5th cooperation plan that has existed between Ukraine and NATO. The plan pictures Ukrainian obligations in reforms of the security sector, which includes the civil control of security agencies and joint projects in the field of emergency prevention and management.[10] For the time being a solid cooperation is being built up between NATO and Ukraine, although the political landscape is such that it is far from a certainty that sufficient political will exists to implement full membership.

Yanukovich, disputes Ukraine's readiness to join NATO. His main argument is that sufficient public support for joining the alliance is lacking. He has suggested that Ukraine should 'take a pause' from the idea of rapid accession. Yanukovich added that 'the time will come when a decision will be made ... For the time being we are looking at enlargement of our cooperation with NATO'.[11] Yanukovich stated that support for NATO had dropped since the era of Kuchma. He gave the figure of 30 percent public support for when he was Prime Minister under Kuchma, but dropped to less than 20 percent under the Orange Coalition and explained that support had risen during his recent term as Premier. There have been accusations that the drop in support is a result of propaganda from the Party of Regions and their Communist allies, which has portrayed NATO as the external enemy and perpetuating the Soviet myth.[12] The *Kyiv Post* editorial would seem to hint at a gap between rhetoric and practice by the Party of Regions and their political allies, which on the one hand stress a willingness to join NATO, but on the other hand work actively to muster public opinion against it.

Russia has also proved to be very vocal on the prospects of Ukraine joining NATO. One Russian mass media outlet, *Moscow News*, went as far as to label Ukraine's plan to join the military alliance as tantamount to embarking on the path to a 'Small Cold War'.

> In the end, Russia will just stare in amazement at the Ukrainian Armed Forces pass under American control and Ukrainian politicians swear allegiance to NATO. And then questions will start to be asked: "Who lost Ukraine?" "Who allowed the enemy to come to our doorstep?" and finally, "Who betrayed the

---

9   'Ukraine-NATO Plan of Action Made Public', Ukrayinksa *Pravda*, www.pravda.com.ua/en/news_print/2003/1/22/2494.htm, 22 January 2003, accessed 19 June 2007.

10   Ukraine Government Approves Plan of Cooperation With NATO, *ITAR-TASS*, http://itar-tass.com, 6 June 2007.

11   'Ukraine "Not Ready" to Join NATO', *BBC News*, http://newsvote.bbc.co.uk, 14 September 2006.

12   'Play NATO Straight', Editorial, *Kyiv Post*, www.kyivpost.com/opinion/editorial/26790/, 19 June 2007.

Motherland?" Amid Russia's de facto encirclement by NATO, there will be a surge in anti-Western mood. The majority of Russian politicians, including the most reasonable and responsible, will be unable to resist such pressure, which will result in a sharp turn toward nationalism. But the West will firmly uphold its interests, responding harshly and cold-bloodedly to Russia's half-hearted and toothless threats. Thus a "small" Cold War will be revived. Ukraine's admission to NATO is a red line that will create a fundamentally new geopolitical situation for Russia.[13]

The author of this article is putting into words a number of Russian perceptions of what NATO represents. Interesting the idea of encirclement of Russia by NATO and the sense of betrayal should Ukraine join the alliance. It also is predicting a number of dire consequences in terms of social development in Russia, but at the same time accusing Russia of only being capable of rhetoric and nothing in terms of concrete practical steps at countering NATO's expansion. In every sense, Ukraine is considered to be 'lost' should it gain membership.

One of the criticisms is that the NATO reforms, although they have been somewhat successful in the armed forces, little else has changed. This relates to other security apparatus, the SBU and Interior Ministry for instance. Both of these institutions have changed very little from the Soviet times and remain non-transparent and non-trusted organizations. An additional problem is a lack of experience and expertise among law makers in the Verkhovna Rada in military and security matters, thus leaving the military circles in effective control of the reform process.[14]

Joining NATO is a major political priority of the former Orange Coalition partners and winners of the Orange Revolution. In a visit to Poland in March 2008, the President of Ukraine Viktor Yushchenko characterized the accession to NATO as being a sovereign right of Ukraine. He also outlined the motivation and reasoning behind the desire. 'For us an accession to NATO is not a matter of choice, but just a matter of time. … I do not see prospects for security and sovereignty of Ukraine without NATO.'[15] Therefore the issue has become a highly symbolic issue in national politics in Ukraine, highlighting the political rift that exists.

The failure of Ukraine to receive an invitation to the Membership Action Plan (MAP) in the NATO summit in Bucharest in April 2008 was a setback, as much psychologically as it is physically. Vladimir Ogryzko, the Ukrainian Foreign

---

13   Markov, S., 'Ukraine's NATO Membership is Path to "Small" Cold War', *Moscow News*, www.mnweekly.ru/national/20070720/55262909-print.html, 20 July 2007.

14   'Security Sector Reform in Ukraine', Bonn International Centre for Conversion, www.bicc.de/ssr_gtz/pdf/ukraine.pdf, accessed 28 September 2007.

15   Accession to NATO Sovereign Right of Ukraine – Yushchenko, *ITAR-TASS*, http://itar-tass.com, 14 March 2008. Even the SBU website contains a document outlining NATO's advantages to Ukraine, to read, please see http://www.ssu.gov.ua/sbu/control/en/publish/article?art_id=83762&cat_id=83642.

Minister, in reference to the number of documents adopted and cooperation stated that 'in essence, the country has already received NATO's Membership Action Plan, although this has not been formalized.' Adding, 'the programme for informing the population about NATO remains on the list of priorities. ... We would rather cut down the number of business trips abroad but we will hold the programme with our teeth'.[16] It seems that the political will to see the task complete has not diminished in spite of the apparent obstacles.

In a rare example of consensus in contemporary Ukrainian politics, Yushchenko, Timoshenko and Yanukovich have all agreed that a nation-wide referendum on the question of accession to NATO MAP is necessary.[17] Yushchenko stated in April 2008 that Ukraine should hold such a referendum within two years.[18] Given the reluctance by NATO in 2008 to offer the MAP to Ukraine, combined with a majority of the local population against the idea of joining, it seems likely to remain a dream for some time to come.

In February 2010 with the confirmation of Yanukovich as President, one of the election pledges came to the forefront of political discussion. Yanukovich pledged to break with the Orange goal of NATO membership in late May 2010. Although at the same time, reaffirming continued (conditional) aspirations towards EU membership.[19] In spite of no longer having on the political agenda NATO membership, Yanukovich has expressed the desire to build cooperation.[20] One of the given motivations for this move is to strengthen Ukraine's neutrality, which prevents it from joining a military bloc.[21] One of Ukraine's declared acts of cooperation with NATO that has been mentioned is to join NATO's rapid reaction force by the end of 2010.[22] It seems that a more nuanced foreign policy is being pursued in order to try and balance Ukraine's various (at times conflicting) foreign policy interests.

---

16   'Ukraine to Hold on to Cooperation with NATO with its Teeth', *ITAR-TASS*, http://itar-tass.com, 25 December 2008.

17   'Ukraine will not join NATO without Referendum – PM Timoshenko', *RIA Novosti*, http://en.rian.ru, 19 January 2008; 'Ukraine Opposition Expects President to Call Referendum on NATO', *ITAR-TASS*, http://itar-tass.com, 28 January 2008; 'Party of Regions Demands Referendum on Ukraine's Accession to NATO MAP', *ITAR-TASS*, http://itar-tass.com, 17 June 2008.

18   'Ukraine May Hold Referendum on NATO in Two Years – Yushchenko', *ITAR-TASS*, http://itar-tass.com, 7 April 2008.

19   'Ukraine Turns Back on Idea of Integration with NATO', *ITAR-TASS*, http://itar-tass.com/NewsID=15185468.html, 1 June 2010.

20   'President: Our Country Not Ready to Join NATO, but We Must Develop Our Partnership', The Official Website of the President of Ukraine, http://www.president.gov.ua/en/news/17247.html, 27 May 2010.

21   Melnichuk, A., 'Parliament Cements Ukraine's Non-Aligned Status', *AP*, 3 June 2010 in Johnson's Russia List, 2010-#108, 3 June 2010.

22   'Ukraine to Join NATO Force this Year Despite New Leader', *RIA Novosti*, http://en.ria.ru/20100507/158907850.html, 7 May 2010.

EU in Ukraine

The European Union has also had a long involvement in Ukraine's development after independence. Since the early 1990s the TACIS programme for international assistance has been working at establishing democracy and a market economy. This is due to be superseded by the European Neighbourhood and Partnership Instrument. EU-Ukraine relations are guided by the Partnership and Cooperation Agreement, which was signed for a 10-year period in 1998 (renewable). There are two sub-committees on this agreement that are of relevance for this work: Sub-Committee on Customs and Cross-Border Cooperation and the Sub-Committee on Justice, Freedom and Security. The Sub-Committee on Customs and Cross-Border Cooperation looks at the issue of cross border cooperation and the provision of relevant technical assistance. It is the role of the Sub-Committee on Justice, Freedom and Security to deal with cooperation and providing assistance (technical, information sharing for instance) on numerous issues associated with border management (crime, terrorism, drug/human smuggling, etc), judicial reform, rule of law and good governance.[23]

Since 1999 the EU has injected 40.2 million Euro into the TACIS cross-border cooperation programme.[24] One of the border control missions that have been running, since 1992, is the European Union Border Assistance Mission. The goal is to monitor and control the situation on the Moldovan-Ukrainian border, which is some 955 km long (of which 470 km of this is controlled by the Transnistrian authorities.[25] This provides the border and customs services with both expertise (from personal contact with EU personnel) and an upgraded technical ability on effective and best practice in border control.

Present Structure of Division of Responsibilities in Border Control

A defined border is one of the signs of statehood. This is especially important as it defines Ukraine, a significant step in the process of state building and giving a definite shape and physical presence of the state. Given Ukraine's history of being absorbed into Russia and then the Soviet Union, there is a strong desire to enjoy all of the trappings of independence. This is not only a symbolic gesture designed to generate distance between Ukraine and the heritage of the Soviet Union, but very much a psychological development as well. The Centre for Peace, Conversion and

---

23   'The EU's Relations with Ukraine', The Institutional Framework, External Relations, http://ec.europa.eu/external_relations/ukraine/intro/index.htm, 27 September 2007.

24   'The EU's Relations with Ukraine', EU Technical Assistance, External Relations, http://ec.europa.eu/external_relations/ukraine/intro/index.htm, 27 September 2007.

25   'European Union Border Assistance Mission', United Nations Development Programme in Ukraine, www.undp.org.ua/?page=projects&projects=35, 27 September 2007.

Foreign Policy of Ukraine gives a good explanation of the significance of border for the nation.

> In the Soviet times, the state border was a symbol of the imperishability of the iron curtain, a guarantor of impermeability of the Soviet society. It served not so much as a means of protection against external threats, but as a barrier for Soviet citizens, whose free communication with the outer world undoubtedly undermined the bases of the regime. The system of state borders of Ukraine was in full measure affected by the Soviet heritage, however the nature of problems and tasks pertaining to their status is new in principle, as it reflects the attempts of our state to gain an appropriate place in the system of regional intercommunications. Without trying to cover all aspects, we consider the problem of borders through the prism of Ukraine's integration policy the problem of international communication and assessment of risks arising from the current, partially undetermined status of state borders.[26]

Ukraine has a border that measures some 6,994 kilometres long; 5,639 kilometres of land border (with Poland, Hungary, Belarus, Romania, Slovakia, Moldova and Russia) and 1,335 kilometres of maritime border.[27] The task of defending and supervising this significant border rests upon the State Border Guard Service of Ukraine. According to given objectives of the State Border Guard Service are being to maintain the 'inviolability of the state border and guarding Ukrainian sovereign rights in its exclusive economic zone'.[28] A number of borders remain as yet not ratified and agreed by Ukraine and some of her neighbours.

The State Border Guard Service is the successor organization of the Soviet Border Troops. As an organization it was first named Ukrainian Border Troops in 1991, which was later subordinated to Ukraine's State Committee for State Border Guarding. It got its present name in March 2003. At the present it is an independent organization that is subordinated to the President of Ukraine. However, during time of war the units come under the command of the Armed Forces of Ukraine.[29]

Ukraine's armed forces currently stand at 125,000 troops in army, 49,100 in the air force, and 13,500 in the navy. Paramilitary organizations in Ukraine include:

---

26 'Borders of Ukraine: An Unfinished Area of a Decade State Building', Centre for Peace, Conversion and Foreign Policy of Ukraine, http://cpcfpu.org.ua/en/projects/borders/papers/problems/document_1, 19 June 2007.

27 'General Characteristics of the State Border of Ukraine', State Border Guard Service of Ukraine, www.pvu.gov.ua/eng/zhdk.htm, 19 June 2007.

28 'Tasks of the State Border Guard Service', State Border Guard Service of Ukraine, www.pvu.gov.ua/eng/zhdk.htm, 19 June 2007. According to the government portal the length of the Ukrainian state border is equal to 7,200 kilometres. See www.kmu.gov.ua/control/en/publish/printable_article?art_id=82588854, 18 June 2007.

29 'State Border Guard Service of Ukraine', Wikipedia, http://en.wikipedia.org/wiki/State_Border_Guard_Service_of_Ukraine, 19 June 2007.

- Interior Ministry Troops – approx. 39,900;
- Border Guards – 45,000 including 14,000 Ukrainian Sea Guard;
- Civil Defence Troops (Ministry of Emergency Situations) – at least 9,500;[30]
- The Ukrainian military has, and still is undergoing drastic reforms. Prime Minister Yulia Timoshenko has promised to end conscription by 2011. This has been criticized by a number of people, including President Yushchenko.[31] A reduction in troop numbers continues as well, from some 700,000 during the Soviet period, down to 191,000 by the end of 2008, to 143,000 by 2011.[32]

One of the current priorities of the Ukrainian government is to strengthen its borders. Recently they adopted a 'Target Programme on Development and Reconstruction of the State Border' that is meant to be fully implemented by 2015 and costing 7 billion UAH. It envisages the construction of 262 new border checkpoints and the reconstruction of 123 existing or old ones. Within the framework of near boundary cooperation with Russia, 144 local border crossings are expected to be opened. Support from the EU and the US government in the programme will be forthcoming, according to the Deputy Head of the State Border Guard Service, Pavlo Shysholin.[33]

The goal of the State Border Guard Service, to become an EU-standard law enforcement body by 2015 is an ambitious one, requiring considerable foreign technical and financial help. Slovakia, Hungary and Poland's entry into the Schengen Zone in December 2007 makes the successful completion of this goal an important one for the EU too. Different governments and organizations are funding some 20 different programmes to the tune of US$28 million. The European Commission is sponsoring some seven programmes at a cost of US$13 million, the US government is sponsoring a further seven programmes for US$15 million, an additional three programmes shall be sponsored by the United nations and the Organization for Security and Cooperation in Europe (OSCE) for US$100,000.[34] Strengthening the Eastern border of the EU is in the interests of both the EU and Ukraine, therefore an SSR programme, such as this, benefit both parties in the form of a more secure border.

---

30   'Military of Ukraine', Wikipedia, http://en.wikipedia.org/wiki/Armed_Forces_of_Ukraine, 19 June 2007.

31   Marone, J., 'Yulia's ARMY Reform Plan Under Fire', *Kyiv Post*, www.kyivpost.com/nation/27669, 24 October 2007.

32   'Verkhovna Rada Reduces Size of Ukrainian Armed Forces', *ITAR-TASS*, http://itar-tass.com, 12 February 2008; 'Ukraine to Downsize Armed Forces in 2008', *RIA Novosti*, http://en.rian.ru, 12 February 2008.

33   'Ukraine to Strengthen its Border', www.kmu.gov.ua/control/en/publish/printable_article?art_id=82588854, 15 June 2007.

34   Pastukhova, A., 'Border Service Adopting EU Standards with Western Funding', *Kyiv Post*, www.kyivpost.com, 27 March 2008.

A senior project specialist with the International Organization for Immigration based in Ukraine, Yuriy Bystro, characterizes the Ukrainian State Border Guard Service as still using Soviet-era standards. Oleksander Panchenko, the head of the International Technical Aid Department of the State Border Guard Service qualified how the EU could help develop border protection, and more specifically the most relevant members of the EU. 'The Hungarian and Polish Border Guards had the same system, mentally and the standards as the Ukrainians do now. ... Their EU transition experience is more valuable to Ukraine than those countries which previously made up the EU.'[35] In this regard, the EU is presented with a unique and powerful hand to play, the experience of its 'new' member states and former Eastern Bloc countries that can assist countries bordering the EU and struggling to cope with a number of changes in the SSR sphere.

One of the problems for Ukrainian entry to NATO is the lack of domestic consensus on the issue. Even the more optimistic polls have a majority of respondents against joining NATO. The Democratic Initiatives Foundation in Ukraine conducted a poll from 5-18 December 2007 among 1800 people. If a referendum was conducted on the issue of joining 53 percent said that they would vote against, and 32 percent for NATO membership. Further, 52 percent of respondents thought that NATO was 'an aggressive imperialistic bloc that would draw Ukraine into military conflicts.'[36] These results have not cooled off Yushchenko's aspirations though, in June 2008 he expressed the wish to convince Ukrainians to join NATO within one year.[37]

To try and resolve the issue, an information campaign has been instituted as a means to boost the profile and popularity of NATO in Ukraine. In November 2008 it was announced that the Ukrainian government was going to conduct a nationwide quiz on NATO via SMS (15 questions on the organization's history and modern global role).[38] The use of an SMS quiz implies that the authorities may be seeking to reach out to and influence a young target audience, i.e. not of the Soviet generation.

Ukraine has been positioning itself closer to the European sphere, one of the rhetorical clues to this came from Anatoliy Zlenko the then Minister of Foreign Affairs (in 2002). In relation to the strengthening of borders, he stated that; 'Ukraine lays claims a place in the united Europe, the place of an Eastern outpost that would simultaneously stabilize and protect Europe.' Zlenko went on to say, in order to make his point, that reception points 'are overfilled with thousands

---

35   Pastukhova, A., 'Border Service Adopting EU Standards with Western Funding', *Kyiv Post*, www.kyivpost.com, 27 March 2008.

36   'Over Half of Ukrainians Against Joining NATO – Survey', *RIA Novosti*, http://en.rian.ru, 24 January 2008.

37   'Yushchenko Hopes to Push NATO Membership Idea Within One Year', *Interfax*, www.interfax.com/3/404345/news.aspx, 19 June 2008.

38   'Ukraine's Government to Conduct Nationwide NATO Quizz via SMS', *RIA Novosti*, http://en.rian.ru, 24 November 2008.

of illegal migrants from Asia and Africa, who are sent home at the cost of the scanty Ukrainian budget'.[39] The implication in Zlenko's statement is that Europe's eastern border goes as far as Ukraine, which serves as a kind of bastion against the problem of illegal migration to Europe. In this manner he tries to emphasize the significance and importance of the Ukrainian borders for the well being of Europe.

Zlenko's statement does still hold significance in terms of the number of illegal migrants and asylum seekers entering the country. The number of foreigners residing legally in Ukraine grew from 108,501 in 2003 to 195,011 in 2006. Russians make up 45 percent, people from the Caucasus, Moldovans and Chinese each accounted for 4 percent, Indian and Iranian expatriates make up 2 percent of the number. In 2003, 916 persons sought asylum in Ukraine, by 2006 (the first nine months only) some 2,101 had sought asylum. Of that figure from 2006, 473 were from India, 359 from Pakistan, followed by Iraq, Palestine and Nigeria. The number of illegal migrants has dropped significantly though, from 17,390 in 2003 to 8,264 in the first nine months of 2006.[40] This potentially represents a problem for the EU as Ukraine is now on the border of the EU, with the entry of Poland, Hungary, Slovakia and Romania. A porous border could allow the entry of some illegal migrants, a significant security concern within the context of the so-called Global War on Terrorism.

A number of contemporary articles appearing in the mass media further highlight the relevance of this sizeable border, which touches or is in close proximity to some of the problem areas affecting Europe. For example one of the border areas of concern is the border with Trans-Dniester. In a BBC article, it stated that there are some 13 enterprises in the region producing arms. According to the article; 'Guns from there have turned up in conflicts around the world. The border with Ukraine is porous, and it is easy for smugglers to traffic goods or arms to the Black Sea port of Odessa, and from there to the rest of the world.'[41] This is but one example, which demonstrates the necessity of a wider interest in Ukraine's ability to define and secure her borders.

There are a number of problems in coming to a resolution in setting the Russian-Ukrainian border, which has been a drawn out and complex process. Often the demarcation of the state border is tied to other problems in relations between the two states, and has at times, been very tense. The Tuzla Dam crisis is a good example of the tensions that exist between the two neighbours, and how quickly this tension can come to the surface under certain circumstances. Tuzla Island, which is located 5.5 kilometres from the Russian mainland in the Sea of

---

39   'Ukraine Seeks to be Europe's "Eastern Outpost"', *Ukrayinska Pravda*, www. pravda.com.ua, 1 November 2002.

40   Aksyonova, M., 'Minorities Feel the Pinch of Racism', Nation, *Kyiv Post*, www. kyivpost.com/nation/27008, 25 July 2007.

41   Reeve, S., 'Trans Border Trans-Dniester', *BBC News*, http://newsvote.bbc.co.uk, 10 May 2005.

Azov, was until 1925 connected to the Russian mainland until a storm severed the connection. The strategic positioning of Tuzla means that the country that controls it, effectively controls a shipping passage in the strait running from the Sea of Azov to Turkey and the Mediterranean Sea. Russia started construction of a dam in the vicinity (on 29 September 2003), and a causeway stretched to within 100 metres of Tuzla. The situation and tension were complicated by the fact that there has been no demarcation of borders in the Strait. On the one hand, Ukraine accused Russia of trying to annex Tuzla by extending the causeway towards. And on the other hand, Russia denied any territorial ambitions in the area, stating that they were only trying to halt coastal degradation of their territory.[42]

Ukraine tended to use the international community as a means of legitimizing their stance on the Tuzla incident. This was especially evident in articles appearing in *Ukrayinska Pravda*. Head of the European Parliament, Jan Wiersma stated that:

> What happens now around Tuzla, probably, originates from the times of the Soviet Union, Khrushchev era, when Crimea and the nearby territories became part of Ukraine, a fact that a lot of Russians can not agree with. But Crimea and the island of Tuzla is a part of Ukraine, and the borders of Ukraine have been recognized by all international community, including the OSCE.[43]

In another article the Ukrainian Foreign Minister, Kostiantyn Hryschenko, told a special Rada commission on the Tuzla incident of foreign support for Ukraine. The main message from him was that foreign states supported Ukraine on the issue, but did not want to interfere in the issue, preferring to leave the matter to be resolved bilaterally.[44] Such expressed support for the Ukrainian position by the international community seemed to boost their resolve on the issue, giving a clear message of support and legitimacy to Ukraine's authorities.

The conflict developed in such a way that there were prospects of an armed conflict developing between the neighbours. Borys Andresiuk, Deputy Chairman of Ukraine's Verkhovna Rada Committee for National Security and Defence, even speculated that there was potential for the incident to grow into a military conflict.[45] There were a number of debates in the Rada, which saw the Russian move as a violation of Ukraine's sovereignty, and at times voted on such symbolic acts of

---

42   'Russia-Ukraine Talks Over Border', http://newsvote.bbc.co.uk, 30 October 2003.

43   'Wiersma: Ukrainian Borders Recognised by International Community', *Ukrayinska Pravda*, 15 October 2003, accessed 19 June 2007.

44   'International Community Supports Ukraine in Kerch Feud, Says Foreign Minister', *Ukrayinska Pravda*, www.pravda.com.ua, 28 October 2003.

45   'MP Fears Tuzla Raw May Grow into Full-Fledged Conflict', *Ukrayinska Pravda*, www.pravda.com.ua, 14 October 2003.

public condemnation.[46] A major problem in the delimitation of the Russia-Ukraine border seems to be an interpretation of the meaning and significance of carrying out the act. For the Ukrainian side it is a matter of formalizing territorial integrity and sovereignty. The Russian view would appear to be associated with seeing the act as erecting a fence between the neighbours, a non-porous and 'artificial' construct that will block free movement. Perhaps relating back to the Soviet times, when a border was viewed as being such an obstacle in order to preserve the existing political and social order.

Tension on the issue of the Russian-Ukrainian border issue was increased in late 2008 with the beginning of provocative political rhetoric on the issue and the symbolization of the problem by the parties. Russia and Ukraine share a common border of 2,295 km (1,974 km land border and 321 km sea border). In late 2008 Russia halted the demarcation process, which prompted a response from the Ukrainian counterparts. The Director of the First Territorial Department at the Ukrainian Foreign Ministry, Leonid Osavolyuk, stated that: 'we will therefore have to take measures concerning the demarcation of our border with Russia ... I do not rule out a unilateral demarcation.'[47] This same threat was re-iterated three months later by Osavolyuk. 'There is no progress. ... The hopes for joint demarcation of the Ukrainian-Russian border are fading.'[48]

In February 2009, further threats were made by the Ukrainian side. The Ukrainian Deputy Foreign Minister, Oleksandr Kupchyshyn was quoted by the UNIAN (Ukrainian) news agency as saying: 'If we fail to agree with Russia [on maritime border demarcation] at a bilateral level, we could apply the international law of the sea.' The move effectively uses the UN international court in order to resolve the dispute. The current maritime border, Ukraine argues, should match the administrative border that existed between the Ukrainian and Russian Soviet Socialist Republics. Russia argues that no such borders existed during the Soviet times, which regulated inland water areas.[49] The politicization of this particular issue makes it a potentially 'hot' topic for some time to come. Ukraine and Russia's lack of progress on the demarcation issue over the last 17 years may imply to need for a neutral intermediary in the process, in order to see some progress.

With the election of Yanukovich to the Ukrainian presidency in early 2010 there seems to have been a shift and some movement on the question of the border's demarcation. President Medvedev of Russia and President Yanukovich of Ukraine signed the demarcation of the Russian-Ukrainian border in May 2010

---

46   'Rada Calls Duma Not to Allow Violation of Ukraine's Sovereignty', *Ukrayinska Pravda*, www.pravda.com.ua, 14 October 2003.

47   'Ukraine Threatens Russia With Unilateral Land Border Demarcation', *Interfax* (Kiev), 24 October 2008. JRL 2008-#197, 29 October 2008.

48   'Ukraine May Demarcate Land Border with Russia Unilaterally – Diplomat', *Interfax* (Kiev), www.interfax.com/3/466771/news.aspx, 27 January 2009.

49   'Ukraine May Refer Maritime Border Row with Russia to UN Court', *RIA Novosti*, http://en.rian.ru, 4 February 2009.

(the agreement on Ukrainian-Russian border infrastructure was signed in 2003).[50] The improving relations with Russia, in this particular case, seem to be paying some dividends.

Questions of Boundaries and Nationalities
During the Soviet and Post-Soviet Era

Ukraine was subjected to harsh repressive measures during the Soviet times, especially during Stalin's time, when efforts were made to eradicate any emerging forms of Ukrainianization. In the period 1 January 1935 until 22 June 1941, it is estimated that there were some 19,840,000 in total were arrested (of which seven million were shot and many of the others perishing in Gulags, two million were shot in the Stalinist Purges and a further five million perished in what is known as the Great Famine).[51] The legacy of such a brutal regime of repression carries with it a significant influence today. The brutal repression in Ukraine was part of *The Kulak Operation* Order #00447, which was signed on 30 July 1937. Aleksandr Uspensky, the Ukrainian People's Commissar of the Interior stated that 'all Ukrainian Poles and Germans were engaged in spying and subversion and that 75-80 percent of Ukrainians were *bourgeois nationalists*'.[52] This would imply an ethnic dimension to the Great Terror existed in Ukraine, as it did in many other parts of the Soviet Union too.

In the wake of the August 1991 coup, which sought to topple the Gorbachev administration by a group of conservative communists, the break-up of the Soviet Union soon began to follow. In December 1991 a referendum was held in the Ukrainian SFSR on independence from the Soviet Union. Of those who voted, 90 percent voted for independence. Although the figure in the Crimean region, where ethnic Russians constitute a majority of the population, 54 percent voted for independence.[53] Even the more Russified parts of Ukraine, situated in the east, some 80 percent still cast a vote to cede from the Soviet Union.[54]

---

50 'President: Border Demarcation Agreement was our Joint Political Decision', Official Website of the President of Ukraine, www.president.ua/en/news/17173.html, 17 May 2010.

51 Bilinsky, Y., 'Basic Factors in Foreign Policy of Ukraine: The Impact of the Soviet Experience' in Starr (ed.) *The Legacy of History in Russia and the New Independent States of Eurasia*. New York: M.E. Sharpe, 1994, pp. 171-191, p. 178.

52 Bordyugov, G., 'The Ethnic Dimension of the Great Terror', *RIA Novosti*, analysis, http://en.rian.ru, 6 August 2007.

53 Plokhy, S., 'Historical Debates and Territorial Claims: Cossack Mythology in the Russian-Ukrainian Border Dispute' in Starr (ed.) *The Legacy of History in Russia and the New Independent States of Eurasia*. New York: M.E. Sharpe, 1994, pp. 147-70, p. 148.

54 Casanova, J., 'Ethno-Linguistic and Religious Pluralism and Democratic Construction in Ukraine' in Rubin and Snyder (eds) *Post-Soviet Political Order: Conflict and State Building*. London: Routledge, 1998, pp. 81-103, p. 83.

According to a 1989 census the ethnic population of Ukraine at the time, consisted of; 75 percent were Ukrainian, some 21 percent (11 million people) Russian, 500,000 Jews, 440,000 Belarusians, 234,000 Bulgarians, 219,000 Poles, 163,000 Hungarians, 135,000 Romanians and others of the population consisting of over 37 million.[55] Thus potentially, there seems to be a possibility for ethnic mobilization on certain issues, especially by the ethnic Russian segment of the population. The next census, after the Soviet one, took place on 5 December 2001. According to the data, Ukraine's population stood at approximately 48.5 million, of which 77.8 percent (37.5 million people) were ethnic Ukrainians and 17.3 percent (8.3 million) were ethnic Russians.[56] This shows a significant drop in the ethnic Russian segment of the Ukrainian population between 1989 and 2001.

Ethnic Russians in Ukraine

The ethnic Russian population in Ukraine has been the cause for some concern, as a potential to rally them for political purposes. However, as demonstrated by the vote for independence in 1991, there seems to be little cohesion amongst this group that are predominantly found in Eastern Ukraine and Crimea. It has been argued that by some that there are a number of reasons that have helped to drain the potential for rebellion.

> Russian speaking regions of Ukraine do not possess a uniform identity conducive to ethnic mobilisation. Rather, linguistic, ethnic, and religious identities overlap unevenly, creating cross-cutting cleavages and a basis for pluralism. These regions have also retained important powers over their economic assets and are able to pursue relations with regions of Russia, especially on economic matters, without raising directly the question of the ethno-nationalist content of state power.[57]

There has been some divergence from the assumption that national groups in Ukraine do not have the power or the will for ethnic mobilization. Different versions of whether ethnic mobilization can be achieved or not appear in the press, most clearly seen between the Ukrainian and Russian press. An article appeared in *RIA Novosti* (Russian state news agency) during the summer of 2006, which warned of a potential territorial split because of a divergence between national politics (of the Orange Coalition) and a significant proportion of eastern Ukraine.

---

55   Casanova, J., 'Ethno-Linguistic and Religious Pluralism and Democratic Construction in Ukraine' in Rubin and Snyder (eds) *Post-Soviet Political Order: Conflict and State Building*. London: Routledge, 1998, pp. 81-103, p. 88.

56   'Demographic Setting', Ministry of Foreign Affairs of Ukraine, www.mfa.gov. ua/mfa/en/publication/content/378.htm, 19 June 2007.

57   Rubin, B.R. and Snyder, J. (eds) *Post-Soviet Political Order: Conflict and State Building*. London: Routledge, 1998, p. 170.

About one-third of Ukraine's population considers Russian its native tongue, but the figure is about 85% in the Crimea, more than 60% in the Lugansk and Donetsk regions, and about 50% in the Kharkov, Zaporozhye, and Odessa regions. The south-eastern regions are strongly critical of the Euro-Atlantic bent in Ukraine's policy, and are keen on promoting close, friendly relations with Russia.[58]

Here the author makes her case for the Russian minority, based upon the premise of a number of areas in Ukraine where they constitute a local majority. Also evident is the criticism aimed at the pro-Western stance of the Orange government, namely the Euro-Atlantic and not a Russian leaning in the new international relations priorities. The article even goes as far as to call for Russian intervention in creating more 'ideal' circumstances to bring about the situation where the Orange government takes into account the views of the eastern parts of the country.

> Geopolitically, Russia should create a situation where the pro-Western Ukrainian government would have to take into account the interests of the eastern parts of the country. As of now, the "Orange" authorities only represent the views of the western Lvov, Ternopol and Ivano-Frankovsk regions and are completely out of touch with the eastern regions.

> But this situation would not benefit Moscow. When Putin spoke about strengthening of Ukraine's territorial integrity, he referred to the risks of the growing ideological divide, which would have unpredictable consequences for Ukrainian unity.[59]

The message of the article is that the pro-Western policy which the Orange coalition is 'forcing' upon the country has the effect of alienating a sizeable proportion of the country. And in doing this, the possibility of territorial division is raised. This could fit with the motivating factors for ethnic mobilization, which did not exist in the 1990s.

However, there usually exists a second side to a story, which in this case will be from the Ukrainian perspective. One such commentary appeared in the newspaper *Kyiv Post* in August 2007. The story covered the issue of ethnic relations in Ukraine and the memory of the Soviet years. It opens with the quote; 'If you want to defeat an enemy, then bring up his children', and vividly describes the Soviet epoch as a 'kind of civil war for Ukraine.' Great effort goes in to detailing the rewriting of history, by the Soviet system. It adds though, like Nazi Germany there were those ordinary people that resisted the system. The author remains optimistic though, that Ukraine is pulling away from its Soviet past and creating its own identity.

---

58   Stanovaya, T., 'Russia Warns Ukraine of the Danger of Disintegration', *RIA Novosti*, http://en.rian.ru, 22 June 2006.

59   Ibid.

Everything that was Ukrainian in the system was rather incidental to it. But, thankfully, nobody calls Ukraine the Ukrainian SSR any more. This name is seen now as even more fictitious than other Soviet myths. It only exists in post-Soviet memory. There is only the former USSR, without much mention of Ukraine as a distinct part of it.

We must recognise the Ukrainian Soviet Socialist Republic as a false otherland, which replaced and served as a substitute for our true Motherland – an independent Ukraine. The half-true Soviet Ukraine is an absolute lie in fact. By rebuilding our consciousness, we can rebuild our nation.

Now, we have a Ukrainian state. Despite its Soviet era, which has not been fully digested by Ukrainian history, Ukraine will be an independent country free of its colonial past.[60]

In regard to the minorities' issue, the author states that they are as much a victim of the Soviet era as Ukraine as it was not free will that brought them there. The general tone of the article though is upbeat and optimistic about Ukraine being able to shake of the relics of the Soviet past and to forge a new and independent Ukrainian state that is free from foreign interference. There has been a tendency to frame history in a somewhat simplistic version of oppressor and victim.

Crimea – Historical Context

Crimea has been a prickly problem for Ukraine. In 1783 Catherine the Great annexed Crimea and it remained a part of Russia until 1954. Ethnic Russians constitute the bulk of the population, Ukrainians make up about 25 percent and Muslim Crimean Tartars form 12 percent.[61] February 1954 saw the removal of the Crimean Oblast from the Russian SFSR and given to the Ukrainian SFSR.[62] This was done on the grounds of Crimea's juxtaposition to Ukraine, and the economic and communications ties between the regions. Although, there was a great amount of emphasis on the aspect of brotherly bonds between the peoples of the Soviet

---

60   Kryvdyk, O., 'Ukraine's Soviet Schism Narrowing', *Kyiv Post*, Opinion/Op-ed, www.kyivpost.com, 9 August 2007.
61   'Regions and Territories: Crimea', *BBC News*, http://newsvote.bbc.co.uk, 7 March 2007.
62   The decision was taken (25 January 1954) and then adopted on 19 February 1954 in a session of the Presidium of the Central Committee of the Communist Party of the Soviet Union. Thirteen of the 27 members were present, which was not enough for a quorum. However, the decision was taken unanimously and the discussion lasted a mere 15 minutes: 'USSR's Nikita Khrushchev Gave Russia's Crimea Away to Ukraine in only 15 Minutes', *Pravda*, http://english.pravda.ru, 19 February 2009.

Union and this was intended to be a token of this notion.[63] This transfer of territory was to set the scene for conflict in the wake of the break up of the Soviet Union. There are a number of Russian politicians and military leaders who regard the area as ancient Russian territory and that the transfer was illegal as it breeched the constitution.

In July 1957, General Secretary of the Communist Party, Nikita Khrushchev announced that each country in the socialist sphere had its own special characteristics, unique customs, which were based upon historic and cultural differences, and national traditions.[64] There were still attempts to create and enforce the stereotype of the Soviet citizen (Homo Sovieticus), but here is acknowledged that all peoples are not identical and equal, by the leader of the Communist Party of the Soviet Union. During the process of the collapse of the Soviet Union, these differences were permitted to come to the surface as there was no authority existing that could effectively suppress these aspirations any more.

Identity and Nationality in the Crimea

The height of tension and conflict between the Crimean region and the Ukrainian authorities did not take long to materialize either. As early as February 1991, the Ukrainian authorities granted an autonomous status to Crimea within the framework of the Ukrainian SSR. This was escalated after the break-up of the Soviet Union and on 6 May 1992 when the Crimean parliament proclaimed independence (although remaining part of Ukraine). The move was met by a harsh response from Kiev, which implied that Ukraine would go to war in order to keep Crimea part of Ukraine. Since 1995-96 tensions have cooled down somewhat, but have not disappeared between the local authorities in Crimea and the central authorities in Kiev.[65] The tensions are not so far under the surface though, as recent events have shown it does not take much to trigger a mobilization of the ethnic Russian population living there.

Russian influence, i.e. the Russification process of Crimea, is still very strong and perpetuated in society. For instance only four out of 240 publications produced in Crimea is in Ukrainian language, a vast majority of publications being in Russian. It is also a strongly Orthodox area, where many profess to be of the Orthodox faith. The Church with the greatest influence is the Moscow Patriarchate branch of the Russian Orthodox Church (and not of the Kievan Patriarchy – independent of Moscow and based in Kiev). The school system is another indicator of the Russianness of the area, 570 of the regions 583 schools are Russian language

---

63   Sullivant, R.S., *Soviet Politics and the Ukraine 1917-57*. New York: Columbia University Press, 1962, p. 285. Crimea was given at the time of the Tricentenial celebrations of the unification of Ukraine and Russia.

64   Ibid., p. 304.

65   Kolsto, P., *Political Construction Sites: Nation-Building in Russia and the Post-Soviet States*. Boulder, CO: Westview Press, 2000, pp. 172-76.

schools. There is the situation that some of the schools are subordinate to the Russian Ministry of Defence.[66] These centres of cultural production are most able and likely to keep reproducing a Russian culture in Crimea, it is unlikely that under these circumstances that a Ukrainian identity can be instituted in an effective manner.

There are efforts to redress this issue on the Crimean peninsula. Under the former Ukrainian President Kuchma, one particular form of 'soft' Ukrainianization policy was implemented. This involved the use of funding selected schools and supplying them with superior teachers, equipment and teaching aids, which taught in the Ukrainian language. Therefore the learning of the Ukrainian language was linked with the quality of education offered by those schools in comparison with the Russian language schools. Since the Orange Revolution of 2004, there has been a more toughened stance on the issue of teaching Ukrainian, which has been characterized by some in Crimea as 'forced Ukrainianization'. This is being attempted at a bureaucratic level, through the use of decrees and legislation from Kiev.[67]

However, debate exists about whether there is in fact a situation of 'forced Ukrainianization' on the Crimean peninsula. One camp says yes, which is demonstrated by a June 2009 poll conducted by the Kiev-based Razumkov Centre, of residents in Crimea. Eighty-five point three percent of respondents believed that there was some kind of 'forced Ukrainianization' on the local population (of Crimea). This seems to be the view at the population level. Another view is held by bureaucrats, who hold a different view. Georgiy Kasianov, director of educational research at the International Renaissance Foundation states that it is only a myth perpetuated by populist politics.

> When they speak of forced Ukrainianization, they point to some decrees of the central government that were never implemented in Crimea, since the Kiev-based Ministry of Education has no direct jurisdiction over Crimean education. … As a rule, directives from Kiev on "Ukrainianization" were never fulfilled. … There is no real state policy directed from Kiev toward the Crimean educational sphere. It is mostly wishful thinking, decrees, and an endless stream of paper.[68]

Although Kasianov has a point with his argument, he does also miss a significant feature of this conflict, which is based upon perception and driven by emotional argumentation. Failure to recognize this aspect or to ignore it could prove to be problematic and not addressing the issues or concern to the Crimean public,

---

66   Shanghina, L., 'The Demographic Situation in Ukraine: Present State, Tendencies, and Predictions', The Ukrainian Centre for Economic and Political Studies named after Olexander Razumkov, www.uceps.org/eng/show/641/, 6 April 2004.

67   Pasechnik, K., 'Crimea: Talking Past Each Other', Transtions On-Line, www.tol.cz, 29 September 2009.

68   Ibid.

regardless of whether these concerns are real or not. They need to be treated as if they are real, even assuming that they are not, as there will be a lack of mutual understanding and communication on this divisive issue otherwise.

Crimean Tartar Question

The Crimean question is further complicated by the Tartar question. Crimea was occupied by the Nazis during the Second World War. Subsequently, Stalin accused the Tartars of collaborating with them. As a result they were deported en masse to Siberia in 1944 when Crimea was recaptured. A great number of those deported did not survive (as many as 40 percent died in the first couple of years of deportation). On 5 September 1967 the Soviet authorities announced a Decree that exonerated the Crimean Tartar of wrongdoing and opened the possibility of their return. In practical terms, a return was not possible until the late 1980s.[69] As the Soviet Union collapsed they were permitted to return, and approximately 250,000 did so. However they suffer from poor housing and high unemployment. The issue of the allocation of land to the Tartars is also another highly contentious issue. Tension and protests over land rights has been the result.[70] Of the 250,000 returnees, there are some 100,000 who have not qualified for Ukrainian citizenship. These people are demanding a special exemption to allow them to vote in parliamentary and local elections.[71] There were moves in mid-2004 by the Ukrainian Rada to address some of the issues. They passed a new bill that included other groups that were exiled (including Germans and Greeks) that would give identical rights of these people to Ukrainian citizens.[72]

A number of obstacles have held up the citizenship issue such as, some countries require a fee to relinquish an existing citizenship. Uzbekistan used to charge US$100 for this service. Economic conditions in Crimea make this difficult as monthly income can be as low as US$10 in some instances, and 64,000 of 136,000 Tartar adults are unemployed. In September 1998 a bilateral agreement was reached between Ukraine and Uzbekistan on the question. As a result some 80,000 Crimean Tartar from Uzbekistan were granted Ukrainian citizenship. The problem still remains with those Crimean Tartar from other CIS countries. There

---

69   Prytula, V., 'Crimean Tartars: The Past Still Haunts', Radio Free Europe Radio Liberty (Unrepresented Nations and Peoples Organisation), www.unpo.org/article. php?id=7125, 6 September 2007.

70   'Regions and Territories: Crimea', *BBC News*, http://newsvote.bbc.co.uk, 7 March 2007. For a comprehensive and concise account of Crimea, see Butkevych, 'Who Has a Right to Crimea', http://infoukes.com/history/crimea/page-12.html, 1997.

71   'Crimean Tartars Demonstrate in Ukraine', *BBC News*, http://news.bbc.co.uk/2/hi/europe/69280.stm, 24 March 1998.

72   Fawkes, H., 'Ukraine to Enforce Equal Rights for Tartars', *BBC News*, http://newsvote.bbc.co.uk, 25 June 2004. The rights relate to provision of land, housing and work. Additionally there would be a ban on discrimination in education, religion and culture.

are still some 90,000 Crimean Tartar who do not possess Ukrainian citizenship.[73] On the surface the problem of citizenship seems to be a bureaucratic one.

Currently, the number of Crimean Tartars living in Crimea is put at 300,000. In 1995 it was estimated that 400-600,000 Crimean Tartars would return. The actual figure of returnees is put at around 50-60,000. However, the Tartar segment of the population, with natural growth plus immigration is the fastest growing ethnic group. And in the next 15-20 years the demographic balance there can change significantly. An alarmist report has predicted a radicalization of the Tartar community. Scenarios have been created and range from a 'Ukrainian Switzerland' to a 'Ukrainian Kosovo' model. This is due to ethnic groups' reactions to what they see as the 'Ukrainianization' of society. It is a defensive reaction, which is aimed at protecting and preserving cultural uniqueness.[74]

From mid-April 2009 some 100-150 Crimean Tartars staged protests, including hunger-strikes outside the Cabinet of Ministers building in Kiev. The aim of the protest was to receive what they saw as being owed to them by law. This protest lasted for one month and 13 days, and was successful in the end, insofar as they got what they came for. The mobilization of the Tartar cause seems to be in the process of becoming much more organized, such as the creation of the civil society organization *Avdet* (Return).[75] Lobbying by the Tartars seems set to intensify in the near future, given some prospect of success coupled with a number of frustrations.

Although some progress is being made in Kiev, the land that is demanded is located in some of the most exclusive and expensive parts of the Black Sea coast. There has been very poor progress made with the local authorities, who are reluctant to hand back the land and appear more inclined to sell this land to businesses. The local authorities on the Crimean peninsula tend to be dominated by ethnic Russians. This situation has brought about an alliance of convenience and mutual interest between Tartars and Ukrainian right-wing political organizations.[76] The various existing political, economic and social problems, mixed with ethnic mobilization can prove to be a recipe for further escalating the current tensions. What took Khrushchev 15 minutes to do on the 25 January 1954 at the session of the Presidium of the Central Committee of the Communist Party of the Soviet Union is going to have consequences that shall continue for the foreseeable future.

---

73   'Crimean Tartar Issue and Recent Election Results', Policy Documentation Centre, No. 21/269, http://pdc.ceu.hu/archive/00001182/01/16.pdf, 27 May 2002.

74   Shanghina, L., 'The Demographic Situation in Ukraine: Present State, Tendencies, and Predictions', The Ukrainian Centre for Economic and Political Studies Named after Olexander Razumkov, www.uceps.org/eng/show/641/, 6 April 2004.

75   'Tartars Seeking Crimean Land', *Kyiv Post*, www.kyivpost.com/nation/42382, 28 May 2009; 'Crimean Tartars Continue Protest, Demand Land', Radio Free Europe Radio Liberty, www.refrl.org, 20 May 2009.

76   'Tartars Seeking Crimean Land', *Kyiv Post*, www.kyivpost.com/nation/42382, 28 May 2009; Judah, B., 'Tartars: Kiev's Anti-Russian Allies', ISN Security Watch, www.isn.ethz.ch, 24 July 2009.

Russian Military Presence and its Effect on Ukraine's Political Map

Background

A significant source of antagonism between a number of countries in the Commonwealth of Independent States and the Russian Federation is the presence of Russian military bases. In the context of Russian-Ukrainian relations, the stationing of the Russian Black Sea fleet in Crimea is a major point of contention between these nations. After the collapse of the Soviet Union, it did not take long before the question of Crimea became a major sticking point. As a number of high ranking Russian politicians and military leaders saw Crimea as historical Russian territory, with many references made to the defence of Sevastopol and the Crimean War of 1853-56.

In April 1992, Vice President Aleksandr Rutskoi made a visit to Crimea. During this visit he asserted that the Black Sea Fleet was and would always remain Russian. Commander of the Black Sea Fleet, Admiral Igor Kasatonov, who in an interview with the newspaper *Literaturnaya Rossiya* in December 1992 was quoted as saying that Russia in any form cannot be imagined without the Black Sea Fleet. And that a Ukrainian takeover of the fleet, its bases and the Black Sea would hurl Russia back three centuries, to times before Peter the Great.[77]

Significant pressure was brought to bear on Ukraine by Russia in an attempt to force a solution to various 'problems' that existed. The then Chairman of the Russian Duma's Committee on Foreign Affairs and International Economic Relations, Vladimir Lukin, in mid January 1992 formulated measures designed to pressure Ukraine. Lukin advocated the simultaneous use of economic and diplomatic pressure on Ukraine; immediately cutting Russian defence contracts with enterprises located in Ukraine, and at the same time exerting diplomatic pressure for the return of Crimea and the Black Sea Fleet.[78] According to one article Russia paid about US$98 million per year for the use of the base and the territory it occupies. To be put into perspective, the US was paying the Philippines some US$2 billion for use of the base at Subic Bay.[79] In recent years, the issue of NATO membership, Russian military facilities and minority issues have become a very tangled and messy interlocking web.

---

77   Plokhy, S., 'Historical Debates and Territorial Claims: Cossack Mythology in the Russian-Ukrainian Border Dispute' in Starr (ed.) *The Legacy of History in Russia and the New Independent States of Eurasia.* New York: M.E. Sharpe, 1994, pp. 147-70, p. 149.

78   Bilinsky, Y., 'Basic Factors in Foreign Policy of Ukraine: The Impact of the Soviet Experience' in Starr (ed.) *The Legacy of History in Russia and the New Independent States of Eurasia.* New York: M.E. Sharpe, 1994, pp. 171-91, pp. 171-2.

79   Losev, I., 'Rage Against Russia', *Ukrayinska Pravda*, www.pravda.com.ua/en/news_print/2005/7/23/650.htm, 10 July 2005.

Moving from the Russian Orbit

However, there has been a gradual move by a number of countries in the Commonwealth of Independent States that are seeking to create distance and independence from Russian influence in the old international structures in the region, and doing this by creating new ones. One such grouping is GUAM (Georgia Ukraine Azerbaijan Moldova). Although it has been stated publicly that GUAM is not an organization that is designed to be reducing Russian influence, it would appear to be just that. Created in 1997, the agenda of GUAM tackles a number of problems that exist in CIS countries' relations with Russia. The GUAM regional summit in June 2007 reveals the agenda of the organization and hints at a number of projects that would suggest moves at the reduction of Russia's ability to influence these countries.

The regional summit was convened in Baku and the agenda included: security, fight against terrorism, economic and humanitarian integration, and ensuring the security of transport corridors. In addition to the member states, The Polish and Lithuanian presidents and a number of other foreign officials were present. The Georgian Foreign Minister, Gela Bezhuashvili stated that 'we agreed to work allowing GUAM to involve their military and police contingent in peacekeeping operations'. And that Georgia 'seeks GUAM peacekeeping forces to be created as soon as possible'.[80] GUAM has stated that it wants to resolve the frozen conflicts in Georgia and Moldova (South Ossetia and Abkhazia in Georgia and Transdnestr in Moldova), which it accuses Russia of artificially provoking. They envisage doing this by replacing Russian troops in the region with GUAM troops.[81] There is a gradual move to remove a number of problematic issues that have existed between the GUAM states and Russia, which have existed since the fall of the Soviet Union.

Russian Black Sea Fleet

To put this situation into a context of Ukraine and problems with Russian military presence, a brief analysis of the situation on the Crimean Peninsula and the Russian Black Sea base is needed. The Black Sea Fleet is a shadow of its former days in the Soviet Union, in 1991 its strength was more than 800 vessels of all types and several hundred combat aircraft. That figure today ranges somewhere in the dozens. Its flagship, the cruiser *Moskva*, was built in 1983 but has not fired its main missiles in some 14 years. There have been no new ships joining the fleet in approximately 10 years. On May 28 1997 Russia and Ukraine signed the

---

80   'GUAM Seeks to Involve its Peacekeeping Contingent – Minister', *ITAR-TASS*, http://itar-tass.com, 18 June 2007; 'GUAM Summit to Open in Baku on Tuesday', *Interfax*, www.interfax.ru, 19 June 2007.

81   'GUAM Regional Group Rounds off its Largest Summit', *RIA Novosti*, http://en.rian.ru, 19 June 2007.

Big Treaty an agreement on the status of the fleet. It lacked legal agreements that regulated some basic issues on the Black Sea Fleet's existence, the result has been frequent disputes at court level. The judgements of which are frequently ignored by the Russian navy as it believes international treaties (such as this) should require a governmental commission. However, the government commissions that convene every six months rarely come to agreement either.[82] The lease of Ukrainian territory is set to expire in the year 2017.

As stated earlier the base is under lease, which Russia pay just under US$100 million. However, this money is not seen by Ukraine as it is deducted from Ukraine's energy debt to Russia. Two airbases and a ship re-supply facility are maintained on the Crimean Peninsula. Although there is a provision to extend the term of lease, Ukraine is insisting on a complete Russian withdrawal by this time.[83] Former Ukrainian Defence Minister and Deputy Minister for National Security, Oleksandr Kuzmuk, stated this point succinctly.

> Ten years have passed since the signing of the agreement. We should now know what has been done at Novorossiysk (construction of Russian naval base to replace loss of bases in Crimea), and what has been done in Sevastopol. We should know what decisions are being taken to prevent a situation, where in 2017 the day comes when not a single mariner, not a single vessel should remain, and all the infrastructure is handed over to Ukraine, but neither the Russian Black Sea Fleet, nor Russia are ready for this. 2017 is the last year of the Russian Black Sea Fleet stay in Ukraine, according to the agreement signed between Russia and Ukraine in 1997.[84]

This statement leaves no room for any alternative interpretation, Ukraine demands a full Russian withdrawal from Crimea by 2017. There have been a number of incidents that have had the effect of heightening tensions. It relates to the tensions and the use of courts in an attempt to affect the outcome of disputes. In January 2007 Ukrainian court bailiffs attempted to seize an installation belonging to the Black Sea Fleet. 'Igor Manikin, the chief court marshal of the Kherson Region arrived today at the Mars-75 radio navigation facility, located in the town of Genichesk. He attempted to forcibly take this installation from the Black Sea Fleet's control', read a statement from the fleet's press service. This was the second incident, the first taking place in June 2006 when Ukrainian bailiffs, together with

---

82   Safanov, V., 'A Sad Anniversary for the Black Sea Fleet', *RIA Novosti*, http://en.rian.ru, 28 May 2007.

83   'Ukraine Insists on Russian Naval Base Withdrawal by 2017', *RIA Novosti*, http://en.rian.ru, 30 May 2007.

84   'Ukrainian Security Official Wants Russian Report on Black Sea Fleet Removal Plan', *Interfax-Ukraine*, 12 June 2007. From Johnson's Russia List, 2007-#133, 13 June 2007.

Interior Ministry and other officials arrived at the building housing the Fleet's hydrographical service in Sevastopol in an attempt to gain control.[85]

Ukrainian youth have also been mobilized in the deadly game. A group of Ukrainian youth activists (called Student Brotherhood) tried to enter the Fleet Headquarters in Sevastopol. 'Today at 9:30 a.m. some 10 young people tried to violate the checkpoint border, but were not allowed to enter the Black Sea Fleet's guarded territory. The fleet command believes that this provocation aims at creating artificial tension around the fleet being based in Ukraine.'[86] Both sides are engaged in provoking the other in a series of political manoeuvres. The Russian business daily newspaper, *Kommersant*, predicted a possible dire turn of events. 'The lighthouse battle which began last week is threatening to develop into a new diplomatic conflict between Moscow and Kiev, which promises to be no less sharp than the recent gas crisis.'[87]

The period of April to May in 2010 saw a number of policy twists by the Yanukovich administration, which differed from the previous Yushchenko regime. It was announced that a 30 percent discount had been offered by Russia on the price of gas to Ukraine.[88] At the same time it was announced that the lease of the Russian Black Sea Fleet was being extended by 25 years, which means its continued presence until 2042.[89] At a joint press conference with Medvedev in Kiev, Yanukovich criticized what he characterized as being the politics of confrontation of the last five years, and the need for a new approach.

> Today, in every region of Ukraine understanding the understanding of stability became crucial, because stability is a factor of improving the economy and people's lives. We must be effective not only in domestic policy. ... Has ever politics of confrontation in international relations been effective? I do not know such a country that would defend its national interests through confrontation. Our policy will always be dominated by the principled stand in defending national interests. We will always adhere to this principle. It will be the basis.[90]

---

85   'Ukraine Attempts to Seize Russian Navy Navigation System', *RIA Novosti*, http://en.rian.ru, 23 January 2007.

86   'Russian Fleet Based in Ukraine Condemns Activists' "Provocation"', *RIA Novosti*, http://en.rian.ru, 28 June 2006.

87   'Press Storm Over Crimea Lighthouse', *BBC News*, http://newsvote.bbc.co.uk, 17 January 2006, accessed 19 June 2007.

88   'Ukraine's Ex-President Slams Naval Base Deal With Russia', *RIA Novosti*, http://en.rian.ru/world/20100422/158705079.html, 22 April 2010.

89   'Russian Black Sea Fleet to Stay in Ukraine', UPI, http://www.upi.com/Top_News/Special/2010/04/21/Russian-Black-Sea-fleet-to-stay-in-Ukraine/UPI-43751271881825/, 21 April 2010.

90   'President: Our Policy Will Always be Based on Protection of National Interests', Official Website of the President of Ukraine, www.president.gov.ua/en/news/17176.html, 17 May 2010.

Ukraine is a divided country and the various existing fractures, if aggravated, could potentially split the country. Hence there seems to be a move from the more ethnically oriented and driven politics of the Yushchenko administration to a seemingly more balanced approach that tries to take the conflicting interests into account.

Protesting NATO Presence

There has been evidence of mobilization of ethnic Russians in Crimea in order to try and disrupt Ukraine's relations with NATO. One such incident involved the Crimean parliament's attempt to ban NATO from its territory, in protest to a planned NATO exercise that was scheduled to run in 2006. In order to create a sense of legitimacy for their cause, the Crimean parliament stated that it had conducted an unofficial referendum on possible membership to the alliance. According to figures given, 58.2 percent of the eligible voters (897,000 people) took part and 98.7 percent of them (885,400 persons) voted against the accession of Ukraine to NATO.[91] The poll was dismissed by Kiev. A statement by the Representative Office of the Ukrainian President in the Crimean Autonomy was brief. 'According to Article 92 of the Ukrainian Constitution, the foreign policy of the state is determined solely by national laws.'[92] Yushchenko dismissed the move as being irrelevant. 'This decision is yet more political speculation. It does not introduce any dramatic changes in Ukraine-NATO relations. Implementation of the plan falls directly within the competence of the central authorities, government, parliament and president.'[93] As a defence for public support of NATO, First Deputy Foreign Minister, Anton Buteiko made note of the results of the elections in 2006.

> I can see no opposition to Ukraine's joining NATO. Individual groups representing certain political forces than ran elections under the slogan *No NATO in Ukraine* have made public statements ... [but] they did not negotiate the barrier [to take up parliamentary seats], so it is incorrect to say that anti-NATO sentiments exist in Ukraine.[94]

Operation Sea Breeze 2006 was set for the summer of 2006 and proved to be a spark that would ignite protests and political action on the issue of NATO and

---

91   'Crimea Residents Distrustful of NATO – Informal Vote', *RIA Novosti*, http://en.rian.ru, 17 December 2006. The vote had no legal consequences.

92   'Crimea's Referendum on NATO Illegal – Ukraine', *RIA Novosti*, http://en.rian.ru, 9 October 2006.

93   'Yushchenko Slams Crimea NATO Decision as "Political Speculation"', *RIA Novosti*, http://en.rian.ru, 6 June 2006.

94   'No Anti-NATO Sentiments in Ukraine – First Deputy FM Buteiko', *RIA Novosti*, http://en.rian.ru, 6 June 2006. The People's Opposition Party, led by Natalia Vitrenko ran on an anti-NATO platform. But the party failed to attain the necessary 3 percent of the vote to secure a seat in parliament.

Ukraine. Initially, the authorities in Kiev and Western partners in the exercise tried to portray the event as not being related to NATO. A NATO spokesman, James Appathuri, stated 'these are bilateral exercises between the US and Ukraine open to NATO allies and partners, but not organized by NATO or funded by NATO'.[95] This statement was echoed by the Defence Ministry; 'The Sea Breeze joint exercises are part of cooperation between the Ukrainian Defence Ministry and the US Department of Defence. These are bilateral exercises designed to raise the combat efficiency of Ukraine's armed forces and have nothing to do with NATO.'[96] A factor that complicated matters was a law passed by the parliament earlier in 2006, which banned foreign military from exercises on the territory of Ukraine.[97]

Statements made by officials after the presence of a US ship at the Crimean port of Feodosiya, tended to be clumsy and contradictory, which had the effect of destroying official credibility. On 28 May 2006 Ukraine's Defence Minister, Anatoly Gritsenko admitted to making 'mistakes' in previous statements and confirmed that a US naval ship *Advantage* had indeed delivered weapons.[98] Earlier the Defence Minister stated that it was 'construction material' for the renovation of a local military training base.[99] The Ukrainian Prosecutor's Office got involved in the situation too. 'The Advantage, which delivered hardware and arms for a military exercise, is not a warship.' It was added that the troops on board the ship were not armed and therefore could not be classed as a military unit.[100] Such excuses are pushing the limits of fact and fiction. The attempts to try and reclassify something like this demonstrate that a significant informational problem is recognized. A problem that is significant enough that it requires action to try and avoid possible embarrassing consequences for the Ukrainian authorities.

Yushchenko ordered law enforcement agencies to maintain public order in Crimea in response to protests at the foreign military presence and to deport any foreigners who had joined the protests.[101] Demonstrations and counter-demonstrations were arranged, anti-NATO ones by the Party of Regions and the pro-NATO demonstrations by Pora Public Movement (which supported the Orange Revolution). Ukraine's Channel 5 reported a clash between the rival demonstrations, in which the numerically superior anti-NATO group won. The

---

95   'Russia Warns Kiev Over NATO Plans', *BBC News*, http://newsvote.bbc.co.uk, 7 June 2006, accessed 19 June 2007.

96   'Sea Breeze Exercise Unrelated to NATO – Ukraine Defence Ministry', *RIA Novosti*, http://en.rian.ru, 2 June 2006.

97   'Ukraine Defence Minister Admits US Ship Brought Arms to Crimea', *RIA Novosti*, http://en.rian.ru, 29 May 2006

98   Ibid.

99   Litovkin, V., 'The Feodosia Blockade: When Enough is Enough', *RIA Novosti*, http://en.rian.ru, 1 June 2006.

100   'Yushchenko Slams Crimea NATO Decision as "Political Speculation"', *RIA Novosti*, http://en.rian.ru, 6 June 2006.

101   'Crimean Parliament Protests Foreign Military Exercise With US', *RIA Novosti*, http://en.rian.ru, 5 June 2006.

anti-NATO demonstrators actually managed to penetrate the security area. 'Today we managed to penetrate the port area and open several containers, where we discovered at least 30 metric tons of weapons and fuses.'[102] The situation got well out of hand for the effective management and organization of the military exercise. Thus a rather humiliating back track was forced upon Kiev, who cancelled the exercise.

Volodymyr Bova, a spokesman for the Ukrainian Navy told the TV station *Era* that 'the cargo, which was delivered on May 27 to Feodosia by the US vessel, was fully loaded on board the vessel, and nothing was left at the port.' A Ukrainian transport ship was used to redeliver the US equipment.[103] Other scheduled military exercises involving forces belonging to NATO members were also cancelled in light of the events that unfolded at Feodosia.[104] The chaotic manner and falsification of information by the Orange government had an effect of not only intensifying the conflict but destroying their reputation. The reputation for the government of Tymoshenko and the President was harmed, among not only Ukrainians, but also perhaps in the eyes of NATO for not being an entirely reliable partner. This certainly is evident by virtue of words not being able to match deeds.

Contemporary Problems in the Ukrainian Politics

The outcome of the Orange Revolution saw a significant change in the orientation of national politics in Ukraine. Attempts to install a nominated successor to the outgoing President Leonid Kuchma ultimately failed as Viktor Yanukovich was eventually ousted by popular protests. Viktor Yushchenko, the opposition figure leader formed a highly fragmented and volatile coalition. The falling popularity of the Orange Coalition saw a strange alliance form between the former adversaries, Yushchenko inviting Yanukovich to lead the government (as Prime Minister). A situation that was forced by not only the sagging public support for the Orange government as conditions for the ordinary people did not change and high expectations were dashed. Thus the situation was making it easy for Yanukovich, now leader of the Party of Regions, to gain popularity.

Even within the Orange Coalition, there was a hint of rivalry to outright hatred. In some cases it seems that the only thing holding political coalitions together was the political reality of the time. That is, if they did not join up then they would lose power. Yulia Mostova, editor of the newspaper Dzerkalo Tizhnya (Mirror of the Week) gave an insight into the politics and events guiding the alliance between

---

102   'NATO Arguments Spark Clashes in Ukraine's Crimea', *RIA Novosti*, http://en.rian.ru, 8 June 2006.

103   'Ukrainian Vessel Removes US NATO Cargo From Crimean Port', *RIA Novosti*, http://en.rian.ru, 22 June 2006.

104   'Ukraine, NATO Postpone Joint Manoeuvres', *RIA Novosti*, http://en.rian.ru, 8 June 2006.

Viktor Yushchenko and Yulia Tymoshenko. In the wake of the elections, according to Mostova, Yushchenko tried to persuade Tymoshenko to release him from his promise. She replied: 'If you do not want to fulfil your obligations, don't. But I won't give in.' And Mostova went on to say that 'the reality of their relationship was hatred'.[105]

The alliance between the two leaders has been marked by tension though, and Yanukovich represents a threat to Yushchenko's presidency. This mutual distrust, tension and ultimately conflict manifested itself in a very open manner recently. A crisis began in April 2007 when Yushchenko dissolved Parliament and called for snap elections in May, but were subsequently moved to June 24 after large numbers of protesters on both sides, took to the streets. Attempts were made by Yushchenko to influence further the composition (and therefore the decisions) of the Ukrainian Constitutional Court,[106] and to force the dissolution of parliament through the sacking of MPs.[107] Yushchenko made a hint of what was to come as early as July 2006 when he addressed MPs to work according to the rules of procedure of the Verkhovna Rada and the Constitution of Ukraine 'otherwise, the Verkhovna Rada will have no prospects'.[108] A large portion of the battle was fought within the confines of the parliament, however, it did eventually spill out beyond after some time. The result though was a lack of movement by both parties within the forum of the conflict that was taking place there.

The trigger to the political crisis was Yanokovich's gaining of more power in the parliament. According to the constitution only factions and not individuals can change sides. However, there were a number of cases in the 11 months before the crisis began, which saw a number of deputies allied with Yushchenko change sides. A critical point being, if Yanukovich and the Party of Regions gain 300 seats of the 450 seat house, then he has the power to overturn presidential vetoes and to oversee

---

105   Mulvey, S., 'Ukraine's Heroes Turn into Foes', *BBC News*, http://newsvote.bbc. co.uk, 1 November 2005. The promise was made by Yushchenko that in case of an election victory Timoshenko was promised the premiership.

106   'Ukraine President Sacks Representative to Constitutional Court', *Interfax*, www.interfax.ru/e/B/politics/28.html?id_issue=11763116, 6 June 2007. The Constitutional Court of Ukraine is composed of 18 judges; the President, Verkhovna Rada and Congress of Judges each nominate 6 judges. They decide upon issues of conformity with the Constitution of Ukraine of the following: laws and other legal acts of the Verkhovna Rada, acts of the President, acts of cabinet ministers, legal acts of the Verkhovna Rada of the Autonomous Republic of Crimea. 'Constitutional Court of Ukraine', Chapter XII, Official Website of the President of Ukraine, http://ww7president.gov.ua/en/content/p_10312_e.html, 19 June 2007.

107   'Ukraine Leaders Set for New Talks', *BBC News*, http://newsvote.bbc.co.uk, 26 May 2007. Eventually the two leaders eventually settled on the date of September 30 to hold the snap parliamentary elections. Ukraine Interior Minister Must be Called to Account – President, *RIA Novosti*, http://en.rian.ru, 30 May 2007.

108   'Parliamentary Crisis 2 (Summary)', Official Website of the President of Ukraine, www.president.gov.ua/en/news/data/print/9444.html, 15 July 2006.

new constitutional changes.[109] This situation threatened to leave Yushchenko into a position where he held no effective power, and was not something he could tolerate if he wanted to have some measure of influence.

Political battles raged on for some time and began to peak when there was a clash over the control of some 40,000 Interior Ministry troops. This came in the wake of the sacking of the prosecutor general, Svyatolslav Piskun. In response, riot police (in defiance of the president) seized the offices of the sacked prosecutor general. The riot troops were controlled by Interior Minister, Vasyl Tsushko, and not by President Yushchenko. Tsushko was an ally of the Prime Minister Viktor Yanukovich. Tsushko went as far as to publicly state that: 'It is a part of the president's entourage, whom I call the junta, which is pushing us towards civil war.'[110] Yushchenko appointed Viktor Shemchuk as the acting prosecutor general. In response to Tsushko's actions, Shemchuk announced that he had launched an investigation into his actions.[111] The President made plans to take control over these troops at a time when there was a deadlock in the struggle.

Publicly at least, both leaders agreed that they would not resort to the use of force in order to resolve the political standoff. In late May 2007, Yanukovich and the Speaker of the Verkhovna Rada, Alexander Morozov, at a press conference ruled out the use of force in resolving the political dispute.[112] Yushchenko's foreign policy adviser, Oleksandr Chalyi reiterated that sentiment on the President's behalf: 'the President has sent a very clear message, that he will never use force to resolve the question.'[113] However, as described earlier both sides have used force or sought to amass the potential to use force to resolve certain aspects of the political crisis that was unfolding.

The crisis came to an end on 27 May 2007 through a political settlement to the crisis, which was agreed upon by both sides (Yushchenko and Yanukovich). It was agreed to hold elections after a series of legal amendments were introduced in parliament in order to prepare for the elections.[114] However, this relies on the good will of the parties involved to hold their word when they have significant differences and mutual hostility towards each other. The pro-presidential and pro-premier factions were given two days to consider a number of draft laws that would

---

109   'Ukraine Rivals in Tense Stand-off', *BBC News*, http://newsvote.bbc.co.uk, 3 April 2007.

110   'Ukraine Leaders Set for New Talks', *BBC News*, http://newsvote.bbc.co.uk, 26 May 2007.

111   'Ukraine Interior Minister Must be Called to Account – President', *RIA Novosti*, http://en.rian.ru, 30 May 2007.

112   'Ukraine not to Use Force to Settle Crisis, PM Says', *RBC News*, www.rbcnews. com/free/20070525174729.shtml, 25 May 2007.

113   Maddox, B., 'I Won't Use Tanks to End Parliament Stand-off, Says Leader', Official Website of the President of Ukraine, www.president.gov.ua/en/news/data/print/15366.html, 26 April 2007.

114   'Yushchenko: Ukraine's Image Tarnished by Power Struggle', *Moscow News*, www.mnweekly.ru/cis/20070607/55257202, 7 June 2007.

allow the snap elections. However, the time passed without any consensus being achieved. Additionally, the parliament voted against the presidential proposal that Tsushko be held to account for his actions.[115] This is not an encouraging sign so soon after the political agreement that was designed to end the conflict that griped Ukraine.

In a summary of the outcome of the political conflict, one can say two things; firstly that it is not yet resolved and secondly it damaged the image of Ukraine. At a news conference Yushchenko spoke of a 'loss of Ukraine's image due to the non-constitutional processes in parliament which stemmed from quarrels and conflicts'. He went on to add that 'Europe would like to see that Ukraine can emerge from the crisis itself while respecting democratic principles'.[116] Predictions for Ukraine's political future are in some cases not particularly optimistic. Mychailo Wynnycyj, a professor of sociology at Kyiv-Mohyla Academy predicts that:

> We will have one political crisis after another. There is likely to be an election almost every year in Ukraine for the next 10 years. ... Politically it is a mess. But as long as the economy continues to grow at the rate it has been, it won't be a significant problem for our country.[117]

One of the factors that have the potential to ensure that the conflict continues is that the sides of this political struggle are unable to gain a clear major in the Verkhovna Rada. Added to this is a provision in the Ukrainian constitution that states that a coalition must form a majority within one month of it starting work. If MPs fail to come to an agreement, the president is entitled to dissolve the parliament and call for new elections.[118] So far, in the run-up to the elections there is a clear tendency by the major parties towards running their campaign upon populist promises and policies.[119] Such a trend is not conducive to longer term political and social stability. The coming election scheduled in September 2007 shall be a test to see whether the political impasse has been solved or whether Ukraine shall lurch from one political crisis to the next as the result of evenly matched opposing political blocs.

The bitter political infighting among the former Orange coalition allies, so openly and publicly, has also had a wider spill over effect. Public trust in politics has fallen to new low levels, which has been compounded by the effects of the

---

115   'Ukraine Rada Fails to Agree Laws to Hold Snap Elections', *RIA Novosti*, http://en.rian.ru, 31 May 2007.

116   'Yushchenko: Ukraine's Image Tarnished by Power Struggle', *Moscow News*, www.mnweekly.ru/cis/20070607/55257202, 7 June 2007.

117   Fawkes, H., 'Kiev Crisis Delayed Not Solved', *BBC News*, http://newsvote.bbc.co.uk, 29 May 2007.

118   'Ukrainian Parliament Takes Recess for Another Week', *RIA Novosti*, http://en.rian.ru, 7 June 2006.

119   Bandera, S., 'Elections Mired in Litigation, Populism', Nation, *Kyiv Post*, www.kyivpost.com/nation/27232/, 15 August 2007.

economic crisis that has affected Ukraine very hard. Yushchenko as a political force is spent,[120] his arbitrary and autocratic style of rule, such as the regular hiring and firing of governments[121] and his inability to resolve pressing economic problems have eroded his public legitimacy. Robert Legvold from Colombia University commented on the effects of the political squabbling among the former partners.

> And that has not only produced a stalemate, political stalemate and an inability to make progress between the executive branch and parliament, but a kind of poisonous, petty political competition among leaders that has alienated the public at large, which is for the most part very unsatisfied with all major political leaders in Ukraine. And that makes it very difficult for the government, even if it were to get its act together, to mobilise the population behind it.[122]

A poll that was conducted in late 2008 confirms the public's disappointment and disillusionment with the results of the Orange Revolution and its unfulfilled promises. The Washington based International Foundation for Electoral Systems (IFES) commissioned the poll, which was conducted by the International Sociology Institute in Kiev (funded by USAID). A total of 1,218 citizens were surveyed in the period 17-28 October 2008. A mere 15 percent of respondents believed that they were living in a democratic society, and 93 percent were disappointed with the economic and political situation in Ukraine. Some 76 percent surveyed also believed Ukraine is heading toward chaos, which compares with 43 percent believing Ukraine to be on the way to stability in 2004 (the figure increased to 47 percent in 2007).[123] The next presidential elections were scheduled for 17 January 2010, currently a political paralysis is gripping Ukraine and is predicted to remain until at least those elections.

In February 2010 Yanukovich was declared the winner of the elections, after a second round of elections that was contested by Timoshenko and Yanukovich. By this time, Yushchenko was no longer a political force and his credibility was in tatters. At the same time, Timoshenko has failed to establish herself as being the leader of what is left of the Orange forces.[124] This may have been the result of a number of factors including an inability to keep many of their key pledges, and

---

120   Yushchenko's popularity rating was lower than 20 percent in 2007 according to: Kuzio, T., 'Counterpoint to the Counterfactual: Another View of the Yushchenko Legacy', Op. ed., *Kyiv Post*, www.kyivpost.com/opinion/oped/27988, 12 December 2007.

121   A number of events bear testimony to this, such as the firing of the Timoshenko government in September 2005 and the hiring of his former political opponent, Yanukovich in August 2006.

122   De Nesnera, A., 'Ukrainians Disillusioned with "Orange Revolution"', *Voice of America*, 26 August 2009. JRL 2009-#159, 27 August 2009.

123   'A Nation Deeply Unhappy', *Kyiv Post*, www.kyivpost.com/nation/30896, 12 November 2008.

124   Druker, J., 'Enigmatic Ressurection in Ukraine', *ISN Network*, http://www.isn. ethz.ch/isn/Current-Affairs/Security-Watch/Detail/?id=112406&lng=en, 9 February 2010.

the economic crisis that crippled the economy. Yanukovich seems to be trying to pursue a balance in domestic and international politics. Although he has pursued the election pledge of dropping the drive for NATO membership, he has already broken another pledge of re-introducing Russian as a second official language.[125]

Conclusion

Ukraine is facing numerous problems in various spheres: economic, social and political, which affects the effective functioning of society adversely. The problems that have been outlined in this chapter also have an impact upon the country's ability to implement a meaningful and lasting Security Sector Reform. Two major problems are apparent though; the assistance and the reforms cannot be approached piecemeal, a comprehensive reform is needed; a trusted and experienced international actor is needed, not only from a point of view of experience, but also not to inflame the existing tensions in Ukraine. For this to come about, outside (foreign) help seems to be the most realistic solution.

In regard to an international partner to help Ukraine through the process of SSR, NATO has the necessary experience and abilities to tackle a number of the military issues, but it becomes problematic with the political sphere (not least of all being many Ukrainians are against NATO membership and suspicious of the organization). The EU is in a somewhat unique position insofar as it does not have the negative connotations of NATO, and has a lot of 'in-house' potential to advise and help carry out the necessary reform measures. An added advantage being a number of the newer EU members (such as Poland and Hungary) have made the transformation from Eastern Bloc satellite states to EU and NATO members, thereby having the direct experience to share with Ukraine.

The issue of Security Sector Reform in contemporary Ukraine is a very important and topical issue for a number of reasons. Ukraine is now a country bordering the EU and NATO countries. It has a long border, including with a number of problem or potentially unstable areas (Transdnestr and Georgia for example). Certainly the problem is recognized and understood by organizations, such as the EU, which actively engage in practical steps in strengthening the border areas. The security and well-being of Ukraine's citizens (and to a less extent some neighbouring countries) is affected by a raft of other complex problems, which at times become intermeshed with other issues in a highly politicized game. There is a lot of unfinished business when it comes to the delineation of borders with a number of neighbours. The setting of international borders is one of the elements and defining features linked to statehood. With regards to the lack of progress in this matter with Russia, this very much seems to be a result of the definition of what a border is and what it stands for. In the Ukrainian case it is a measure of

125 'Analysis: Yanukovych Tightens Grip, So What Now for Ukraine?', *Kyiv Post*, www.kyivpost.com/news/nation/detail/68860/, 7 June 2010.

statehood and independence after some 300 years of being swallowed up. For Russia, a defined border seems to indicate that a barrier or impermeable wall or barrier is erected and it becomes a symbolic obstacle in relations.

There is a strong link between the past and the present, exercising a strong influence in the manner in which certain problems are created and handled today. For this reason it is essential that at least a basic understanding of Ukrainian history is dealt with in order to make some sense out of the, at times, seemingly non-logical actions of some of the actors involved in the national scene. Perceptions, images and events of suffering and victimization are prevalent in contemporary political discourse. This is especially so when it comes to dealing with the history of the Soviet Union. Events such as the Great Famine, deportations of ethnic groups under Stalin's orders and the change in ethnic composition as a result of migration in the Soviet Union have altered the ethnic balance of power in Ukraine.

Prospects for ethnic mobilization that at the beginning of Ukraine's independence was negligible due to a civic approach to citizenship and engaging in an inclusive manner that did not alienate any ethnic group, has been replaced by ethnic tension. This is especially evident on the national level between eastern (Russian dominated) and western (Ukrainian dominated) Ukraine, and also on the Crimean Peninsula. The stopping of the NATO exercises in 2006 saw just how effective ethnic mobilization can get when they are well organized. Thus posing not only an embarrassing situation for the politicians in Kiev, but perhaps if left unchecked, putting at risk the territorial integrity of the republic.

National politics is also a significant problem presently. The deadlock that has come about a mere two to three years after the victory of the Orange Revolution, has meant that any form of effective running of the state and long term policy planning have disappeared. Instead it has been replaced by populist rhetoric and policies, which are intended to keep those who hold power in as long as possible. Furthermore, the even matching of strength of the opposing political factions makes the prospect of any resolution to the political chaos unlikely, at least in the short term.

Some of the primary reasons for slow progress or failure in SSR in Ukraine relate to the lack of inter-agency cooperation and a lack of political will. There would appear to be a perception among various government agencies and ministries that they act in isolation and fail to consider that what they do may have an impact upon another agency. This can lead to a situation that creates an environment of competition, instead of the necessary cooperation. This has been clearly seen, especially in relations between the President and the Prime Minister. Due to the ideological split that has occurred in Ukrainian politics in the wake of the Orange Revolution, there is a lack of clear leadership and political engagement to drive processes, such as SSR, as the issue of political power is much more of a pressing issue that is wrapped in self-interest and self-preservation.

An important point in the SSR process is to start with identifying the current threats being faced, and to structure the forces in a way to effectively meet these challenges. This process is very much in the early stages in Ukraine and may prove to be a problem if not dealt with effectively. The publication of a defence white paper is an encouraging sign of progress though. Another related problem is the lack of knowledge and experience among parliamentary deputies in the defence and security sector, this leaves the military as the experts in the field and in effect reduces the level of democratic oversight and control of the armed forces. NATO and EU efforts in this area have met with some success at the grass roots level in the ministries and departments concerned, but further efforts are needed in the area of raising the level of knowledge and professionalism at the political level. The recent changes in Ukraine's political environment, especially the reaffirmation of the non-aligned status offers the EU to play a central role in assisting in SSR in all of its aspects (defence, law enforcement, economic and political).

References

Beyme, K. von, *Transition to Democracy in Eastern Europe*. London: Macmillan Press, 1996.

Chumak, V., 'Security Sector Reform in Ukraine'. Analytical Report, Kiev, International Centre for Policy Studies, February 2007.

Dawisha, K. and Parrott, B. (eds) *The Consolidation of Democracy in East-Central Europe*. Cambridge: Cambridge University Press, 1997.

Karatnycky, A., Motyl, A. and Graybow, C. (eds) *Nations in Transit: Civil Society, Democracy and Markets in East Central Europe and the Newly Independent States (1998)*. New Brunswick: Freedom House, 1999.

Kolsto, P., *Political Construction Sites: Nation-Building in Russia and the Post-Soviet States*. Boulder, CO: Westview Press, 2000.

Roth, C. (ed.) *Understanding and Supporting Security Sector Reform*. London: Department for International Development, 1997.

Rubin, B.R. and Snyder, J. (eds) *Post-Soviet Political Order: Conflict and State Building*. London: Routledge, 1998.

Rudnytsky, I.L., *Essays in Modern Ukrainian History*. Harvard: Harvard University Press, 1987.

Rudnytsky, I.L. and Himka, J.-P. (eds) *Rethinking Ukrainian History*. Edmonton: University of Toronto Press, 1981.

Sakwa, R., *Russian Politics and Society*, 3rd edition. London: Routledge, 2002.

'Security Sector Reform in Ukraine'. Bonn International Centre for Conversion, www.bicc.de/ssr_gtz/pdf/ukraine.pdf, accessed 28 September 2007.

Starr, S.F. (ed.) *The Legacy of History in Russia and the New Independent States of Eurasia*. New York: M.E. Sharpe, 1994.

Sullivant, R.S., *Soviet Politics and the Ukraine 1917-57*. New York: Columbia University Press, 1962.

Chapter 11

The Control of Small Arms and Light Weapons in Ukraine: The Need for Strengthened International Security Sector Reform

Andrea Johansson

Introduction

The purpose of this chapter is to investigate the possibilities and constraints for international Security Sector Reform (SSR) support to Ukraine in the field of small arms and light weapons (SALW).[1] SALW cause the deaths of hundreds of thousands of people every year, which is far higher than the casualty count from conventional weapons. It is estimated that there are 500 million weapons in circulation world-wide and the question of how to control the flood of small arms and light weapons has risen quickly on the arms control and disarmament agenda during the last decade. For many reasons, this is also one of the more complicated arms control and disarmament issues to deal with. There is a large number of producers of SALW, but also huge weaponry stocks left over from the end of the Cold War, which make the supply-side difficult to control. Small arms and light weapons are easy to transport, hard to trace and quite simple to keep in circulation for a long time. The grey and black markets of such weapons are often linked to organized crime, drug trafficking and activities of several non-state actors. In addition, national norms for firearms possession and use differ between countries.[2]

Many countries in the former Soviet Union have huge stocks of SALW. Some of these countries, like Tajikistan would be categorized as a post conflict country

---

1 So far no internationally agreed definition of small arms and light weapons exists. Broadly speaking, small arms are often defined as weapons constructed for use by individuals (revolvers, rifles, assault rifles, machine-guns and mounted grenade launchers). Light weapons are also portable, but need to be transported by light vehicles or pack animal and require a crew or team to operate (portable anti-aircraft guns, anti-tank guns, anti-aircraft missile systems, landmines, ammunition and explosives etc.). Krause, K., 17 May 1998.

2 Krause, K., 17 May 1998.

by Hänggi, while others like Ukraine would be considered post-authoritarian. In some instances the Security Sectors of these post-authoritarian countries, have been unable or unwilling to control SALW according to the standards of the international community. This has affected the countries own security when SALW have ended up in the hands of criminals or terrorists. Furthermore other countries' security has been threatened, when weapons have been sold to rebels or guerrillas in conflict areas. As will be described in this chapter, Ukraine is unfortunately a good example of a post-authoritarian state, with an unreformed Security Sector, which has been unable to control its stocks of SALW or its export of them.

The international community has been involved in different projects all over the world trying to improve the control of SALW. In Ukraine, other countries in the former Soviet Union and the Balkans, the EU, OSCE and NATO have been the most active regional actors in this matter and some actions could be interpreted as efforts to achieve SSR. However, the EU is quite untested when it comes to SSR in a context of SALW in non-conflict countries, but Ukraine is one of its first projects.[3]

Still, important questions remain to be discussed further: what are the *reform needs* in a post-authoritarian country as Ukraine, which *means* have been used to improve the control of SALW and which *results* have been achieved so far? To answer these questions, this chapter will analyse the actors of Ukraine's Security Sector responsible for the control of SALW and identify its weak links as well as the reform needs. The second part of the chapter will examine the efforts of NATO, EU and OSCE to improve the control of SALW by implementing SSR and the results. These analyses will provide a basis for a concluding discussion of constraints and possibilities for SSR in terms of improving the control of SALW in a post-authoritarian state like Ukraine.

Background

A country's national *Security Sector*[4] is an important player in the international fight against the spread of SALW. For example, the army is responsible for the control over its weaponry resources and preventing them from leaking out into the society. Other key players are the police, which investigate any criminal activities, like for instance arms brokering and the judicial institutions, which are in charge

---

3   The organizations will be more thoroughly described in the second half of the chapter, including recommendations of further reading.

4   There is no definition of what a Security Sector consists of. Some researchers consider it only to include the army and police and others prefer wider definitions, which include both state and non-state actors (Heiner Hänggi's 'Conceptualising Security Sector Reform and Reconstruction'). In this chapter a broad definition will be used, mainly because the control of SALW involves several actors and a narrow definition would exclude crucial actors as oversight authorities, the judicial system, NGOs etc.

of implementing legislation correctly interconnected to SALW and prosecuting those who break the law. Oversight authorities, like the Security Services and the State Border Guards, are often responsible for arms deliveries ending up with the correct end-user as well as controlling imports. Of course, the government and parliament are important actors, since they control these institutions, work out policies (production, export etc.) and make laws.

Non state actors could also be categorized as parts of the Security Sector or at least as actors affecting it.[5] Nongovernmental organizations' efforts could for instance increase good governance and transparency in the state sectors improving the control of SALW. In conclusion, the control of SALW depends on several actors in the Security Sector. If the Security Sector is not capable of controlling the spread of SALW (and thereby its side effects[6]) or is not willing to do so, the Security Sector might not be able to fulfil its duty to provide security to the state or its people. As has sometimes been the case regarding the export of SALW, actors in the Security Sector could even take advantage of their position by for example participate in illegal arms export, which is economically profitable. A dysfunctional Security Sector is a point of departure for SSR, which is described in this chapter as a means to solve the issues of lack of security and good governance with a holistic approach.[7]

Heiner Hänggi has divided the general needs of SSR into three categories of receiving countries according to the following contexts: developmental, post-authoritarian and post-conflict states.[8] In a SSR-SALW perspective, most research has been done so far on post-conflict situations (demand countries) and especially on how to disarm, demobilize and reintegrate (DDR) soldiers. DDR is sometimes discussed as a part of SSR and seen as a precondition to be able to implement SSR. Focus in this kind of research is how to provide security to the people, stop armed violence in a conflict torn society and create the necessary conditions for a country's security forces to regain the legitimate use of force.[9] However, as Hänggi points out there are other categories of states that need SSR. In a context of controlling SALW these countries have not gained much research attention so far.

5　Hänggi, Heiner.

6　For further information of problems caused by or related to SALW, see K. Krause 'The Challenge of Small Arms and Light Weapons', 1998.

7　Hänggi, Heiner pp. 1-4.

8　Hänggi, Heiner, p. 5.

9　See for example: Wille, C., 2006. 'Stabilizing Cambodia: Small Arms Control and Secuity Sector Reform' in *Small Arms Survey 2006: Unfinished Business*; Bryden, A. and Heiner H. (eds) 2005. 'Security Governance and Post-Conflict Peace Building'. Geneva: Geneva Centre for the Democratic Control of Armed Forces; UNDDR 'SALW Control, Security & Development'. Available at: http://www.unddr.org; Beeck, C., 2006; 'Re-Paving the Road to Peace: Analysis of the Implementation of DDR in Aceh Province Indonesia'. Available at: http://www.bicc.de; Bryden, A., 2007. 'Understanding the DDR-SSR Nexus – Building Sustainable Peace in Africa'. Available at: http://www.dcaf.ch/.

Origins of the SALW Surplus in Ukraine

The Soviet Legacy

On 24 August 1991 the Verkhovna Rada, Ukraine's parliament, passed a resolution that nationalized all military formations, including armaments and military stocks earlier controlled by Moscow. Ukraine's Soviet inheritance had made the newly independent country in charge of the third largest army in the world. During the Soviet era the Ukrainian territory had been divided into three military districts, which belonged to the second echelon of the Warsaw Pact. Five ground armies, one army corps, four air armies, one air defence army, the Black Sea fleet, one rocket army, 21 divisions (infantry, tank and artillery), three airborne brigades and many support units including over 780,000 troops. Moreover, because of Ukraine's strategic geographic position almost two thousand nuclear warheads (the world's third largest nuclear arsenal) had been placed on the territory. In addition to the Ministry of Defence's military resources, the Ministry of Interior controlled approximately 130 000 troops (the border guard, the police etc.) at the beginning of independence.

When Soviet troops retreated from Central Europe, large quantities of military equipment and armaments were dumped in Ukraine. Nor the Soviet army or any other institution had developed an organization for surplus destruction; instead the problem was solved by storing the weapons and the ammunition. This method had been used since the First World War. Hence, Ukrainian stocks were overfilled with obsolete ammunition and weapons from two world wars in addition to the weaponry stocks acquired during the Cold War. Official statistics from the Ministry of Defence (MoD) show that there are approximately seven million SALW and 2.5 million tons ammunition of varying calibres stockpiled all over the country, including several hundred millions of rounds of small arms ammunition.[10] Because of insufficient Ukrainian documentation, the correct figures might be higher, perhaps even twice as much.[11] These statistics do not include those arms and ammunition which are in use. In Ukraine each ministry is responsible for its own weapons and the largest quantities of SALW belong to the MoD and the Ministry of Interior (MoI), however no data is available on the holdings of the last-mentioned.

In spite of its enormous military forces, large quantities of small arms, light weapons, nuclear warheads and conventional weapons, Ukraine's military power in reality was rather weak in the beginning 1990s. A large amount of the material was of a poor standard and several units were unfit for active services. Upholding this machinery was a heavy burden for the already stretched economy of the country and the need for reform became evident. However, the authorities had no experience in governing on the national level, since this task was managed

---

10   *Radio Free Europe*, 15 June 2006.
11   Griffiths, H., 02.2007.

by Moscow during the Soviet era. In the middle of the 1990s force reduction and reorganization became necessary to reduce the economic burden, but also to prevent and combat 'new' post cold war threats (terrorism, illegal immigration etc.) which to a greater extent already had emerged on the security agendas in the Western Europe. Force reductions are still an ongoing project, which means that the surplus of small arms and light weapons will increase further. At a rough estimate 20,000 personnel could be relieved from their services if the weaponry stocks were substantially reduced, since they require close guarding.[12]

Surplus Policy

At least 184 storage sites (bunkers, salt mines and storage outside) of ammunition, some including SALW, are located in Ukraine. The official policy to decide which of these depots would be declared surplus, have been related to what the armed forces need. In case of surplus declaration, the weaponry would either be destroyed or exported. However, between 1993 and 2003 the type of weaponry, the age of ammunition and suitability of the storage facility were the most used criteria in this process. Regarding SALW, only obsolete guns and rifles aging back to WWII were declared surplus and destroyed during this period.[13]

In the 1980s 'disposal of arms' had become a known concept in the Soviet Union, but at that time in a context of nuclear weapons. Ten years later conventional weapons were included in these discussions; nevertheless it took additionally ten years for the newer models of small arms and light weapons to end up on the agenda. In 1993 the Ukrainian government made a resolution on conventional weapons, which was intended to coordinate the entire chain of disposal activities, including the process of surplus declaration, activities of contractors, and provisions of funds for destruction. Three amendments to this resolution were made, but still efforts of the Ukrainian government failed. Only a fraction of the earmarked money for disposal was paid out. Foreign companies were contracted to destroy ammunition; a process from which they could extract valuable materials from. Since they focused on economic profits, no measures were taken to dispose non-profitable agents, as explosives, which were left at the storage sites. Small calibre ammunition for SALW on the other hand did not pose an immediate security threat as obsolete larger calibre ammunition and rockets risking to explode. Therefore, the government did not prioritize small calibre ammunition and consequently no financial resources were allocated to develop destruction facilities for this kind of ammunition.[14]

The questionable methods of destruction of larger calibre ammunition went on until 2004, when a depot near Melitopol exploded. As an outcome of the disaster, the Ukrainian government suspended the foreign contractors and once again

---

12   Chumak, V., 02.2007.
13   Griffiths, H., 02.2007.
14   Polyakov, L., 2005.

acknowledged the security threat posed by the depots of obsolete ammunition, which still are located near nuclear power plants, big cities and gas pipelines. The lack of financial resources necessary to be able to address the problem has forced the government to search for international economic support from the EU, OSCE and NATO.

The SALW Industry

At least one-third of the Soviet Military Industrial complex was located in Ukraine. A majority of these companies had unique technological capabilities. As in most cases in the USSR, the production was controlled and coordinated by Moscow. On paper Ukraine inherited a huge industry from the Soviet Union and some experts thought that the country had the best opportunities and capabilities among the former Soviet Republics for a positive economic development. However, Ukraine lacked central structures for command and experience in planning on the national level. In addition the factories were dependent on components produced by other newly independent countries with similar problems as Ukraine. The economic climate deterred as necessary reforms were not realized by the politicians, which resulted in high inflation, privatization in a stalemate and sinking real wages.

Despite the large military industrial complex sited in Ukraine, no industrial facilities or designing bureaus were specialized in developing or producing SALW. In the late 1990s Ukrainian politicians started to show interest in the SALW industry. Valentin Badrak, director of the Ukrainian Centre for Army, Conversion and Disarmament, argues that there were mainly two reasons for the emerging political interest. To begin with there was a need to upgrade some of the small arms used by forces controlled by the Ministry of Interior. Even more important, there was an increasing demand for small calibre ammunition, since Ukraine had exported large quantities of small arms and light weapons during the decade.[15] Today there are about twenty factories and design bureaus, financed by the national budget, which develop and produce SALW, including ammunition.[16]

The entire arms industry is troubled by the fact that there is almost no domestic market in Ukraine (approximately 95 percent of the production is exported). Consequently, the future for this industrial sector is a matter of uncertainty.[17] Ukraine is still the tenth largest arms exporter in the world,[18] but this top-ranking is not a result of the domestic manufacturing of SALW. In comparison to other East European countries the production is quite small and therefore the business in SALW is still a matter of selling of weaponry stocks. The authorities and companies have made clear that SALW production is not a priority in the arms industry because of the current hard competition on the world market.

15	Global Security.org [n.d.].
16	Global Marketing System [n.d.].
17	*Zerkalo Nedeli*, 6 October 2006.
18	*Kyiv Post*, 3 September 2009.

The only exception is ammunition for small arms and light weapons, which is considered to be a lucrative business with great potential.[19] Unfortunately there are no official statistics or information on the quantities manufactured or who the customers are.

Shortcomings in the Control of SALW

Lack of Legislation and Governmental Weaknesses

During Ukraine's first years as an independent country, arms export lacked legislation, codes of conduct and organizational structures. Since the Ukrainian forces did not need the enormous Soviet arsenal, but financial resources, the authorities decided to sell of large quantities, including SALW. In the opposite to the Soviet arms export, which was often used as an instrument to influence conflicts in the Third World by supplying one side with weapons, Ukrainian politicians were only interested in economic profit. Because of the defective export control system, it is hard to say where and what was exported. At a rough estimate SALW and other types of arms worth three billion US dollars (perhaps even more) were sold to foreign clients.[20] In addition, between 1992 and 1998 Ukraine lost 32 billion US dollars in military assets, partly through theft, discount arms sales and lack of oversight and regulation.[21]

A number of reports published[22] since the 1990s have revealed Ukrainian illicit arms transfers,[23] which have given the country a reputation of being one of the most active illegal arms suppliers in the international community. In many cases the responsible authorities turned a blind eye to weapons sales by corrupt individuals or dealers to inappropriate end-users. Between the years of 1997 and 2000 some figures suggest that the illegal export was even greater than the legal one. Small arms and light weapons originating from Ukrainian stockpiles have ended up in conflict zones in Africa (Liberia, Sierra Leone and Angola), the Middle East and the Balkans. There is also evidence of illegal exports to these countries in the form of documented seizures of shipments.[24]

---

19   Badrak, V., 2001.
20   Bailes et al. 11.2003.
21   International Alert [n.d.].
22   See for example: UN, 9 July 2001 'U.N. Conference on Small Arms Trafficking, New York 9 July 2001'. Available at: http://www.hrw.org. International Alert, 'Small Arms Control in Ukraine'. Available at: http://www.international-alert.org.
23   Illicit arms transfers are often interpreted as arms export to individuals or groups (embargoed states, criminals, terrorists etc.), who are not allowed to possess or buy weapons. This does not mean that it is necessarily an illegal activity in the country where for example the arms dealer lives or the business is performed.
24   International Alert [n.d.].

Ukrainian citizens have also acted as brokers or middlemen in arms trading networks all over the Eastern Europe.[25] One of the most notorious arms brokers, Leonin Minin, was arrested in Italy in the year of 2000. Evidence showed that he had supplied Liberia and Sierra Leone with 113 tonnes of weapons and 13 million rounds of small arms ammunition. Since the shipments had not passed through Italy, he had to be released and was never convicted.[26]

In December 2005 a parliamentary commission lead by Serhiy Sinchenko started an investigation of illegal arms transfers and ammunitions sales to other countries. The investigation came to the conclusion that illegal arms sales peaked in 1996. According to the commission the only person who knew the extent of the illegal arms transfers was Volodymyr Gorbulin, the former secretary of the National Security and Defence Council of Ukraine (NSDC). The results were handed over to the General Prosecutor's Office for supplementary investigation, but nobody has been prosecuted so far. A number of rumours that top Ukrainian officials and leaders (working for the Ukrainian Security Service, the border guard and the NSDC) have been engaged in illegal arms trade have circulated during the decades. Ukraine's former president Leonid Kuchma and several prosecutors flatly denied such allegations, but anonymous sources working for the SBU claimed that they have not been telling the truth. Earlier inquiries of such allegations have both been buried and forgotten or have not provided enough evidence for charging anyone.[27]

The Export Control System and Reform Efforts

The Ukrainian government and the responsible authorities of SALW have assured that they follow the norms and practices of arms export and are willing to cooperate with international organization and foreign countries on questions concerning SALW. As a member of the UN, Ukraine has guaranteed its commitment to the UN 2001 'Program of Action to Prevent, Combat and Eradicate the Illicit Trade in Small Arms and Light Weapons in all its Aspects'. Ukraine is also committed to the Wassenaar Arrangement,[28] the OSCE's SALW Document[29] and the EU Code of Conduct on Arms Exports. Furthermore, the CIS countries, including Ukraine, share information about exports of MANPADS.

In order to enhance the control system, the government decided to limit the number of authorized exporters in the beginning of the new millennium. The

---

25 Synovitz, R., 03.2000.
26 *Oxfam Briefing Note*, 15 June 2006.
27 *Moscow Kommersant*, 8 December 2001.
28 For more information about the Wassenaar Arrangement visit http://www.was senaar.org/.
29 See OSCE below.

remaining exporters of SALW are Ukrspetsexport[30] and TASKO. Moreover, several new laws have been introduced and one of the most important entered into force on February 2003: 'The Law of Ukraine on State Control of International Transfers of Goods Designated for Military Purposes and Dual-Use Goods'. This law aims to prevent terrorist and other elements to obtain this kind of weapons and to regulate state control. Additionally, SALW as well as their components, materials and equipment designed for development and production are regulated by this law. Furthermore, it covers activities related to international transfers, like intermediary (brokerage) services, production as well as scientific and technical collaboration.

The present control system consists of several Ukrainian authorities, which are responsible for different parts of the arms export monitoring. The State Export Control Service (SECS) checks the exporter's application against companies known as violators of international principles and determine weather to grant or refuse a permit to export SALW. Additionally, the SECS reports every three months to the President and the Prime Minister. The decision is always preceded by an interdepartmental examination including different state authorities and the Committee for Policy on Military-Technical Cooperation and Export Control, which oversees SECS. On the other hand the National Security and Defence Council supervise the Committee. Finally, all documents are examined by the State Export Control Service, the Ministry of Foreign Affairs and the Security Service of Ukraine (SBU). Furthermore, the SBU investigate suspected export control violations and smuggling activities and is also responsible for protecting state secrets and technical information during the international transfer of controlled goods.

There are particularly two commissions in the parliament which are interested in the arms export: the Rada Commission on Defence and State Security and the Rada Commission on Foreign Affairs. The commissions' insight and influence in arms export is though limited.[31]

When president Viktor Yushchenko came into power after the Orange Revolution 2004, one of his campaign promises to fulfil was to improve the arms export control system and to restore Ukraine's reputation as an ill-conceived exporter. His ambition was to make the weapon export transparent and urged the state-owned Ukrspetsexport to operate 'with clean hands and within the law'.[32] Instead of simple trade and overhauling of Soviet-designed surplus arms, he stated that focus should be on manufacturing weapons. As a first step toward transparency, the president ordered an audit of Ukrspetsexport financial records. In 2006 another sign of improvement became clear, when the Ukrainian government published a

---

30   Ukrspetsexport and its daughter companies are since then responsible for all Ukrainian arms import and export.

31   For more information on the Ukrainian Export Control System, visit www.dsecu. gov.ua.

32   Jane's Intelligence Review, 1 July 2005.

report of Ukraine's arms transfers carried out during the year of 2004. The report revealed that especially different kinds of small arms (machine-guns, rifles, pistols etc.) had been exported to countries in North America, Africa, Caucasus and Europe. Since then, three additional yearly reports have been published, which give information on number, type and destination of Ukrainian SALW exports. The figures shows that between 2004 and 2007, 721,777 SALW units have been sold to 27 countries. As mentioned above, the ammunition industry is seen as a more lucrative sector than manufacturing weapons, but figures of the exported amount are not available.[33]

Recent Accusations of Illicit Arms Transfers and Critique of the Control System

Accusations of Ukrainian involvement in illicit arms transfers have decreased significantly the last couple of years, although new ones still keep coming up. In August 2009, a report by the British Parliament revealed that the Ukrainian State Service for Export Control had licensed British registered companies to export light weapons from Soviet stockpiles. The list of end-users, provided by the Ukrainian Ministry of Foreign Affairs, included countries in Africa which were embargoed. According to the report, the list lacked information on when the license was granted and the type of goods or their value. Moreover, it was impossible to decide whether the arms were shipped directly from Ukraine to the end-users, or whether they were transferred via the UK.[34] The spokesman for the Ukrainian State Export Control responded to the accusations that Ukrainian law only allowed Ukrainian companies to be licensed and that the government body had acted accordingly. The problem was explained to be that the verb 'to license' in English could mean having permission or a contract for something, but that did not necessary include a government-approved paper.[35]

However, the British report concluded that the Ukrainian export control system was inefficient because of weakness in the parliamentary and public oversight. For example, ad hoc Commissions to investigate suspected abuses of the licensing systems have been arranged, but the deliberations have been held in private and only the findings of the Commission have been published, not its full report. Further investigations on the suspected illicit arms transfers will be carried out by British authorities.

Political – Institutional Obstacles

Changes in the allocation of influence in the arms business are nothing new in Ukrainian political circles, which is one of the remaining strongholds of the

---

33   *Ukrainian Government*, 3 June 2006.

34   House of Commons, Business and Enterprise, Defence, Foreign Affairs and International Development Committees, 19 August 2009.

35   *Kyiv Post*, 3 September 2009.

president. During the years of independence, the appointment of Ukrspetsexport's Chief Executive Officer (CEO) has always been a symbol of this struggle for power. The arms business is the only sphere where the National Security and Defence Council, all uniformed government branches, and secret and intelligence services cooperate. Moreover, military technical cooperation is seen as a useful foreign policy tool. The government passed a resolution in 2006, changing the procedure to nominate Ukrspetsexport's CEO, which will put the government, instead of the Committee for military-technical cooperation and export control policies in charge of preparing all decisions on arms trade and military-technical cooperation. Since this Committee operates under the president, his actual influence would decrease. Nevertheless, the struggle for influence continues as the constitution leaves room for interpretations. Valentin Badrak, at the Centre for Army, Conversion and Disarmament Studies, claims that the resolution has changed nothing so far.[36]

In March 2007 a new proposal was submitted by the National Security and Defence Council, which suggested a degradation of Ukrspetsexport and the creation of another executive body under the Cabinet of Ministers. If the reform had been accomplished, the power and control of arms export and production would have been concentrated in this new executive body. Ukrspetsexport would have developed into a concern, but would still have been part of the planned executive body.[37]

In conclusion, the struggle for power between political fractions in Ukraine since 2004 has also affected the arms industry in large as well as the arms export, which have been important tools in this combat. Further changes in the present arms export control system and military industrial complex might therefore not come as a surprise depending on whom future elections bring to power.

The Reform Needs

The Ukrainian control system of SALW has been improved the last decade, but several factors still exist, which contribute to the risk of illicit arms transfers, originating from either surplus weaponry stocks or the SALW industry.[38]

The struggle between political fractions in Ukraine has affected the arms industry as well as the export. Therefore, the Security Sector has to be depoliticized, to be able to function most effectively. Furthermore, several of the authorities, which are responsible for the control of SALW in some matter, remain to be reformed. For example, the SBU has gained little attention and lacks transparency. The current organization of SBU makes it a useful power tool for political purposes and the officials' loyalty is rewarded by a free hand to engage in shadow business and practice corruption. Ukraine's history of illicit arms transfers have often involved individuals working for the SBU using their positions to earn

---

36   Radio Free Europe, 15 June 2006.
37   *Zerkalo Nedeli*, 17-23 March 2007.
38   Griffiths, H., 02.2007.

big money.[39] However, a comprehensive review of the security services is under way, as well as enhancement of the legislation.[40] The SECS and the Border Guard are still to be fully reformed as well, regarding transparency and how they perform its work.[41]

Ukraine has improved its legal systems and continues to adapt it to international norms, even though some work is still to be done. Furthermore the judicial system needs to be improved for more independence from political influence and get a strengthened capacity for investigating illicit arms transfers and certifying that infringements will be put on trial.

However, one of the most alarming problems in Ukraine is the level of corruption in all political and administrative layers. Ukraine is placed number 134 (in companion with Pakistan and Nicaragua) out of 180 countries on the Transparency International's corruption index.[42] As long as the level of corruption is sky-high, there are no guarantees that the control authorities of SALW act within the law. Therefore, the work against corruption has to be prioritized in the Security Sector.

Another reform need refers to the openness and transparency of the arms export. The Ukrainian parliament has very little oversight of arms export[43] and the civil society's participation in questions regarding SALW transfers has been modest. Generally, SALW issues are not identified as a priority by the NGO's, there is a lack of public interest and open public debates are uncommon in Ukraine. Therefore the level of NGO oversight is unsatisfactory. Nevertheless, there are two exceptions which make the future look a bit brighter: the Razumkov Centre and the Kiev-based International Centre for Policy Studies (ICPS). The former NGO have focused on researching the problems relating to surplus SALW and ammunition, striving to identify priority areas on which international cooperation and assistance should concentrate. ICPS collaborates with the British nongovernmental organization Saferworld on a thorough analysis of Ukraine's export control system. Their aim is also to work out a project intended to develop parliamentary oversight.[44] However, these initiatives are only fractions of what needs to be done.

The media in Ukraine has become much more independent in Ukraine since the Orange revolution in 2004.[45] During the last years journalists have been able to work more freely, compared to the Kuchma regime. The relationship between the media and authorities and companies involved in arms export is still to be

---

39   Chumak, V., 02.2007; Griffiths, H., 02.2007.
40   Chumak, V., 02.2007, p. 34.
41   Griffiths, H., 02.2007.
42   *Transparency International*, 2009.
43   *Safer World Organisation*, 04.2007.
44   For more information about the projects, visit the organisations' homepages: http://www.saferworld.org and http://www.icps.kiev.ua.
45   Freedom House Organisation [n.d.].

improved in order to bring about transparency in the arms trade in Ukraine. It is rather unusual for the responsible authorities to discuss issues like arms export and illicit arms transfers in the media, which would have the potential to improve the openness of this sector.

In conclusion, international organizations could further improve the control of SALW in Ukraine by advocating the following reforms:

- Measures aimed at depoliticizing the Security Sector as a way to stabilize the arms control system;
- Improving the judicial system for more independence from political influence and strengthened capacity for investigating illicit arms transfers and certifying that infringements will be put on trial, as well as implement work against corruption;
- More involvement of the parliament in the arms export control systems;
- More support is needed to non-governmental organizations and research institutions in order to increase the information about this rather non existing question in the Ukrainian society, which would affect openness and transparency positively.

The International Community in Ukraine

In the late 1990s, the International Community started to show interest in security threats associated with easy access to small arms and light weapons. So far focus has been on conflict torn countries, however states as Ukraine, with huge amounts of surplus SALW have recently also ended up on the agenda of the International Community. The EU, NATO and OSCE have all made efforts to improve Ukraine's control of SALW by reforming the Security Sector. The second part of this chapter will therefore try to identify these organizations' aims and strategies to reform Ukraine, as well as the results of their efforts. The analysis will be followed by a discussion on possibilities and constraints for international Security Sector Reform (SSR) support to Ukraine in the field of SALW.

The OSCE, SALW and SSR

The OSCE states that SALW are the most easily acquired weapons, which are used in armed conflicts by both states and non-state actors. Therefore the OSCE seeks to ensure that weapons do not leak from the legal market, by advocating different methods to control the production, transfer and stockpiling of SALW, including the destruction of surplus arms. The largest source of worry is the weaponry stocks left over from the Cold War, which also are perceived as humanitarian and environmental risks by the organization. In 2003 the threat of terrorist gaining access to SALW (especially Manportable Air Defence Systems, MANPADS) were added to the OSCE strategy.[46]

The OSCE was one of the first international organizations to initiate a discussion on the threats posed by SALW. In November 2000, the OSCE adopted a *Document on Small Arms and Light Weapons*, which established standards for controlling, manufacturing, marking, transferring and stockpiling of SALW. Furthermore, the document also includes a set of measures for use in post-conflict situations. Every year the member states are supposed to exchange information on national procedures of stockpile management and security, the amount of seized and destroyed SALW as well as imports and exports of SALW within the OSCE. Some of the most important state responsibilities according to the document are combating illicit trafficking, contributing to the reduction and prevention of the excessive and accumulation uncontrolled spread of SALW, exercising due restraint to make sure that small arms are manufactured, transferred and held only in accordance with legitimate defence and security needs and building confidence, security and transparency.[47] As a result of this document, a best practices guide was created in 2003, which describes national marking systems of SALW; national procedures for the control of manufacture; national export and import policy; national control of brokering activities; national procedures for stockpile-management and security; definitions for indicators of a surplus; techniques and procedures for destruction; and small arms measures as part of disarmament, demobilization and reintegration.[48]

A state is only bound to the OSCE document on SALW in a political sense, not legally, which of course is also the case regarding the handbook. Because of its legal status, the OSCE does not deal with arms control issues directly and a member country has to request assistance. The organization is though involved in various politico-military activities like confidence- and security-building measures aimed at fostering trust among member states as well as projects giving assistance on the destruction of SALW and ammunition.

The OSCE in Ukraine

Ukraine became a member of the OSCE in 1992 and during the years two field operations have contributed to the establishment of a variety of projects. Ukraine takes part in meetings regarding SALW and, as mentioned above, the country has acknowledged the principles of the *Document on Small Arms and Light Weapons*. It is rather unclear how the OSCE document and handbook have affected Ukraine's security sector and policy on SALW, since there are no studies on this topic.

---

46   OSCE [n.d.] (d).
47   OSCE, 24 November 2000.
48   OSCE [n.d.] (a).

Since one of the OSCE's priorities is SALW stockpiles, it has been involved in different projects across Eastern Europe and Central Asia,[49] collecting weapons and destroying them.

However, Ukrainian politicians have not requested assistance on SALW destruction, but help clearing the site of unexploded material following the explosion at an ammunition storage site in Novobogdanivka (6 May 2004) and dispose a highly toxic (both to humans and the environment) liquid rocket fuel component known as mélange. The outcome of the first project on unexploded material was a success, therefore similar projects are planned to be executed.[50]

The OSCE is involved in different projects, which is supposed to reform Ukraine's security sector, though none of them are explicitly aimed at improving the control of SALW. For example, the OSCE has helped Ukraine to improve border security and rule of law, prevent corruption, promote transparency in the government and democratic governance procedures, and implement programs to retrain discharged military personnel. The OSCE presents a range of its activities and assistance in Ukraine on its website – http://www.osce.org/ukraine/17089. html (accessed 1 June 2010).

NATO, SALW and SSR

In 1999 NATO created an ad hoc working group within the Euro-Atlantic Partnership Council to work on issues related to the spread of small arms and light weapons. The Alliance did not develop a special programme, instead it urged the members and Partner Countries to contribute to the '2001 UN Programme of Action to prevent, combat and eradicate the illicit trade in Small Arms and Light Weapons in All Its Aspects'.[51] So far, the members of the NATO have done so through the Trust Fund, established in the year 2000, which is available for all countries taking part in the Partnership for Peace (PfP) programme. This was from the beginning meant to provide assistance to countries that needed help to destroy landmines, but during the years this fund has also come to include disposal of surplus stockpiles (SALW, conventional ammunition etc.). According to the Trust Funds policy, the presence of large quantities of SALW and ammunition represents a threat to Partner Countries and their population as well as the wider region. The destruction of SALW is therefore regarded to be an effective method to reduce this threat and is conceived as a practical tool to support defence reform and the fight against terrorism, supporting NATO's ambitions to improve security and stability across the Euro Atlantic Area.[52]

---

49   For example Armenia, Azerbaijan, Belarus, Kazakhstan, Moldova, Russia, Tajikistan and Uzbekistan.
50   OSCE [n.d.] (c).
51   *NATO Handbook*, 15 October 2002; *NATO/EAPC* [n.d.].
52   NATO Publications [n.d.].

NATO in Ukraine

Ukraine was the first country of the former Soviet Union to join the PfP in 1994 and three years later it signed the Special Partnership Charter. The Ukrainian government has since then uttered its wishes to join the Alliance, but at the same time necessary reforms have not been realized and both political and public support is low. In addition, Ukraine's geopolitical position between NATO and Russia makes future relations to the Alliance a matter of uncertainty (see chapters 9 and 10 from Bynander and Simons in this volume for more detail on the subject). However, Ukraine has provided different joint NATO peace operations with personnel and every year a Target Plan is signed by both parties.

In 2001 Ukraine approached NATO for financial assistance on destruction of ammunition. The Netherlands and the United Kingdom on the other hand called attention to the dangers of SALW stockpiles in the country and in 2002 a feasibility study were established in which the NATO International Secretariat, NAMSA, American, British and Ukrainian experts, as well as the Ukrainian Ministry of Defence participated. The study identified best practices of destruction, available methods and costs and started the process of declaring SALW surplus. When the study was completed, the international political tension over the alleged sale of Kolchuga air defence system to Iraq with a possible involvement of the former Ukrainian president Kuchma and difficulties regarding state sovereignty and weaponry stockpiles became evident, the project was halted. Ukraine's political relations with NATO became frosty and no country was interested in being a lead nation as long as the government was unwilling to destroy SALW. As time went by and several ammunitions depots exploded making the need for economic assistance acute, the government changed its mind on SALW disposal and negotiations were resumed.[53] The USA stepped in and promised to be the lead nation and provide the project with considerable funds if MANPADS would be available for delineation as surplus and destruction. It was argued that 'MANPADS, in particular, represent a potential serious threat to civil and military aviation if they fall into the wrong hands'.[54]

The Trust Fund project started in 2005 and aimed to last for 12 years. During this period 133,000 tons ammunition, 1.5 million SALW and 1000 MANPADS would be destroyed. As a lead nation the US is responsible for arranging sufficient donations to cover costs. NAMSA is the executive body and the Ukrainian authorities on the other hand are in charge of logistics etc. After an initial good progress, discussions with the Ukrainian points of contact became unproductive, forcing the Deputy Minister of Defence to step in. The parliamentary elections in 2006 created an air of uncertainty, since the constellation of the team might be

---

53   *NATO*, 14 April 2005.
54   Ibid.

changed and overall the political situation in Ukraine was of concern because of its likely impact on the project.[55]

A report from 2006 by Hugh Griffiths on the projects result so far revealed that one negative side effect of the project had might been that the western participators had encouraged a sense in certain quarters of the MoD that MANPADS and Kalashnikovs were worth more than their actual value on the commercial market and should be withheld from being declared surplus. For example, the Supreme Headquarters Allied Powers Europe (SHAPE) supported initiatives to acquire large quantities of AK-47 derivatives and T-72 tank ammunition for the new Iraqi security forces. In addition, some of this weaponry exported in 2005 had not been registered in Ukraine's yearly export report. However, Griffiths argued the project had had a positive influence on Ukrainian surplus decision-making and it had founded important working relationships between the NATO and the MoD.[56]

The problems with the project continued until the second half of 2009. Internal Ukrainian political, legislative and financial obstacles had resulted in delays in securing the required government-level approvals, despite formal and informal efforts of several institutions of NATO, the USA State Department and the European Council Presidency.[57] Furthermore, the Ukrainians had offered SALW for destruction, but in spite of the MoD's assurances of the release of them, the ministry failed to fulfil its promises.[58] However, in July 2009, a change in the Governments attitude to the project was noted. The MoD stated that its was prepared to release 54,000 SALW to the project for destruction and further releases were expected in the near future, although no further MANPADS would be available for destruction in this phase. Additionally, ammunition destruction had finally started and progress had been better than expected by NAMSA. The Lead Nation, the USA, has indicated that if Ukraine would meet its obligations, it would consider extending the project until 31 December 2010 (first phase), secure extra funding to enable the planned destruction of 15 000 tonnes of ammunition and begin negotiations for a follow-on, second phase.[59]

In addition to the SALW destruction project, the NATO is also involved in reforming the Security Sector of Ukraine responsible for the control of SALW. For example the Alliance urges the Ukrainian government to implement a Partnership Action Plan on terrorism, including strengthening efforts to ensure strict control over arms export and take part in international export regimes. Moreover, the adaptation of national legislation in accordance with the EU Code of Conduct on Arms Export has especially been advocated. NATO has helped Ukraine to transform and streamline the Border Guard, but preventing arms trafficking has not been identified as a top priority in this work. In the Action Plan 2006, the

---

55   *NATO*, first-fourth periodic reports on the NAMSA project.
56   Griffiths, H., 02.2007.
57   More information about the EU's involvement in the project will follow below.
58   *NATO*, 2009a.
59   *NATO*, 2009b.

Alliance for the first time mentioned the need to reform the Ukrainian Security Service (SBU) and the State Export Service (SES). It was suggested that a NATO-Ukraine expert working group would be established to address these requirements. NATO has held consultation with Ukraine on transparency and public oversight over the SBU, but the reform plans concerning the SES seem to have come to nothing, as these have not been discussed in the Action Plans since then.[60] Overall, NATO strivings to reform Ukraine's Security Sector in large is a top priority and consultations with international partners, particularly NATO itself and its allies, are often the suggested method to reach the desired goal.[61]

The EU, SALW and SSR

The EU policy on SALW related issues has developed gradually since 1998 when the first framework to tackle the threat of SALW accumulation was prepared by the European Council. This was renewed in 2002 and the latest update was made in 2005 resulting in the 'EU Strategy to combat illicit accumulation and trafficking of SALW and their ammunition'.

The document is interconnected with the 'European Security Strategy 2003' (ESS), since four out of five post cold war challenges (terrorism, conflicts, state failure and organized crime[62]) mentioned in ESS are said to be worsened by SALW.

The widely spread of SALW is considered to be a growing threat to security and peace processes in conflict areas. These kinds of conflicts are acknowledged to be a problem all over the world, but Africa is identified as the most affected continent. The EU has therefore participated in different aid programs, both containing elements of disarmament, demobilization and reintegration (DDR) and security sector reform in this part of the world. However, the EU's actions have mostly been reactive, but according to the new strategy the European Council intend to work with preventive measurements to a larger extent. One way of doing this is focusing on the supply side, which to a large extent are related to SALW stockpiles in Eastern and South Eastern Europe left over from the Cold War, but also cheap and insufficiently controlled manufacturing located in the same geographic area. The European Council has suggested several instruments in the struggle against accumulation of SALW in terms of SSR: Member States' civilian and military capabilities, CFSP and ESDP instruments (as well as the Code of Conduct on Arms Exports[63]), other external action instruments and police, customs and judiciary action within the EU. The strategy also advocates that issues

---

60   *NATO*, 2005; *NATO*, 2006.

61   *NATO*, 2009c.

62   The fifth threat is proliferation of weapons of mass destructions. European Council, 12 December 2003.

63   For more information about *The EU's Code of Conduct on Arms Export*, visit http://www.consilium.europa.eu.

regarding SALW could be incorporated in treaties with other countries, which in the Ukrainian case would be the European Neighbourhood Policy (ENP). In December 2008 the European council adopted a reference article on SALW to be inserted in agreements with third countries and concluded that negotiations on the non-proliferation of WMD could be complemented with a separate article on SALW.

The EU in Ukraine

The first bilateral agreements between Ukraine and the EU were settled in the 1990's. Ukraine has for a long time uttered its wishes to join the EU, but these have not been fulfilled and the government has to be content with being a member of the ENP for the time being. Relations between the two parties have nonetheless grown stronger after the Orange Revolution and after Ukraine became an adjacent neighbour in 2004 to the Union, when Poland, Slovenia and Hungary's became members of the EU.[64]

The first notion of the EU's interest in SALW related issues in Ukraine is documented in the 'European Council Common Strategy of 11 December 1999 on Ukraine'.[65] The Council intended to explore the possibilities of creating regular expert level Troika conferences with Ukraine in the margins of CFSP working groups on disarmament, non-proliferation and export of conventional arms. One of the purposes of these meetings would have been to set up cooperation between the EU and Ukraine in the field of non-proliferation of small arms and light weapons. Considerations were also made on how to prevent trafficking of small arms, which was thought to be a source of instability for Ukraine and neighbouring countries. The European Council suggested that a Joint Action would might be possible to draw up, that would include reinforcing control capacities of police and custom services, tackle this kind of criminality in training courses and develop exchange of information between the EU and Europol Member States in order to enhance the analysis on criminal activity regarding SALW. The proposals have not been taken any further and no official agreement between the Europol and Ukraine exists.

The Union has expressed concern on several occasions, about Ukrainian arms export to conflict zones and requested Ukraine to subscribe to the principles of the 'EU Code of Conduct on Arms Exports', something that also have been

---

64 EU relations with Ukraine are based on the 1998 Partnership and Co-operation agreement. In 2001 a separated document was established in the field of justice, freedom and security called the EU Action Plan on Justice and Home Affairs with Ukraine, which prioritize readmission and migration, border management, the fight against money laundering, trafficking in human beings and drugs as well as corruption, preventing and fighting sexual exploitation of children and child pornography. The ENP Action Plan was adopted in 2005 by Ukraine and is gradually implemented.

65 *Official Journal of the European Communities*, 23 December 1999.

pointed out in the Action Plan for Justice and Home Affairs.[66] The Ukrainians have accepted to join the above mentioned meetings (the first was held in 2000) exchanging information on arms embargoes and countries/regions of concern, latest developments in arms export policy and legislation. In 2005 Ukraine agreed to 'take due account of the content and principles of the EU Code of Conduct on Arms Exports' in its Action Plan with the EU (adopted February 2005).

In the 'ENP Action Plan 2004' (prepared by the Commission), Ukraine and the EU is recommended to 'further develop co-operation in the fight against the trafficking of firearms',[67] as well as 'address threats for security, public health and environment posed by Ukrainian stockpiles of old ammunition, inter alia anti personnel land mines'.[68] The 'ENPI Eastern Regional Indicative Programme 2007-2010' (intended to complement the Country Strategy Papers produced for each country in the region) mentions priority support for five strategic categories. One of these categories is composed of anti-personnel landmines, explosive remnants of war, small arms and light weapons in the context of organized crime. This is seen as a serious challenge, worsened by the fact that large parts of the region constitute key smuggling and trafficking routes for illicit small arms and light weapons from insufficiently controlled stocks.[69] On the other hand, 'The Country Strategy Paper 2007-2013' refers to Ukrainian stockpiles of SALW, but only in terms of the need for destruction and allocated economic resources for assistance to perform this work.[70] This strategy was a result of a decision made by the European Council in 2005, to join the NAMSA project.[71] A financial contribution to the first phase of the project was seen as a possible solution to reduce the risks associated to the accumulation of large quantities of SALW and ammunition.[72]

This decision to join the NAMSA project was explained by the new EU strategy to prevent surplus sales of SALW to conflict torn areas, as mentioned above. By donating one million Euros for purchase and installation of equipment designed for long-term SALW and larger calibre ammunition destruction to the project, the EU could fulfil its wishes as well as Ukraine's. In 'The Second Progress Report on the implementation of the EU Strategy to Combat Illicit Accumulation and Trafficking of SALW and their Ammunition 2006',[73] the European Commission reported that Ukraine's Ministries of Defence, Foreign Affairs and Emergencies welcomed its support 'to work on a comprehensive Ukraine Action Plan tackling the

---

66   *Official Journal of the European Union*, 29 March 2003.

67   European Commission, 2004.

68   European Commission, 2004.

69   The other four categories are: i) Networks, in particular transport and energy networks; ii) Environment and forestry; iii) Border and migration management, the fight against international crime, and customs; iv) People-to-people activities, information and support. European Commission, 2006a.

70   European Commission, 2006.

71   *Official Journal of the European Union*, 1 December 2005.

72   *Official Journal of the European Union*, 1 December 2005.

73   Council of the European Union, 12 December 2006.

problems of surplus weapons and ammunition in a transparent and comprehensive manner.[74] As already have been mentioned above, the SALW destruction project faced several years of problems, due to political and economic obstacles. The EU has been involved in the negotiations with Ukraine to solve these problems and has threatened to leave the project and withdraw its economic support on several occasions.[75]

Except for the SALW destruction project, the EU supports the reform of the Ukrainian Border Guard and the work to improve border control, but the arguments brought forward to do this is related to stop illegal immigrants, rather than preventing arms smuggling. The EUBAM project initiated in 2005 on the Ukrainian and Moldovan borders aims to put a stop to smuggling, trafficking and customs fraud, although illegal transfers of SALW so far do not seem as a problem.[76] The EU also encourages good governance, an enhanced judicial system free from corruption and transparency in all levels of state administration. That kind of projects might improve for example the system of arms export as a side effect, but the EU has no specific intentions to improve the control of SALW by these efforts.[77]

Conclusions: Possibilities and Constraints for International SSR in the Field of Ukrainian SALW

Ukraine is a new challenge for the international community, when it comes to SSR and SALW. Organizations as the EU and OSCE have greater experience from conflict areas, than from post-authoritarian countries with an unreformed Security Sector, which is not interested or incapable of controlling its resources of SALW. The analysis of the EU, NATO and OSCE has showed that mainly two means have been used to try to reform Ukraine's Security Sector; destruction of SALW and policy documents/discussions. None of the organizations have tried to apply a holistic SSR approach on Ukraine, though they are able to do it, since they all are involved in different parts of Ukraine's Security Sector. They use documents and meetings to discuss best practices of arms export, but there is so much more that could be included in the realm of practical application rather than diplomatic rhetoric. Ukraine has been willing to accept different international documents, however some questions still remain.

Destruction of SALW is a well-known procedure by all old members of the EU and NATO. Furthermore, the same strategy has also been used in post-conflict

---

74   Council of the European Union, 12 December 2006.

75   *NATO*, 2009a.

76   European Union, 12.2005, EUBAM, 2006.

77   To see the official document on EU strategy from 2006 to combat the illegal trafficking of SALW and ammunition go to http://register.consilium.europa.eu/pdf/en/06/st05/st05319.en06.pdf.

countries and it is a concrete method to attack the problem. Hopefully, the NAMSA project in Ukraine has not only destroyed weapons, but also started to foster a sanctioned surplus policy within the Ukrainian authorities which they have lacked. This potential policy change, would rather have to be understood as a positive bi-effect, since the organizations seems to focus more on the elimination of SALW, than the implementation of a surplus policy that sees excess SALW destroyed.

The ambitious NAMSA project has as mentioned encountered difficulties because of political instability in Ukraine and financial issues. During 2008 and 2009 Ukraine has suffered from the world economic crisis and perhaps disposal of SALW has not been a prioritized topic. Moreover, Ukraine did not request assistance on the destruction of SALW, but on dangerous and obsolete ammunition, because it lacked the necessary resources itself. That is, the politicians of Ukraine were probably not particularly motivated to destroy SALW from the beginning. How could then the international community motivate a country as Ukraine? The NAMSA project has tried to bargain as mentioned. When the project has been stalled, high level politicians have stepped in to negotiate. It is quite unclear exactly what made Ukraine change its minds in 2009, but perhaps something even more valuable than the destruction of obsolete ammunition was at stake. The EU and NATO have the advantage that they could offer a country as Ukraine something more or put pressure on it (the carrot or the whip), since the organizations are involved in several projects in Ukraine and the country is dependent on them in a number of aspects. However, when the OSCE agrees to destroy ammunition in Ukraine without demanding anything in return, it risks undermining the other organizations bargaining strategy. Therefore, international actors have to be coordinated.

Another problem that the NAMSA project has had to face is the Ukrainian political instability. Additionally, the entire Security Sector and arms industry are more or less involved in this struggle. Could the international community do anything to prevent this? Perhaps by trying to depoliticize the Security Sector, but it is quite difficult and intricate to try to influence the Ukrainian internal political struggles. The organizations could at least try to make sure that the project is sanctioned in all political fractions, to make it survive any changes in the political sphere.

References

Badrak, V., 'State Control Over Sensitive Exports in Ukraine'. *Eksport Vooruzheniy Journal* 4, 2001.
Bailes, A.J.K. et al., 'Relics of Cold War – Europe's Challenge, Ukraine's Experience'. SIPRI Policy Paper, No. 6, November 2003.
Centre for International Cooperation and Security, 03.2005, 'Assessing and Reviewing the Impact of Small Arms Projects on Arms Availability and Poverty'. Retrieved 20 May 2007 from http://www.bradford.ac.uk.

Chumak, V., 'Security Sector Reform in Ukraine – Analytical Report'. International Centre for Policy Studies. Available at: http://www.icps.kiev.ua, February 2007.

Council of the European Union, 12 December 2006, 'Second Progress Report on the Implementation of the EU Strategy to Combat Illicit Accumulation and Trafficking of SALW and their Ammunition'. Retrieved 12 July 2007 from http://register.consilium.europa.eu.

EUBAM, 2006, 'Annual Report – European Union Border Assistance Mission to Moldova and Ukraine: 2005/2006'. Retrieved 1 August 2007 from http://www.eubam.org.

Eurasia Daily Monitor, 24 January 2005, 'Did Ukraine's Security Service Really Prevent Bloodshed During the Orange Revolution?' Retrieved 6 July 2007 from http://www.taraskuzio.net.

European Commission, 2004, 'Recommendation on the Implementation of the EU-Ukraine Action Plan'. Retrieved 28 June 2007 from http://ec.europa.eu.

European Commission, 2006, 'European Neighbourhood and Partnership Instrument – Ukraine Country Strategy Paper 2007-2013'. Retrieved 10 July 2007 from http://ec.europa.eu.

European Commission, 2006a, 'European Neighbourhood and Partnership Instrument Eastern Regional Programme Strategy Paper 2007-2013'. Retrieved 10 July 2007 from http://ec.europa.eu.

European Council, 1998, 'The EU Code of Conduct on Arms exports'. Available at: http://www.consilium.europa.eu.

European Council, 12.12.2003, 'A Secure Europe in a Better World – European Security Strategy'. Retrieved 3 July 2007 from http://www.consilium.europa.eu.

European Union, 12.2005, 'Factsheet – EU Border Assistance Mission to Moldova and Ukraine'. Retrieved 1 August 2007 from http://www.consilium.europa.eu.

Financial Times, 25 May 2007, 'EU Urges Ukraine Rivals to Avoid Violence'. Retrieved 1 June 2007 from http://www.ft.com.

Freedom House Organisation [n.d.], 'Table 4. Independent Media Ratings History and Regional Breakdown'. Retrieved 16 July 2007 from http://www.freedomhouse.hu.

Global Marketing System [n.d.], 'Leading Ukrainian Companies Database – Tasko, Corporation'. Retrieved 2 June 2007 from http://www.rada.com.ua/eng/catalog/.

Global Security [n.d.], 'Ukraine Defence Industry'. Retrieved 20 August 2007 from http://www.globalsecurity.org/military.

Griffiths, H., 02.2007, 'In the Interests of All – Negotiated Surplus Decision-Making in Ukraine'. Small Arms Survey.

Hänggi, H., 'Chapter 1: Conceptualising Security Sector Reform and Reconstruction', *Reform and Reconstruction of the Security Sector*, Münster, Geneva, 2004.

House of Commons, Business and Enterprise, Defence, Foreign Affairs and International Development Committees, 19 August 2009, 'Scrutiny of Arms

Export Controls (2009): UK Strategic Export Controls Annual Report 2007, Quarterly Reports for 2008, licensing policy and review of export control legislation'. Available at: www.publications.parliament.uk.

Interfax, 27 May 2004, 'Ukrainian Authorities Arrest Explosives Traffickers'. Retrieved 15 July 2007 from http://nisat.org.

International Alert [n.d.], 'Small Arms Control in Ukraine'. Retrieved 10 May 2007 from http://www.international-alert.org.

International Press Institute, 2003, 'World Press Freedom Review 2003 – Ukraine'. Retrieved 28 June 2007 from http://www.freemedia.at.

Jane's Intelligence Review, 1 July 2005, 'Curbing Arms Industry is Vital for Ukraine's NATO Ambitions'. Retrieved 3 May 2007 from http://www.janes. com.

Krause, K., 'The Challenge of Small Arms and Light Weapons'. Retrieved 20 April 2007 from http://isn.ethz.ch, 17 May 1998.

Kyiv Post, 3 September 2009, 'British Investigate Murky Arms Deal Involving Ukraine, Embargoed Nation'.

Moscow Kommersant, 8 December 2001, 'Reports Implicating Ukraine Security Chief'.

NATO, 14 April 2005, 'Proposal for the Destruction of Conventional Ammunition, Small Arms and Light Weapons, and Man-potable Air Defence Systems in Ukraine'.

NATO, 2005, 'NATO-Ukraine Annual Target Plan for 2006 in the Framework of NATO-Ukraine Action Plan'. Retrieved 7 July 2007 from http://www.nato. int.

NATO, 2006, 'NATO-Ukraine Annual Target Plan for the Year 2007 in the Framework of NATO-Ukraine Action Plan'. Retrieved 7 July 2007 from http:// www.nato.int.

NATO, 2009a, '14th Periodic Report on the NATO/PfP Trust Fund Project for the Destruction of Conventional Ammunition, Small Arms and Light Weapons, and Man-Portable Air Defence Systems in Ukraine'.

NATO, 2009b, '15th Periodic Report on the NATO/PfP Trust Fund Project for the Destruction of Conventional Ammunition, Small Arms and Light Weapons, and Man-Portable Air Defence Systems in Ukraine'.

NATO, 2009c, 'NATO-Ukraine Annual Target Plan for 2009 in the Framework of NATO-Ukraine Action Plan'.

NATO/EAPC [n.d.], 'Executive Summary of the EAPC Contribution to the UN Follow-up Conference'. Retrieved 1 July 2007 from http://disarmament. un.org.

NATO Handbook, 15 October 2002, 'Chapter 6: Arms Control, Disarmament and Non-proliferation'. Retrieved 25 June 2007 from http://www.nato.int.

NATO Publications [n.d.], 'Trust Fund Projects – Promoting Security and Defence reform'. Retrieved 28 June 2007 from http://www.nato.int.

Official Journal of the European Communities, 15 January 1999, 'Joint Action of 17 December 1998 to Combat the Destabilising Accumulation and Spread of

Small Arms and Light Weapons'. Retrieved 10 May 2007 from http://eur-lex. europa.eu.

Official Journal of the European Communities, 23 December 1999, 'European Council Common Strategy of 11 December 1999 on Ukraine (1999/877/ CFSP)'. Retrieved 1 July 2007 from http://eur-lex.europa.eu.

Official Journal of the European Union, 29 March 2003, 'EU Action Plan on Justice and Home Affairs in Ukraine'. Retrieved 1 July 2007 from http://eur-lex.europa.eu.

Official Journal of the European Union, 1 December 2005, 'Council Decision 2005/852/CFSP of 29 November 2005 for the Destruction of Small Arms and Light Weapons (SALW) and their Ammunition in Ukraine'. Retrieved 12 July 2007 from http://eur-lex.europa.eu.

OSCE [n.d.](a), 'Handbook of Best Practices on Small Arms and Light Weapons'. Retrieved 29 May 2007 from http://www.osce.org.

OSCE [n.d.](b), 'Forum for Security Co-operation, Anti-terrorism'. Retrieved 29 May 2007 from http://www.osce.org/fsc.

OSCE [n.d.](c), 'Forum for Security Co-operation, Assistance Projects – Ukraine'. Retrieved 28 May 2007 from http://www.osce.org/fsc.

OSCE [n.d.](d), 'Working Together to Enhance Security and Stability – OSCE Projects on SALW and Conventional Ammunition'. Retrieved 27 May 2007 from http://www.osce.org.

OSCE, 24 November 2000, 'OSCE Document on Small Arms and Light Weapons'. Retrieved 28 May 2007 from http://www.osce.org.

Oxfam Briefing Note, 15 June 2006, 'Ammunition: the Fuel of Conflict'. Retrieved 20 May 2007 from http://www.oxfam.org.

Ploughshares, 3.2001, 'Security Sector Reform and the Demand for Small Arms and Light Weapons'. Retrieved 15 May 2007 from http://www.ploughshares.ca.

Polyakov, L., 'Aging Stocks of Ammunition and SALW in Ukraine – Risks and Challenges'. Bonn International Centre for Conversion, Paper 41. Available at: http://www.bicc.org, 2005.

Radio Free Europe, 15 June 2006, 'World: Illicit Ammunition Trade Fuels Conflicts'. Retrieved 12 August 2007 from http://www.rferl.org.

Ryerson University, SAFER-net, 22 August 2003, 'Ukraine'. Retrieved 7 July 2007 from http://www.ryerson.ca/SAFER-Net.

Safer World Organisation, 04.2007, 'Ukrainian MPs Visit UK Parliament'. Retrieved 4 June 2007 from http://www.saferworld.org.uk.

Shelley, L. [n.d.], 'Organized Crime and Corruption in Ukraine: Impediments to the Development of a Free Market Economy'. Retrieved 7 April 2007 from http://www.demokratizatsiya.org.

Small Arms Net [n.d.], 'Definition of Small Arms and Light Weapons'. Retrieved 28 April 2007 from www.smallarmsnet.org/definition.htm.

Small Arms Survey [n.d.], 'Reform of the State Security Forces and Small Arms Component'. Retrieved 15 August 2007 from http://www.smallarmssurvey. org.

Strekal, O., 'Civil Control Over the National Security Policymaking Process in Ukraine'. Retrieved 8 July 2007 from http://www.nato.int, 1997.

Synovitz, R., 'UN: Eastern Europe's Arms Trade Violates Sanctions'. Radio Free Europe. Available at: http://www.rferl.org, March 2000.

Transparency International, 2009, 'Corruption Perceptions Index 2009'. Available at: http://www.transparency.org.

Ukrainian Government, 3 June 2006, 'Державна служба експортного контролю України – Інформація про обсяги міжнародних передач озброєнь, здійснених Україною у 2004 році'. Retrieved 15 June 2006 from http://www. dsecu.gov.ua.

Zerkalo Nedeli, 17-23 June 2006, 'A New Epoch of Arms and Armaments Results in Tougher Play'. Retrieved 10 July 2007 from http://www.mw.ua.

Zerkalo Nedeli, 6 October 2006, 'Apple of Arms Discord'. Retrieved 11 June 2007 from http://www.mw.ua.

Zerkalo Nedeli, 17-23 March 2007, 'Scramble for Control of Arms Business'. Retrieved 11 July 2007 from http://www.mw.ua.

Chapter 12
Missed Opportunities: The European Union and Security Sector Reform in Afghanistan

Mark Sedra[1]

Introduction

In US President Barack Obama's December 2009 West Point Address in which he laid out his plan to stabilize Afghanistan through a troop and civilian surge, he clearly pointed to an exit strategy of the US and international community. The mission, he said, of the 30,000 new US troops he would be deploying to Afghanistan would not solely be to disrupt and destroy the Taliban, but to 'help create the conditions for the United States to transfer responsibility to the Afghans'.[2] The process to develop the Afghan National Security Forces (ANSF) to which President Obama was referring is the central component of the country's security sector reform (SSR) agenda whose aim is to transform the security and justice architecture of the state, ensuring not only that it is more efficient and effective, but governed and managed in accordance with democratic norms and international standards. The problem was, as Obama put it, that US forces have lacked 'the full support they need to effectively train and partner with the Afghan Security Forces and better secure the population'.[3] This was both recognition of the limited and disappointing achievements of the SSR process and an expression of frustration over the insufficiency of allied – primarily European – contributions to it.

Although by 2010 the US was, by the sheer force of the resource levels it was contributing, the clear leader and driver of the SSR process in Afghanistan, disbursing over US\$25 billion to the training of the ANSF from 2002-2010, the process had started out as a genuinely multilateral enterprise, with European states playing a leading and indispensable role. In the spring of 2002, a lead nation framework was inaugurated under the auspices of the G8 to oversee and underwrite the development and transformation of the Afghan security sector, with European states playing a central role. Germany, Italy and Great Britain were tasked under

---

1   Mark Sedra is a Senior Fellow at the Centre for International Governance Innovation (CIGI) and teaches at the University of Waterloo.
2   President Barack Obama, 'The Way Forward in Afghanistan and Pakistan', speech delivered on 1 December 2009 at US Military Academy, West Point, NY. Available at: http://www.msnbc.msn.com/id/34231058/ns/politics-white_house/, accessed 15 June 2010.
3   Ibid.

the framework to spearhead reforms in the areas of policing, justice, and counter-narcotics respectively, with the United States and Japan taking on lead nation responsibilities for military reform and demilitarization. While this turf setting exercise certainly succeeded in tying the five donors to their individual areas of responsibility, it was not able to ensure that adequate resource levels were invested in each, nor did it establish a mechanism to facilitate process wide coordination.

Over the subsequent five years the SSR process would stall and even flounder, with noticeable progress made only in the area of military reform, attributable to both the sizable contribution of resources made by the US and the decision to build the Afghan National Army (ANA) from scratch rather than work with broken and tainted existing structures and actors. One can legitimately speak of several lost years in the other pillars of the SSR agenda, where not only was progress slow, but in some areas ground was lost. This can be attributed to two broad factors: First, the international community failed to adequately assess the scale of the problems and challenges that existed in Afghanistan. The needs assessments undertaken by the IMF and World Bank with support from the UN prior to the December 2001 Tokyo Donor Conference severely underestimated the resource levels needed to reconstruct Afghanistan, a factor both of the insufficient time available to undertake these studies and the inhospitable nature of the security conditions in Afghanistan where the war was still wrapping up. In the security sphere, close observers of Afghanistan in 2001 have described the naïveté of donor assumptions that the security situation would improve on its own and that Afghan war fatigue would trump political and strategic drivers of conflict, not to mention factional and ethnic tensions, to solidify the peace.

The light footprint approach to state building adopted by the international community in Afghanistan was both an outgrowth of this faith in the inherent stability of the post-Taliban political order and a reflection of the reticence of the US and other key donors, including the European states, to establish an international trusteeship akin to that in Bosnia-Herzegovina or Timor-Leste. The light footprint, which sought to emphasize Afghan ownership and leadership – a difficult proposition in a politically fragmented state facing massive capacity – ensured that the SSR process, like other aspects of the state building agenda, would lack both adequate resources and political will to make tangible progress.

Secondly, European and other key donor states lacked the appropriate institutional mechanisms to deliver the necessary aid and assistance to the field in a timely manner, particularly once the security situation began to deteriorate. Countries like Germany, for instance, lacked the institutional systems and structures to rapidly deploy and sustain large numbers of police officers in Afghanistan.

The false start for the SSR process coupled with the sharp rise of insurgent activity distorted the SSR agenda. Always primarily fixated on the development of the ANSF, the SSR process since 2007 could best be described as a subset of the NATO-led counter insurgency (COIN) strategy rather than a part of the country's state building process. Of the resources dedicated to SSR, the vast majority go to the training and equipping of the ANSF, not to developing the justice system, building governance structures, and promoting civil society engagement in the security arena, all critical dimensions of the SSR concept. Even within the ANSF the process has been heavily militarized, with police development aimed more at creating 'little soldiers' than community police.[4] In fact, SSR specialists would be hard-pressed to refer to the process in Afghanistan as SSR at all, as it features few of the distinctive elements that distinguish SSR from previous forms of security assistance.

European states engaged in the Afghan SSR process, recognize these shortcomings, directing their criticisms at flawed US planning rather than their own strategies and approaches. Considering that Europe remains the conceptual home for the SSR model, with the US only now beginning to embrace it, its inability to organize an effective response to the problems of the Afghan SSR agenda is all the more striking and disappointing.

One way in which Europe could have exercised greater influence and leverage over the direction of SSR in Afghanistan would have been to expand its engagement in the process. However, despite the achievement of greater unity of effort among European SSR stakeholders through the creation of the EUPOL mission in 2007, European engagement in the process did not increase substantially. While bureaucratic deadlocks and inadequate institutional mechanisms at the EU level have obstructed the development of EUPOL, it has been a lack of political commitment among prominent member states that has most impeded its work.

Afghanistan is not lost and SSR is not dead. It remains the lynchpin of the state building and COIN strategies, and despite the false start, limited progress in some areas has been made. Nonetheless, an uphill battle remains, with SSR facing specific and potent challenges ranging from fiscal sustainability to ethnic and political fragmentation. With the insurgency escalating, it is understandable that some donors would seek to instrumentalize SSR as a means to expedite the stabilization of the country. Experience has shown though, as reflected in SSR doctrine, that co-opting the reforming security sector to achieve short-term political and security goals may bring some immediate gains but can have disastrous long-term ramifications, particularly for democratic development, human-rights protection and peace-building. Militarized security and justice institutions tend to create new fault lines of conflict rather than break down existing ones. Afghanistan may be a particularly challenging case of SSR, but it also reflects some of the fundamental contradictions and weaknesses of the SSR concept, namely the wide gap between the model's normative principles and implementation realities.

---

4   Bailey, D.H. and Perito, R.M., *The Police in War: Fighting Insurgency, Terrorism and Violent Crime*. Boulder: Lynne Reinner, 2009.

The State of Afghanistan's SSR Process in 2010

It cannot be said that insufficient resources has been the main impediment to SSR in Afghanistan; the US had spent over US$25 billion on the ANSF by 2010 and the Pentagon has submitted a budget request for a further $11.6 billion for 2011.[5] This dwarfs the approximately US$1.4 billion committed by the European Commission and key EU states to the process between 2002 and 2010.[6] While overall resource levels have increased significantly as the process has developed, serious questions can be asked about how the money has been allocated. Only a small fraction of the funds spent on SSR, less than five percent, have been dedicated to judicial/ legal reform, prison reform and the promotion of good governance within the security sector. As a result, these areas have lagged far behind the ANSF in their development and been a drag on the entire security sector.

While a lack of money has not been a major problem for Afghanistan's SSR agenda, a gap in human resources, in the form of trainers and mentors for the ANP and ANA, has been. As of early 2010 there was a gap of 4,000 army and police mentors, with the US filling the vast majority of mentor slots in the force.[7] European states in particular have been singled out by the US and NATO secretariat for their failure to adequately fill mentor positions for the ANSF.

One of the most pressing problems facing the SSR process is the significant levels of wastage and leakage of aid, either through corruption or simple mismanagement. This is perhaps not surprising considering the strong pressure on donor agencies to spend money quickly coupled with the low absorptive capacity and high rates of corruption in the Afghan state. For instance, tens of thousands of weapons delivered to both the Afghan National Police (ANP) and Afghan National Army (ANA) have gone unaccounted for over the past five years, many of which

---

5   Tarnoff, C., *Afghanistan: US Foreign Assistance* (Washington, DC: Congressional Research Service, 5 March 2010); United States Department of Defense, Overview: Fiscal Year 2011 Budget Request (Washington, DC: United States Department of Defence, February 2010).

6   North Atlantic Treaty Organization (NATO) (2010), 'Fact Sheet: NATO's Police Operational Mentor and Liaison Teams (POMLTs) June 2010'. Available at: http://www.isaf. nato.int/images/stories/File/factsheets-june/JUne%202010-Fact%20Sheet%20POMLT. pdf; Government of Germany (2007), 'Funding for Police Assistance in Afghanistan Tripled'. Available at: http://www.auswaertiges-amt.de/diplo/en/Aussenpolitik/Regionale Schwerpunkte/AfghanistanZentralasien/AktuelleArtikel/071115-Erhoehung-Polizei mittel,navCtx=252166.html; Government of Germany (2010), 'International Support for an Effective Afghan Police Force'. Available at: http://www.auswaertiges-amt.de/ diplo/en/Aussenpolitik/RegionaleSchwerpunkte/AfghanistanZentralasien/Polizeiaufbau. html; European Union (2010), 'EU Police Mission in Afghanistan (EUPOL) Factsheet'. Available at: http://www.consilium.europa.eu/uedocs/cms_data/docs/missionPress/files/10 0218%20FACTSHEET%20EUPOL%20Afghanistan%20-%20version%2017_EN.pdf (all accessed 16 June 2010).

7   Reuters, 'US Makes Urgent Appeal to NATO on Afghan Training', 4 February 2010.

are believed to have found their way into the hands of insurgents via the black market.[8] Despite wide publicity and awareness of this problem since 2004-05, asset management structures within the ANA and ANP remained underdeveloped and a serious problem in 2010.

The ANA is often touted as the success story of the Afghan SSR process, having reached a force size of roughly 100,000 by mid-2010 and showing significant competence and professionalism in operations. However, as 2010 reports of the Centre for International Governance Innovation (CIGI) and the International Crisis Group (ICG) showed, this rosy image is far too simplistic and even misleading.[9] The reports laid bare some of the imposing challenges faced by the force, including high rates of attrition, ethnic factionalism and poor logistics. Even still, the ANA remains far ahead of both the ANP and the judicial system in terms of its development.

In a startling admission in the spring of 2010, Lt. Gen William B. Caldwell IV, who leads the NATO Training Mission-Afghanistan (NTM-A), the body that oversees the training and development of the ANSF, asserted that barely 25 percent of the 92,000 ANP currently on duty had received formal training.[10] In fact, the NTM-A cites as one of their major achievements the reversal of the ANP training formula from deploy and then train to train and then deploy. This raises serious questions about the tens of thousands of young Afghans that the US-funded police training program, run out of eight training centres across the country, has graduated over the past five years. A significant number have been killed, with the casualty rate for the ANP 3-4 times that of the ANA, while others merely went home with their weapons, contributing to an attrition rate measured at 25-30 percent per annum.[11] The other answer may be that many of those police never existed. They are 'ghost police', part of the numbers game in Afghanistan perpetuated by ANP commanders to pilfer salaries and donor agencies and private contractors to demonstrate progress to impatient governments at home.

Even a cursory glance at some of the statistics regarding the ANP demonstrates the scale of the challenge that exists for the force, with up to 70 percent believed to be illiterate, 80 percent engaged in some form of corruption or criminality, and up to 50 percent users of illegal narcotics. In light of these realities it is of little the surprise that the police have not been able to fulfil their part of the clear,

8 Bhatia M. and Sedra, M., *Afghanistan, Arms and Conflict: Armed Groups, Disarmament and Security in a Post-War Society*. New York: Routledge, 2008.

9 International Crisis Group (ICG), 'A Force in Fragments: Reconstituting the Afghan National Army', Asia Report No. 190, Brussels, INCG, 12 May 2010; Centre for International Governance Innovation (CIGI), 'Security Sector Reform Monitor: Afghanistan', No. 3, Waterloo, Canada, CIGI, May 2010.

10 Miller, T.C., Hosenball, M. and Moreau, R., 'The Gang that Couldn't Shoot Straight', *Newsweek*, 29 March 2010.

11 Maj-Gen Mike Ward, 'NATO Response to "The Illusion of Police Reform"', Blog – Dispatches from the Field: Perspectives on the Afghanistan Conflict. Available at: http://www.cigionline.org/blogs/2010/4/nato-response-illusion-police-reform.

hold and build COIN strategy, namely holding and securing territory that have been cleared of insurgents.

Considering the functional limitations and even basic incompetence of the ANP, it would seem logical that donors would prioritize training as a means to raise the quality of the force to something approaching international standards. However, the pressures to get boots on the ground, to produce 'little soldiers' to relieve pressure on NATO troops in the war against the Taliban has seemingly trumped the genuine needs of the ANP. As a result, basic training was streamlined in 2010 from eight to six weeks. According to NATO officials, the actual period of instruction did not change, due to longer training days and reduced weekends. However, when you consider that police in Iraq receive twelve weeks of training and the only effective branch of the Afghan police (the specialized Afghan Civil Order Police) receive sixteen, the insufficiency of the six week training cycle is apparent.[12]

In spite of the setbacks experienced by the police reform process over the past eight years, some developments since 2008 – namely the launch of the well-conceived Focused District Development training program and the appointment of the acclaimed reformist Haneef Atmar as Interior Minister – generated some hope that the process could be turning a corner. In an institution lacking effective leadership and rife with corruption, the appointment in late 2008 of Atmar, credited with moulding two effective government ministries – Education and Rural Rehabilitation and Development – was heralded as a breakthrough. As with many breakthroughs in Afghanistan's though, it was short-lived, as President Karzai dismissed Atmar along with popular Intelligence Chief Amrullah Saleh in June 2010, allegedly over security breakdowns in Kabul during the National Peace Jirga in the same month, but believed to be part of an effort of Karzai to consolidate his political support base within the government. Regardless of the motives, the dismissal leaves the Ministry of Interior and in fact the entire SSR process adrift once again, devoid of a reliable local partner that could place an Afghan stamp on the process.

The Afghan justice and penitentiary systems have not fared much better than the police in terms of implementing reform. Almost every facet of the justice system from human capacity in the form of trained jurists to infrastructure such as courthouses and pre-trial detention facilities are lacking. A majority of the country's judges have had no formal legal education, in *sharia* or secular law, with some lacking even secondary school education. Corruption is endemic and it is common for justice offices at the local level to be captured or co-opted by local strongmen. According to a number of surveys over the past eight years, only a fraction of the country's prisons come close to meeting basic human rights standards.[13] Reform

---

12   In Canada and several other Western donor countries basic training for police officers is roughly 24 weeks in duration.

13   Hodes, C. and Sedra, M., 'The Search for Security in Post-Taliban Afghanistan'. IISS Adelphi Paper 391. New York: Routledge, 2007.

initiatives that have been undertaken in the judicial and prison systems have tended to be small scale and ad hoc, with some notable achievements having been made in law collection and infrastructural development. The shortcomings of the judicial system have prompted a majority of Afghans, in the range of 80-90 percent, to look to informal or traditional structures and actors to resolve their disputes. They tend to be viewed as more affordable, trustworthy, geographically accessible, and locally legitimate than formal bodies. However, few initiatives have been launched to reconcile formal and informal structures and build a relationship of complementarity between them. This may be do to the reluctance of state judicial institutions in Afghanistan to recognize the legitimacy of informal systems, with the Afghan Supreme Court openly resisting notions of ceding authority to non-state justice actors. This resistance to embracing the realities on the ground typifies the challenges and contradictions within Afghanistan's judicial reform process.

The problems confronting Afghanistan's SSR process in 2010 are largely unchanged from those pondered in 2002, reflecting the inability of reform stakeholders to alter course or adapt effectively to the difficult conditions that have prevailed. Perhaps the most prominent problem facing the process has been the adverse security environment and the steady growth of the Taliban-led insurgency. Complex processes of institutional transformation like SSR are difficult enough to undertake in ideal security and political conditions, let alone amidst a war. The SSR model itself was not designed to operate in conditions of acute insecurity, but rather in stable political and security environments like those which prevailed in the states of the former Soviet Union following the collapse of the Berlin Wall or in post-Apartheid South Africa. The ongoing conflict in Afghanistan has distorted the SSR process in a number of ways. First, it has altered the timelines for the process; what is inherently a long-term process is characteristically viewed in Afghanistan as a short-term remedy for insecurity and a weapon against the insurgency. Second, it places enormous pressure on the nascent security structures, actors and institutions being developed or reformed. New police and military forces are deployed straight from the training ground to the front lines, leaving no time to gain experience on the job, become acclimatized to their duties, and receive in-service training and mentoring. Finally, it has changed the roles and mandates of the security institutions. The police, for instance, have been transformed from community police to auxiliary soldiers or paramilitary fighters. Experience has shown that short-termist approaches to SSR, rather than nurturing democratically accountable and rights respecting security institutions, can breed security force impunity, corruption and politicization, signs of which are already beginning to emerge in Afghanistan.

The second major challenge can be described broadly as a lack of political commitment or will among the major SSR stakeholders. Political will in the affirmative refers to the ability or willingness of a political actor to expend political capital or take risks to achieve a particular policy outcome. Since SSR invariably alters the balance of power within the recipient country, robust political will is required among all stakeholders to deter potential spoilers in the process and overcome any challenges they may present. In the Afghan case, President Karzai has not displayed the requisite political will to move the process forward. This has been reflected in his choice of appointments, tolerating a string of inefficient, unqualified and even corrupt officials at the highest levels in the security establishment, particularly within the senior ranks of the Ministry of Interior and ANP. The only effective reformist Ministers the Ministry of Interior has had since 2001, Ali Jalali and Haneef Atmar, did not remain at there posts long enough to effect the type of structural change required. In the case of Jalali his resignation was motivated partly out of frustration over the President's interference in the appointments process for the ANP. Karzai's juggling of appointments, aimed at appeasing local strongmen and consolidating his support base, has paralysed efforts to de-factionalize the Ministry and crack down on corruption and graft.

Another sign of Karzai's tepid commitment to the SSR process is his tolerance of corruption and links to the drug trade within the security establishment. The absence of Afghan political will reflects and contributes to the ownership and leadership gap within the process. With the executive branch showing little interest in the type of comprehensive reforms demanded by the SSR process, there are few incentives for Afghan state officials to take up the mantel. Moreover, with the government tolerating unqualified actors in key security sector posts, the capability of state offices to implement the complex reforms entailed in SSR is highly limited.

The third challenge relates to the sustainability of reforms in the security sector. The Afghan National Development Strategy states the problem simply: ' ... the international community has imported models of security forces that impose costs Afghanistan may not be able to sustain'.[14] Even according to the most optimistic projections concerning the growth of Afghan revenue generating capacity over the coming decade, the country cannot hope to cover is recurrent security expenditure, which in 2009/10 represented roughly 200 percent of Afghan domestic revenues, for at least another decade.[15] An examination of historical precedent shows that when the state has been unable to pay its security forces, typically due to the withdrawal of foreign subsidies – whether British, Soviet or now American – the security sector has collapsed and conflict has ensured.

The international community is indeed, as several analysts have pointed out, recreating a rentier state in Afghanistan, with the Afghan government dependent on international aid and human resources to survive. It would be wishful thinking to suggest that a self-sufficient state apparatus, capable of containing insecurity, establishing a monopoly over the use of coercive force, and providing basic services to the population, could be created within in a mere eight years, especially considering that Afghanistan is one of the poorest countries in the world – second to the bottom in the UNDP's 2009 Human Development Index – and just emerged

---

14   Interim Afghanistan National Development Strategy (I-ANDS), 2006.
15   Figures taken from the website of the General Budget Directorate of the Afghan Ministry of Finance. Available at: http://www.budgetmof.gov.af/, accessed 17 June 2010.

from a brutal civil war that lasted more than two decades. However, it is still crucial to consider issues of sustainability over the long-term, to ensure that when the international community does leave Afghanistan the Afghan government possesses the resources and institutional tools to sustain the state. The painful reality for most Western donor states is that even after international troops leave Afghanistan, the core security donors will have to foot the bill for the comprehensive security apparatus that they helped to create for the foreseeable future. Failing to do so would only expedite the collapse of the Afghan state, mirroring historical experience. After all, in-sourcing the security of Afghanistan to the country's own security forces makes is much more economical for donor states than maintaining an open-ended troop deployment. According to Afghan Defence Minister Rahim Wardak, for the amount of money that the US and its NATO allies are spending in Afghanistan to deploy their forces for one year, they could train and equip a an ANA of 400,000 and sustain it for a decade.[16]

Europe's Contribution to SSR

European states have played a prominent role in the Afghan SSR process, serving as lead nations for three of its five pillars; however, this European face on the process belies the fairly limited impact it has had on its direction. It was, in fact, the failure of the European lead nations, patricianly Germany and Italy in the areas of policing and judicial reform to show the necessary ambition, commitment and resolve to effect real change that led to the breakdown of the lead nation system and the emergence of clear US ownership over the entire process. Even the EUPOL mission, formed after the US had effectively assumed control over the process, has struggled to garner the necessary resources from EU member states to fulfil its limited mandate. One can see the declining EU role in SSR in Afghanistan as a missed opportunity to forcefully present a European model of security assistance, with European states having been at the forefront of the development of the SSR concept over the past decade.

From the outset of the SSR process, resources were a main impediment to effective European engagement. It appears in hindsight that when Germany accepted lead nation status for police reform it did not adequately grasp the scale or urgency of the challenge that the task presented, something its early interventions reflected. Germany's first major initiative was the re-establishment of the National Police Academy, which provides university level education for a future cadre of senior officers. This was a laudable initiative, but little thought was given to the scores of rank and file patrolmen across the country, most of whom are illiterate and

---

16   Council on Foreign Relations (CFR), 'Afghan Defense Chief Unhappy with Obama Plan', Interview of Afghan Defence Minister, Gen Abdul Rahim Wardak by Greg Bruno, 16 April 2009. Available at: http://www.cfr.org/publication/19116/afghan_defense_chief_unhappy_with_obama_plan.html, accessed 17 June 2010.

lack any formal instruction in policing techniques, and who are the main providers of security at the grass roots level. The limitations of the German commitment are reflected in its funding disbursements, with Germany committing only €12 million per year from 2002 to 2007 and roughly €160 million from 2008-10, a paltry sum compared to the $6 billion the US contributed from 2002 to 2009, Moreover, Germany's human resource contribution did not come close to meeting the needs of the situation, with the German Police Project Office comprising only 25 officers in 2002 as well as one civilian strategic advisor responsible for the reform of the entire Ministry of Interior, comprising over 75,000 employees.[17]

The US responded to the gaps in the police reform process by gradually, and somewhat reluctantly at first, expanding their role in it from 2003 onwards, forming a set of regional training centres to train rank and file officers. US-German communication, however, did not develop at the same pace as the growth of US engagement. In fact, up until 2006-07, the relationship between the US police reform program and the GPPO was strained with very little communication and collaboration, a reflection of German anxieties over US infringement on their turf and US consternation over inadequate German investment in the process.

The situation in the judicial sector was not much better with the relationship between the Italian and US judicial reform missions openly hostile at times, as much a factor of the personalities of senior program managers as irreconcilable differences in program structures and approaches. Certainly, however, one of the primary drivers of coordination gaps in the rule of law sector as a whole were the differing legal and policing traditions of the European stakeholders and the United States. With the US coming from a common law legal tradition and featuring a decentralized police force and the Italians and Germans emanating from civil code based legal systems with national police agencies, their programming featured, at times, and fundamentally different messages. This had the effect of sending contradictory signals to the Afghans, wasting scarce resources and fostering mutual tensions.

The situation only began to improve in 2007 with the formation of the EUPOL mission and the establishment of the International Police Coordination Board (IPCB), which, despite evolving into a rather ineffective body, did introduce a mechanism for communication and collaboration. These developments were followed by a number of senior level cross appointments and secondments between the Coalition Security Transition Command-Afghanistan – the US military body responsible for SSR that was replaced by the NATO Training Mission-Afghanistan in November 2009 – and EUPOL that helped to facilitate greater communication and collaboration at the working level. Yet, despite improved collaboration, US frustration over the paucity of the EU commitment to the process has persisted.

The most powerful indicator of the mixed EU political commitment to the process has been the inability of EUPOL to fill its mandated staff quota of 400.

---

17   Hodes, C. and Sedra, M., *The Search for Security in Post-Taliban Afghanistan*. Oxford: Routledge, 2007.

As of June 2010, only 265 of the 400 staff slots were filled, the majority of which are based in Kabul. EU restrictions over the deployment of civilian personnel to insecure areas of the country have prevented EUPOL from establishing a critical cross-country presence. These staffing shortfalls undercut the ability of the mission to fulfil its mandate: to 'significantly contribute to the establishment under Afghan ownership of suitable and effective civilian policing arrangements, which will ensure appropriate interaction with the wider criminal justice system'.[18] The mission saw itself as fulfilling part of an informal division of responsibility in the rule of law reform process, with the US focusing on short-term training and institutional development while EUPOL emphasized long-term issues of sustainability and structural change.

Further challenging the EU's ability to fulfil this mandate and perceived role has been a problem of leadership. There have been three different chiefs of the EUPOL mission since its inauguration in June 2007, one leaving due to personality differences with the EU Special Representative who exercises political direction over the body. This has prevented the development of critical continuity in approach and leadership.

Some of these problems of resource shortfalls can seen as a result of competing priorities, such as the EU policing mission in Kosovo, that have stretched scarce resources, as well as the unpopularity of the Afghan mission in many European states. It can also, however, be attributed to the immaturity and insufficiency of structures and procedures at the headquarters level in Brussels and individual European capitals to rapidly respond to such crises, in this case to identify, recruit and deploy qualified civilian SSR experts rapidly.

While EUPOL and European SSR assistance to Afghanistan in general has made some modest gains it has largely failed to live up to its mandate and promise. In particular the EU's potential role as a check on US SSR short-termism is immensely important, but it has not committed the resources or achieved the type of impact in the security sector that would endow it with the credibility to constructively criticize its large partner. As one of the main drivers of the SSR concept globally and with genuine security interests at stake in Afghanistan, more could have been expected from Europe.

Conclusion

In many respects, the type of security assistance being provided to Afghanistan's security and justice institutions does not fit well under the rubric of security sector reform. The overwhelming focus of the process on training and equipping the ANSF defies the core principles of SSR, namely the need for a holistic agenda, a focus on

---

18   Quoted in Gross, E., 'Security Sector Reform in Afghanistan: The EU's Contribution'. Occasional Paper No. 78, Brussels, European Union Institute for Security Studies, April 2009, p. 29.

governance and a long-term outlook. The gradual hitching of the SSR process to the COIN bandwagon is understandable in light of the escalating insurgency and growing pressure to rapidly improve security and political conditions, but such a distortion of the model can have deleterious long term ramifications, namely an over-militarized sector that is fiscally unsustainable and highly politicized. In other words, within the security sector this process could be laying the seeds for the future unravelling of the state.

There is a need to decouple the SSR process from the COIN machine. This doesn't mean that the security and justice institutions should be built in a vacuum, without consideration of the war that currently grips Afghanistan, only that wartime conditions and circumstances should not dictate the shape and orientation of those institutions. For instance, justice and governance structures should no longer be neglected in favour of getting boots on the ground and the police should be seen through a community policing prism rather than a paramilitary one. In the present environment in 2010, with the Taliban insurgency gaining ground, this is a rather dramatic shift in approach and may seem counter-intuitive to some. However, if NATO and the international community is interested in creating a state capable of upholding the human security of its population and not merely containing the threats Afghanistan could pose to the outside world – an assumption that is by no means clear – than it must take a more holistic, balanced and long-term SSR approach. Europe should be at the forefront of efforts to encourage a re-conceptualization or re-focusing of security sector assistance.

Achieving this about face in strategy may be too late as the state-building process approaches its tenth year, and the security and political situation shows few signs of turning around. The Afghan experience has yielded a number of important lessons both for the EU and the concept more generally. First, European states and other SSR donors need to develop more sophisticated structures to deliver SSR assistance in a timely manner, particularly mechanisms to rapidly deploy SSR expertise in the field and to deliver funds. Second, the Afghan case shows that there may be a need to re-visit the conceptual model for SSR as it applies to post-conflict settings. Conventional SSR as outlined in documents like the OECD-DAC handbook is in many ways unfeasible in complex post-conflict settings. More nuanced, flexible and adaptable frameworks attuned to such difficult settings are needed to bridge the policy-practice gap that has marred the SSR concept.

Afghanistan may demonstrate above all else the need for realism and modesty in reform goals. The international community was never going to succeed in transforming a broken and underdeveloped security sector into an effective, Western-modelled system within five or even ten years. This is not a justification for a pared down expedient approach focusing on the security forces, but rather a reminder that SSR is a long-term evolutionary process that demands long-term engagement, generational in the case of Afghanistan. In other words it is a marathon not a sprint. Committing to such a long-term process runs contrary to current Western donor orthodoxy, but is a necessity to achieve any level of success in such contexts. If that sort of commitment cannot be made, donors are best advised not to engage at all, because half measures can do harm. Afghanistan shows that current SSR implementation approaches simply don't work, something that the paucity of successful post-conflict SSR cases around the world confirms. Europe can and should be a leader in utilizing the lessons learned from Afghanistan to re-frame the SSR model.

References

Bailey, D.H. and Perito, R.M., *The Police in War: Fighting Insurgency, Terrorism and Violent Crime*. Boulder: Lynne Reinner, 2009.

Bhatia, M. and Sedra, M., *Afghanistan, Arms and Conflict: Armed groups, Disarmament and Security in a Post-War Society*. New York: Routledge, 2008.

Bruno, G., Council on Foreign Relations (CFR), 'Afghan Defense Chief Unhappy with Obama Plan', Interview of Afghan Defence Minister, Gen Abdul Rahim Wardak, 16 April 2009. Available at: http://www.cfr.org/publication/19116/afghan_defense_chief_unhappy_with_obama_plan.html, accessed 17 June 2010.

Centre for International Governance Innovation (CIGI), 'Security Sector Reform Monitor: Afghanistan', No. 3, Waterloo, Canada, CIGI, May 2010.

European Union, 'EU Police Mission in Afghanistan (EUPOL) Factsheet', 2010. Available at: http://www.consilium.europa.eu/uedocs/cms_data/docs/missionPress/files/100218%20FACTSHEET%20EUPOL%20Afghanistan%20-%20version%2017_EN.pdf, accessed on 16 June 2010.

Government of Germany, 'Funding for Police Assistance in Afghanistan Tripled', 2007. Available at: http://www.auswaertiges-amt.de/diplo/en/Aussenpolitik/RegionaleSchwerpunkte/AfghanistanZentralasien/AktuelleArtikel/071115-Erhoehung-Polizeimittel,navCtx=252166.html, accessed on 16 June 2010.

Government of Germany, 'International Support for an Effective Afghan Police Force', 2010. Available at: http://www.auswaertiges-amt.de/diplo/en/Aussenpolitik/RegionaleSchwerpunkte/AfghanistanZentralasien/Polizeiauf bau.html, accessed on 16 June 2010.

Gross, E., 'Security Sector Reform in Afghanistan: The EU's Contribution'. Occasional Paper No. 78, Brussels, European Union Institute for Security Studies, April 2009.

Hodes, C. and Sedra, M., *The Search for Security in Post-Taliban Afghanistan*. New York: Routledge, 2007.

Interim Afghanistan National Development Strategy (I-ANDS), 2006.

International Crisis Group (ICG), 'A Force in Fragments: Reconstituting the Afghan National Army', Asia Report No. 190, Brussels, INCG, 12 May 2010.

North Atlantic Treaty Organization (NATO), 'Fact Sheet: NATO's Police Operational Mentor and Liaison Teams (POMLTs) June 2010'. Available at: http://www.isaf.nato.int/images/stories/File/factsheets-june/JUne%202010-Fact%20Sheet%20POMLT.pdf, 16 June 2010.

Tarnoff, C. 'Afghanistan: US Foreign Assistance'. Washington, DC: Congressional Research Service, 5 March 2010.

United States Department of Defence, 'Overview: Fiscal Year 2011 Budget Request'. Washington, DC: United States Department of Defence, February 2010.

Ward, Maj-Gen M., 'NATO Response to "The Illusion of Police Reform"', Blog – Dispatches from the Field: Perspectives on the Afghanistan Conflict. Available at: http://www.cigionline.org/blogs/2010/4/nato-response-illusion-police-reform.

Chapter 13

Security Sector Reform in Sub-Saharan Africa: A New Playground, Different Rules, New Players?[1]

Magnus Jörgel

… but what is Security Sector *Reform?* Do we have any security, or should it be insecurity reform? Do you know about the Transformers, that kids play with, that is what we should have, something dark and ugly that could be made into a nice toy in an instance, yes a transformation, that is it …[2]

Introduction

This chapter will discuss the Sub-Saharan Africa context for the concept of security sector reform (SSR). A picture is drawn of a different, and difficult, environment, SSR in Sub-Saharan Africa. It will also try to give new input to the ongoing research and discussion about the potentials and impacts of, and on, SSR related issues. The chapter provides some snapshots from Sub-Saharan Africa and its conflicts, rather than a complete overview. It does not pretend to give answers to how SSR should be framed and implemented. It will however point out some possible considerations that could be used to take us a step further in conceptualizing SSR and maybe even more importantly draw some practical conclusions for the development of SSR. The impediments facing SSR in Sub-Saharan Africa include for example the unfamiliar cultural setting, the complexity of the conflicts, the lack of state capacity, the citizen's insecurity and the resistance against change from the security sector itself and the individuals connected to it. These problems will be highlighted by insights and illustrations mainly drawn from Sierra Leone, Liberia and the Democratic Republic of Congo (DRC).

---

1   This work draws on the findings from my own research and the main argument in this chapter agrees with the findings of, among others, J. Kayode Fayemi, Funmi Olonisakin, Alan Bryden and from the research done by ISS in South Africa. It also draws on the writings of Mats Utas. The first hand empiric data used in this article have been collected for my research in Sierra Leone and DRC during April 2002, December 2003, October-November 2005, April-May 2006 and August 2007.

2   Discussion with informants in Bunia, the Democratic Republic of Congo, 6 December 2003.

Several challenges confront states in Sub-Saharan Africa when it comes to SSR; many states are fragile and just recently out of conflict, many states have limited capacity to deal with major initiatives such as reforming a state apparatus. An ethnographic understanding of social maps is crucial for understanding the particulars of these societies. However, it takes time, it may take unorthodox methods and it may not provide all the answers wanted, but it will in the end provide the answers, or questions, *needed*. The weak state, or rather the absence of a well functioning state, is a major factor in the fundaments for SSR. If the state has little control over its territory, or does not have monopoly on violence, it is extremely difficult to start and calibrate the reform of security.

The concept of SSR in a Sub-Saharan African setting is fairly well thought through, it goes well beyond reforming the military and police forces, and it accommodates areas such as social security and individual security. SSR also encompasses institutions and management of the security sector, as well as the capacity per se to provide security to the state and society.[3] The capacity to reform is also interconnected with the overall standard of living, state finance and individual ability of state leaders to rally popular support for reform activities. Since the concept of SSR is in its essence a 'Eurocentric' idea, there might be a need to underline the importance of a good understanding of the particulars when SSR is put in a different context, the Sub-Saharan Africa region. A useful reminder and guide is for example the construction of four clusters around which transformation processes can be managed; cultural, human, political and organizational.

Looking at these factors and how they interact is important in understanding how to target SSR effectively. Firstly, most commonly the security sector, i.e. military, police and other actors who are permitted to use some form of lethal violence,[4] is such an integrated part of the state that it is almost impossible to distinguish between the different actors. A major overhaul of one part of the state have such impact on other parts, those informal networks that holds the state together and sustains the more formal structures, are at risk of being ripped apart. A perilous road most politicians would be unwilling to take.[5]

What seems to be one of the key elements in reformation programmes is the fact that the programme as such implies a shift in power. A power structure that is actually built by, and on, the very people that must take part in the reformation is a precarious situation for the reformist. If there is no, or limited, knowledge and understanding of this it is difficult to see how any progress can be made. The mapping of the different networks, social bonds and informal structures, down

---

3   See for example Bryden, A. and Fluri, P., *Security Sector Reform; Institutions, Society and Good Governance*. Baden-Baden: Nomos, 2003.

4   See 'DAC Handbook on SSR: Supporting Security and Justice'. Paris: OECD, 2007 edition, pp. 7-8.

5   For a discussion on informal, shadow, networks see for example Jörgel, M. and Utas, M., 'The Mano River Basin Area: Formal and Informal Security Providers in Liberia, Guinea and Sierra Leone', FOI-R-2418-SE, ISSN 1650-1942, 2007.

to individual level, is crucial, time consuming and difficult, but essential. This is probably not a key issue for Sub-Saharan Africa alone, but might be of particular importance in this region. The social network in places where extreme poverty and violent conflict are as frequent and prevalent as in Sub-Saharan Africa, the individual positioning in a social network, and the navigation in the network, becomes not only important, it becomes the way of living.[6] It is very important to realize the need to balance the pressing need for change with the need to do this sensitive, there is no benefits from a SSR programme that in the end actually alienates citizens from their security forces.

Secondly, the legacy of colonial rule and the new social context that it often brought on states in Africa must also be taken into account. Many of the structures existing today are not African per se, but mirrors colonial powers wishes to rule by proxy, and to structure colonies in ways that were easy to understand, and manage, for colonial civil servants.[7]

Thirdly, culture and economy must be linked. SSR should acknowledge the import of 'soft issues', such as value systems, democratic principles and gender issues.[8] A particular socio-economic reality is the issue of youth[9] is probably one of the most important ones when discussing SSR, at least in a Sub-Saharan setting, it is quite easy and rather common, to get caught up with policy discussions and institutionalized reform work, and forgetting the more long term, issues of giving youth an alternative to the work and future of soldiering. Without clear alternatives in forms of education and an achievable overall acceptable standard of living, the disgruntled young ex-combatants will never see civil life, however reformed, as a real alternative to the life as a soldier. The biggest challenge in SSR, and any other attempts to reform, or transform, societies, is to get a clear picture of what former belligerents really need. Basic education is at the top of the list with most ex combatants; unfortunately, this is a lengthy project and therefore in most cases not bothered with.

The level of financial resources to undertake SSR projects on a national level, without international support, is very limited in most Sub-Saharan African countries, and popular support for projects concerning reform of the security sector, when hundreds of millions are still living in poverty or extreme poverty, can be difficult to muster. Even if transformation of the police force and judicial

---

6 For a discussion on 'social navigation' see Utas, M. and Jörgel, M., 'The West Side Boys: Military Navigation in the Sierra Leone Civil War', *Journal of Modern African Studies* 46(3), 2008, pp. 487-511.

7 For an insight in the colonial legacy see for example Mbembe, A., *On the Post Colony*. Los Angeles: University of California Press, 2001.

8 Williams, R., 'African Armed Forces and the Challenges of Security Sector Reform', *Journal of Security Sector Management*, March 2005.

9 For an overview on marginalized youth and rebels see Utas, M. and Christiansen, V., *Navigating Youth Generating Adulthood: Social Becoming in an African Context*. Uppsala: Nordic Africa Institute, 2006; and Richards, P., *Fighting for the Rain Forest: War, Youth, & Resources in Sierra Leone*. Portsmouth, NH: Heinemann, 1996.

sector is badly needed in many countries, the issue of schools, sanitation and clean water might seem more important and urgent for the government to address.

If SSR ever is to be seen as a positive driving force in the overall transforming going on in Sub-Saharan Africa today, holistic approaches and clear messages that a well functioning security sector gives stability to all other projects and reform work is imperative for development and international finance.

Background

The specifics of the conflict in Sierra Leone and DRC that have implications for SSR needs to be run-through briefly, this will however not be a historic expose, it will only act as a starting point for my discussion.

One important aspect of the Sierra Leonean contemporary problems is found in the 1960-70s. The All Peoples Party (APC) embarks on a journey towards a one-party state, formally declared in 1971. The oppressive rule that follows effectively militarizes the country. On the one hand, the Royal Sierra Leonean Armed Forces (RSLAF) is weakened, and the Special Security Division (SSD) and the Internal Security Unit (ISU) are formed as alternative security forces. In the 1990s, the army had, for all practical purposes, ceased to be a security tool for the government.[10] This together with an overall deinstitutionalizing process of the government leads to a situation in which local militias, rebel groups, foreign armed forces, mercenaries and armed thugs all see their chance to advance economic or political ambitions.[11] The formalization of violence together with a total lack of public insight in finance and other state business led to a free fall decline of living standard and a totally demoralized, unprofessional and politicized security force.[12] When the Revolutionary United Front (RUF) attacks Sierra Leone from Liberia (beginning in March 1991), it is almost a completion of the downward spiral of privatization of violence that had occurred for almost 20 years. The state had no real possibilities to defend it's territory and this led to the extremely confused war in the country, a war where state security forces fights on the state side at day and on the rebel side at night, where mercenaries fight for one side one week and acts as private security firms the next, where militias start as local defence forces and ends up as major national parts in the conflict. This, together with a regional and international involvement from both individual states, regional security complexes, business men, the Economic Community of West African States (ECOWAS), and

---

10   See for an example Horn, A., Olonisakin, F. and Peak, G., 'United Kingdom-Led Security Sector Reform in Sierra Leone', *Civil Wars* 8(2), June 2006, pp. 109-23.

11   See for example Fayemi, K., Abdullah, I., Richards, P. and Bangura, Y. for detailed discussions on the militarization of Sierra Leone in Abdel-Fatau Musah and J. Kayode Fayemi, *Mercenaries: An African Security Dilemma*. London: Pluto Press, 2000.

12   Osman Gbla in ISS Monograph Series No. 135, May 2007.

UN gives the specifics for a very difficult transition from war to peace, and a SSR project maybe more complex than ever before.

In order to understand the wider picture of SSR and the flow on effect of reform, the regional aspect needs to be taken into account in terms of its approach and influence. The conflict in DRC has its own logic and particular problems, in the 1990s DRC was in fact a nation in total chaos, the government in Kinshasa could not in any way be seen as having control over the country, a country as big as Western Europe with a population of over 60 million. As Sierra Leone, part of contemporary conflict in DRC has its legacy in history, the violence and domination by King Leopold II has marked the country in terms of both cruelty and political unrest. The situation after independence was not improving in any important way, if anything it fell into deeper hopelessness. President Mobutu Sese Seko ruled with two major goals, to enrich himself and to make his project of 'Zaireization' a success.[13] None of which succeeded, Mobutu himself was killed and his Zaire project came to a complete standstill. Laurent Kabila, a rebellion leader from the Eastern part of DRC, overthrew Mobutu. Under the leadership of Kabila DRC fell into even worse circumstances, called 'Africa's first World War',[14] DRC was ripped apart with conflict between Kabila and Rwanda and Uganda. The riches in Eastern DRC was exploited by international companies, and Angola, South Africa and others were involved in the conflict as well as private military companies, mercenaries, smugglers and ordinary thugs. The fighting between national armies, rebel groups, proxies and different security forces made the conflict almost impossible to solve or understand. In 2001, Laurent Kabila was assassinated and his son Joseph Kabila took over as president, after intensive international pressure a peace agreement was signed in Sun City, South Africa, in 2002. What is interesting with this agreement is that it tries to provide a framework for DDR and SSR; it even goes as far as to give the basis for elections and a democratic government. Unfortunately, it was never fully understood how difficult it would prove to be to get former rebel leaders and antagonists to sit in the same government, and it was probably not understood how difficult it would be to integrate former enemies in the new national army. The war truly did divide the country in three parts, Kinshasa, Eastern DRC and the rest.

The Playground

The weak state, or rather the absence of a well functioning state, is a major factor in the fundaments for SSR. The citizen is left to the whims of security entrepreneurs, warlords and brute force by anybody with an AK-47. In addition, since there is an

---

13 For a detailed overview of the DRC history and contemporary conflicts see for example Turner, T., *The Congo Wars – Conflict, Myth, Reality*. London/New York: NYZed Books, 2007.

14 Madeleine Albright.

abundance of AK-47s in Sub-Saharan Africa (almost 8 per person in Chad)[15] one basis for SSR must be a comprehensive, overarching, approach. It is not only the armed functions that need to be reformed it must be a total overview of the state capacity. The judicial branch must be able to ensure the people adequate cover and protection. The police must have the capacity not only to protect but also to serve the citizen. When starting to reintegrate society and to re-build the state, SSR must address all these functions. However, the obstacles are immense and embedded in everyday life.

One example of the difficulties to uphold a good reputation towards the public in Sierra Leone is the question of police salaries. A police officer in Sierra Leone is paid about US$50, which is finished when house rent is paid for. Thereafter she, or he, must locate additional funding for food, school fees, clothes, transportation, and all other expenses the family has. The additional funding, needed to survive and cater for your family, comes to a large extent from bribes taken from people the police officer is supposed to serve. An impossible situation for all, the pay is outrageously low.

The police officer, of course, does not *want* to pressure people into paying for services they actually are entitled to, or should be adequately paid for so that they could cater for themselves. The police officer does not want to force the public to pay to avoid being harassed, and the public, also self evident, does not think much of the police officer who actually steals their money. Unfortunately, this is a situation not specific for the Sierra Leonean Police (SLP), it is in general terms the same in the RSLAF. However, one must give credit to the work by Great Britain. There has been a tremendous amount of aid, help, conceptual discussions and practical projects gone into the Sierra Leonean police and armed force. The British have training teams in place for the army and there is constant help from British police officers towards the police. But the under funding and thereby the inability to break up old networks of corruption and nepotism has meant that the situation today is far from good – in practical terms it is as bad as it was before the war.

Is there any hope of bringing in ex-rebels, militias and other fractions into the new army, and if so, how is it done? The process of disarming and demobilize the different warring fractions in Sierra Leone was a taunting task. From the beginning, it was almost impossible to organize because of the sheer volume of ex-combatants and arms floating around the country. However, the process managed to disarm and demobilize, at least to an extent where the international community could say that it had done its share. Unfortunately, large portions of the combatants have gone from being a 'someone', even if this meant to be in charge of a roadblock armed with an AK-47, to become a 'no one', an unemployed, disgruntled and angry youth. This has shown to be an enormous problem, a problem that actually surfaced during the elections 2007 in Sierra Leone. Many of the former soldiers, rebels and other violent groupings took up 'security' posts for the political parties,

---

15   Nelson Alusala, ISS monograph, No. 129, March 2007, p. 57.

their senior commanders became 'chief security' and the demobilized networks was put to formal use once again.[16]

Transforming the Actors

In Sierra Leone, under the initial process of SSR, the reintegration process of ex combatants, the focus on 'quick fixes', limited by short-term financing and poor management have produced thousands of marginalized youth, with strong adverse sentiment towards the police, military and political system as a whole. The notion that former rebels would be satisfied with training as carpenters, or trained in soap making can be seen as a funny joke, but it was what was offered to the vast majority of demobilized soldiers.[17] If there is something that people in Sub-Saharan Africa is taught to do it is carpentry and other skills such as soap making. What would be needed were skills such as computer literacy, advanced mechanics and advanced management training, and maybe most important, basic education.

Much more complicated to do, both in terms of needed level of teachers, amount of time and level of financing, but none the less, what were offered was not what was needed. The ex-combatants were fooled and used during the war, they were fooled after the war ended and they are fooled today. This of course one of the background factors to why they have been so interested in preserving their networks.

Former rebel groups such as the West Side Boys have kept their command structure in place, the soldiers still work together, the social network from 'the bush' is brought into Freetown and the possibilities to mobilize the group is all to present, as shown during the election period. If there had been an alternative, a viable and sought after alternative, an overwhelming majority of the now marginalized youths would of course take it. Unfortunately, there is a lack of political will, and capacity to bring this about. With a better understanding of the reality for those groups, there could be a good chance to incorporate them in peacetime society in a way that would make them a productive positive force, instead of a potential destabilizing one.

What is even more troublesome is the fact that this is far from the only example of the difficulties in bringing together different warring factions after a conflict. It is very common to have the integration process stated and described in the peace agreement, unfortunately often without proper understanding of the difficulties and the practical specifics of the opposing parties in the conflict. The 'Brassage'[18]

---

16 Observations from research trip during elections in Sierra Leone 2007.

17 See Utas, M., 'Building a Future? The Re-Integration and Remarginalisation of Youth in Liberia' in Richards (ed.) *No Peace, No War: An Anthropology of Contemporary Armed Conflicts.* Oxford: James Currey, 2005, pp. 137-54.

18 The word means 'brewing', to bring together or melt together, originally from Belgian French.

in the Democratic Republic of Congo (DRC) is just another example of the same problem. The numbers alone makes the problem clear, as of today there are some 150 000 armed soldiers in DRC.[19] This is supposed to become a targeted national armed force of about preferably 70,000 organized in 18, brigade size units.[20] The new armed forces of the DRC will hold soldiers from all old factions. The problem is, apart from the fact that there were at least nine major rebel groups in eastern DRC alone, not counting various Mai-Mai groups and others, that the leaders make up for their lost fighters by recruiting new ones, sometimes among the children in the region.[21] The 'Brassage', has in practice actually brought about more, and new, child soldiers – a side effect not often discussed.[22] To further show the problems in DRC in regard to SSR, General Nkunda[23] have proposed a new way of forming the brigades in eastern DRC, a so called 'Mixage', a local mix of troops in Eastern DRC, not going through the transition training and not being deployed outside of its home territory. This has actually been implemented to some degree and in the North Kivu where there are two 'Mixage' brigades deployed. General Nkunda is clearly provoking the DRC government, using the SSR project for his own benefit and for his own specific goals.[24]

The overall work in DRC in regards to SSR have been slow, full of internal conflicts and it is still very much to be proven if there is real progress towards a new integrated national armed force.[25] The army still have not completed the 'Brassage' of more than six brigade formations out of a planned total of eighteen, and in the east, armed rebels still roam free. In DRC, as in most examples of post conflict situations in Sub-Saharan post war situations, there has been a focus on the military, leaving the police force, especially in the country side, neglected and without any real possibilities to perform their duties. The police in DRC have historically never been in a position to provide even the basic service to the people. To even further diminish the police force it was not even a provision in the Sun City Peace Agreement to create a national well functioning police force. It was very much left as a fragmented, ill-equipped institution without any proper

---

19   This is a highly contested and unreliable figure, Prof. Roger Kibasomba states in ISS Occasional Paper 119, December 2005, that there can be as many as 350,000 ex combatants in DRC.

20   International Crisis Group, Africa Report No. 104, 13 February 2006.

21   IRIN, 30 November 2006 (www.irinnews.org/report.aspx?reportid= 62256), ISS (www.iss.co.za/Af/profiles/DRCongo/SecInfo.html) both accessed 24 September 2007.

22   Amnesty International, AFR 62/009/206 (press release).

23   General Laurent Nkunda was brought to international attention following the massacres in Kisangani 2002; he has come back to eastern DRC from South Africa where he was supposed to enrol for university studies. For a detailed study of General Nkunda see ISS Situation Report, 3 September 2007, Henri Boshoff.

24   Henri Boshoff, ISS today, 22 March 2007.

25   www.iss.co.za/pubs/ASR/13no4/AWBoshoff.htm (accessed 24 September 2007), www.oxfam.org/en/policy/briefingpapers/bp97_MONUC_mandate_renewal_070216 (accessed 24 September 2007).

national management.[26] On a local level there are even more problems facing the SSR process in DRC, since the allocated, long-term finances for the new armed forces only seems to manage about 2,200 soldiers per brigade instead of planned 3500, local leaders have been reluctant to send their best troops through transition training, keeping them back to form a tool for substantial freedom of action, at their immediate disposal.[27]

International Assistance, Intervention and Provision of Support

The few positive signs in Sierra Leone when it comes to the reformation of the armed forces are largely due to the British lead International Military Assistance Training Teams (IMATT), The RSLAF seems to be somewhat more disciplined than pre-1998. However, even with the essential, pivotal, British impact there seems to be a long way to go before RSLAF, as a whole, have reached any kind of international standard when it comes to professionalism and capacity.[28] The importance of a 'leading nation' with a long-term strategy and a long-term commitment is clearly proven by the British example in Sierra Leone. If we do not apply a minimum of 10-15 year time frame for SSR activities there will be no measurable amount of long-term progress, maybe quite the opposite we will only help in making corruption and mismanaging permanent. The old, corrupted, network benefits immensely from short term funding, without accountability and with distorted transparency.

To make the context even more difficult there is a definite regional aspect on SSR, taking West Africa as an example, ECOWAS have put a range of initiatives at the table, both at its own initiative and on African Union (AU) initiative. Here the possibilities for controversies between regional representatives, national governments and international experts are manifold. In Sierra Leone, there is the British involvement in SSR through IMATT and various initiatives within the police, ECOWAS wants to have a say about the implementation of an early warning system, the Sierra Leone government has its Good Governance and Public Service Programme and the Sierra Leone vision 2025 as part of its guiding principles. ECOWAS has, as of now, no framework of its own on SSR but relies heavenly on German military advisers on the issue.[29] As a result, there are ample possibilities for misunderstanding and confusion. A clear overarching framework, leading from AU, through regional bodies to national governments would greatly

---

26   International Crisis Group, Africa Report No. 104, 13 February 2006.

27   Ibid.

28   RSLAF do participate in UN missions, but this is only with specially trained units and officers.

29   The OECD DAC handbook on SSR, 2007 edition, is one of the basic, overarching, blueprints used in Sub-Sahara Africa.

improve the effectiveness and coordination of SSR on an international level.[30] The regional aspect can be pushed even further, the conflicts in Western Africa are to a large extent cross-border conflicts in one aspect or another. This is not always in terms of official involvement by states but in practical terms, staging areas and logistical support are often placed across borders. Another important factor in the regional aspect is the circulation, and recirculation, of arms. This is in nature an international business, and often depends on cross border access. The involvement in, and support of, different conflicts in West Africa calls for a regional approach to SSR, and if this is not acknowledged there is a definite risk of problems to spill over to another country rather than being contained and solved at it's starting point.

The Difficulties of Ending Conflicts

Some focus should be placed on the formal aspect of the provisions for SSR within the different agreements leading to the formal end of the conflict. Without a firm blueprint for SSR, included in the formal agreement, a lack of purpose may prevail. One such formal agreement was made in the Liberian Accra Peace Agreement,[31] where it was clearly stated how the reform work was supposed to be phased, who were supposed to be part of the new armed forces, how the new force were to be trained and so on. The SSR work in Liberia is still in a too early phase to be judged proper. The problems arising in Liberia is largely the same as in Sierra Leone, and to be successful the government must provide a decent alternative for the pre-agreement soldier. It is not enough to talk about the coming better; it must be shown, preferably today. In Liberia there had been quite some despondency from the former rebel soldiers, not much progress have been shown in terms of improvements of their living standards or status within society, a large group have therefore set up camp in one of the larger plantations outside Monrovia. The comfort of your old network is much more worth than the promises from the government.

There is also the question of constitutional framework, and the need for it to be in place to allow the different players to know what rules apply. The principles for civil-military cooperation, the issue of civilian control over the security sector and a fundamental understanding of democratic methods of working are some examples of basic blueprints that need to be produced, discussed and agreed upon. The demilitarization of a nation coming out of conflict is maybe even a greater challenge than the reconstruction and reform of various security players. In this part of SSR the police play a major role as it is in most cases closer to the people, it has the job of dealing with day-to-day violence and it has great influence for the overall wellbeing of the citizen. It is therefore rather disappointing that the police

---

30   For details see Ishola Williams in ISS Monograph Series No. 135, May 2007.
31   www.usip.org/library/pa/liberia_08182003_toc.html (accessed 24 September 2007).

have received much lesser attention than the armed forces in most SSR projects. In the order of priority, the police are often at the bottom of the list. The police in Sierra Leone which is still under funded, without proper equipment and training, and still lacks the popular support it needs to fulfil its purpose.[32] The problem of the dysfunctional judiciary system in Sierra Leone is also worsening the problem of how the public views the Sierra Leone police force. The public knowledge about how 'big men' are let loose by the court and the person reporting the crime committed by the 'big man' is himself punished by losing his job doesn't make for a cordial cooperation between police and the public.

The Playground Transformed

The greater problem of demilitarization, in terms of not only disarmament but also rather the notion and change of mindset, is put to the forefront when the issue of ownership of the SSR project comes up. The reformation of armed forces and police forces must be seen as a national concern, there must never be any uncertainty of whether the SSR is in the hands of the nation itself, the government, or a foreign body.[33] This might seem perfectly clear, and all can agree on this, but since the financing, management and decision-making very often lays in other hands than the government itself, it can not be stressed enough that every possible measure must be taken to ensure that the ownership is firmly national. This is a problem faced by many agencies involved in development aid work as the low capacity of the nation itself, makes it difficult to put overall management outside of your own organization. It is however crucial in SSR, that the ownership itself indicates the national control over, and incorporation of, armed forces and police. Since there is great dissociation between many security players and the people from the beginning, even before the actual conflict breaks out, the ownership of the process of SSR is an important factor for the long-term success of SSR.

The improvement of *both* service and capacity towards the local communities is key to bring the different actors within the security sector and their employers, the people, closer. However, the police and the work it fulfils cannot be seen as a separate part from the judicial system. In broad outline, one has to take into consideration the law making process, the court system, the correction services and how the overall system is accountable towards the public. There are of course also the issues of border control, immigration processes and the refugee movements in the region. Since the Mano River Region in many aspects is to be considered as an intertwined economic and conflict area, where trade, movements of people and export of violence always have been done without much regard for formal borders or authorities, those issues will be of great importance for the public and not only the governments in the region. The management of all this will in the end show

---

32 Discussion with Osman Gbla, 2 September 2007
33 As have been the case in Sierra Leone in regards to IMATT.

the level of trust and confidence there is between the security arrangements and the people, and will ultimately decide the final success of SSR.[34]

The transformation from a militarized society to peacetime governance will put the issue of recruitment into the security sector without nepotism and other forms of corrupt access to enrolment into the forefront. The case of Sierra Leone shows that there can be progress in certain areas, the move away from the card system[35] under Siaka Stevens rule, by which the freefall of security forces intensified, to a modern knowledge and ability based admission system has so far proven to heighten the standard of the military and police at least on an individual level.[36]

The management of SSR, although it might be managed from the outside in the short run, must in the end be managed and owned by the nation itself. There is no other way that the government can get popular support for fundamental change, but to be in control over the process and accountable for its progress. Even if the capacity to manage the SSR at the national level is low at the beginning of the project, it is important to have a clear view on how capacity building should grow parallel with the SSR. There is a need for both capacity building i.e. from new capacity, but also for an examination of how capacity actually is used. This applies both to individual knowledge and to institutional outreach. The process must balance both international, outside help and national progress. Coordination of efforts are essential in this regard, capacity increase in individual proficiency that cannot be used by the institution is of limited value. This must not be confused with the importance of having a lead nation, ownership of the process and coordination and ability to put pressure on the international community.

Conclusion

The wish to design institutions and to reform the security sector has proven much more difficult than anyone could imagine when the first experience took place in 1970, after the civil war in Nigeria. The challenges have proven phenomenal and the solutions have been slow to come about. Nevertheless, no matter how difficult there has been progress, new ideas have been put on the table and actual reformation has been made. It is important to acknowledge that the term and the conception of SSR is a recent one; it was actually only in 1997 that Claire Short introduced the term SSR. From this perspective there has been quite some progress

---

34   For a historical, and contemporary, overview on civil-military relations in Sub-Saharan Africa (specifically Sierra Leone) see Ngoma, N., 'Civil-Military Relations in Africa: Navigating Uncharted Waters', *African Security Review* 15(4), 2006, pp. 98-111; and Cox, T.S., *Civil-Military Relations in Sierra Leone: A Case-Study of Soldiers in African Politics*. Cambridge, MA: Harvard University Press, 1976.

35   The card system meant that local governors could nominate people from their own group to join the armed forces, loyal but rarely the best for the position.

36   Osman Gbla in ISS Monograph Series No. 135, May 2007.

made both in practical and conceptual terms. To be able to tackle all problems facing SSR projects one could divide SSR into four different aspects, political, institutional, economic and societal. The four aspects, managed in a cohesive and transparent way, might be a way to divide the overwhelming project into more manageable sub sections. The most important caveat here would then be that the sub sections needs a strong, uniting, leadership so that the balance and sequencing all leads to the final goal.[37]

However, quite a few practical issues need to be addressed, discussed and implemented in SSR projects as soon as possible. Among them, there is for an example an urgent need for an overall closer relationship between politicians, the security sector and citizens. There is also a need for a much stronger commitment from the international community for long-term cooperation on security sector issues and there is definitely a need for a much better understanding of the socio-political context in which the SSR takes place. To understand the root causes of the conflict is of fundamental importance for a wise implementation of SSR projects, a well-mapped sociological context is well-spent efforts. The complex conflict situation in Sub-Saharan Africa with a multitude of different warring parties, militias, local defence forces, private security firms, rebel groups, different special security units within the police and military, special presidential guards and armed robbers requires a much more holistic approach than hitherto used. To accommodate such diverse actors, in a context with only basic, limited, capacities, it takes a well-formulated inclusive framework to make progress.

There are probably a couple of specific fundaments to be used as guiding principles when it comes to SSR and Sub-Saharan Africa. The need for long-term cooperation and endurance is a foundation for any reform work. There should be a 10-15 year strategy for all reform projects, fully funded and with clear milestones to fulfil. A strong cooperation, preferably with a 'lead nation' must be formed for the start-up period. The British in Sierra Leone might stand as an example, even if the UN, AU or EU takes on the responsibility for a SSR project on national level the need for a bilateral partner cannot be stressed enough. SSR in weak states are much more than reform work on military, police, and other security players. The need for a true reformation of state management, a fulfilment of judicial basic needs and a functioning welfare strategy for the individual citizens, are crucial determinants for the success of SSR.

What is often overseen is the simple fact that within SSR, the security sector is not an institution, for the citizen it is the very core of safe living, the very thing that makes it possible to send kids to school. This only comes about when a sustainable reform agenda is fully owned by the state itself. There is a definite need for a deeper, primary sourced research on SSR in the Sub-Saharan setting, primarily on factors such as rebel groups' incorporation and participation in SSR

---

37   Jane Chanaa, 'Security Sector Reform: Issues, Challenges and Prospects'. IISS Adelphi Paper 344 (2002).

and the influence of 'shadow' networks[38] on the process. An in depth survey of the differences, and similarities, between a 'Western' oriented approach to SSR and an 'African' one, would also have benefits for a better understanding, and cooperation, between specifically European and African countries.

SSR in a Sub-Saharan African setting is not another game, it is played by the same basic rules but there are definitely some new players around, and there is a difference in context and culture, and those differences needs to be taken in serious account. A stronger focus on the transformation, more than reformation, and an even stronger focus on coherent, multidiscipline, pragmatic and comprehensive long-term approaches would take us further within the field of SSR. It takes a smart kid to carry the Transformers from the imaginary world into the real one, as it takes a smart adult to take concepts out of the policy discussion, bringing them to practical use.

References

Amnesty International, AFR 62/009/206.

Baker, B., *African Anarchy: Is it the States, Regimes, or Societies that are Collapsing?* 19(3), 2002, pp. 131-38.

Biro, D., 'The (Un)bearable Lightness of ... Violence: Warlordism as an Alternative Form of Governance in the "Westphalian Periphery"' in Tobias Debiel and Lambach (eds) *State Failure Revisited II: Actors of Violence and Alternative Forms of Governance.* INEF Report 89/2007, Essen, University of Duisburg, 2007, pp. 7-49.

Bryden, A. and Fluri, P., *Security Sector Reform; Institutions, Society and Good Governance.* Baden-Baden: Nomos, 2003.

Chanaa, J., 'Security Sector Reform: Issues, Challenges and Prospects'. IISS Adelphi Paper 344, 2002.

Cox, T.S., *Civil-Military Relations in Sierra Leone: A Case-Study of Soldiers in African Politics.* Cambridge, MA: Harvard University Press, 1976.

DAC Handbook on SSR: Supporting Security and Justice. Paris: OECD, 2007.

Horn, A., Olonisakin, F. and Peak, G., 'United Kingdom-Led Security Sector Reform in Sierra Leone', *Civil Wars* 8(2), June 2006, pp. 109-23.

International Crisis Group, Africa Report No. 104, 13 February 2006.

---

38   For a discussion on informal, shadow, networks see for example Baker, B., 'African Anarchy: Is it the States, Regimes, or Societies that are Collapsing?' 19(3), 2002, pp. 131-38; Biro, D., 'The (Un)bearable Lightness of ... Violence: Warlordism as an Alternative Form of Governance in the "Westphalian Periphery"' in Tobias Debiel and Daniel Lambach (eds) *State Failure Revisited II: Actors of Violence and Alternative Forms of Governance.* INEF Report 89/2007, Essen, University of Duisburg, 2007, pp. 7-49; Utas, M. and Jörgel, M., 'The Mano River Basin Area: Formal and Informal Security Providers in Liberia, Guinea and Sierra Leone', FOI-R--2418—SE, Stockholm, FOI, 2007.

ISS Monograph No. 129, March 2007.

ISS Monograph Series No. 135, May 2007.

Mbembe, A., *On the Post Colony*. Los Angeles: University of California Press, 2001.

Musah, A.-F. and Fayemi, J.K., *Mercenaries: An African Security Dilemma*. London: Pluto Press, 2000.

Ngoma, N., 'Civil-Military Relations in Africa: Navigating Uncharted Waters', *African Security Review* 15(4), 2006, pp. 98-111.

Richards, P., *Fighting for the Rain Forest: War, Youth, & Resources in Sierra Leone*. Portsmouth, NH: Heinemann, 1996.

Turner, T., *The Congo Wars – Conflict, Myth, Reality*. London/New York: NYZed Books, 2007.

Utas, M., 'Building a Future? The Re-Integration and Remarginalisation of Youth in Liberia' in Paul Richards (ed.) *No Peace, No War: An Anthropology of Contemporary Armed Conflicts*. Oxford: James Currey, 2005, pp. 137-54.

Utas, M. and Christiansen, V., *Navigating Youth Generating Adulthood: Social Becoming in an African Context*. Uppsala: Nordic Africa Institute, 2006.

Utas, M. and Jörgel, M., *The Mano River Basin Area: Formal and Informal Security Providers in Liberia, Guinea and Sierra Leone*. FOI-R--2418—SE, Stockholm, FOI, 2007.

Utas, M. and Jörgel, M., 'The West Side Boys: Military Navigation in the Sierra Leone Civil War', *Journal of Modern African Studies* 46(3), 2008, pp. 487-511.

Williams, R., 'African Armed Forces and the Challenges of Security Sector Reform', *Journal of Security Sector Management*, March 2005.

Chapter 14

The European Union and SSR in Guinea-Bissau

Caroline Bahnson

Background

Guinea-Bissau is a small West-African country, which gained independence only in 1974 and after an 11-year-long liberation war with Portugal. Its short post-independence history has been turbulent, with several successful and attempted *coup d'états*, no Head of State having finished a full term, and three Chiefs of General Defence Staff assassinated. A short but intense civil war in 1998-99 left the already fragile and poor state in a dire situation with the massive destruction of social and economic infrastructure, a further decline in economic indicators, and public institutions ever more weakened.

A couple of key patterns have characterized the politics and history of the country. First of all, the popular guerrilla war against the Portuguese colonial power left the country with an influential group of former combatants whose evolving internal alliances and enmities have continued to shape the political landscape. Secondly, the Armed Forces have through the respect gained during the war and a subsequent sense of entitlement remained a politicized and controlling actor in Bissau-Guinean power struggles. Especially the relationship between the holders of the Presidency and the Chief of General Defence Staff (CGDS) has been problematic. As later examples, in March 2009, a bomb killed CGDS General Tagme in his office after which, in the early hours of the following day, army officers killed President Vieira in his home. Furthermore, in April 2010, the country's first CGDS who had not participated in the war of liberation was arrested along with – albeit briefly – the Prime Minister by the former's own deputy. In spite of the extreme measure, both the President and the Prime Minister have refrained from intervening in the mutiny. Thirdly, the instability has resulted in a general lack of governance, and subsequent collapse of state institutions, including the justice and penal system, the control of the territory as well as the formal economy.[1]

The political nature of the armed forces established during the war for independence has hence continued to shape the history and governance of the country to present day. Personal, ethnic and political rivalries have led to strong divisions within the army which have continued to be exploited for political

---

1   For an overview of Guinea-Bissau history and current state, see e.g. International Crisis Group, 'Guinea-Bissau: In Need of a State'. Africa Report No. 142, 2 July 2008 or http://news.bbc.co.uk/1/hi/world/africa/country_profiles/1043287.stm.

purposes.[2] The armed forces are reputedly also intricately involved in the trafficking of drugs, facilitating the transfer of the goods from Latin America dropped at the ill-guarded territory of Guinea-Bissau through to Europe. While the extent of the problem is disputed (many commentators and media outlets have already named the country a narco-state) there is no doubt that even a relatively limited influx of cash affects the balances of power and incentives in a poor state like Guinea-Bissau. In summary, by 2005 Guinea-Bissau had a security sector that was, among other things, marked by armed forces that were intricately linked to the political system, while posing a huge burden on the fragile and cash-strapped state by being too many, too old, too senior and poorly trained.[3] The lack of budgetary transparency makes it difficult to assess its actual cost to the state, but one of the more conservative estimations guesses that the military absorbs 25 percent of the country's annual budget.[4] The respect given to former liberation war fighters and their continued influential role in all spheres of society made it politically impossible to send them home in face of minimal pensions.

While being less influential, the police had never added much benefit to internal security of the country. In 2005, the police constituted a plethora of forces, under several different ministries and with overlapping and ill-defined mandates. There was a lack of an adequate legal framework, as well as even a minimum of resources or actual geographic coverage of the country. Corruption and abuse of power was rampant thus constituting a menace rather than service to the citizens of Guinea-Bissau. The justice system, which up until the nineties was seen as a branch of political power, also provided very little service to the population. Underfunding, corruption and inadequacies of infrastructure along with the fact that the country had no prisons meant that neither criminal nor civil justice was excised.[5]

The National Security Sector Reform Plan

In 2005, the relative stability brought by an alliance between President Vieira and CGDS General Tagme and a general fatigue of the military-political struggles among the population, led the UN peacebuilding mission in Guinea-Bissau (UNOGBIS) to investigate the possibilities of reforming the security sector. The need for General Tagme to help the older of his troops out of the armed forces

---

2   See e.g. International Crisis Group, 'Guinea-Bissau: Beyond the Rule of the Gun'. Africa Briefing No. 61, 25 June 2009.

3   The actual number and demography of the military was actually unknown until a census was carried out as part of the security sector reform in 2008. The census confirmed the general picture: of a total of 4,458 members, half were between 40 and 60, 5.5 percent older than 60 (including four members above 80), and only 6 members younger than 20 years of age. Forty-two percent were officers, 13 percent non-commissioned officers, 25 percent corporals and 20 percent troops.

4   International Crisis Group, Africa Briefing No. 61.

5   Government of Guinea-Bissau, 'Restructuring and Modernisation of the Defence and Security Sector: Strategy Document', Geneva, 7 and 8 November 2006.

while retaining the role as protector provided an important incentive for him to agree to such reform.[6]

With the help of the British Security Sector Development Team (SSDAT), a national security sector reform strategy was drafted during 2006 to be presented at a donor conference. The idea was to produce a document whose conclusions were based on a wide consultative process, however, the actual work stalled until the date of the conference was set and was therefore done under greater haste and with fewer participants than desired.[7]

Nevertheless, the strategy was finalized and presented to donors in Geneva as planned in November 2006. The document summarized the situation in the defence, security and justice sector and then outlined a number of key objectives; namely: a) resizing the defence and security sector by bringing it in line with the country's needs and economic capacities; b) modernizing the sector in line with its role; c) clarifying the status of former national freedom fighters; d) strengthening the participation of the sector in consolidating sub-regional security; e) building capacities and enhancing efficiency in the justice sector, f) mobilizing national and international resources for investment in the sector; and g) involving civil society in the implementation of reform in the sector.[8]

In more concrete terms, the strategy defined the target number of troops resulting from the downsizing of the armed forces, as well as for the integration of a number of the various security forces into a national guard.

A Steering Committee headed by the Minister of Defence and comprising relevant representatives of the Government, civil society and the international community was to be responsible for overseeing compliance with the political and strategic principles of the reform. Ideas to have a technical coordination committee and a separate support office for implementation were merged into the Steering Committee Secretariat, composed of representatives of the Ministry of Defence (Head of the Secretariat), Ministry of Interior, Ministry of Ex-combatants, Ministry of Justice and Armed Forces Headquarters.

While being a good start to tackling the many problems of the security sector in Guinea-Bissau, the strategy fell short on a number of key issues. For one, the issue of security sector governance was largely ignored in spite of it being at the core of the problems experienced by the country since independence. Hence the strategy did not envisage any activities to be undertaken as attempts to re-focus the blurred line between the military and politics, either through strengthening the Government's own accountability institutions nor those of external oversight mechanisms such as parliament, the media and civil society.

The area of justice reform was also treated almost as an afterthought, with very few links to the other sectors. In addition, the strategy was developed at a time when

---

6   In fact, the word *reforma* primarily means retirement in Portuguese.

7   SSDAT Report, December 2006.

8   Government of Guinea-Bissau, 'Restructuring and Modernisation of the Defence and Security Sector: Strategy Document', Geneva, 7 and 8 November 2006.

the international community had just started focusing on Guinea-Bissau as transit hub for the narcotics trade between South America and Europe and counter-narcotics measures were therefore not explicitly included as an issue in the final document.

EU Support to SSR in Guinea-Bissau

The lack of a strong engagement from any one bilateral partner and the fact that the European Commission[9] was already the largest donor in Guinea-Bissau facilitated its decision to support SSR. The field was at this point a rising priority on the international community's agenda generally, and specifically regarding Guinea-Bissau which with its size and perceived complexity of the challenges resulted in an idea that 'if we cannot do it there, we can do it nowhere' in reference to places like the Democratic Republic of Congo and Afghanistan. For a country that was not in the immediate post-conflict phase, it was hence unusual that the European Union decided to engage all its available instruments: the European Development Fund (EDF), the Instrument for Stability (IfS), and the Common Foreign and Security Policy (CFSP).

European Development Fund

The European Commission commenced its investments in the security sector already after the 1998-1999 conflict, where it along with the World Bank, the African Development Bank, the Netherlands and Sweden invested €3 million in a DDR program (PDDRI), which demobilized and provided reinsertion benefits to approximately 4,000 members of the military, paramilitary and militia forces.[10] While in general not considered to be a success in terms of impact, the project also fell short of providing benefits to the entire target group. Before the presentation of the national strategy, the European Commission also signed a financing agreement for €6.6 million with the Government in early 2006 to support the justice and legislative institutions (*Programme d'Appui aux Organes de Souveraineté et à l'Etat de Droit*, also known as PAOSED).[11]

However, it was not until the adoption of the national SSR strategy in November 2006 that the EU decided to get involved more comprehensively in the reform efforts of the security sector. In the first instance, this resulted in the development of a €7.7 million project, *Programme d'Appui à la Reforme du Secteur Sécuritaire* (PARSS) which aimed to address one of the key sticking points of the reform

---

9   The author uses EC and Commission in a synonymous sense.

10   Convention de Financement entre la Commission Européenne et La République de Guinée Bissau, *Appui à la Reforme du Secteur Sécuritaire, GUB 008/06, IXème FED.*

11   Convention de Financement entre la Commission Européenne et La République de Guinée Bissau, *Programme d'Appui aux Organes de Souveraineté et à l'Etat de Droit, GUB 002/05, IXème FED.*

described above, namely how to encourage the downsize of the armed forces. Hence, the project had two main components. The largest component would set up modalities for compensation to the members of the armed and security forces that would leave as part of the reform, either as cash benefits through a pension fund for those who had reached the official retirement age or as reintegration assistance for those younger. A second smaller component was designed to cover the remaining caseload from the PDRRI of combatants from the Liberation War who had already left the army and would therefore not benefit from the first component. The programme was designed to be implemented through the national implementation and coordination structure, and for programme staff to be located with the Steering Committee Secretariat.[12]

Finally, the EC pledged another €2 million in December 2007 at an international conference on combating drug trafficking in Guinea-Bissau. This contribution was given to the UNODC to finance their initial operations to implement a counter-narcotics action plan.

Instrument for Stability

The EC was keenly aware that the time between the national and international adoption of the strategy and the realistic point when PARSS' technical assistance could be in place risked losing the momentum gained. In addition, at the time of the conception of the project, it was deemed that in order to implement the strategy, a number of issues would have to be addressed such as gaps in the legal framework, and the lack of reliable and exhaustive censuses for the different security services and ex-combatants. As the Commission deemed the political commitment of the then government favourable and the situation on the ground relative stable, it looked into how to provide more rapid support so that the reform process could move forward. The External Relations of the Commission approved to use the Instrument for Stability mechanism to finance a technical assistance project hence aimed at supporting Guinea Bissau in its security sector reform during its initial phase.

Three advisers were to be placed in the national structure for one year to facilitate institutional support and capacity building in the security sector, and the preparation of schemes to be used for the PARSS project.[13]

Council of the European Union

Meanwhile, the United Kingdom was looking for a way to continue their support to the process they had helped father through the SSDAT. Realizing the lack of

---

12   Convention de Financement entre la Commission Européenne et La République de Guinée Bissau, *Appui à la Reforme du Secteur Sécuritaire, GUB 008/06, IXème FED.*

13   European Commission, Terms of Reference, Technical Assistance in support of SSR in Guinea-Bissau, EC Instrument for Stability, 2007.

capacity within Guinea-Bissau to break down, plan and implement the ambitious SSR plan, it was suggested that the European Council set up a cross-cutting CFSP mission to assist the Government in moving this process along. A first assessment mission was conducted in May 2007[14] and a joint one with the Commission took place in October 2007. With strong support from Portugal who held the EU Presidency at the time, a limited one-year mandate to support the development of specific action plans was adopted by member states in February 2008.[15] As the first of its kind, it was to include both military and civilian advisers to allow it 'to provide local authorities with advice and assistance on SSR in the Republic of Guinea Bissau, in order to contribute to creating the conditions for implementation of the National SSR Strategy'[16] in all three key sectors: military, police and justice. The idea of such a broad mission scope was initially not welcomed by the European Commission and especially the inclusion of a justice component was seen as trespassing into traditional Commission turf.

Implementation Experience

Working with the Bissau-Guinean Government and administration with its notorious lethargy and covert lines of authority, all the European interventions came off to a rough start. The company that won the bid to implement the justice programme struggled to get established and develop realizable work plans and only managed to disburse a fraction of its budget in its first three years of implementation. While benefiting to a certain degree of input from the IfS, the SSR project got stalled first from the inception problems and lack of capacity facing the Steering Committee Secretariat that was in charge of execution of the project on behalf of the Government, and later on getting enough qualified bids for the technical assistance component. It thus took 1.5 years between the Commission signed the financing convention and the arrival of the technical assistants. Getting the IfS team in place also took longer than originally anticipated, and it was not fully staffed until four months after the arrival of the first adviser. As they were to be based in a new national structure whose mandate at the time of their arrival was still unclear and with no infrastructure at its disposal, the advisers struggled to find its entry points and gain the confidence of interlocutors.

The CFSP mission also came off to a very slow start attributable to a couple of key factors. First of all, the planning and preparation process was done mainly in Brussels, with minimal presence in Bissau between the scoping mission resulting in the agreement with the Government, and finally the arrival of the first staff in April 2008. In practical terms this meant that staffing, basic procurement process and setting up of a proper headquarters took well into the first year of the mission's

---

14   Council Joint Action 2008/112/CFSP of 12 February 2008.

15   Council Joint Action 2008/112/CFSP of 12 February 2008.

16   Council Joint Action 2008/112/CFSP of 12 February 2008.

mandate, slowing down certain activities and monopolizing energy that should have been spent elsewhere. More seriously however, was the fact that most of the Bissau-Guinean counterparts had forgotten the objectives of the mandate – and in the case of the Minister of Justice the mission itself[17] – by the time of arrival, requiring the mission to overcome significant suspicion among key stakeholders and to restart building relationships from scratch. Secondly, the Council itself and the incoming mission members arguable had unrealistic expectations about the level of appropriation of the mission mandate by the various branches of Government. With a prevailing belief that the fact that the mission had been authorized by the Head of State would automatically entail full-hearted cooperation from all counterparts, initially caused a great deal of frustration and confusion.

The actual work and progress on the various aspects of reform varied significantly across sectors and over time.

For the reasons described above, the restructuring of the defence remained one of the trickiest aspects of the reform – presumably the reason why the Minister of Defence had been given the role of Head of the SSR Steering Committee. The elevated position of the CGDS meant that the factual hierarchy within the Ministry of Defence did not correspond to the official one and that the CGDS was not subjected to decisions taken by Minister. While being less obvious after the assassination of General Tagme, this fact did not change significantly. While the Minister would undertake all the discussions, negotiations and decisions related to the reform, this could at all times be countered by the armed forces, making planning and implementation close to impossible.

It was also on the defence reform that the national strategy proved most controversial. Contrary to reality, the military leadership claimed that they had not been properly consulted when the document had been drafted,[18] and true to tradition, did not seem to worry about the fact that it had been approved by a democratically elected Parliament. This lack of adherence to the overall structure and direction of the reform made it particularly difficult for the EUSSR to gain access to information, including the results of a census carried out by UNDP which were the foundation upon which to restructure the forces. In general, the mission faced continuous low-key resistance from General Tagme and his staff hindering the advancement of translating the strategy into concrete implementation plans that could be followed up by national and international actors.

The Chief of General Defence Staff (CGDS) following the assassination of General Tagme, was significantly more interested in the reform so in combination with a change of EU SSR senior military adviser, this allowed for a restart in the assistance to the defence reform, and the mission was well advanced in fulfilling its mandate when the military order changed again in April 2010.

The integration of eight different forces into four, and the complete lack of an appropriate legal framework made the restructuring of the security forces

---

17 Author's discussion with the Minister of Justice.
18 Author's conversations with two different CGDSs and other high ranking officers.

technically more difficult than the army reform, albeit politically much more straight forward. This made it easier to tackle for the technically-focused EU SSR mission and its advisers took advantage of the lack of strong national leadership to attack the issues head-on. A joint commission of the Ministry of Interior, the EU SSR and bilateral police advisers developed a comprehensive set of laws for the public order police as well as the new National Guard, which was approved by the Council of Ministers and at the time of writing awaits approval by Parliament.

For the EC, the main concern related to the police was to obtain the necessary background data for including the future lay-offs in their pension and integration programme and a census was envisioned to supplement the data from the military census. While this had originally been planned to be undertaken by the PARSS as part of its supportive activities,[19] the fact that the Commission's public administration reform project was on the verge of implementing a general census for the civil service led to a decision of joining the two. While this made sense as a principle as well as for reasons of economy of scale, neither the public administration experts, nor the Steering Committee Secretariat were thrilled about the arrangement. While the Secretariat wished to be able to quality control the process and results (and receive their part of the per diem while conducting the census), the project staff, not being part of the SSR structure or agenda, saw the involvement of the Secretariat as a layer of additional politicized complication to a logistically complex, but in essence technical task. Cooperation between the two was hence mainly done through the facilitation of the IfS, which also acted as link between the public administration project and PARSS, the other EDF project depending on the data.

Following the example set by the National Strategy, the justice interventions funded by the international community featured only peripheral to the SSR agenda. Limited international support to the sector was instigated before the development of the 2006 strategy, and the projects in place were disinclined to subject themselves to a holistic process that most justice practitioners did not consider themselves to be part of. The view that justice is not a subsector to SSR was also shared by the initial team leader of PAOSED.

The drug trafficking agenda and the keen donor interest in this particular area quickly came to dominate the justice reform process. It could have tied the justice sector more closely to the rest of the reform framework, as it was a clear example of cross-cutting dependencies between the various security forces, the military and the justice and penal system. However, either because the Ministry of Justice consciously wanted to keep control of the resources earmarked for the counter-narcotics action plan or simply because this objective was not mentioned specifically in the strategy, the efforts were not integrated with the rest of the reform process. Unlike the progress being made in the area of defence, and police, the plans were discussed at neither Steering Committee nor Secretariat level, and instead a separate coordination structure was put in place to steer these efforts.

---

19   PARSS Financing Convention.

Challenges and Opportunities

The process of reforming the security sector in Guinea-Bissau is still in its early phases, and so is the European engagement. Almost three years of operation have nonetheless revealed a number of challenges and opportunities for continued European support to the reform in Guinea-Bissau in particular and possibly for similar efforts in other countries.

Coherence of EU Approach

In spite of ample potential for turf wars between the various EU instruments, cooperation did in fact not prove difficult on the ground. Division of labour with regards to the armed and security forces was clear enough with the EU SSR dealing with the soldiers in active service, while the Commission would be occupying themselves with the ones leaving. Overlap in the area of justice which had been the most contentious issue in Brussels due to it being a traditional domain of the Commission was minimal, probably partly due to the weak capacity and implementation problems of PAOSED and the limited scope of the EU SSR's prosecution focus and collaboration progressed relatively smoothly. In the initial phase of the EU SSR mission, the members of the IfS team worked closely with the EU SSR advisers giving briefings and providing them with relevant national and international contacts and documents. This close relationship continued to the end of the IfS project period, both with regard to more day-to-day operational cooperation, to the IfS participating and providing substantial input into visiting Council missions from Brussels, evaluation missions and research. This cooperation was matched at the strategic level, where the Head of Mission and the EC Delegate met regularly to discuss issues of concern to the progress of the SSR agenda, with the latter subsequently being one of the biggest proponents for extensions of the EU SSR mission mandate. This strong inter-organizational support was subsequently picked up in Brussels to an extent that the Commission warned member states that it would have to reconsider the EDF financing of SSR if a new ESDP mission was not approved by the Council when discussed in Madrid in early 2010.[20]

While the 'bilateral' cooperation between the various instruments worked well, this never resulted in a holistic approach. For example, while the EU SSR prosecution adviser and IfS coordinator collaborated with PAOSED, the project staff never agreed to see justice as being part of the SSR domain, and hence shied away from participating fully in the general SSR coordination forum. In addition, stronger linkages with another EDF project working towards reform of the public administration in general were never established, and constituted a lost opportunity to strengthen the otherwise weak governance and accountability aspects of the overall reform and the European approach hereto. The lack of a clear European vision also allowed for individual member states to use the narcotic

---

20   Discussions with Commission and Council employees.

agenda to distract attention from how to tackle SSR as an aspect of economic and governance development.

Political Nature of SSR and Mitigation of Associated Risks

While there might be a conceptual understanding within the European Union that SSR is in essence a political endeavour, the instruments more readily available to the organization when engaging in such efforts are either those used for development assistance in general (Commission) or sector specific technical assistance (Council). The reform of the security sector in Guinea-Bissau having low priority as a foreign policy issue was therefore in general tackled as a purely financial and technical issue, investing heavily in technical assistance, infrastructure and equipment to military, police and justice. While many of challenges of the security sector were indeed in great need of such assistance, the heart of problem was more complex and required significant 'political investment' from national as well as international players. Such type of investment was minimal from the European actors. The Commission Delegation did not have a dedicated political section nor a more analytical governance team and the Head of Delegation was in effect the only interface with the Bissau-Guinean political system. The IfS had a broader process mandate and access to certain key players, but had not significant clout due to their consultancy attachment to the EU and limited human and financial resources. The EU SSR had a pragmatic Head of Mission with little diplomatic experience and only one political adviser who was concurrently the mission's reporting, public affairs and protocol officer. The lack of 'investment' in political steering and engagement at the top EU level and in the capacity to generate profound and up-to-date political analyses on the ground diminished the impact of the technical and financial investments as well as exposed the EU to a number of risks.

Dealing with core state functions, both the Commission and the Council recognized that 'political will' was a prerequisite for their interventions, and cites it as being present at the conceptualization of their respective interventions.[21] However, in reality this will was only assumed through the existence of the national strategy for SSR and that the Government had expressed agreement of the necessity of SSR. Beyond this, little effort was put into analysing key questions such as a) whose will was in fact legitimate considering the country's informal hierarchy, b) whether this will went beyond mere rhetoric, c) its change over time and d) its consequences for the European interventions and expected benefits. Once the EDF and the Council had made commitments to engage, critical examination and continuous testing of the relevance and efficacy of their activities waned, in spite of the dramatic events occurring during their presence in the country. In the end, the EU along with the general international response to the limping nature

---

21   Convention de Financement, PARSS, Annex II, p. 13, IfS Terms of Reference, p. 7, EU SSR Joint Action.

of the SSR process was mirroring that of the national structures, i.e. rhetorical support and stress of importance, while in reality shying away from engaging in difficult dialogues and potentially taking tough and unpopular decisions. Financial and technical support was largely decoupled from performance or progress and the Government knew that if it made a real push to succeed it would be doubtful that external resources would increase – and vice versa, stalling did not seem to discourage donors.

The analysis of the probability and potential impact of unintended negative consequences and subsequent adoption of risk mitigation measures were downplayed by both the Commission and the Council. In particular the security sector's strong interdependency with democratic governance and legitimacy was set aside by the EU's technical sectorial focus and not least attempts to gain short term advances risked in the long run to undermine the fundamental need for the subjugation of the armed forces to the control of civil authorities. The dilemma is highlighted by the ESDP approach to the military leadership. One of the key issues to be addressed by the reform of the security sector was the unusual standing and influence of the military – and specifically the CGDS – in politics. As the most politically difficult part of the CFSP mandate was the reform of the armed forces, it was decided to appoint a European General as Head of Mission to facilitate access to and respect by the CGDS, considering his general lack of regard for civilian authority. As a result the mission either ignored or failed to fully comprehend that the CGDS was indeed a political actor rather than a General submitted to the leadership of the sitting Government as any other civil servant. Along with most international delegations, the mission would bypass the Minister of Defence and deal directly with the General, hereby endorsing and in effect supporting his unofficial status and allowing the short-term need for access to undermine the long-term democratic governance objective.

The EC exposed itself to a different kind of risk in its efforts to set up the pension fund for retiring personnel from the armed and security forces. This fund was very much on General Tagme's agenda, but was additionally backed by a majority of Guinea-Bissau's elite, many of which were former fighters themselves. Their expectation was that the international community would fund 100 percent of their salary plus additional perks like free cars and housing – an entitlement guaranteed by law but never enacted due to lack of resources. The censuses of the forces and calculations based on life expectancy and the level of salaries[22] made it clear that the European contribution would only cover a part of these expectations. While advocating for other donors to support the fund, the Commission refrained from engaging with the Government on such sensitive questions as the politicians' responsibility to lower expectations of beneficiaries hereby risking political capital *vis-à-vis* a strong interest group. The Commission similarly stayed clear of the question as to who should be responsible for choosing the beneficiaries in the case

---

22   The salaries of Army officers of the ranks of major and above are significantly higher than salary levels of other senior civil servants.

of insufficient resources, a key political issue entailing the possibility to create allegiances as well as change balances of power between the various groups. The strength of the Commission's development work had been in its infrastructure projects, where say one good road is useful even if many other roads in the country remain to be repaired. However, in case of providing pensions for ex-militaries, partial funding could pose a bigger challenge to stability than no funding, and hence is a risk needing pre-emptive attention.

Realistic Assessment of Resources Required for SSR

Reforming the security sector in fragile states and post-conflict settings are complicated and long-term affairs. If ambitions are higher than mere train-and-equip programmes, the process is likely to be characterized by a stop-and-go nature full of surprises and with a need to re-assess assumptions on a continuous basis. From a Brussels perspective the rationale for the EU architecture was reasonable: using the EDF for long-term engagement and the IfS and the ESDP framework to address what appeared to be specific obstacles or challenges to the process. Hence, one-year mandates for the two endeavours seemed appropriate so as to go in, fix the problem, and leave again. Unfortunately, key assumptions of the context in which these teams were to operate, not least related to the Government's readiness and ability to carry forward the reform were overly optimistic. The final definitions of the length of mandates were in the end based on the political and bureaucratic realities in Brussels rather than Bissau, leading to unrealistic expectations in terms of needed time and resources.

The case of European investment in SSR in Guinea-Bissau in essence demonstrates the resource dilemma the European Union faces when it decides to intervene in this sector. The need for adequate political investment is described above as well as the risks associated with financial investments that do not cover the entire target group such as the pension fund. In addition, the EU exposed itself to a reputational risks associated with the quality of technical assistance that they provided to the process. While technical assistance is one of the main aspects of international support to the SSR, it is only as good as the technical assistants deployed. The current secondment regime used by the Council to staff its advisory missions make sense from fiduciary and internal European political concerns, but are not always conducive to achieving the objectives of the missions on the ground. It is difficult to find technically and personally qualified people who are willing to work in a difficult environment like Guinea-Bissau, and have sufficient language skills to work substantially with national counterparts. People who do not fulfil the requirements are sent anyway. In the best case this is a waste of resources, but can in the worst case be counter-productive and discredit international efforts in general.

Institutional Approaches and the Power of Personalities

By working with agents of Government, it was natural for the EU to base its working modalities on an institutional approach. However, in Guinea-Bissau one cannot underestimate the importance of individuals, and how past alliances and enmities play a pivotal role in the conduct of public policy and administration. The one-year mandates given to both the IfS and the EU SSR miscalculated the time needed to build relationships and win the confidence of key counterparts. The IfS overcame this to a certain extent by basing itself in the Secretariat premises which had been renovated using the IfS funds for office rent. The PARSS likewise co-located and had additional budget lines to support concrete activities carried out by the Secretariat. The lack of project funding and the fact that the EU SSR advisers did not co-locate with their national counterparts made their contribution to the relevant actors diffuse, and initially raised doubts among Bissau-Guineans of their usefulness. This was not helped by a frequent turn-over of ministers and key interlocutors[23] whose first instinct would be to ask for technical assistants to 'show me the money'. Over time and with patience the mission did form key working relationship that carried forward the tasks, however, having access to at least seed money for projects would have helped the mission greatly.

Way Ahead

Security sector reform in Guinea-Bissau and the European support to this is still at an early stage. While significant technical progress has been made in producing concrete implementation plans in the relevant sectors, immense challenges remain regarding the political, governance, and not least budgetary foundations of the reform.

The latest incident of mutiny within the Armed Forces and its consequences for the democratic leadership of the country in general, and the security sector in particular are still not fully realized at the time of writing. Neither is the international, and herein the European, response to this. At the moment the President and Prime Minister are downplaying the gravity of the event, hereby allowing the key actors such at the EU and the UN to do the same, and hence continue their programmes unabatedly. How the events of April will shape the debate within the Council of the European Union regarding the continuation of an ESDP mission will be particularly telling of the organization's acknowledgement of the complexities of their assumptions allowing for success. Conditionalities for the establishment of a new mission were agreed between Member States, such as the legislative passing of the legal packages prepared with the help of the EU SSR. This will not have been done in time, and there is a high probability that the

---

23   In the first two years of the mission's life, it dealt with three different Presidents, three different Ministers of Defence and Interior and two Chiefs of General Defence Staff.

institutional inertia will lead to an extension disregarding both their conditionality and the current legitimacy gap in the top of the Armed Forces.[24]

Unlike the case of e.g. Sierra Leone, no EU member states has been inclined to engage substantially either bilaterally or through the EU in Guinea-Bissau, leading the EU to apply a rather ad-hoc approach to its support. The EU should be able to act strategically and decisively without a bilateral driver, and Guinea-Bissau will in the coming period be an interesting test case for the effects of the Lisbon Treaty and the creation of a common European External Action Service which would take on a bigger diplomatic responsibility. Bissau only hosts three European embassies, placing a large burden on them with the rotating presidencies. This will mean the Delegation will have to take on the political role of a unified EU representation as well, expanding from the technical focus that it previously held. The larger role being given to the Delegation has the potential of adding needed mid- and long-term diplomatic and political capacity for analysis and influence to the approach to changing the current status of the security forces in Guinea-Bissau.

References

Convention de Financement, PARSS, Annex II, p. 13, IfS Terms of Reference, p. 7, EUSSR Joint Action.

Convention de Financement entre la Commission Européenne et La République de Guinée Bissau, *Appui à la Reforme du Secteur Sécuritaire, GUB 008/06, IXème FED.*

Convention de Financement entre la Commission Européenne et La République de Guinée Bissau, *Programme d'Appui aux Organes de Souveraineté et à l'Etat de Droit, GUB 002/05, IXème FED.*

Council Joint Action 2008/112/CFSP of 12 February 2008.

European Commission, Terms of Reference, Technical Assistance in support of SSR in Guinea-Bissau, EC Instrument for Stability, 2007.

Government of Guinea-Bissau, 'Restructuring and Modernisation of the Defence and Security Sector: Strategy Document', Geneva, 7 and 8 November 2006.

International Crisis Group, Africa Briefing No. 61.

International Crisis Group, 'Guinea-Bissau: Beyond the Rule of the Gun'. Africa Briefing No. 61, 25 June 2009.

International Crisis Group, 'Guinea-Bissau: In need of a State'. Africa Report No. 142, 2 July 2008.

SSDAT Report, December 2006.

---

24   Author's discussions with Council staff and civil servants from Member States.

Chapter 15

Liberian Vigilantes: Informal Security Provision on the Margins of Security Sector Reform[1]

Ana Kantor and Mariam Persson

Introduction

Time and time again African states have been found weak, non-functioning or even mere territorial frames for hosting its citizens. The formal institutions of African states have failed to gain, or even seek legitimacy and respect of its inhabitants and proven to be incapable of providing its citizens with basic security. As a result, mistrust in these formal institutions and authorities have made people turn to alternative solutions to cope with their everyday lives and safeguard their basic human security. Yet international donors and others, who aim to contribute to the strengthening of the security context in such African states, have seldom managed to look beyond the official facade of the state and its formal security institutions in order to gain an in-depth understanding of how informal networks operate. As this chapter aims to show, this western tendency to treat the non-state security context as a negligible factor will unavoidably have serious consequences. By not acknowledging the informal sphere, one undoubtedly fails to recognize the very actors and mechanisms that African citizens, more often than not, rely on for their basic security.

From a donor and western perspective, post-conflict states are often understood as weak and fragile political realities. Conflict is perceived as the main source contributing to the loss of state authority and endemic instability, fostering an internal security environment of anarchy and chaos with regional and international repercussions. It is often *assumed* that *nothing works* in these societies and that the institutions that safeguard individuals must be built from scratch. The widely prescribed antidote for conflict affected countries usually involves some sort of measures injecting democratic institutional-building to reconstruct (and at times create for the first time) state capacity. While these processes may be necessary and well-intentioned, they are also lengthy and costly. In fact, various studies point out that post-conflict state building results are less than impressive, particularly in the

1 The research for this article was financed by the Folke Bernadotte Academy and a version of this article has been previously published by the Folke Bernadotte Academy internal report series.

growing and ever-expanding field of security sector reform.[2] Security sector reform (SSR) strategies are meant to assist the creation of state security institutions that are responsive to the security needs of individuals. Security related state-building efforts have generally concentrated on the apparently obvious (or at least readily discernible) actors and state institutions.[3] This approach, however, is quite contrary to the admittedly fairly recent and widely recognized argument that state-centric security approaches are insufficient for grappling with on-the-ground realities of security provision. As Bruce Baker argues, current security sector reform practices are based 'on two false assumptions, namely: that the post-conflict state is able (or even willing) to deliver policing to a majority of its population; and that [the post-conflict state] is the principal actor in policing provision'.[4]

This chapter argues that any attempt to reform state security institutions as a means of improving overall security must start with a thorough investigation of the current security context. However, during this process of security mapping, informal actors cannot be neglected. Often this very sector not only exists, but also effectively functions and continuously adapts to contextual realities. One must therefore consider the informal networks of security provision and the recognition of non-state security actors that ordinary citizens, in addition to formal security providers, must navigate on an everyday basis. In doing so it also becomes easier to identify the hidden links between these formal and informal networks that at various levels interact, complement, or even compete with each other. The focus of this chapter is to explore and describe informal security organizations (mainly community watch and vigilante groups) in modern-day Liberia, a country that at the moment is undergoing security sector reform with major assistance from the international community.

As this chapter will show, vigilantism in Liberia captures a range of interacting political, social, economic, local and international factors and dynamics. It also seeks to shed light on some of the links between informal security actors and the formal sphere, which are seldom studied. By deepening the understanding of Liberia's complex security setting, vigilante activities can be understood as something neither legal, nor something completely illegal, but rather a dynamic response to a variety of needs, including security. One of the main findings in this

---

2   See studies such as Peake, G., Scheye, E. and Hills, A., 'Conclusions' in *Managing Insecurity. Field Experiences of Security Sector Reform*. New York: Routledge, 2008, p. 165; Call, C.T. and Cousens, E., *Ending Wars and Building Peace: Coping with Crisis*. New York: International Peace Academy, 2007, pp. 8-9; Call, C.T. with Wyeth, V., *Building States to Build Peace*. Boulder: Lynne Rienner Publishers, 2008.

3   From a security sector reform perspective, the core security actors include: the military, police, border guards, the executive, the legislative (and its security related specialized committees), relevant government ministries (i.e. Ministry of Defence, Justice, Internal Affairs, Finance), and increasingly some relevant civil society groups.

4   Baker, B. (a), 'The Future of SSR is Non-state', Paper presented at 'The Future of SSR', e-conference organized by Centre for International Governance Innovation CIGI, Waterloo, Canada, 4-8 May 2009.

chapter is that these informal groups of security providers, both in urban and rural settings, perceive the state's provision of security as something complementary to their *own* security provision. In fact, the real gatekeepers to Liberia's criminal justice system are the vigilante groups, not the formal security providers, who apprehend suspected criminals and assess their guilt within the confines of the local communities.

Methodology

Given the difficulty of accessing and working with informal networks, some caveats are required to explain the methodology of this chapter. The data for this chapter was collected in Liberia during February and March of 2009. The study draws heavily on interviews carried out with informally organized security groups found in various neighbourhoods in urban Monrovia, in Montserrado County, and in the rural city of Voinjama, in Lofa County. Respondents were interviewed in semi-structured interviews, either in groups and/or individually, and were asked to answer open-ended questions about their perceptions of who provides security for their communities. Additionally, respondents answered questions regarding the characteristics of their organized security groups, the security threats in their communities, and their relationship to the formal security actors. Furthermore, the study draws on interviews with local NGOs' staff, official law enforcement personnel, and other official actors intimately acquainted with the reform of the Liberia National Police (LNP) and the security situation in Liberia. Other sources of data include official reports from the UN, NGOs, and daily newspapers and contemporary academic publications on informal security provision in Africa. While the interviews yielded much insight into the diverse views and methods of informal security organizing, they only capture a limited aspect of the nature and function of these organizations. Yet by shedding light on some of these aspects, this chapter will contribute to a more nuanced understanding of the complex web of formal and informal security networks creating the contemporary security setting in Liberia, which will also provide some critical reflection on the current SSR strategies.

Outline of the Chapter

The second section outlines the conceptual frameworks of this study and identifies some important definitions underpinning this investigation. It describes the concept of security sector reform and presents theories on informal networks of security provision. It also describes and reviews current academic knowledge on vigilantism. This section also aims to explain the importance of informality in African countries and how vigilantism often becomes a natural part of the security landscape. The third section briefly traces Liberia's peace process and the reform of the security sector. It provides an overview of the police reform process and the challenges to policing in Liberia. This section elaborates on the strategies employed and provides a context to the formal provision of security. The fourth section delves into the various cases of community organized watch groups and vigilantes, based upon interviews carried out in the areas of Monrovia and Voinjama. Apart from describing vigilantism and self-initiated security provision in Liberia, issues such as violence, legitimacy, and the chains of command, including the positions of youth, elders and ex-combatants are discussed. The final section makes some policy recommendations for security sector reform programming, highlighting how and why knowledge on informal security realities is of vital strategic relevance when planning and implementing current and future security sector reform programs.

Conceptual Framework

Security Sector Reform

Security sector reform (SSR) emerged as a conceptual and policy tool to address the idea, among other things, that development could not occur without security and justice, and vice versa. Donor states acknowledged that, particularly in post-conflict countries, the sources of insecurity were not only poverty and inequality but also a security system incapable of protecting its citizens. In some of these societies, it was precisely the military or the police that were the main causes of insecurity. Without achieving a basic level of security, reconstruction work (such as building schools and roads) was difficult and thus the basic foundations of democracy could not be established. Hence, SSR emerged as a policy to reform, reconstruct or build security institutions with a 'people-centred approach'. Over the past 15 years, donor states and international organizations have embarked on ambitious, challenging projects that have tried to shape and support security related institutions into agencies, which are responsive to citizens' needs, and which operate effectively and efficiently, according to principles of democratic governance.

The security system of any given nation is composed of a variety of actors and institutions. In fact, some define it as 'all groups in society that are capable of using force as well as the institutions that manage, direct, oversee and monitor them, and otherwise play a role in the development of a country's security policy and the provision of its security'.[5] In theory, these include government oversight bodies (such as the Ministry of Defence or Parliament), judicial and penal institutions (such as courts, prosecutors, correctional services), and non-state security actors (such as private security companies, civil society groups, guerrilla armies, and civil defence patrols). In practice, however, most SSR programs

---

5 Law, D. and Myshlovska, O., 'The Evolution of the Concepts of Security Sector Reform and Security Governance: The EU Perspective' in Spence and Fluri (eds) *The European Union and Security Sector Reform*. London: John Harper, 2008. p. 6.

target the core security agencies, particularly two of them: the military and the police. SSR activities have focused on building the state and its institutions, often ignoring the fact that supporting these institutions does not necessarily lead to security strategies and outcomes that are in fact people-centred. Additionally, the strategy of focusing on the military and the police, contradict the principles of efficiency and economic sustainability, as building these institutions from scratch is an incredibly resource intensive endeavour, particularly for post-conflict states. Experience has also shown that SSR programs are seldom coordinated and that reforms are sectoral rather than all-encompassing of the entire security panorama. Reforms should supposedly be carried out in a way that is complementary to or in line with other sectors. So supporting the development of police services without supporting at the same time the criminal justice system will, for example, have a limited impact on SSR.

There has been significant progress in understanding the fact that SSR programs must take a 'multi-layered or multi-stakeholder approach' – based on the insight that the state often lacks the capacity of being the sole provider of justice and security. Recognizing that post-conflict states may have capacity deficits, may not be viewed as legitimate, and '… historically may have never exercised full sovereign authority over its territory', the OECD recognizes that 'the design of justice and security development indeed requires a multi-layered approach that provides assistance to a range of legitimate state and non-state providers at the multiple points at which actual day-to-day service delivery occurs'.[6] Despite this, as Baker and Scheye note, non-state systems are routinely overlooked by SSR programs.[7] There is little available in SSR policy circles describing the actual role, capacity, and interest of non-state security actors. Baker and Scheye add that 'more often than not, non-state actors are perceived to be purveyors of injustice and insecurity, though little empirical effort has been made to distinguish between different types of non-state actors'.[8] By not truly understanding the nature or characteristics of non-state security actors, SSR programs have excluded individuals who at times have gained more public trust and legitimacy than the formal security agencies. Hence, opportunities for strengthening functioning security mechanisms are limited when the role of non-state security actors is not fully understood or simply neglected.

---

6   OECD Handbook on Security System Reform, 2007, pp. 67-68.

7   Baker, B. and Scheye, E., 'Multi-Layered Justice and Security Delivery in Post-Conflict and Fragile States', *Conflict*, Security and Development Group 7(4), December 2007, p. 505.

8   Ibid.

Informal Networks of Security Provision

In western democracies, the implied assumption is that security and safety are a public good, and it is up to the state to 'deliver' this service. As power and authority rests with the state, mapping out security provision is a fairly straight-forward task of analysing state institutions and bureaucracies. However, using only this perspective to analyse security provision in many non-western states poses the risk of misunderstanding complex power relations. One can claim that in African states, as in many other parts of the non-western world, official state structures and institutions may often be only one of the relevant players within a multi-actor, multi-faceted security configuration. In fact, the state and non-state actors may share the distribution of 'public goods'.[9] As Baker argues, in this context, the state 'has to share authority, legitimacy and capacity with other structures'.[10] Hence, any analysis of the security setting must thereby also take the 'informal' reality into account.

In Western Africa, most activities are shaped by informal networks made up by a multitude of actors, *inter alia*: politicians, military, businessmen, NGOs, national and international organizations, secret societies, religious leaders, warlords, trade unions, etc.[11] Support and authorization of these informal networks often enable the formal mechanisms to function and operate.[12] It is within the informal sphere that the security landscape is defined. In examining security providers in the Mano River Basin area, Jörgel and Utas claim that the informal structures make up about 80 percent of all security providers and they determine the nature of the formal institutions and how they are used. According to them, actors within the informal structures navigate the formal structures and use them as a vehicle to further their own political and economic interests. In real political terms, the formal structures thereby become a mere shadow image of the informal reality.[13]

Mapping informal networks – in particular, informal security networks – is often a challenging task. As Jörgel and Utas have pointed out, these structures cannot easily be unravelled, traced or understood – as they are a complex, ever changing web of links. Moreover, actors operating within formal spheres, who often have links to informal structures and non-state security actors, wish to keep these ties hidden. Having connections to security actors outside the formal state apparatus is not considered a suitable picture to present to the western donor world.[14] Nonetheless, the security panorama remains incomplete if the legal and 'illegal' providers of security are not properly considered.

---

9   Baker (a).
10   Ibid.
11   Jörgel, M. and Utas, M., 'The Mano River Basin Area – Formal and Informal Security Providers in Liberia, Guinea and Sierra Leone', *FOI Defence Analysis*, 2007, p. 8.
12   Ibid.
13   Ibid., p. 12.
14   Ibid.

Understanding Vigilantism

As has been pointed out by Bruce Baker, organized activities, whether by the state or non-state groups, that seek to ensure the maintenance of communal order, security and peace in Africa through elements of prevention, deterrence, investigation of breaches and punishment are surprisingly largely understudied. What is evident from his studies is that policing in Africa is not a monopoly of the state police. Policing is carried out by formal and informal agencies outside the realm of the police and often outside the realm of the state.[15] Yet, 'non-state policing', as Baker calls this type of informal security provision, is a valuable asset for advancing safety and security among the poor,[16] especially since poor communities tend to be excluded from formal security provision.

In fact when it comes to security, African citizens have a range of alternatives and actors (state and non-state, legal and illegal) that they must navigate in order to secure their everyday protection.[17] Moreover, evidence also points to the fact that African citizens rarely see formal and informal security provisions as mutually exclusive categories. Baker, for example, argues that as people move about their daily business or as the time of the day changes, people also move from one sphere of security agency to another one, which may be better suited for their protection at that very moment.[18] In this sense formal and informal security providers are all part of a complex pattern of overlapping actors that from a citizens' point of view interact and complement each other, rather than appearing as incompatible alternatives. In that light it is interesting to see under what circumstances people choose one alternative over another. Nevertheless, it is precisely this analysis of the multiplicity of choices that is often neglected when initiating security sector reform processes, as reforms to security actors solely focus on state agencies.

One form of non-state policing that is often cast aside, although it plays a significant part in the security context, is vigilantism. While there is no precise scholarly definition or understanding of what vigilantism exactly is, generally it is understood as a form of protection by organizations or movements, which seek to provide security for their local communities. More precisely, Abrahams' comprehensive definition describes vigilantism as 'an organized attempt by a group of 'ordinary citizens' to enforce norms and maintain law and order on behalf of their communities, often by resorting to violence, in the perceived absence of effective official state action through the police and courts'.[19] Vigilante-

---

15 Baker, B., *Multi-Choice Policing in Africa.* Nordiska Afrikainstitutet, 2008, p. 100.

16 Ibid., p. 5.

17 Some of the choices include mob violence, religious police, civil defence force, etc. For a detailed list of multi choice policing see Baker, 2008, p. 79.

18 Baker, 2008, p. 27.

19 Abrahams, R., 'What's in a Name? Some Thoughts on the Vocabulary of Vigilantism and Related Form of "Informal Criminal Justice"' in Feenan (ed.) *Informal Criminal Justice.* Aldershot: Ashgate, 2003, p. 26.

type organizations have existed in many cultures, in past and present times, in both rural and urban settings. Modern-day empirics suggest that often vigilante outcomes are particularly violent and sometimes lethal.[20] Various studies also point to the effectiveness of these groups, and there are well-documented cases where vigilante success led to a dramatic decrease in crime.[21] Of course, as the literature also demonstrates: 'The history of vigilantism is filled with cases of mistaken identity, in which the wrong person was made to pay for someone else's misdeeds.'[22]

Vigilante-type organizations often emerge when there is the perception of increased criminality or social deviance which threatens social order.[23] These groups flourish not only in places where states lack capacity to protect citizens from crime, but also where the state itself is believed to be corrupt or untrustworthy.[24] Deep mistrust of the state and formal security providers, driven by the inability of the police to provide basic security and protect its citizens' human rights, further encourages vigilantism. Daniel Nina, for example, has argued that vigilantism arises from the perception that the state is doing nothing to guarantee the safety of a community. Accordingly when communities' demands on the state to do something are considered to have been ignored, actions of vigilantism occur. The state is thereby seen as a limited player with regard to crime prevention and when it comes to guaranteeing citizens' security.[25] But despite this, as argued by David Pratten, vigilantism can not merely be explained as a popular response to the vacuum left by state collapse, failure or instrumentalized disorder.[26] Such connections to the formal sphere are more complex than that. According to Buur and Jensen although vigilante organizations often claim to be based outside and in opposition to an ineffective or even predatory state, they are involved in state-like performances like security enforcement to such extent that it causes a renegotiation of the boundaries between state and society. It thereby becomes difficult to distinguish between what

---

20   Adinkrah, M., 'Vigilante Homicides in Contemporary Ghana', *Journal of Criminal Justice* 33, 2005, p. 415; see also Allen, F.G., 'Vigilante Justice in Jamaica: The Community Against Crime', *International Journal of Comparative and Applied Criminal Justice* 21, 1997.

21   See studies such as Buur, L., 'Crime and Punishment on the Margins of the Post-Apartheid State', *Anthropology and Humanism* 28(1), 2003; Oomen, B., 'Vigilantism or Alternative Citizenship? The Rise of Mapogo a Mathamaga', *African Studies* 63(2), December 2004; Abrahams, R., 'Sungusungu: Village Vigilante Groups in Tanzania', *African Affairs* 86, 1987.

22   Adinkrah, 2005, p. 415.

23   Ibid.

24   Heald, S., 'Controlling Crime and Corruption from Below: Sungusungu in Kenya', *International Relations* 21, 2007, p. 183.

25   Nina, D., 'Dirty Harry is Back: Vigilantism in South Africa – The (Re)Emergence of "Good" and "Bad" Community', *African Security Review* 9(1), 2000.

26   Pratten, D. (a), 'The Politics of Protection: Perspectives on Vigilantism in Nigeria', *Africa* 78(1), 2008, p. 8.

is the state and what is not. Vigilante groups operate at the frontier of the state, blurring the boundaries between the state and what normally falls outside of it. According to Buur and Jensen, authority should be seen as not necessarily lodged in particular institutions but as practices performed by different groups which can employ several and different registers. For instance, state representatives can, and do, sometimes use vigilante organizations for legally sanctioned violence.[27] Vigilantism can thus often be accepted at local levels of the state since it addresses issues of security and moral order that are relevant to people living on the margin, beyond the reach of the formal state apparatus.[28]

The public image of these groups often presents a one-sided picture of vigilante groups. They are often described as mere brutal and undisciplined mobs or crowds consisting of mostly young people without any clear social or political identity and as emotional and spontaneous. However, this simplified image may in fact hinder us from fully understanding the complexity of the vigilante phenomenon. Buur and Jensen argue that vigilantism should be seen as a form of local everyday policing. Even though it should be recognized that vigilante groups, in different ways, challenge the rule of law and the state's monopoly of using legitimate force and often severely infringe on citizen's rights, Buur and Jensen suggest that vigilantism cannot be reduced to either expressions of the mob or to mere antidotes to formal law.[29] In fact, Pratten argues that often vigilante activities are not solely focused on security; vigilantism serves a range of other functions in a community, such as disciplining children, sponsoring unemployed youth, recovering debts, and screening political candidates.[30] In line with these arguments, this study recognizes the complexity of vigilantism, and looks beyond the one-sided picture of these movements as brutal gangs. This perspective is crucial in understanding why non-state security provision often is a rational choice for many African citizens. In order to help nuance the picture, it is also important to comprehend this phenomenon in relation to the formal state security provision. Vigilantism and informal security provision cannot be reduced to formal and state controlled security's antithesis, the relation between the formal and informal is in this sense much more convoluted.

A Background to Security Sector Reform in Liberia

In August 2003 in Accra, the Comprehensive Peace Agreement (CPA) was signed by the warring parties of Liberia, after the two Liberian civil wars between 1989-

---

27 Buur, L. and Jensen, S., 'Vigilantism and the Policing of Everyday Life in South Africa', *African Studies* 63(2), 2004. p. 144.

28 Ibid., p. 139.

29 Buur and Jensen, 2004, p. 140.

30 Pratten, D. (b), 'The Thief Eats his Shame: Practice and Power in Nigerian Vigilantism', *Africa* 78(1), 2008, p. 65.

1996 and 1999-2003.[31] Following the resignation of the former rebel-leader of the National Patriotic Front of Liberia (NPFL) and later Liberian president Charles Taylor, in September of the same year, the United Nations Mission in Liberia (UNMIL) was established to monitor the ceasefire agreement and support other aspects of the CPA, including the security sector reform. More specifically, Security Council Resolution 1509 (2003) stipulated that one of the mandates of UNMIL should be to 'assist the transitional government of Liberia in monitoring and restructuring the police force of Liberia, consistent with democratic policing, to develop a civilian police training program, and to otherwise assist in the training of civilian police'.[32] UNMIL took the leading role in the reform of the Liberia National Police (LNP) and other civilian security state agencies (such as the Immigration Force, the Special Security Services, and the border patrol), while the United States focused on reforming the Armed Forces of Liberia (AFL). Security sector reform in Liberia from the outset has presented an enormous challenge. Rebuilding the police, the armed forces, and other security institutions was undertaken in the context of socio-economic and political collapse, fuelled by fourteen years of civil war and a massive scale humanitarian crisis. Among other things, SSR has meant addressing a security sector that historically has been dysfunctional, politicized, and beyond the ruling elite inexperienced in protecting Liberian citizens. Coupled with these issues is Liberia's weak judicial system, including the lack of basic infrastructure and few resources in the courts and prisons.

The Right Strategy? The Right Institutions?

Liberia is progressively restoring peace and stability, while attempting to also consolidate democracy. The recently produced National Security Strategy[33] and Pillar I[34] in Liberia's Poverty Reduction Strategy[35] are attempts by the government to comprehensively address security matters, particularly formal security institutions, in ways that are congruent with governance and professionalism. The total recreation of the Armed Forces of Liberia (AFL), according to some, appears

---

31   For a more detailed account of Liberia's civil wars and transition to peace see Moran, M.H., *Liberia. The Violence of Democracy.* Philadelphia: University of Pennsylvania Press, 2006; Adebajo, A., *Building Peace in West Africa. Liberia, Sierra Leone and Guinea-Bissau.* Boulder: Lynne Rienner Publishers, 2002.

32   United Nations Security Council Resolution 1509. S/RES/1509 (2003) p. 4.

33   Government of Liberia, 'National Security Strategy of the Republic of Liberia', January 2008.

34   Four main sectors of intervention, or 'pillars' were identified in Liberia's Poverty Reduction Strategy Paper: (I) Security; (II) Economic Revitalization; (III) Governance and the Rule of Law; and (IV) Infrastructure and Basic Services.

35   International Monetary Fund, 'Liberia: Poverty Reduction Strategy Paper', July 2008, IMF Country Report No. 08/219.

to be a provisional success.[36] Several military bases have undergone refurbishing with the assistance of American contractors. The vetting and recruitment program of the AFL appear to have been well run, and over 2,000 recruits have undergone basic training. The Liberia National Police (LNP) did not undergo such an effective vetting process, something that will be discussed later in this paper, but has made some other important achievements. To date, over 3,600 officers have been trained by UNMIL, and much of that training in the Police Academy is now being conducted by Liberian officers. Additionally, within the LNP there is a Professional Services Unit, which is increasingly trying to address internal affairs and to deal with cases of police misconduct.

Yet despite some important achievements, the SSR process has been problematic and at times policy has been misguided and not prioritized in dealing with the current security environment of Liberia. Many in Liberia argue that the international community and the national government have focused too much on the armed forces, considering the fact that their budget is disproportionately larger than the LNP's.[37] The lack of resources has detrimentally affected the capacity of the LNP, something that will be discussed below, and as a result citizens are not being protected, especially from crime. Additionally, other security agencies (such as the Ministry of Security, the National Security Agency, and the National Bureau of Investigation) have been virtually untouched. Considering the abusive past of the AFL, it is understandable that reform efforts address the undisciplined and politicized ways of the armed forces and firmly establish civilian control. Upon the signing of the peace accord, Liberia, like many other post-conflict settings, has faced new security challenges mainly in the form of theft, burglary, assault and rape. The increasing number of land and property disputes has also intensified ethnic tensions and resulted in outbreaks of violence.[38] Bearing in mind that the LNP is the formally recognized as the primary law enforcement body in the country, one must question whether it has received sufficient attention.

The absence of a comprehensive and 'whole-of-government' approach to SSR is also evident by the lack of coordination efforts. An example of this can be seen in Liberia's Poverty Reduction Strategy: while Pillar I addresses security issues, Pillar III addresses rule of law matters. This distinction, evident throughout SSR programs in Liberia, is a setback because the police and the criminal justice system will only be as effective as their counterparts. Thus far, the justice system, the courts, and prisons have undergone limited reform. In fact, corruption in the judicial system is endemic; there are massive case backlogs and prolonged

---

36 International Crisis Group, 'Liberia: Uneven Progress in Security Sector Reform', Report No. 148, 13 January 2009, p. 9.

37 Alloycious, D., 'Liberia: "Police's Budget Can't Fight Crime"', 7 July 2008, AllAfrica, available at: http://allafrica.com/stories/200807071359.html, accessed 13 August 2009, 13:05.

38 'National Security Strategy of Liberia', p. 22, Interview with UN official, Monrovia, March 5, 2009.

pre-trial detentions, and often suspects are released without ever going to trial.[39] Hence, successful apprehension of a criminal by the police is often insufficient to keep criminals permanently off the streets. The Ministry of Justice is technically responsible for coordinating security sector reforms. Presently there is no such capacity, although there have been discussions to create such a role.[40]

Despite the fact that the reforms have been uncoordinated, they have at the same time, ironically, been centralized and state-centric. Other relevant security actors (such as private security companies, customary chiefs, and to some extent ex-AFL soldiers and former police officers) have been largely left out of reform discussions. Reform efforts, such as the creation of the police's armed elite Emergency Response Unit (ERU), have mainly occurred in the capital Monrovia and have not taken into account that 40 percent of Liberians live in rural areas.[41] There has been a proposal to create County Security Councils and District Security Councils, which would allow local security agencies, civil society and other government agencies the opportunity to discuss and actively participate in national security issues. However, to date, such efforts remain to be implemented. Police representation outside of Monrovia has improved, but is still limited. In rural areas, for example, the number of active police officers at times was merely 30 in Bomi County and 54 in Bong County.[42] The Professional Services Unit is based at the police headquarters, and so one must wonder how internal affairs investigations are conducted outside the capital. Similarly the AFL, as of yet, has not been deployed throughout Liberia. UNMIL troops and the armed UN Formed Police Units are still the primary actors safeguarding rural areas when conflicts break out.

Policing without Police

Policing inadequacies in Liberia are most commonly explained by the fact that they are under-resourced. Across Liberia police officers, government representatives, and citizens widely agree that the LNP has funding and logistical problems. It is not uncommon to walk into a police depot and find that there are no radios, computers, office supplies, toilets, or electricity. Officers do not have batons, gas, or handcuffs, and many use their personal mobile phones to communicate with each other and with police headquarters. Vehicles are scarce, as is fuel. In Lofa County, for

---

39   'Liberia. Warnings Against Mob Justice', *Africa Research Bulletin*, 1-31 October 2006, p. 16831.

40   Interview with Dr. Thomas Jaye, Governance Commission, Monrovia, 12 March 2009.

41   Liberia has a population of about three million. Source: Population Division of the Department of Economic and Social Affairs of the United Nations Secretariat, 'World Population Prospects: The 2006 Revision and World Urbanization Prospects: The 2007 Revision', http://esa.un.org/unup, 20 April 2009, 08:09:54.

42   Baker, B. (b), *Resource Constraint and Policy in Liberia's Post-Conflict Policing.* Forthcoming, 2009, p. 7.

example, a deputy police commander said that there was only one vehicle available in an area with about 250,000 inhabitants.[43] Most often the vehicle was used to transport the police commander to and from Lofa and Monrovia. Without cars, the police cannot respond rapidly. They are not able to transport suspected criminals, nor are they able to patrol. UNPOL officers often report that they spend their time chauffeuring LNP officers. Needless to say, forensic investigation equipment and capabilities are almost non-existent. This often results in not having enough or proper evidence to hold suspects for trial. Important achievements (such as the LNP's newly formed Women and Children's Protection Section) are undermined by chronic understaffing and limited resources.[44]

One of the more problematic issues for the LNP is that there are insufficient officers for the security needs of the country, especially since officers are unarmed. The political decision to create an unarmed LNP was not necessarily incorrect, considering its past misuse of power and force. Yet, a completely unarmed police officer faced with criminals armed with machetes or guns is rarely able to stop them or even protect themselves. As a result, there are some areas that the police are unable or unwilling to patrol. Given this, and the fact that police officers take home a pay check of a little bit more than U$70 per month (after deducting insurance and other fees), patrolling the streets at the cost of risking one's life is understandably unappealing. Furthermore, since these wages are so low and realistically cannot financially support a police officer, corruption becomes a tool for survival.

A New Face on the Old LNP or an Old Face on the New LNP?

It is unsurprising that public confidence in the new LNP, while it has improved, is still low. There have been efforts to make LNP into a more effective, people centred-service; however, it is widely recognized that security sector reform is a long term process. The reality is that it will take many years, if not decades, for the LNP to build expertise, consolidate practices, and gain the necessary respect to effectively carry out policing functions. Yet, the increased crime and sense of insecurity only further deteriorates the LNP's legitimacy and reputation. In a fieldwork survey, 76 percent of Liberians responded that the most important actor ensuring their personal safety was UNMIL, while only 18 percent felt the same of the Liberia National Police.[45] Many interviewees cited cases where the

---

43 Interview with a local deputy police commander, Voinjama, March 2009.

44 US Department of State, Liberia, Bureau of Democracy, Human Rights, and Labour, 6 March 2007. Available at: http://www.state.gov/g/drl/rls/hrrpt/2006/78742.htm 2009-04-21.

45 Judy Smith-Höhn, 'Multi-Level Security Provision in Post-Conflict Societies: Local Perspectives from Liberia and Sierra Leone'. Paper for the AEGIS European Conference on African Studies, 'African Alternatives: Initiative and Creativity beyond Current Constraints', 2007, p. 5.

police took hours to arrive to a crime scene and then often were unable to properly investigate or even solve the case. Public perception of the LNP is not just based on its apparent lack of capacity and inability to respond to criminal activities, but also on their assessment of the police reform process. Many believe that the LNP is still made up of 'dirty cops'. Part of this problem is associated to the vetting process of the LNP – which for many Liberians and international observers was a failure.[46] It is widely acknowledged that the vetting procedures did not effectively weed out past perpetrators of human rights. At the same time, some argue that the deactivation process removed too many qualified senior police officers, leaving significant managerial gaps in the LNP, as well as removing proper role models for younger officers. One international police officer, assisting the LNP with internal affairs, believes that an additional problem is the fact that the remaining senior officers that were actually left behind are corrupt and 'contaminate' the new recruits.[47]

Liberians also acknowledge that the new LNP does not embody principles of accountability and good governance, as SSR efforts set out to do – in fact the LNP to a certain extent is arguably a politicized security agency. 'The the President of Liberia (Ellen Sirleaf-Johnson) has been directly responsible for the appointment of not only the Inspector General (IG) but also of various police commissioners, only one of which is an actual professional police officer.'[48] The appointment of Beatrice Munah-Sieh, a former New Jersey teacher with no police experience, to Inspector General created great controversy and questioned the direction of the LNP. Moreover, critical opinions of this presidential decision were accentuated, when President Ellen Sirleaf-Johnson 'punished' Munah-Sieh for a 'grave incident' by granting her a month of training in the United States, despite recommendations calling for her resignation.[49] One of the latest controversies was the political appointment of an advisor to the LNP's Inspector General, who was the former Police Director under Charles Taylor's administration and has a poor human rights record, which is well-documented.[50]

There are also plenty of media reports pointing to cases of police misconduct.[51] This also includes higher echelons within the LNP, who were found stealing fuel

46   International Crisis Group. January 2009, p. 17.

47   Interview with UNPOL officer previously stationed in Liberia, Stockholm, February 2009.

48   Interview with an international police officer, Monrovia, 3 March 2009.

49   This incident resulted in a bloody shoot-out between the LNP and the Seaport Police with apparent knowledge of the Inspector General. See 'Decision on Freeport Probe Must be Clear', *The Analyst Newspaper*, 7 August 2007; Thomas-Queh, J., 'The Police in Question: A Grave Security Pitfall To be Reckoned With?' *The Perspective*, Atlanta Georgia, 18 July 2008.

50   Sorbor George, 'Taylor's Police Director to advise LNP', Star Radio Liberia, Thursday, 12 February 2009.

51   Fahn, P.A., 'Liberia: President Sirleaf Fuels Debate on Police', October 2008, BBC World Service Trust, available at: http://www.communicatingjustice.org/en/

or abusing their authority and influence. In many cases, these police officers are inadequately disciplined.[52] An American contractor, working on justice reform issues, accounted for cases of severe police misconduct, where the police officers were 'untouchable' due to their extensive ties to important and powerful people – 'big men'.[53] In one case, the internal investigation was obstructed by other security institutions, including the National Security Agency and the National Bureau of Investigation, which prevented the prosecution of the corrupt officer. Despite efforts to hold the police accountable, misconduct is often treated with impunity and the LNP is a tool for political manipulation to reward and protect a few. To illustrate this belief amongst Liberians, the LNP's newly formed ERUs (Emergency Response Units) are in Monrovia better known as 'Ellen's Response Units', after their close relations to the president.

Community Policing through Community Watch Groups or Vigilantes?

Recently, there has been much attention devoted to the use of 'community-oriented policing' strategies, particularly in police reform efforts in post-conflict countries. Liberia is no exception. Donor-driven community-oriented policing programs aim at creating improved coordination and communication between the police and those being policed. Through 'consultative efforts' in the areas patrolled, police are able to, in theory, discern the needs and priorities of a specific community. In Liberia, in order to both improve policing capacity and public perceptions of the police, Community Policing Forums (CPF) were set up to link police and communities. However, the results of such forums are mixed. Many argue that the CPFs are not sufficiently supported by the police.[54] In some cases, criminals identified by community members are not dealt with. Additionally, CPF members complain that the forums are run on a completely voluntary basis with little or no assistance from the government – members must also pay for their own stationary, mobile phones, flashlights, etc. Nonetheless, Community Policing Forums have become especially important in Monrovia. Through the CPFs' channels, the LNP encouraged the creation of community watch groups, with the purpose of apprehending criminals. In the face of growing crime and violence and given the police's inability to deal with lawlessness, the former Minister of Justice Frances Johnson Morris in 2006 called on Liberians 'to organize themselves into community watch teams or vigilante groups',[55] Soon after the Minister's statement, UNMIL's police commissioner stated: 'we have to forget the word vigilante and focus on

---

stories/04102008_liberia_president_sirleaf_fuels_debate_police, accessed 13 August 2009 13:14.

52   Interview with an American justice reform contractor, Monrovia, 5 March 2009.

53   For a discussion on 'big men' and their ability to achieve and maintain power and control through social networks see Jörgel and Utas, 2007.

54   Interview with local NGOs working on security issues, Monrovia, 2 March 2009.

55   'Liberia Calls for Citizen Vigilantes to Fight Crime', *AlertNet*, 6 September 2006.

community policing forums that were created by the LNP supported by UNMIL' and added that people should not patrol the streets.[56] Despite of trying to take back her statement, the Minister of Justice tapped into a phenomenon that already existed in Liberia: people using self-help solutions to insecurity. The following section provides a description of these groups, their manner of operating, and their status between the formal and informal.

Vigilantes in Liberia – Local Defenders or Menace to Society?

The web of security provision in Liberia is complex and multi-dimensional. At one level, reforms are in the process of creating state-driven central institutions tasked with maintaining security and enforcing law and order. At the same time, the sources of security (and insecurity) in Liberia exist outside formal state structures, at times competing with them, and at times part of a multifaceted continuum of relationships and networks. Whether in rural Lofa or in the inner city neighbourhoods of Monrovia, public security occurs beyond the legal authority of the Liberia National Police. In these different contexts, groups of ordinary citizens (usually young men) organize themselves along different structures, sometimes with formal permission from the authorities, identifying themselves as 'neighbourhood/community watch groups' or 'vigilantes'.

For this study interviews were conducted with participants from six loosely defined conglomerations of groups that have distinctly organized themselves according to their communities' security needs and capabilities. Some of the groups were made up of members of the same ethnic groups, but the majority of them seemed to organize themselves according to locality. Three of them, the Mandingo Group, the Loma Group, and the Bazzi Quarter group operated in Voinjama, although the latter had ceased to operate at the time when the interviews were carried out. Voinjama, the capital of Lofa County, is a small city located in the heavily-forested north-western part of Liberia bordering Guinea and Sierra Leone. Situated in Liberia's rich agricultural and diamond-mining area, the city of Voinjama was a prosperous and booming city before the two civil wars. However, Voinjama was heavily affected by the wars. In fact, it was here the Liberians United for Reconciliation and Democracy (LURD) rebels launched its campaign against President Charles Taylor during the second war. Voinjama changed hands several times during the years of fierce fighting. When disarmament finally came in 2004, much of the once flourishing city had been destroyed by the heavily artillery. Today, Voinjama, with the third largest numbers of ex-combatants in Liberia, is now struggling with poverty and high unemployment rates. Many of the bullet-scarred houses are still painted with names of rebel groups, which bear witness to the brutal war that raged here not so long ago.

---

56   UNMIL. 'Weekly Press Briefing', 13 September 2006. Available at: http://unmil. org/1article.asp?id=1630&zdoc=1, accessed 7 October 2009, 17:50.

For this study, three urban groups were also interviewed in the capital city Monrovia: the Paynesville Group and the Congo Town Group operating in the suburbs of Monrovia, and the Sinkor Group operating in the city centre (a short distance from the UNMIL Headquarters). Monrovia, as much of the country, was left in ruins after the two civil wars. During the second civil war, the capital was extensively damaged in 2003 during the major military confrontation between the Liberian Armed Forces and the LURD rebels. Poverty, unemployment, heavy criminality and illiteracy are among the many everyday challenges in the marginalized areas where interviews took place. As this research has shown, young men[57] both in the urban and rural settings believed the state's provision of security, at best, to be something complementary to their *own* security provision. It is evident that these vigilante groups, and not the formal security providers, were the real gatekeepers of Liberia's criminal justice system and, in some situations, of the corrections system too.

The Origins of Liberian Vigilantes

The one common trait among all groups studied in this chapter is that their *raison d'être* is simple and consistent, 'The state has failed us; therefore, we've taken on the task of defending our community ourselves.'[58] Since the end of the civil war in 2003, the crime rate has remained high as is typical in post-conflict settings. As one of the informants said, 'The houses of our neighbourhoods get burglarized almost every night here. The criminals are often organized and they come in armed gangs.'[59] The most common security issue reported during our interviews was crime in the form of burglary and theft. While spousal abuse, rape, and, to a certain extent, murders are also significant security threats, these were generally less discussed by the informants. In Voinjama, an elderly chief reported that in the past young men would sell marijuana, fostering a climate for further criminality. However, this stopped when the community watch group reported such activities to the police. According to these group members, criminality after the war greatly increased due to poverty and the lack of opportunities for ex-combatants and for those people returning from neighbouring countries after the war. In Voinjama, the various group members that were interviewed believed that more than half of all the criminals came from neighbouring Guinea in hope of reaping some of the US dollars readily available in Liberia. Another explanation was that criminals in

---

57   In the vigilante or community watch groups interviewed for this study no women were active members. Women could have supportive roles but did not patrol the streets at night time. Nonetheless, young women may actually take a more active part in similar security settings, but are perhaps less visible due to the prevalent gender structures.

58   Interviews with vigilante and community watch groups conducted during March 2009 in Monrovia and Voinjama.

59   Interview with a vigilante member in Monrovia, March 2009.

Monrovia often hid in the rural areas (such as those in Lofa County), knowing well that the police with its limited resources would not be able to find them.[60]

Patrolling the streets then had become a necessity to a non-functioning and absent police force. The young men interviewed expressed their frustration over the fact that the police did not have the capacity, resources, and sometimes even the willingness to prevent burglary, rape, abuse and other crimes in their communities. Despite the creation of Community Policing Forums in some of the neighbourhoods where the interviewed vigilante groups operated, many of respondents expressed dissatisfaction with the actual involvement and unwillingness of the police to address specific community security issues. Many respondents claimed that it took several hours for the police to arrive to the crime scene, if they showed up at all. In the Bazzi Quarter, a maze-like neighbourhood, with narrow alley ways, informants reported that the unarmed police rarely, if ever, entered the area, especially at night. Several group members did hold a general belief that the Liberia National Police had somewhat improved, but not enough to keep them safe. However, all groups reported that police corruption was endemic and in the words of a Mandigo Group informant, 'There are still some *ugly* officers'.[61] Some were believed to harbour criminals or even share dwellings with them. Some, he added, are criminals themselves, often involved in 'gangster' like activities, dealing marijuana and cocaine. The demand of bribes was a regular occurrence, and people almost accepted it as part of the daily routine, knowing well that the police officers were underpaid. In light of these circumstances, the young men felt that they had to organize themselves because the police were not trustworthy.[62]

Modes of Operation

Although the modes of action somewhat varied among the community watch groups and the vigilantes interviewed here, there were several similarities. Usually patrols were made up of groups of 10-20 young men who met after dusk (any time from 9pm to 12am) to patrol specific areas until the morning hours (until about 2am or 6am). While these young men patrolled in the strictest sense, or were 'hanging out' with their friends, they kept a vigilant eye on their surroundings and for possible trouble and 'rogues'.[63] These patrols stopped and interrogated any stranger that entered their neighbourhood. Upon asking one of the group leaders how these men know who is a stranger, he said: 'The youth know exactly who belongs and who doesn't belong in the community.' Some groups claimed to use passwords at night in order to verify that a person actually belonged to a specific community. However, once a person was deemed suspicious, the group would

---

60   Interviews with vigilante and community watch groups in Voinjama, March 2009.
61   Interview with a community watch group member in Voinjama, March 2009.
62   Interviews with vigilante and community watch groups in Voinjama, March 2009.
63   This is the term used by Liberians to describe thieves or criminals.

question the individual to find out their motive or intention for being in that area. If they found the explanation acceptable, they would let them go or escort them to where they claimed they were going. However, if the person in question seemed 'up to no good', then other actions were taken. 'Depending on the nature of the crime, we either punish him ourselves or take him to the police.'[64]

The specific course of action taken by different vigilante groups, when faced with a criminal or a potential one, seemed to greatly vary from group to group. Those groups that had approval from the police to operate as 'community watch groups' clearly recognized that 'even criminals have rights' and 'with power comes responsibility.' In these cases, the criminals were then escorted to the police depot, although often without any actual evidence collected except for the testimony given by the vigilante group member(s). However, almost all 'formally registered' community watch groups and vigilante groups interviewed in this study eventually admitted that the captured person was never immediately, and not always, brought to the police. As noted above, an individual's guilt or innocence was often determined on the spot after an interrogation, and sometimes, so was their punishment.[65]

Despite the fact that there is currently no war in Liberia, violence is clearly an everyday reality for these groups, particularly in urban areas. Patrolling the streets of Monrovia is a dangerous undertaking, and group members such as those in Sinkor report that they themselves have often been injured when facing criminals. As a result, they have armed themselves with machetes and iron bars, claiming that the criminals often were better equipped than they were. Consequently they felt forced to respond with armed violence. In his article on Nigerian vigilantes, Baker also touches upon this issue of escalating violence. He argues that the most fundamental response to the use of force is counterforce. Despite the fact that citizens arm themselves, criminals continue their illegal activities while preparing themselves with the intention to meet defensive violence with violence. However, criminal violence not only drives people to defend themselves but also retaliate in anger.[66] When this happens, the escalation of violence is often unavoidable. The 'defensive violence' of the Liberian vigilantes could thereby be seen both as a response, a consequence, and a contributing factor to the structural and physical violence of everyday life in Liberia.

These aspects highlight that the existence of vigilante groups leads to a number of negative consequences. The most obvious one is when these groups become more of a threat, rather than the defenders of the community. The unpredictable nature of these groups can become particularly exacerbated when the young men patrol the streets under the influence of alcohol or drugs, or when their vigilante

---

64   Interviews with vigilante and community watch groups conducted during March 2009 in Monrovia and Voinjama.

65   Ibid.

66   Baker, B., 'When the Bakassi Boys Came: Eastern Nigeria Confronts Vigilantism', *Journal of Contemporary African Studies* 20(2), 223-44, 2002, pp. 238, 242.

ways become profitable; for example, when they resort to extortion or other gang-like activities. On the one hand, there is much evidence that 'so-called' suspects' rights are severely violated by these methods and the manner in which they are apprehended. But on the other hand, one can wonder who is protecting the rights of the community members who live in constant fear from burglary and other crimes.

One pattern that seems to have emerged from the interviews is the issue of escalating violence. As previously noted, the increase in violent methods was not only a reaction to better armed criminals, but also a result of frustration. Almost all of the community watch group members mentioned that they felt a strong sense of frustration about the fact that apprehended criminals were not properly dealt with by the police or the courts, and that in many cases they were released after a day or two. In their defence, the formal authorities explained that often these groups would apprehend a suspected criminal and bring the person to the police without any concrete evidence. They also claimed that the group members were not willing to follow up these cases and/or testify against the suspected criminals in court. In short, vigilante groups seemed more willing to take the law into their own hands, rather than to hand over the suspected criminal to an inefficient, corrupt police force. This clearly demonstrates an area where better communication and increased awareness between the police and the community watch groups could lead to a possible reduction of violence and mob justice.

Organization and Chains of Command:
The Role of Elders, Youth, and Ex-Combatants

As mentioned above, vigilante and community watch groups' self-expressed purpose and reason for existing are generally consistent from group to group; however, the organizational structure and chains of command significantly differed between the groups interviewed for this study. In Voinjama, all of the interviewed groups had strong ties to their respective traditional chief. Likewise, the position of elders was also deemed important in these communities. In the Mandingo Group, a relative to the Mandingo chief, had, with police permission, organized his community's watch group. He was an elder or someone who could be described as a 'big man', characterized by his close ties to the chief, and a high social status (that is, was married and was able to afford a house, something that was impossible for the social category of youth). Due to his strong sense of commitment for the local community, and his ability to create a network of dependants, he had taken on the responsibility of organizing protection for the community. This form of organization can be understood by the concept of 'big men and networks' used by Jörgel and Utas to explain the logic of patron-client relations in African countries where the mutual dependency between 'big men' and clients determine how social relations are constructed. By creating networks of dependants, a 'big man' is able to manifest his/her power while the clients in return for giving support also receive favours.[67]

Within the Mandingo community this organizational structure provides mutual benefits for the 'big men' and the youth. As the community watch group leader explained, this was also a way to occupy the youth of his area – young unemployed men – some of whom were ex-combatants. In his opinion, getting the youth to participate in the watch group was a way to keep them out of crime and to make them feel that they contributed to the community. The Mandingo Group was highly organized. This may be related to the fact that Voinjama, as a former LURD stronghold, with many of its fighters from the Mandingo community, still had lingering military organizational structures in place. Not only did the Mandingo group collect fees from families ($20LD) and shops ($50LD), but the 'Team Head of the Community Watch Group' kept a detailed roster of all the young men involved in patrolling the area. Furthermore, the group had two other additional team leaders – a security advisory and a coordinator.

The young men of the Mandingo group answered to the team head and the other elders, and were not allowed to take any decisions themselves, on what to do with captured suspects. In this case, power and influence are clearly limited by the traditional power structures. Yet during the war these structures had often been eroded when youth rebels suddenly achieved powerful positions. However, this chain of command was often complicated. The team head noted that it was difficult to convince the young men to not take the law into their own hands.

Yet in other settings, the power structures and the group compositions were completely different. Just as the war in some sense had empowered youth and challenged the traditional authority of elders, the vigilante movements could offer young men influential positions in their neighbourhoods.[68] In one of the vigilante groups in central Monrovia, the elders of the community had no direct influence over the group's activities. The young men, from various ethnic backgrounds, who had organized the group, had chosen their leader because he was well-respected and popular in their neighbourhood – a former and well-known elite basketball player. He and a few young men close to him were responsible for taking decisions and implementing them; that is, they did not need to consult the neighbourhood elders first. This group also admitted to cooperating with other vigilante groups, when necessary, especially in light of organized gangs. Vigilantism for many from this group was an 'extra-curricular' activity that they participated in after they had finished their studies or their day jobs.

A former vigilante leader in Paynesville, Monrovia, described yet another structure of organization. He himself had been appointed as the leader of his neighbourhood vigilante group by the elders of the community and was thereby

---

67 Jörgel and Utas, 2007, p. 13.

68 As argued by Mats Utas (2005), the Liberian Civil War temporarily created new opportunities for people who had earlier been marginalized. Young people from marginalized backgrounds became field commanders and strongmen in their communities.

responsible for a group of 50 young men. Whenever they arrested a suspected criminal, they were supposed to bring the person to the elders so that they could decide whether the person should be brought to the police or not. However, this did not always occur. Frustration over the fact that the 'suspected criminal' they had captured was often released by the police and seldom prosecuted, drove them to punishing the suspect themselves, without involving either the police or the elders. As the vigilante leader expressed, 'We had a rule in my neighbourhood: the fourth time a guy was caught committing a crime something really bad happened to him, and if his crime was serious we killed him.' These young men, often unemployed or marginalized, could thereby suddenly hold very influential positions when serving as vigilantes.

Ex-combatants also appeared to have a special position within several of the vigilante and community watch groups. In the Mandingo community watch group in Voinjama a former high level LURD commander held the position of security advisor. With long experience from the Liberian civil wars (first as an officer within the Liberian Army then as a LURD commander), he was well-known in the Lofa County: respected by some, feared by others. Nevertheless, he had significant influence over the community watch groups, as he together with the leader was responsible for choosing, organizing and training the young men. He picked certain men because they were former LURD combatants and already had training; others because he trusted them and had known them since they were children. Even though other vigilante and community watch groups were not mainly composed of ex-combatants, similar structures and chains of command prevailed. Recent research has shown that LURD combatants continued to have a strong influence in Lofa County after the war had come to an end. When villages in the county were repopulated in 2004 and 2005, former LURD commanders assumed policing roles and were assisted by dozens of young combatants. However, these well-armed combatants with little supervision actually became a security risk. Nonetheless, several communities still accepted this security arrangement during this period, probably under the assumption that with former LURD soldiers in the community, they were less likely to fall victim to LURD attacks.[69]

The informants in these groups mentioned both the advantages and the difficulties of having ex-combatants in their groups. As a former vigilante group leader from Monrovia explained, he always needed to have some ex-combatants in his groups because of their fearless attitude and because they were not afraid to use violence when necessary. He further added that having ex-combatants in his group meant that others became reluctant to commit crimes in his neighbourhood, knowing well that these young men with combat experience were capable of dealing with criminals. These young men were fearless and others feared them, and thus they effectively deterred crime just by their presence. Such statements were made by members of the other groups as well. Yet, ex-combatants also

---

69   Hill, R., Temin, J. and Pacholek, L., 'Building Security Where there is No Security', *Journal of Peacebuilding & Development* 3(2), 2007, pp. 43-44.

caused problems for their vigilante groups. Their past experiences from the war and fearless attitude towards violence made them unpredictable and difficult to control, and sometimes under the influence of alcohol and drugs this became even worse. They were often more likely to respond with violence, and could therefore put the entire group at risk.[70]

As much of the research has shown, ex-combatants are often one of the most vulnerable groups in post-conflict societies often facing marginalization, exclusion and stigmatization after war.[71] In particular, there has been much discussion regarding the fact that the DDR (disarmament, demobilization, and reintegration) process in Liberia did not adequately address or satisfy the needs of ex-combatants.[72] The reintegration phase has been challenging. One group of ex-combatants, during interviews, mentioned that the psycho-social dimension and (re)integration into the labour force have been very problematic for them. As a result, they further added, many ex-combatants in Liberia found it very difficult to make a transition into a life that did not deal, in one way or another, with 'security matters'.[73] Ex-combatants could thereby easily be mobilized in new security settings as members of chains of commands and structures which often remained after the war. However, their participation in these community watch groups, as shown above, can bring both advantages and disadvantages. On the one hand, providing job opportunities for the young people in a community, can strengthen the security situation (depending on the situation and the individual), and provide the first step to reintegrating young ex-combatants into civilian life. On the other hand, organized ex-combatants in vigilante or community watch groups can essentially contribute to maintaining rebel structures and chains of commands, further impeding the reintegration process. Another concern given the highly organized structures of some of these groups is the fact that these informal security networks could easily be remobilized if armed conflict would arise again in Liberia.

---

70   Interviews with vigilante and community watch groups conducted during March 2009 in Monrovia and Voinjama.

71   See for example Utas, 2005, on the situation of young ex-combatants in Liberia and how they more often faced re-marginalization rather than re-integration in the aftermath of war.

72   See studies such as Jennings, K.M., 'The Struggle to Satisfy: DDR Through the Eyes of Ex-combatants in Liberia', *International Peacekeeping* 14(2), April 2007, pp. 204-218; Hill, R., Taylor, G. and Temin, J., *Would You Fight Again? Understanding Liberian Ex-Combatant Reintegration.* United States Institute for Peace, Special Report 211, September 2008.

73   Interviews with ex-combatants, Monrovia, February 2009.

Legitimate Violence? Relations to Community,
Criminality and Formal Security Actors

The community and the vigilantes appear to have a symbiotic relationship. Despite whatever feelings or thoughts ordinary citizens have about these groups, people often resort to them when there is a problem; for example, when their house has been burglarized or when a crime is in progress. At the same time the vigilantes may rely on the community for information on who is doing what, how someone was able to afford a new stereo or television, or who came in sudden possession of money. Some groups appear to have a more formalized backing from their communities, sometimes in the form of food, coffee, flash lights, mobile phones or 'small small money'. Whether these contributions are given out of free will, fear, or pressure is of course difficult to determine. However, this type of support appears to be important for the sustainability of these groups. The Bazzi Quarter Group, for example, claimed to have stopped patrolling because the community no longer wanted to or could support them financially. As previously mentioned, the highly organized Mandingo Group received significant support from their community.

Our findings from the Liberian context indicate that ordinary citizens generally considered vigilantes and informal security providers as a natural, or unavoidable, part of the security landscape. Although vigilante practices are often officially condemned, local opinions on the phenomenon could be quite different. Other research on vigilantism in Nigeria shows that there is often a sharp division of opinion about the legitimacy of people threatening, or carrying out, vigilante assaults on those perceived as criminals. Therefore, to simply call vigilantism 'deviant' is problematic since the practice does in fact have widespread support.[74] In Nigeria, a very large number of people do not regard vigilantism as deviant in the way that the federal government and the legal institutions do – that is, as a criminal act. The different views on vigilantism thereby become a struggle over norms of internal security and the right to determine 'proper' conduct.[75] Moreover, the use of violence by vigilante groups is something that is accepted. As noted by Jensen when researching vigilantism and everyday policing in South Africa, violence occupies a highly ambivalent position in this context since it can be perceived as legitimate if it occurs as a response to an original illegitimate use of violence.[76] Therefore, the violence committed by the vigilantes is not only justified as a response of counter-violence by the vigilantes themselves but is also perceived as such by the local communities, and thereby as legitimate actions.

---

74   Baker, 2002, p. 224.

75   Ibid., p. 242.

76   Jensen, S., 'Security and Violence on the Frontier of the State: Vigilant citizens in Nkomazi, South Africa' in Ahluwalia et al. (eds) *Violence and Non-Violence in Africa*, 2007, p. 119.

Nevertheless, the lines between those considered criminals and those claiming to be vigilantes are often blurred. Pratten describes the case of a vigilante group in Nigeria that had been initiated by a former gang member who claimed to be tired of being blamed for the thefts in his village. He felt he could clear his name by 'turning vigilante'.[77] Hence, it seems rational for community members, in an effort to gain some form of control over criminal elements, to accept such persons if they 'turned vigilante' in order to keep the 'criminals' on their side.

The relationship between community watch groups and vigilantes and the Liberia National Police is more complicated. The vigilantes at times get into trouble with the police. A leader of one of the groups said that he been arrested and severely abused by the police after having caught a criminal and 'rightfully' beaten him up. Also, the police are often involved in cases where vigilantes have mistakenly assaulted someone (which happens often). In theory, community watch groups are allowed to exist and operate – provided that they officially register with the police and abide by the law. However, no one in Liberia seems to know the exact rules governing their behaviour. According to a United Nations staff member, who works on community policing issues, the community watch groups are not supposed to patrol the streets, but rather just keep a watchful eye over their communities. Additionally, they are not supposed to receive financial or other support from their communities, nor are they to receive any additional resources from the police. However, a senior LNP officer admitted to providing these groups with flashlights, for example. Additionally, a very high-ranking officer within LNP Headquarters stated that they try to provide office space where the groups can operate and organize themselves. At the same time, most police officers discourage vigilante violence. While these groups do not have any formal clearance for their activities and their actions are illegal, many claim they have the silent approval of the police. What further complicates the issue is that many formally registered and supported community watch groups take the law into their own hands, in the same manner than non-registered groups. These groups are able to carry out the work that the unarmed LNP is often unable to do. As one informant from a vigilante group in Monrovia declared, 'They know what we do and they need us – they need our work.'[78]

Whether these groups are local defenders acting where the state has failed, or whether they are a menace to society has been debated before. Such questions have, for example, been asked by scholars looking at private initiatives for security in various parts of Africa. As Gore and Pratten argue, vigilantism in Nigeria expresses a lack of confidence in the capacity of the state to offer security, but does not project a revolutionary or anti-state message. Nor is state sponsorship

---

77 Pratten (b), 2008, p. 70.
78 Interviews with vigilante and community watch groups conducted during March 2009 in Monrovia.

of vigilantes something especially new in this context.[79] Or as pointed out by Christian Lund, on the one hand vigilantes in Nigeria often portray themselves as the 'antithesis' of the state which is believed to be something removed from the local arena, seeking legitimacy for their actions in their non-state status. Yet, on the other hand they often act within the formal structure of the state, as in the case of being 'commissioned' by the state to carry out police matters.[80]

Despite the fact that the representatives of state and informal security providers often tried to distance themselves from each other (the former more than the latter), this investigation has revealed that they were both part of the same system. The links between the formal security system and the informal security providers were clearly present even though they appeared hidden whenever the official picture was presented. The vigilantes and the community watch groups, sometimes with formal approval and sometimes without, did the work the police could not or would not do, sometimes with devastating consequences. They were the first to apprehend, judge, and often castigate suspected offenders, with punishments that in the worst-case scenarios could lead to brutal beatings or even death. It was evident that the informal security actors were providing security in areas where the state police never entered, and these networks provided important functions for ordinary citizens. For such citizens – forced to find ways of protecting themselves – having to rely on informal security actors was a risky option, but so, too, was depending on the formal security system.

Implications for SSR policy: The Hidden Security Links

This chapter shows that vigilantes, like other forms of informal security provider networks, are an important part of the Liberian security context. Unlike other security and justice sectors in Liberia, these groups actually function. Perhaps they do not operate exactly according western standards, but they act with purpose and motivation to rid their communities of crime. Also, considering the financial, human resources and legitimacy issues of post-conflict environments, community watch groups can perhaps, using fewer resources, do what state institutions cannot. For example, with minimal financial support (e.g., small food contributions or a little pocket money), vigilante groups would be more willing and able to protect their communities, something they might do anyway.

Informal security actors hence present both opportunities and challenges for international donors and aid agencies. On the one hand, they are a constant fixture of the everyday security and insecurity landscape, even though they have not been incorporated into the 'formal' policy on security and policing. Although

---

79   Gore, C. and Pratten, D., 'The Politics of Plunder: The Rhetorics of Order and Disorder in Southern Nigeria', *African Affairs* 102, 211-240, 2003, p. 232.

80   Lund, C., 'Twilight Institutions: Public Authority and Local Politics in Africa', *Development and Change* 37(4), 685-705, 2006, p. 688.

not often openly admitted, these groups operate with the police's knowledge and silent consent and will continue to do so in light of a poor functioning police and criminal justice system. If donors are truly committed to policies that aim to improve the human security of the local populations, then these groups (and the 'services' they render) must be taken into account. Rather than approach security and justice projects with the perspective of *'what does not work'* or *'what is missing'*, donors should examine *'what exists already'* and ask themselves *'why is it working'* and *'how can we support and improve it'*. Such questions will lead to more sustainable, locally-supported, realistic SSR strategies.

Additional research is needed, particularly to fully understand the role of these groups in various settings. This may mean following the development, on an ongoing basis, of a specific group to better understand how they adapt or change to Liberia's security setting. More specifically, criteria could be developed in order to better assess the function, effectiveness, and interests of these groups. In the cases where these groups effectively work with the local police authority, more assistance could be given to these structures so that they can strengthen their cooperation with the police rather than work against them or impede their work. Such arrangements could also serve to create greater local accountability, transparency, and legitimacy of the local police.

On the other hand, addressing the negative consequences of these groups is more challenging. As this chapter has discussed, the increased use of violence by these groups is problematic and only serves to further fuel a sense of insecurity and instability. As has been identified, much of this violence (as well as mob violence) has emerged in reaction to the frustration felt with the lack of consequences or punishment given to 'suspected criminals'. There appears to be a lack of information amongst vigilante groups, but even within the larger community, about the criminal justice process. Many of the respondents were under the impression that once a criminal is caught and handed over to the police, then their involvement was over. Despite the fact that there have been public campaigns informing citizens, many are still unaware that they must follow up their cases with the police and/or that they must go to court and testify. Citizen's lack of knowledge about how the security system works simply intensifies the feeling of disempowerment, which only increases frustration and resentment with the local police (the most visible expression of government authority). While the existence of community policing forums may eventually remedy some of these issues, local communities may still feel that they have not been adequately supported or maintained by the LNP. This issue will also need to be addressed.

In addition, these vigilante groups are the most culturally and geographically viable option for addressing a specific community's safety needs and tie better into traditional structures than state-driven policing. This is particularly true if one considers places like Voinjama, where many of the women do not communicate in English and thus are unable to communicate with the local police (who are often men from other parts of the country); the reliance on security depends on such groups. This also illustrates the necessity, or at least relevance, of recruiting police officers and placing them back in their own home communities. While there is a risk that such arrangement could further encourage corruption and favouritism (which is happening anyway whether police officers are from the area or not), bringing officers that know their communities and are willing to safeguard them could facilitate building the legitimacy of the new police service.

In the case of Liberia, it is evident that a multi-layered approach to SSR has not been taken. The focus has been on institution-building, particularly those of the police and the military, while ignoring the role of the poorly understood vigilante and community watch groups. Yet the need to incorporate these groups into the wider conceptual and practical understanding of security service delivery has been echoed by others. For example, the academic and former Liberian President Amos Sawyer argues that Liberia must consider systems of polycentric governance. A polycentric system of democratic governance means that rather than looking at policy and institutional choices in dichotomies (such as centralized or decentralized, formal or informal), one should look at a variety of institutions and agents '... within the context of certain kinds of things. The analysis should begin by asking what kind of goods and services do we want to provide, and how can we best provide them in a given setting?'[81] This system considers that there are multiple centres of limited or shared authority at multiple levels of governance, capable of providing and producing a variety of public goods and services. Sawyer argues that while central governments may be more efficient at providing some goods, local institutions, NGOs, and even the private sector may be better at delivering others. The challenge, he notes 'is to identify and establish a governing system that allows for a mix of all of these institutional arrangements: local/national, private/public'.[82] Finally, Sawyer argues that, 'Instead of trying to fit everything into a standard Weberian model, [polycentric governance] provides opportunities to build on what people themselves want to do. Instead of telling people that their ways of doing things is wrong and does not fit into our theory of state, the concept of polycentric governance attempts to evolve a theory of state that is based on the realities on the ground.'[83]

Similarly, Baker and Scheye argue,

> If we are interested in improving the experience of justice and security of the end user, it seems misguided to focus the *majority* of SSR effort on reforming the state security and justice agencies. It would make more sense to recognize the nature and composition of the post-conflict and fragile state without imposing it an idealized Western conception of what the state should be: acknowledge its inherent weaknesses and limitations; accept the ways in which state and non-state actors inter-penetrate, mingle, and merge; and then, attempt to strengthen

---

81   Andersen, L., 'Democratic Governance in Post-Conflict Liberia – An Interview with Dr. Amos Sawyer'. DIIS Working Paper No. 2007, 20, October 2007, pp. 11-12.

82   Ibid., p. 12.

83   Ibid., p. 14.

the performance of those who actually deliver most of the security and justice in addition to building state capacities.[84]

The implication for donors wanting to support SSR strategies is clear: support programs that may not necessarily resemble western institutions, as well as practices or actors who may not fit into the preferred criteria. This may not mean supporting all informal security actors, but it means carefully identifying and supporting those who can effectively deliver the security needs of the local population, particularly in the short-term when state institutions are deemed illegitimate or ineffective. In turn, this has the potential to improve the overall security environment in the longer run, as well as build support and legitimacy in the formal state security providers.

Concluding Remarks

Vigilante-like groups are just one of the many informal state security and justice actors operating in Liberia. In fact, on a day to day basis most Liberians find themselves navigating a continuum of choices for both their security and justice needs. While this chapter cannot make definite conclusions about all vigilante groups in Liberia, it has attempted to shed some light on these under-examined security actors. This chapter has identified a number of issues in relation to non-state security actors that should be further researched in order to improve SSR initiatives. First of all, vigilante groups do not appear to be an isolated phenomenon in Liberia. Since a number of non-state initiatives for creating security exist (like the groups presented in this chapter), the international community must find ways to identify and map them out in order to lay the foundation for a sustainable and efficient security sector reform. Furthermore these groups need to be included when programs for SSR are planned and implemented. Therefore strategies on the ways to work with, rather than against, these groups within the SSR-programmes must be prepared. To enable this, more research is needed to understand how these groups operate and, more importantly, how they are perceived and used by their communities. Additionally, it would be fruitful to better understand how these groups' perceptions of justice interact with the customary justice system.

As this case has shown, the emergence and existence of these groups is very much context dependent – not only because the Liberian state has failed to secure its citizens, but also because these groups have tangible benefits for the youths that participate in them. This is an important reminder of the inherent link between security and development. The extent to which such contributions are beneficial to the communities should also be studied on a case-by-case basis. If security sector reform programs are to have any lasting impact or success in Liberia, it is evident

---

84   Baker and Scheye 2007, p. 514.

that they must recognize the reality that security provision in Liberia is carried out by actors that are both formal and informal.

References

Abrahams, R., 'Sungusungu: Village Vigilante Groups in Tanzania', *African Affairs*, 86, 1987.

Abrahams, R. 'What's in a Name? Some Thoughts on the Vocabulary of Vigilantism and Related Forms of "Informal Criminal Justice"' in Feenan (ed.) *Informal Criminal Justice*. Aldershot: Ashgate, 2003.

Adebajo, A., *Buiilding Peace in West Africa. Liberia, Sierra Leone and Guinea-Bissau*. Boulder: Lynne Rienner Publishers, 2002.

Adinkrah, M., 'Vigilante Homicides in Contemporary Ghana', *Journal of Criminal Justice* 33, 2005.

Africa Research Bulletin, 'Liberia: Warnings Against Mob Justice', 1-31 October 2006.

AlertNet, 'Liberia Calls for Citizen Vigilantes to Fight Crime', 6 September 2006.

Allen, F.G., 'Vigilante Justice in Jamaica: The Community Against Crime', *International Journal of Comparative and Applied Criminal Justice* 21, 1997.

Alloycious, D., 'Liberia: Police's Budget Can't Fight Crime', 7 July 2008, AllAfrica, available at: http://allafrica.com/stories/200807071359.html, accessed 13/08/2009, 13:05.

Andersen, L., 'Democratic Governance in Post-Conflict Liberia – An Interview with Dr. Amos Sawyer'. DIIS Working Paper No. 2007, 20, October 2007.

Baker, B., 'When the Bakassi Boys Came: Eastern Nigeria Confronts Vigilantism', *Journal of Contemporary African Studies*, 20(2), 2002, 223-44.

Baker, B., 'Multi-Choice Policing in Africa', Nordiska Afrikainstitutet, 2008.

Baker, B. (a), 'The Future is SSR is Non-State'. Paper presented at 'The Future of SSR', e-conference organized by Centre for International Governance Innovation CIGI, Waterloo, Canada, 4-8 May 2009.

Baker, B. (b), *Resource Constraint and Policy in Liberia's Post-Conflict Policing*. Forthcoming, 2009.

Baker, B. and Scheye, E., 'Multi-Layered Justice and Security Delivery in Post-Conflict and Fragile States', *Conflict*, Security and Development Group 7(4), December 2007.

Buur, L., 'Crime and Punishment on the Margins of the Post-Apartheid State', *Anthropology and Humanism* 28(1), 2003.

Buur, L. and Jensen, S., 'Vigilantism and the Policing of Everyday Life in South Africa', *African Studies* 63(2), 2004.

Call, C.T. and Cousens, E., *Ending Wars and Building Peace: Coping with Crisis*. New York: International Peace Academy, 2007.

Call, C.T. and Wyeth, V., *Building States to Build Peace*. Boulder: Lynne Rienner Publishers, 2008.

Fahn, P.A., 'Liberia: President Sirleaf Fuels Debate on Police', October 2008, BBC World Service Trust, available at: http://www.communicatingjustice.org/en/stories/04102008_liberia_president_sirleaf_fuels_debate_police, accessed 8/13/2009, 13:14.

Gore, C. and Pratten, D., 'The Politics of Plunder: The Rhetorics of Order and Disorder in Southern Nigeria', *African Affairs* 102, 2003, 211-40.

Government of Liberia, 'National Security Strategy of the Republic of Liberia', January 2008.

Heald, S., 'Controlling Crime and Corruption from Below: Sungusungu in Kenya', *International Relations* 21, 2007.

Hill, R., Taylor, G. and Temin, J., 'Would You Fight Again? Understanding Liberian Ex-Combatant Reintegration', United States Institute for Peace, Special Report 211, September 2008.

Hill, R., Temin, J. and Pacholek, L., 'Building Security Where There is No Security', *Journal of Peacebuilding & Development* 3(2), 2007.

International Crisis Group, 'Liberia: Uneven Progress in Security Sector Reform'. Report No. 148, 13 January 2009.

International Monetary Fund, 'Liberia: Poverty Reduction Strategy Paper', July 2008, IMF Country Report No. 08/219.

Jennings, K.M., 'The Struggle to Satisfy: DDR Through the Eyes of Ex-Combatants in Liberia', *International Peacekeeping* 14(2), April 2007, pp. 204-18.

Jensen, S., 'Security and Violence on the Frontier of the State: Vigilant Citizens in Nkomazi, South Africa' in Ahluwalia et al. (eds) *Violence and Non-Violence in Africa*. London: Routledge, 2007.

Jörgel, M. and Utas, M., 'The Mano River Basin Area – Formal and Informal Security Providers in Liberia, Guinea and Sierra Leone', *FOI Defence Analysis*, 2007.

Law, D. and Myshlovska, O., 'The Evolution of the Concepts of Security Sector Reform and Security Governance: The EU Perspective' in Spence and Fluri (eds) *The European Union and Security Sector Reform*. London: John Harper, 2008.

Lund, C., 'Twilight Institutions: Public Authority and Local Politics in Africa', *Development and Change* 37(4), 685-705, 2006.

Moran, M.H., *Liberia: The Violence of Democracy*. Philadelphia: University of Pennsylvania Press, 2006.

National Security Strategy of Liberia, Interview with UN official, Monrovia, 5 March 2009, pp. 22.

Nina, D., 'Dirty Harry is Back: Vigilantism in South Africa – The (Re)Emergence of "Good" and "Bad" Community', *African Security Review* 9(1), 2000.

OECD Handbook on Security System Reform, 2007.

Oomen, B., 'Vigilantism or Alternative Citizenship? The Rise of Mapogo a Mathamaga', *African Studies* 63(2), December 2004.

Peake, G., Scheye, E. and Hills, A., 'Conclusions' in Peake, Scheye and Hills (eds) *Managing Insecurity. Field Experiences of Security Sector Reform.* New York: Routledge, 2008.

Population Division of the Department of Economic and Social Affairs of the United Nations Secretariat, 'World Population Prospects: The 2006 Revision and World Urbanization Prospects: The 2007 Revision', http://esa.un.org/unup, accessed 20 April 2009, 08:09:54.

Pratten, D. (a), 'The Politics of Protection: Perspectives on Vigilantism in Nigeria', *Africa* 78(1), 2008.

Pratten, D. (b), 'The Thief Eats his Shame: Practice and Power in Nigerian Vigilantism', *Africa* 78(1), 2008.

Smith-Höhn, J., 'Multi-Level Security Provision in Post-Conflict Societies: Local Perspectives from Liberia and Sierra Leone'. Paper for the AEGIS European Conference on African Studies, 'African Alternatives: Initiative and Creativity beyond Current Constraints', 2007.

Sorbor G., 'Taylor's Police Director to Advise LNP', Star Radio Liberia, 12 February 2009.

The Analyst Newspaper, 'Decision on Freeport Probe Must be Clear', 7 August 2007.

Thomas-Queh, J., 'The Police in Question: A Grave Security Pitfall to be Reckoned With?', *The Perspective*, Atlanta Georgia, 18 July 2008.

United Nations Security Council Resolution 1509, S/RES/1509 (2003), p. 4.

United Nations Mission in Liberia, 'Weekly Press Briefing', 13 September 2006. Available at: http://unmil.org/1article.asp?id=1630&zdoc=1, accessed 7 October 2009, 17:50.

US Department of State, 'Liberia, Bureau of Democracy, Human Rights, and Labor', 6 March 2007. Available at: http://www.state.gov/g/drl/rls/hrrpt/2006/78742.htm, accessed 21 April 2009.

Utas, M., 'Building a Future? The Reintegration & Remarginalisation of Youth in Liberia' in Richard (ed.) *No Peace No War: An Anthology of Contemporary Armed Conflicts.* Ohio: Ohio University Press, 2005.

Interviews

Interview with UNPOL officer previously stationed in Liberia, Stockholm, February 2009.

Interviews with ex-combatants, Monrovia, February 2009.

Interview with local NGOs working on security issues, Monrovia, March 2, 2009.

Interview with an international police officer, Monrovia, March 3, 2009.

Interview with an American justice reform contractor, Monrovia, March 5, 2009.

Interview with Dr. Thomas Jaye, Governance Commission, Monrovia, March 12, 2009.

Interview with a local deputy police commander, Voinjama, March 2009.

Interviews with vigilante members and community watch groups conducted during March 2009 in Monrovia and Voinjama.

Conclusion:
Challenges and Opportunities – Towards a Comprehensive EU SSR Policy and Practice

Magnus Ekengren and Greg Simons

This volume contains some 15 different chapters that cover a wide range of aspects and perspectives on SSR and the European Union's past, current and future role in this sphere. A number of the case study chapters are quite critical of the current efforts at SSR, especially in the context of the missions on the African continent.

The task of summing up the knowledge contained in this work is going to be done in two stages. Firstly, we shall undertake the summarizing of this knowledge and lessons on the basis of individual chapters (within regional frameworks, e.g. Baltic Sea Region, Africa, Balkans, Former Soviet Union and Central Asia) in order to get an appreciation of the tactical and operational aspects of SSR. Then the task of teasing out the common knowledge and lessons shall commence in order to gain an insight into the strategic picture.

In the introduction, we introduced the idea of the three Ps (policy, policies and practice) as a means to view and link the information contained within this book. Up until now, the EU has handled its own internal experiences of SSR pretty well regarding the first two Ps. It has been made clear that a policy grounded on a comprehensive and regional approach is needed, and policies have been developed for international SSR support. As of yet however, there has not been a sensitivity and flexibility built in its policies to the specificities of recipient countries. This necessitates the following:

1. To be more open and alert to the particulars and specifics of recipients;
2. To develop tools that facilitate a more flexible and sensitive approach that at the same time sets institutional frameworks for a close dialogue, formulation of recipients' needs, conditions for EU aid, and the evaluation of missions.

This is a curious turn of events. In the 1990s this is exactly what the EU did with the candidate countries; there was a close dialogue, there were also clearly defined goals that each candidate country needed to fulfil, which was in the framework of that country's constitutional and historical background. This necessitates asking, why the third P (practice) is missing within the contemporary context of EU SSR missions?

The Regional Perspective

Nordic-Baltic States and Poland

What were in reality the factors that altered the basis for – in Stålvant's words – 'a regional dialogue between governments and peoples' ('regionalization') in the Baltic Sea Area? One of the most important conclusions that can be drawn from the Baltic Sea experiences is that good reform results are born out of multilateral efforts within overlapping but not duplicating frameworks able to foster close networks of cooperation between supporters and partners of SSR. Another explanation of the successful outcome was the invention of many different institutional responses at the sub-regional level; the Barents Euro Arctic Council, the Arctic Council and the EU's 'Northern Dimension' to name the most important. These early and all-embracing institutions facilitated exchange and cooperation not only among governments but at all levels of society. At the same time it was important for the Baltic partner states early to prepare for meeting the different demands inserted in existing organizations' security reform activity (for example, NATO's focus on security and the EU's and UN's on development).

Another Nordic-Baltic experience was the broad scope and complexity of working methods in the field of SSR. In fact, the many practitioners involved in what today is called SSR activities did not then identify them as such. Strong mutual understanding between donors and receivers was a key to efficient international coordination and for the apprehension of what models of cooperation would work and why. In this regard it was also essential for each individual state – Estonia, Latvia and Lithuania – to use insights from regional best practices and lessons learned about the links between security, peace, democracy, the transformation of government and development. Here many benevolent factors in individual states acted together for the common good. For example, successful Swedish support of the SSR in the Baltic States was to a large extent due to the fact that Sweden adapted its internal broad concept of 'total defence' into a useful external tool for SSR support. Again, the supporters' own experiences seem to be an important factor behind efficient SSR.

Another key driving force facilitating SSR is, according to Stålvant, the early evolution of common regional interests. Early international conventions and sector specific goals such as 'comprehensive environmental security' paved the way for a solid material foundation of trade and exchange. The 'Common Baltic Sea' became a shared responsibility and gathered a broad range of governmental participants, including Russia, as well as representatives from civil society, the NGO-community and business. The protection of the environment often functioned as a smallest common denominator and point of departure for discussion of other common challenges. The strategic goal for the Nordic-Baltic States was security – a goal to be achieved with as little explicit reference to security cooperation as possible. The method was to down-play talks about security, focus on trade, transnational networking and environmental threats ('soft security') and invent institutional responses. In line with the traditional EU method, the Nordic-Baltic States created security by not talking about it.

The main lesson that can be drawn from the *Polish* experiences is, in the view of Patoka, that the primary condition of security sector reform is political and economic stability. SSR is a time-demanding process and therefore implementation ought to be conducted in conditions making possible long-term planning for all actors involved in reforms. Three more particular conclusions can be drawn from Poland's SSR. *First*, it is of crucial importance to clearly define the distribution of authority and responsibility between actors involved in SSR. These reforms are the core component of national security policy, therefore, the definition of authority must be subject to legal and constitutional norms. To achieve such goals, SSR should be elaborated in representative parliamentarian fora and intra-governmental working groups. These organs should have the right and means to evaluate the progress of reform as well as to postulate correction of legal and executive acts. *Second*, budgets of all actors ought to be designed in harmony with the SSR strategy. Especially, the defence budget should be constructed in accordance with the strategy of military industry reforms as well as long-term planning conducted by agencies responsible for crisis management and management of civilian emergencies. *Third*, core international organizations, as well as regional political and military alliances, should act as a stimulator of SSR by imposing obligations on their member states and conditionalities on candidate states. One of the aims of these obligations and constraints should be to foster a regional security arena.

The Nordic-Baltic governments have decided that time is ripe to discuss the possibilities of a deepening of SSR cooperation among these states when confronted with a rapidly growing demand of SSR support elsewhere. Already today the Nordic-Baltic countries coordinate SSR activities in the Ukraine and in the Western Balkans.[1] In a next, strategic step of closer cooperation it seems only natural for these states to look back to their common recent history for inspiration in the shaping of efficient and sustainable international SSR.

The European Union

How should the EU best realize its unique SSR potential? Alyson Bailes' view on the EU's SSR potential is mixed. On the one hand she expresses concern about the fact that the EU can not simply externalize its internal security success story to the rest of the world, or at least not to many countries in need of SSR in for example Africa or Asia. And this for several reasons: *firstly*, these countries might not need the SSR Europe has managed to carry out during the 1990s, or indeed since the 1950s. Some of them are faced with traditional, territorial military threats where defence reform for post-national relations and international humanitarian missions will not be the most needed. *Secondly*, because the Union will have internal difficulties of agreeing on what national models the EU SSR should be moulded. According to Bailes, the

---

1   Tolgfors (2007).

challenge will be great with regard to the need to coordinate EU member states efforts and Union projects. *Thirdly*, the incentive of membership in the EU or NATO does not exist which seriously weakens the important 'soft power' tool with which the Union has pursued its SSR in Europe. On the other hand, the EU *does*, according to Bailes, need to preserve the image stemming from its internal life of being strict on good governance and democracy as a prerequisite for support of SSR in any country/region of the world. The conclusion of Bailes is that we should be careful to use our European model for prescribing reforms of defence substance but instead focus on *how* things are reformed and with *what goals* when it comes to further democracy and governance. But the fact is that this is also easier said than done owing to the fact that the two dimensions are so closely linked. To what extent can they be separated? How to agree on EU SSR programmes?

Spence, Britz and Ekengren try to answer these questions. Spence sees the main potential of EU SSR in the Union's traditional regional approach to security reform which encompasses both method and goals. The advantage is that the Union can share SSR responsibility with its member states and thus does not need to find absolute consensus for a uniform European approach. National models can co-exist with Union approaches and member states could delegate particular SSR tasks to the EU on which there are agreement. Increasing Union engagement will in time pull member states SSR in the same direction towards an SSR driven by a 'European interest', that can be more 'value' based than national interests.

In this way the EU will, according to Spence, prove a more efficient SSR actor due to the fact that it is not being seen by global partners as pursuing its own narrow strategic security goals. The 'European interest' is a much vaguer goal of assisting other countries into models 'we feel comfortable with' – in the words of Spence. He seems to means that the Union should refrain from enter into discussions of what kind of defence that or that partner country should possess. Emphasis on democracy and development goals for all reforms – on *how* things are reformed – will in the long run lead to the changes in defence substance preferred by the Union.

Also Britz points to the long term capacity and regional dimension as the greatest assets of the Union in SSR. The aim of EU SSR is broad security referring both to the protection of states and citizens, and as a consequence perhaps also 'societal security'. Britz discusses potential tensions between different parts of EU SSR policy. On the one hand, the SSR focused on good governance and development led by the Commission, and on the other, the emphasis on security and crisis management in the Common Security and Defence Policy under the Council. She recapitulates the EU Policy framework for Security sector reform (Council Conclusions, 12 June 2006, paragraph 1) where emphasis is put on 'the fact that SSR is a holistic, multi-sector, and long term process encompassing the overall functioning of the security system as part of governance reforms'. The EU underlines strong national ownership: nationally/regionally owned participatory reform processes designed to strengthen good governance, democratic norms, the rule of law, and the respect and promotion of human rights. The concrete substance must of course be shaped in view of needs in receiving states/regions and the possibilities of donors. In the words of the EU Council: 'A case by case analysis based on a situation specific approach is always needed to assess whether any proposed activities are most properly carried out through ESDP or Community action or a combination of both' (Council Conclusions, 12 June 2006, paragraph 4).

Ekengren shows that a lot remains to be done in the EU institutions and national administration for an effective Union able to deal with the widening and transboundary security concept. The question of whether the Union will be able to think anew and bridge the gap between internal and external security agents will be of tremendous importance for its international SSR. The key to success is not only the ability of the Union think innovatively on security, but member states' readiness to pool and share sovereignty with the Union in widening security fields. EU international SSR has to be in tune with the organization's increasingly stronger focus on the protection of humans, citizens and society. One should be careful not to jeopardize the Union's reform capacity by short term security objectives. The EU has a great potential to renew SSR for a new global security landscape by projecting its own internal work. This includes its traditional ability to link efforts for security, development and democracy together in innovative ways and regional solutions – a quality that make the Union a particularly well suited SSR actor. The overall aim of supporting SSR should be to enhance developing countries' capabilities to handle threats to both internal and external security in a way that is consistent with democratic norms and international Human Rights principles, good governance, and international law. At the same time, it is crucial not to reinvent the wheel. There are already many experiences from the EU, OECD, UN and NATO/ PfP that can be used in elaborating more coherent strategies. Ekengren's chapter also points to an increasingly important role of SSR in CSDP. The challenge for the Union will be to transform its military and civilian missions into longer term SSR engagements whenever possible.

It is an historical challenge for the EU member states to live up to new security objectives set through the Union. However, the biggest challenge is perhaps not to immediately define a common, uniform view of what SSR is among the member states. Instead the Union should now find 'niches' of SSR that best could complement the member states and at the same time be a longer term driving force for both more harmonized 'European' SSR and innovation in national creation of SSR resources. The Union might for example establish SSR guidelines and head line goals for national administrations to fulfil by listing capacities in the same way as is done in the area of military and civil crisis management. Can the Union be successful in this endeavour it will help generating resources for individual national SSR action as well as common EU efforts. As pointed out by Spence, in the area of security policy and SSR it is the totality of EU and member state action that constitute the European whole – the 'total security output of Europe'.

One of the most important conclusions that can be drawn from the Nordic-Baltic-EU sections of the report concerns today's fundamentally new demands on national abilities to provide resources for international SSR. EU member states need to invent systems able to mobilize human and material resources from a broad spectrum of national administration. Cross-departmental SSR strategies need to be elaborated that in time might transform into more permanent ministerial structures and 'stand-by' resources encompassing foreign policy, defence, crisis management, development, justice and rule of law experts. Our analysis of the SSR needs reveal the contours of evolving governmental structures beyond the traditional division between internal order (ministry of justice), external security and development (foreign ministry) and external defence (ministry of defence).[2] That is, post-national government adapted to the needs stemming from multilateral SSR for a rapidly changing security landscape where national sovereignty is giving way for global SSR cooperation.

The Western Balkans

What insights can be drawn from the experiences of SSR in the Western Balkans? The analysis of Juncos and Collantes-Celador clearly shows how current problems of international coordination originate in a lack of coherent long term strategy and incentives for local actors to pursue reforms. The particularly severe transboundary issues of the Western Balkans are of course a stumbling block for a stronger regional approach to SSR. The authors point to the fact that international SSR actors have managed to stabilize the region but that much remains to be done in order to proceed to the other processes explaining the Nordic-Baltic success; regionalization and normalization. Much remains to be done also when it comes to defining a clear division of responsibility between the authorities of SSR in the region – one of the main Polish lessons.

The necessary bottom-up processes for a regionalization are weak in the Western Balkans. One of the main factors behind this situation is the lack of trust between national and ethnic communities putting obstacles to exchanges as well as the setting of common objectives. The benevolent pluralism of ideas, actors and organizational solutions that could be found in the Baltic Sea area is in the Western Balkans contrasted by ethnic plurality and local stakeholders with narrow self- interests. Most importantly, Balkan civil society is not geared towards transnational networking for obvious reasons. In contrast to the Baltic States, these states have fought recent wars with each other and popular sentiments are still very much affected by these experiences. Juncos and Collantes-Celador do not mention any signs of transnational networks of cities and local municipalities – an element that constituted the foundation for the Baltic Sea region. This is very worrisome. Twinning arrangements between order and border authorities – including the police, border guards, and civil protection agencies – helped to both re-established national sovereignty in the Baltic States and sew the region together.

---

2   The creation of 'European Expert Teams' for SSR will further this process (Council of the European Union 2008).

The consequences for regional cooperation are many. Unlike the Baltic Sea area where disputes and 'fuzzy borders of competence' in Stålvant's words, were turned into justifications for meetings and organs, regional problems in the Western Balkans are still comprehended as obstacles to dialogue. The unsettled geographical borders lead to not only a politicization of 'technical' issues but to cross–border criminality with ethnic overtones and tensions. In this way the potential of organized crime as a legitimate challenge for the region as a whole can not be exploited for the common good. While there were very strong endogenous factors favouring reform in the Baltic Sea area, the driving forces in the Western Balkans are almost exclusively external actors. While the external SSR actors in the former region played the role of facilitators and source of inspiration they are in the latter functioning as imposer and controller.

Before regionalization processes have led to enduring stability, it will be very difficult for the Western Balkans to enter into a phase of normalization where the states are treated as equal partners and an 'asset' in the combating of international threats. Not until Croatia, Bosnia and Herzegovina, Albania and Kosovo have ceased to be a source of instability, the international community can divert more attention to other security issues and hot spots. The normalization that took place in the Baltic Sea region in the form of EU and NATO membership meant that the sub-regional cooperation entered into a less intensive phase. The EU institutions, including the European Commission no longer accorded the same instrumental utility to the sub-regional cooperation. The secretariats and institutions for Baltic Sea cooperation took on more normal public tasks.

How can today's SSR be shaped to overcome these differences in conditions between the Western Balkans and the Baltic Sea area? How to avoid 'securitized SSR' – the ad hoc management of immediate threats and crises at the detriment of long term objectives? Juncos and Collantes-Celador point to the need for greater economic assistance in order to foster a stronger basis for local ownership and the linking of security measures to larger structural and social reforms. They argue that without a socio-economic development and a more relaxed visa regime international SSR will have very small possibilities to foster the confidence building arrangements for trust that are so well needed. They strongly underline the need for a longer term strategic approach to the SSR activities, including more effective international implementation and assessment. The EU member states should strengthen their support and provide freedoms to the Western Balkans in order to prepare these states for their inclusion into the Union. A heavy responsibility falls on the shoulder of the political leadership in the EU states who has to meet the pedagogical challenge of explaining to their electorates the necessities of Balkan reform and the provision of appropriate resources. They have to explain the great security gains for France, Sweden and others that are achieved through SSR in the Western Balkans.

Even though the conditions between the Western Balkans and the Baltic Sea differ, there are important lessons from the latter region that *can* be applied. For example, international pluralism of actors is a good thing provided they are guided with a clear strategic goal they have in common. The Nordic-Baltic experiences also suggest the establishment of systematic needs assessment by the local actors that should serve as a basis for a close and institutionalized dialogue with international partners. To this end a plethora of organs for meetings and dialogue between all reform actors in the region should be established. These organs should also create frameworks for clear implementation and assessment criteria for SSR similar to the EU's method for evaluating the fulfilment of its '*acquis*' in the enlargement negotiations. This in order to clarify the advantages and duties following from a closer relationship to the EU and avoid today's 'blame game' between Union supporters and critics in the region. Free trade agreements should be worked out as soon as possible between the countries in the region and with the EU.

Ukraine

Fredrik Bynander, Greg Simons and Andrea Johansson present a broad overview of conditions and possible future areas for SSR in Ukraine. Bynander calls for a sensitivity of external actors of the great issue at stake in SSR support to Ukraine, namely the country's security identity. Ukraine's security policy choices will constitute the core of the political debate in coming years. The result is difficult to predict. A strategic SSR approach setting clear long term goals in common would make it easier for international actors to adapt, prioritize and streamline support in accordance with these decisive Ukrainian developments. Bynander also wants to raise our awareness of the risk of clashes between the EU and NATO engagement in the country. An explanation of the successful parallel management of these organizations by Estonia, Latvia, Lithuania and Poland is of course that they were driven by obligations arising from membership. But a key to success was also these countries' early establishment of strategies of their own that helped them to make the most of external support in the pursuing of their national and regional goals. Ukraine should try to draw on this example to the largest possible extent.

Simons shows the importance of an in-depth understanding of the historical and geographical issues in today's Ukraine for the shaping of efficient SSR. Without an overall approach considering the politics of boundaries, nationalities and external relations – what the Ukrainian actors in government and opposition deem necessary for security – international SSR will continue to play a very limited role for change in the security sector.

There are many concrete implications for SSR that external actors can draw from history and politics. One key element would be to help Ukraine to formulate regional cooperation goals that could guide security sector reform. This help should be shaped so as to promote today's initiatives towards a regionalization including Georgia, Ukraine, Azerbaijan and Moldova (GUAM) while at the same time foster confidence-building measures with Russia. Here, the EU experience of setting up a multitude of organs and fora with overlapping and inclusive membership could inspire. SSR should to an increasing extent be discussed and shaped within regional fora such as the existing GUAM, Council for Baltic Sea States, the

European Neighbourhood Policy of the EU, Black Sea Economic Cooperation, Common Wealth of Independent States (CIS), Euro-Atlantic Partnership Council, Partnership for Peace, but also new organs for broad regional participation from a wide range of society, including NGOs, civil society, think tanks, business. These institutions should identify common regional challenges and discuss tools for opening up exchange and combating common security threats.

Another key task for international SSR actors is to help Ukraine to shape its borders for statehood – necessary for security as well as symbolic reasons – in a way that minimize the risk of creating barriers to regional cooperation. A natural point of departure is of course to strengthen the support of the EU's border control assistance to Ukraine for control and cross-border cooperation.[3] The Nordic-Baltic example can here be an inspiration for fostering twinning arrangements between order and border authorities for the exchange of expertise and techniques with neighbours both within and outside the Union. That is, an SSR support for a border management policy for security and safety *and* the facilitation and safe carrying out of trade and exchange. As a first step the international community could jointly and together with all concerned Ukrainian authorities and in close dialogue with other establishments and think tanks in Ukraine work out a proposal for a general plan for the reform of borders. This plan could constitute one of the cornerstones for the establishment of multilateral meetings and organs for regional solutions.

Simons' overview of what NATO and the EU have achieved so far with regard to SSR points out promising roads for further reform. He refers to progress at the grass roots level in the ministries that now needs to 'trickle up' to higher political level. In the perspective of Nordic-Baltic cooperation of the 1990s the SSR issue should be further politicized to gain momentum but not 'securitized' in a way that risks excluding partners that could fear international intrusion and sovereignty losses in sensitive internal fields. It will now be crucial for international actors to identify Ukrainian and regional proponents and (potential) allies of NATO and EU SSR that can be part of processes of stabilization and regionalization for normalization. These should be involved in multilateral settings to an increasing degree and with the aim of formulating common regional goals. Shorter term aims for international actors should, like in the case of the Baltic Sea area and the Western Balkans, now give way for strategic security goals set for and *by* the region.

Furthermore, inter-ministerial and inter-agency cooperation should be promoted in Ukraine through SSR not only for particular issue specific reasons but as a way to help creating more coherent government able to define longer term objectives and defence priorities. Clearer state priorities would considerably facilitate international actors' strategic support. A focus on intra-governmental cooperation should include also the broadening of SSR efforts to other ministries than the Ministry of Defence such as the Interior Ministry and the security police

---

3   Cf. the EU Border Assistance Mission to the Republic of Moldova and Ukraine (EUBAM), initiated 2005.

(SBU). Today different ministries pursue security reform in different form and pace. A broader involvement of Ukrainian government might trigger off spill over effects between ministries that could speed up the reform process.

Perhaps the main lesson that can be drawn from Simons' chapter is that the weaker incentives of NATO or EU membership, the more international SSR has to consider the particularities of national politics and structures in the search for reform partners and dynamics. Less clear cut external aims and conditions for reform support open up for domestic interpretations and disputes of the directions for change. A regional approach to SSR engaging Ukrainian, regional and international actors should aim at limiting the politics of border and nationalities by establishing common regional goals and frameworks for the reform of borders and their management. The recent announcement by the newly elected Ukrainian President Viktor Yanukovich, whereby NATO membership (but not cooperation) is off the national agenda, offers the EU a moment to become fully engaged at a point in time when Ukraine is affirming its neutral (non-aligned) status.

Andrea Johansson shows the depth of the problem of small arms and light weapons (SALW) in Ukraine and that the problems can not be solved without a broad approach to SSR. On the other hand she portrays the field as a potentially very productive area for international SSR support. Closer EU cooperation for SSR in the SALW sector would serve many purposes. It could provide a regional input for regional goals such as preventing regional destabilization and the spread of weapons from Ukraine for 'extra-regional conflict intervention' – two of the main purposes of international SSR in SALW according to Johansson. It could contribute to stabilizing the region by enhancing transparency and oversight. A strengthened EU role could aim at supporting existing international codes of conduct in SALW and provide a much needed impetus for international organizations, for example in relation to the NATO initiative of 2006 and the translation of the OSCE handbook 'Document on Small Arms and Light Weapons'. It could also be a useful tool for convincing the Ukrainian government of the importance to follow the EU code of conduct on Arms Export and elaborating a more developed policy in the field within the ENP Action Plan of 2004. The Nordic-Baltic experiences could be used to strengthen the EU's work on a comprehensive Ukraine Action Plan for problems of surplus weapons. In the light of Johansson's analysis, perhaps the most important task for EU cooperation would be to bring up SALW as a fundamental issue for Ukrainian and regional stability that could only be up-rooted by broad and persistent SSR efforts. In this way the EU states would help shifting the focus of the international community towards the supply side of SALW and bring a necessary regional dimension to SALW.

The 2010 presidential elections in Ukraine have seen another shift in Ukrainian policy and international relations. There has been a shift away from Yushchenko's Euro-Atlantic integration programme, which included state objectives of joining the EU and NATO. Yanukovich has kept the goal of eventual membership to the EU, but has dropped the goal of NATO, although pledging to remain 'engaged' with NATO. On a rhetorical level this is justified through maintaining Ukraine's non-aligned status, on a more practical level this may reflect the delicate political balance in Ukraine. Relations with Russia have improved considerably since the confrontational stance taken by Yushchenko (Timoshenko ultimately developed good relations with Russia), and this new policy has resulted in movement on demarcation of the Russian-Ukrainian border, a 25-year-extension for the Russian Black Sea Fleet lease and discounted gas prices for Ukraine. Such shifts provide the EU with a number of opportunities in developing their relations and engagement in the region, including in the sphere of SSR.

Afghanistan

In the chapter by Sedra we learn that current international SSR is attempting to draw Afghanistan deeper into a process of stabilization. However, the strong focus on immediate stabilization needs is put at the detriment of longer terms aims, making it very difficult to predict if and when the country can move to broader frameworks of action such as regionalization and normalization. One thing is however clear in the view of Sedra and that is that the donor side can help improving conditions by a holistic approach to SSR. Sedra points to the Union as a particularly well-placed actor due to its broad security conception including the judicial sector and potential as long term partner for Afghanistan. Closer EU cooperation could function as a driving force for the international generation of resources as well as a strengthened direct role for the Union through its police mission in the country (EUPOL, since 2007).

Africa

Jörgel puts emphasis on the need for longer term strategy (10-15 years) for international engagements in Sub-Saharan Africa. The problems of a fragile state apparatus call for a holistic SSR approach (judicial system, police, welfare strategy etc). Without the support of a whole range of state functions there is little chance that SSR – that today mainly is scattered in the defence sector – will be successful. Without an in-depth understanding of the many different actors' driving forces in the region it will be very difficult for the international community to shape efficient SSR. The 'African oriented approach to SSR' should according to Jörgel, per definition be a holistic one. The need for security sector transformation rather than reformation is another lesson that can be drawn from the African example. Only through strong leadership for Western SSR (Jörgel suggests 'lead nation') in the region can actions be successful and results sustainable.

In the chapter by Bahnson, the state of SSR in one of the most challenging environments is laid bare. Guinea-Bissau is an extremely challenging environment for trying to implement SSR and the EU is experiencing a number of problems in its mission there. The country has been racked by political and economic instability since its independence in 1974 (due in no small part to civil war and *coup d'état* attempts). Bahnson sees that Guinea-Bissau is a test case for the EU

SSR programme, with the attitude if it cannot be done there it cannot be done anywhere. This means that there is a lot at stake in this particular mission that has gained a lot of symbolic value as a result.

In terms of cooperation among the donor agencies there has been a remarkable amount of harmony, in spite of the potential for turf wars. However, the EU effort has been let down in a number of areas. Underestimating the value and effects of politics on the process has been one of the shortcomings. This refers not only to the politics between the donors and Guinea-Bissau, but also politics among the individual donors as well, not to mention the domestic politics at play within the country. Persson and Kantor had similar findings in relation to their case study on Liberia where informal political networks projected significant power. This situation is particularly crucial to understand, where in the African context informal institutions maybe the functioning system in place of an absent or weak formal system, which donors may overlook.

The African chapters also point to the need to fully understand what is needed on the ground, in what quantity and by which time. There can be a tendency to underestimate what is needed in terms of resources (human, financial and material) and the time needed in order to bring about meaningful and lasting SSR. This partly is reliant upon understanding the context of the country and its people, but there also needs to be an appreciation of the regional situation (instability in a neighbouring country may have a spill over effect in the recipient country). Additionally, the specific needs and priorities of the country, its civil population and civil service need to be clearly identified and prioritized. An understanding of the local perspective needs to be established, which is clearly brought out by Kantor, Persson, Bahnson and Jörgel in their respective chapters.

Common Lessons and Knowledge: Building the Strategic Picture

There has been a wealth of information provided above, which gives the reader an impression of the operational and tactical level of SSR in the different regions and contexts. The aim now is to build upon this and create an overview of the strategic level, the challenges and the possibilities for the EU in solidifying and improving its position as a leading world actor in SSR.

Basically the question concerns how we can learn from earlier experiences to improve implementation despite the many differences in the political preconditions for SSR. As shown in this book, SSR in development countries where it is aimed to secure physical and social infrastructure and normal economic activity will always have many differences to cases where the SSR purpose is the democratization of defence and security structures that have been under authoritarian rule. The aim of the categories presented in the Introduction was exactly to improve the basis for a more comprehensive framework for analysis and learning.

The emphasis on three Ps (policy, polices and practice) provides a framework that strengthens the focus on implementation. Thereby it complements today's discussion where we see an evolving common understanding of the policy concept and a growing consensus on the need to shape policies for SSR in a coherent and mutually reinforcing way.

The pyramid shaped diagram of the spheres of SSR (assistance and aid, capacity building and state building) was presented as a way to differentiate between types of assistance that risk being misleadingly lumped together under the broad SSR concept. But the aim was also to illustrate the influences between the different components. The diagram shows that the three spheres are not isolated parts of the SSR whole. There are interactions and flow-on effects from each of these groupings that touch the others. Neglect one aspect, and it may exert a negative influence on the sectors that are being targeted. Therefore, instead of treating each aspect in isolation, which has been 'artificially' imposed, a holistic approach should be undertaken. Thus at the same time as the politics might differ from one sphere to another it is important to conceive of them as a whole due to the fact that international donors and recipient states increasingly are engaged in all of them. There is over time often a need to shift the balance of support from immediate assistance over medium-term capacity building into longer term state building.

The illustration of the components of SSR represents the various tasks at hand, and the three Ps represent the components that constitute the means with which to accomplish those tasks. But again, this does not necessarily mean that all of the aspects of SSR are treated in equal proportion, there may be more emphasis needed on one of the three at the expense of the others in a particular mission. The only implication is that the process should be viewed from the perspective of a whole rather than as unconnected tasks of the process. To make the decision if an emphasis on whether one particular aspect needs more attention, a full and accurate situational awareness needs to be established.

It must also be understood that security is not only or primarily about ensuring the continuation or survival of governments and bureaucracies, it is also about ensuring a good standard of living for a country's citizens; to be free from forms of oppression and physical violence and poverty (free from fear and want). In other words to have their basic life needs met. Therefore evaluation of the missions forms a very critical aspect of SSR. What was done well? What needs improving? Were the goals of the programme met? In taking this approach a sense of good governance, transparency and accountability are built in to the process.

A long-term, comprehensive perspective needs to be considered and understood from day one, and not only 'discovered' when things start to go wrong. For instance, there needs to be a clear delineation, on a case by case basis, of assigned leadership and responsibility roles on SSR missions. This is needed in order to head off turf wars and stovepiping issues that may otherwise occur in case of any inherent ambiguities that may be present. The effective targeting of needs and resources, and leadership of a mission increases the chances of achieving the desired results through reducing the amount of uncertainty and risk involved.

A question was posed in the beginning of this conclusion. Why is there an apparent lack of the third P, practice, in EU SSR? One possible explanation for the relative weakness of this component is due to the heavy efforts going into the making of policy and policies, at the expense of implementation and politics on the ground. Decisions are made and priorities assigned from the political process, which has a tendency to focus on the short-term perspective (agreements within the EU and the election cycle for example). Therefore practice becomes tied to and a product of the politics of policy-making. In the process of coming to consensus on an issue, such as establishing an SSR project, the project becomes one of compromise between the various parties involved in the process, on both the recipient and donor side. As such, it is not necessarily the best solution that is agreed upon, but the one that can be accepted among the various parties involved.

Another reason could be that the EU has not (as yet) distinguished between the three components in its SSR policy to a sufficient degree. As pointed out in the Introduction it is essential that the level of expectations stands in proportion to what the Union aims at and is capable to carry out in practice. By adopting general and vague SSR policies that gives the impression that the Union's engagement cover also longer term state building – while it in reality is shaped for assistance – is a recipe for failed expectations, both at the EU and the receiving end. A more clear differentiation between the three spheres could help to better match the EU's political goals with the SSR resources provided on the ground and avoid an 'expectation-capability gap'. This would also make it easier for the recipients to figure out what is exactly expected and required from them in the different spheres of EU SSR support. Moreover, a clear distinction improves the possibilities for efficient generation and provision of national SSR resources for EU use. The practical implementation challenges in the realm of assistance and aid, which involve a particular set of actors on both ends, are quite different from the ones of state building.

Another question taken up in the Introduction was whether it is possible and useful to create an SSR template that can be applied to all cases. This book has shown the great risks of using a general template given the specifics of local conditions. The division of SSR into three components opens up for a more realistic framework for learning. There are probably greater possibilities to detect patterns in each respective sphere from which generally applicable SSR lessons can be drawn than to define a full 'pyramid' model. Indeed, the cases in this book indicate that there are assistance and capacity building experiences, such as the ones in Ukraine and Western Balkans, on which general recommendations for the future can be based. For example, it seems as there is always and everywhere a great risk of supporting a capacity building that is not very firmly rooted in domestic reformers' immediate needs. In capacity-building and assistance our cases show that it is important generally to quickly establish a 'win-win' situation. The SALW weapons programme and the development of border security in Ukraine is good case of an SSR where there are clear self- interests on both the donor and the recipient side. This is a good starting point, especially given that both parties stand to 'win' if it is successful, thus there is strong mutual motivation towards the goals of the programme. Success in these two spheres of the pyramid is, based upon the results of the case studies, more likely when it involves early mutual dialogue and partnership towards clearly defined goals.

In the sphere of state building SSR partners should in the light of the results be much more careful to ground their actions on historical and geographical analogies. The book has shown that in terms of transferring the values of democracy, transparency and accountability issues, the engagement with the Baltic States has been one of the more successful examples. In a period of just 13 years the Baltic States went from being a part of the Soviet Union (1991), its political, military and economic system to being members of the EU (2004) and NATO (2004). This was done through a close dialogue and partnership. This is also the case with Poland. But due to its size – it is a much larger state than the Baltic countries – there are limits to the comparisons with these states. SSR partners should be careful not to draw too far-reaching lessons from other states experiences in order to avoid the underestimation of the time, cost and needs that still has meant that Polish SSR is not completely resolved.

There has been a period of intense and comprehensive SSR for state building in the Western Balkans as well. The challenges here were greater than in the Baltic States and Poland owing to the bitter civil war. Moreover, this has not been based on a dialogue, rather by strict oversight by an assigned special representative with extensive executive powers. Therefore this case can be seen as one involving an uneven relationship, which has attempted to impose 'state' standards. A significant problem in the Western Balkans, which differs from the Baltic Sea region, is the issue of regionalization. The civil war and violent break-up of Yugoslavia makes any basis of regional development difficult due to the inherent animosities. Another big difference between the preconditions for state building efforts was that the Baltic States and Poland were united in the position to engage in Euro-Atlantic integration.

However, the Western Balkans, Ukraine, Poland and the Baltic States do have in common a functioning state system and bureaucracy (even if it was corrupt and weak, the formal institutions of the state did exist). This provided and facilitated a point of contact between donors and recipients, which is much more problematic in Afghanistan and has in some cases been shown to barely exist in some of the African cases.

Afghanistan has proved, in terms of implementing an SSR programme, to be the most challenging environment. It is currently being subjected to an insurgency that is gaining increasing strength and a lack of consensus among the donors/contributors engaged there (with regards to a strategic plan). The regime that is supported politically and economically is both weak and corrupt. It is the sole case in this volume where SSR is being attempted under the conditions of armed conflict. The complexities and number of actors involved in this case necessitates a cautious and carefully considered approach, not least when it comes to SSR for state building.

The African case studies have shown that at times it is necessary to engage with informal institutions owing to the fact that formal state institutions either do not exist or do not function. To do this successfully though, one must have a thorough understanding of the background of the politics and history of the country concerned as well as an appreciation of the regional dynamics at play (instability across a border may affect stability and efforts within the intended recipient country). To engage with an inappropriate informal actor may cost the programme legitimacy or hinder the ability to attain the stated objectives. All of the cases given also bring out the issue that a true partnership between donor and recipient is needed in order to better the chances of addressing the root problems.

Finally the cases have clarified many links between the three SSR spheres and the strategic goals of 'stabilization', 'regionalization', 'normalization', explained to us by Stålvant. Not least they have shown that it is crucial to apply a comprehensive approach encompassing all three components in all these three phases of development. Receiving states and regions need assistance, capacity and long term state building support throughout the long and often winding road towards normalization. The European Union is uniquely well placed to offer that support.

State-building has been placed at the head of the three (state-building, capacity building, and assistance and aid) SSR spheres. This is due to the fact that once the donor has completed the programme, and the recipient is to stand on their own, it is the institutions of the newly reconstructed state that shall give guidance and govern the system. Therefore the transference of good values and governance are crucial, in addition to increasing the capacity-building (or actually establishing one) of the state institutions in an organizational and philosophical sense. The actual aid and assistance provides the state and its institutions with the physical capability of discharging their duties.

References

Council of the European Union, Security Sector Reform – draft document on deployable European expert teams, 21 October 2008, doc 14576/1/08 REV 1, Brussels, 21 October 2008.

Tolgfors, S., 'Enhanced Nordic Cooperation in a Euro-Atlantic Context', speech by Sten Tolgfors, Swedish Minister for Defence, at the Swedish Atlantic Council conference. Karlberg Palace, Stockholm, 9 November 2007.

Epilogue: Central Insights and Recommendations for EU SSR

Magnus Ekengren

In the light of the main lessons drawn from the experiences highlighted in this volume to improve international SSR and realize the potential of EU SSR this epilogue offers a number of suggestions and recommendations. These recommendations include perspectives and insights into policy, obstacles to efficient polices and implementation, and potential paths to overcome them. They are also a brief summary of the book, which makes me indebted to all of its co-authors.

SSR General

- There is a need for a comprehensive approach to SSR, encompassing a clear policy concept, mutually reinforcing polices (for democracy, development, security) and a strong focus on practical implementation.
- It is essential that SSR is carried out on the basis of partnership with democratic reformers in receiving states.
- SSR cooperation should be based on systematic and regular needs assessments by the local actors.
- SSR should mainly be shaped with the aim of fostering processes for democratization, transparency and good governance, rather than prescribing security and defence substance.
- SSR should be carried out in very close relation to polices for democratization, development and free trade.
- SSR should be embedded in broader reform programmes where explicit security and defence aims are only one reform component.
- SSR should entail components of civic and civil security and enhanced capacities for emergency management and non-military threats.
- Three components normally constitute SSR support: state building, capacity building and aid and assistance.
- The three components should be separated to clarify assisting states' goals and capacities and what is exactly required of the recipient country.

- It is important that the level of expectation, both at receiving and assisting ends, stands in proportion to the aims and capabilities of the donor. This in order to avoid an 'expectation-capability' gap.
- The three components (state- and capacity building and aid and assistance) are mutually influencing each other. Neglect one aspect and it may exert a negative influence on the sectors that are being targeted. The three 'spheres' should be conceived of as a whole.
- There is over time often a need to shift the balance of support from immediate assistance over medium-term capacity building into longer term state building.
- To make the decision if an emphasis on whether one particular component needs more attention, a full and accurate situational awareness needs to be established.
- It is easier to draw lessons for the future from earlier international SSR experiences in the sphere of assistance and capacity building than in the sphere of state building, where the specifics of local conditions should be considered to a higher degree.
- Whenever appropriate SSR should be carried out through multilateral efforts that help bring SSR beyond narrow national self-interests of donor countries.
- Coordination between international donors should be strengthened and systematized.

Elements for a Regional SSR Approach

- Regional approaches offer a more comprehensive means of approaching the SSR problematic.
- Common regional or sub-regional challenges for SSR partners should be identified early.
- Clear strategic regional goals should be set for major SSR activities. These could include measures for meeting common non-security as well as security challenges and the establishment of joint fora and organs.
- SSR partners should try to ensure the early adoption of regional objectives by the authorities of receiving nations and local ownership of projects.
- SSR should aim at involving many multi-lateral actors and providing a pluralism of international, regional and sub-regional organizations, organs and meeting places. SSR should be used for inspiring and inventing institutional responses and security arrangements at regional and sub-regional level.
- SSR should foster frameworks for the sharing of best regional practices of democracy, good governance, security and defence.
- The donor states should adapt their own governmental structures for broad, multinational and effective input into international SSR.

The European Union and SSR

General

- The EU member states need to find formulas that all of them can agree upon. There is a strong need for visionary thinking on which to base long term Union strategies and programmes for SSR.
- The European Union should elaborate its SSR so as to provide a clear added value to its member states.
- The Union should find 'niches' of SSR that best could complement the member states and at the same time be a driving force for both innovation in national SSR and more harmonized 'European' SSR.
- Whenever appropriate SSR should be carried out through the Union – in itself a model for institutionalized SSR and regional security community.
- In dialogue the EU should always infuse as much as possible of its post-national philosophy of regional achievements into its SSR support. Regional solutions are in demand.
- By embedding in practice the EU's 'own' SSR experiences, positive benefits may abound to a state or region in need.
- A great asset and source of legitimacy in world affairs is the normative role of the EU. Without drawing on the qualities of its internal dimension and without a close link to its own broadening security agenda it is perhaps doubtful whether the Union will be an efficient – or even a requested SSR actor – around the globe. One such normative role is to further the Community method of creating regional security communities when shaping an EU SSR policy.
- Sub-regional succesful experiences, such as the Nordic-Baltic one, should be a source of inspiration and initiative for the EU's SSR policy.
- The fact that EU SSR should be 'holistic, multi-sector, and long term' evokes the question of capacity and priority. The Union might need to point out specific international regions and organizations for support where it wants to be particularly active in order get all its instruments to work in parallel for success.
- Cooperation and coordination with other international organizations such as NATO and the UN are essential for successful EU SSR. The goal should be an efficient division of labour. This does not necessarily mean a division in the form of a special responsibility of each organization for individual receiving states. There are often political advantages of having several international donors involved in the same country/region.
- The EU SSR is not an isolated concept. It is paralleled by 'defence reform' efforts at both the national and alliance levels (NATO) and by SSR concepts developed by the United Nations. Parallels need to be worked out, identified and debated.

- There is a public interest in promoting knowledge of the EU's understanding of security sector reform as both a concept, and a programme to be implemented.

Capacity

- The SSR implications for trade, aid and security are not (yet) reflected in EU policy-making and analysis, nor in institutions and operational planning. The process should be shaped so as to mutually reinforce each component part.
- The EU needs to overcome the division between sectors and policies and build on the long tradition of Commission work in the field.
- The EU SSR concept rested mainly on two pillars: ESDP missions (thus a post-conflict element) and EC development aid. The new CSDP offers the possibility for a comprehensive EU SSR in other parts of the world.
- 'Mainstreaming' SSR into other EU areas of cooperation should not mean that the SSR problem is perceived of as 'solved' and could be taken away from the top of the agenda.
- EU member states and regional interest groups should be closely involved in the implementation of the EU SSR.
- EU resources depend on the preparedness of its institutions and member states to surmount traditional barriers between development, security and justice support. In this way they could serve as an example for other donor countries.
- Effective implementation depends on the EU's ability to promote democratic oversight in an holistic approach to SSR that links the defence, police, justice and border and emergency management sectors in recepient states.

Methods

- The Europan Expert Teams for SSR should be developed further. There is a strong need for joint standards and training in the EU member states to make the pool of deployable teams effective.
- The SSR programming dialogue should involve partner countries in need at a very early stage. Participation should be ensured in the EU Country and Regional Strategy papers and Actions plans. Planning should allow for receiving states to participate in various forms.
- For effective implementation, the EU should establish conditionalities and benchmarks for its partner countries, but avoid the risk of being perceived as an agent imposing EU or 'Western values'. Based on local ownership, these SSR conditionalities could well become 'EU SSR Guidelines' to be fulfilled by partner states through yearly 'National Actions Plans'. The

European Commission should then together with the Council assess and evaluate recipients' fulfilment on a regular basis.

- EU Guidelines and National Actions Plans should also entail programmes for training, joint expert pools as well as specific country activities.
- To manage the system of guidelines and action plans and ensure continuity and close dialogue with partners, joint SSR Coordination Committees should be set up.
- The EU and its member states should promote the establishment of a similar system of SSR guidelines in other international fora and organizations.
- The Union could for example assist partner organizations, such as the AU, to establish 'AU SSR Guidelines'.
- The EU should promote SSR cooperation between international regional organizations (EU-AU, EU-ASEAN etc), as well as sub-regional organizations ('twin regions').
- The EU should include 'SSR chapters' in its policy dialogue with other states and regions and its association agreements.
- Both governmental and nongovernmental research institutes and 'think tanks' should help to watch over the implementation of EU SSR, to identify lessons learned, and present policy recommendations. There is a joint interest to cooperate in the following areas:
    - Documentation of the EU SSR policy in its implementation; identification of lessons learned and 'good practice in the making'; policy recommendations.
    - Comparison of the EU SSR with parallel work in sub-regional and international organizations.
    - Policy recommendations/support for international and sub-regional organizations.
    - Development of implementation tools (such as assessment tools, handbooks, guidelines, teaching/training units) on the EU SSR concept.
    - Analysis of the EU SSR concept, identification of what has been left out.
    - Evaluation of EU SSR missions.
    - Anticipation of EU SSR missions (early warning): needs assessments.
    - Joint monitoring/publication programmes (*EU SSR Watch*) on the development of the EU SSR concept and its implementation in CSDP missions and policy programmes such as the European Neighbourhood Policy.

Index

Figures are indicated by bold page numbers.